Broadway Yearbook, 2001–2002

The Broadway Yearbook Series

by Steven Suskin

Previous Titles

Broadway Yearbook, 1999–2000
Broadway Yearbook, 2000–2001

2001
2002
BROADWAY
YEARBOOK

Steven Suskin

OXFORD
UNIVERSITY PRESS

2003

OXFORD
UNIVERSITY PRESS

Oxford   New York

Auckland   Bangkok   Buenos Aires   Cape Town   Chennai
Dar es Salaam   Delhi   Hong Kong   Istanbul   Karachi   Kolkata
Kuala Lumpur   Madrid   Melbourne   Mexico City   Mumbai
Nairobi   São Paulo   Shanghai   Taipei   Tokyo   Toronto

Published by Oxford University Press, Inc.
198 Madison Avenue, New York, New York 10016

www.oup.com

Oxford is a registered trademark of Oxford University Press

ISBN 0-19-515876-8; 0-19-515877-6 (pbk.)
ISSN 1473-933X

1 3 5 7 9 8 6 4 2

Printed in the United States of America
on acid-free paper

For

Helen, Johanna,

and Charlie

Contents

Curtain Calls

Broadway Yearbook, 2001–2002

The Curtain Rises

The 2001–2002 Broadway season was the most difficult in memory. The events of September 11 cast a large shadow on the nation and the world. Compared with the overall situation, the problems of any particular industry are of minor importance; but it was a hard time for people around Broadway to be entertaining, and entertained.

Broadway curtains rose once more after a two-day, three-performance cancellation, but nothing was the same. Business was understandably dismal; the total gross for the week of the attacks, with most shows giving only five performances, was $3,647,734. (Thirty-six percent of the business came from three shows that began the week with strong advance sales, *The Lion King*, *42nd Street*, and *The Producers*; the latter, alone, accounted for 15 percent of the week's total.) This compared with $9,603,505 for the week ending September 9—which in itself had been a bad week, falling from $11,586,215 the week before.

Business on Broadway was already declining even before the attacks, due to a poor economic outlook and a related reduction in incoming tourists. *Variety* had an extended story about the grim prospects for the fall, complete with gloomy prognostications from top theatre executives, in the issue that hit the newsstands on September 10. (One major producer was quoted as saying "it's times like now—September, October and through to January—that things are going to be put to the test.")

Five shows shuttered immediately; they were doing marginal business, anyway. Additional expected closings were averted, thanks to an effective advertising campaign combined with steep discounting. Advance sales, though—except for the biggest hits—did not recover. The Broadway economy has always been led by sellouts; people buy tickets to a show they are only vaguely interested in seeing because they want to go to the theatre on a given date and can't get seats for their top choices. The longer seats remain available for the biggest hits, the harder it is to sell tickets for other shows.

A word should be said, in passing, about the people of the theatre industry. As the weekend of that fateful week arrived, with the country in mourning and the fire still smoldering fifty blocks away, the casts of twenty-three Broadway shows dragged themselves into their dressing rooms, put on their makeup, and forced themselves before the footlights —not an easy thing to do. This applies not only to onstage performers but also to stagehands, musicians, wardrobe, managers, press agents, and other backstage personnel. The spirit in evidence onstage, at this most disheartening time, was heartening.

Moving from matters economic to artistic, the 2001–2002 season was a marked disappointment. The 2000–2001 season was dominated by *The Producers*, which received the most phenomenal critical and audience response in memory. This was accompanied by a second musical comedy hit, *The Full Monty*. (The latter was severely weakened by *The Producers*, settling for a moderately profitable run of less than two years.) On the nonmusical side, there were two major crowd-pleasing moneymakers, the multiple award winner *Proof* and the popular comedy hit *The Tale of the Allergist's Wife*.

The 2001–2002 season featured nothing of particular interest, other than the cyclonic whirlwind that breezed onto Broadway under the title *Elaine Stritch at Liberty*. The musical output was especially weak, with the Tony Award going to a poorly received show that even its supporters admitted was flawed. The nonmusical offerings were somewhat more noteworthy, with three intriguing but problematic works struggling for attention.

What most onlookers tended to overlook was that 2001–2002 *did* contain two major successes: a musical that might well prove more profitable than *The Producers* and a play that was a hotter ticket than *Proof* by far. The musical, *Mamma Mia!*, received mixed-to-unfavorable reviews, being a triumph of nostalgia-targeted marketing over art. The play, *The Graduate*, got the very worst reviews of the entire season: ten-out-of-ten pans, as tabulated in our critical scorecard. *The Graduate* nevertheless outgrossed all of the year's plays and half of the musicals.

Six shows in addition to *Mamma Mia!* and *The Graduate* managed to recoup their investments before season's end, which is an impressive number. (The 1997–1998 season had only two.) The 2001–2002 hits included limited engagements of three relatively inexpensive, one-person shows, but even so; eight of the season's twenty-six commercially produced ventures earned a profit, with another five potentially likely to join the moneymakers. This can only be seen as a positive statistic, regardless of artistic quality.

It was a season of one-person shows, with six opening on Broadway. (Based on a season of thirty-five official Broadway openings, that's roughly one out of six.) Five came clustered in a row, no less, the entire output from December through February. Add in three two-character plays, and you have nine shows—more than a quarter of the Broadway season—with a grand total of twelve actors.

This might seem an ominous trend, driven by excessive production costs and a lack of investors. In some ways, it was. However, these nine shows included my choice for the best Broadway offering of the season, the aforementioned *Elaine Stritch at Liberty*. Also in the group were three other entertainments with four additional dazzling performances, from Barbara Cook, John Leguizamo, Jeffrey Wright, and Mos Def. So let's not fear shows with small casts, only shows with small talents.

The thirty-five shows included fourteen revivals; not the largest number ever—the 1995–1996 season had seventeen—but the most in five years. As has been the case in recent seasons, March and April—between the spring thaw and the Tony nomination deadline—were overcrowded with openings; seventeen shows, half of the annual crop, within eight weeks. There was far from enough business to go around, with the shows ganging up on each other and discount offers abounding.

Total Broadway gross sales (as usually defined, after deduction of commissions and certain union benefits) for the season were $642,545,026; total attendance was 10,958,432, with an average ticket price of $58.63. Sales and attendance were down from 2000–2001, when the totals were $665,424,767 and 11,937,962, respectively. The ticket price, needless to say, was up from 2000–2001, when it had been $55.75.

The dropoff of $20 million in the gross was not a surprise; the week of the terrorist attack counted for a $6 million deficit alone. Still, this was the first time since the 1985–1986 season that the total gross fell. Without the $3 increase in the average ticket price, it would have been an even steeper drop. More indicative of the situation was the falloff in total attendance from 11,937,962 to 10,958,432. That's 8.2 percent, or one million fewer tickets; the lowest attendance since 1997–1998, and the first drop in attendance since 1990–1991.

Playing weeks were 1,430, the lowest level since 1996–1997 and the first time this figure dropped since 1991–1992. (Playing weeks represent the total number of individual weeks that performances were given over the course of the season, in all Broadway theatres combined.) Ten of the thirty-eight Broadway theatres were dark for more than half of 2001–2002; the Minskoff was empty the entire season, with the marquee from

The Adventures of Tom Sawyer—which closed May 13, 2001—haunting Forty-fifth Street until the summer of 2002. (The Minskoff finally reopened in October 2002 with previews of *Dance of the Vampires*, after seventy-four dark weeks.) Seven other houses were dark for eight months or more, including desirable theatres like the Booth, the Broadway, and the Richard Rodgers.

Ticket prices continued their inevitable climb. *The Producers*, with typical bravado, raised their top ticket to $100 on the day after they opened in mid-April 2001. (They actually charged $99, onto which patrons were compelled to add a buck for so-called theatre restoration.) This price was matched in 2001–2002 by *Mamma Mia!*, *Into the Woods*, and the reigning *Lion King*. More astoundingly, some long-running musicals that weren't doing especially strong business saw fit to raise their price to $95. The standard for nonmusicals became $75 (or $76.25, with the restoration charge), which had been tentatively introduced in 2000–2001 (but not by *Proof* or *The Allergist*). One play, the limited engagement of *The Crucible*, charged $86 and managed to sell extremely well —although not well enough, it seems, to quite recoup their high costs.

The Producers can also be blamed for a second development. Broadway Inner Circle, a for-profit agency formed by some of the *Producers* producers, placed prime seats for their show on sale to the general public for $480. ("When you got it," to quote Max Bialystock Brooks, "flaunt it.") The prime seat scheme was adopted by four other shows in early 2002. This was understandable in the case of hot tickets like *The Graduate* and *The Crucible*, both of which charged $250; it was more of a stretch for the long-running revivals of *Chicago* and *Cabaret*, which offered seats for $180.

One foresees that more and more prime seats for hit shows will be withheld from general circulation, in favor of fat cats and the expense account crowd. While this sounds like a terribly greedy act on the part of producers and theatre owners, the fact is that illegal scalpers and brokers have been selling tickets to hits at bloated prices since the days of Flo Ziegfeld. Starting with *The Producers*, some of this money is finally getting into the pockets of investors and royalty recipients. Which is a small victory, anyway.

Broadway Yearbook 2001–2002 presents an analytical discussion of each show that opened on Broadway between May 28, 2001, and May 26, 2002. I have also deemed it fitting to include certain non-Broadway productions of importance, such as the Meryl Streep–Mike Nichols *Seagull* and the City Center Encores! series. The shows are discussed in chronological order; an alphabetical arrangement might make it easier to browse through to find a specific show, but it seems pertinent to have the reader discover each show in the same order as the critics. Timing—that is, competition on the date of opening—is a significant factor in the reception and fate of Broadway shows.

The opening-night credits and cast list are followed by a discussion of the production. I neither ask nor expect the reader to necessarily agree with my opinions. You will no doubt concur with some and not others, hopefully more of the former than the latter. Taste is individual, or at least it should be. I have tried to be consistent in my opinions and to support my arguments (in the nonargumentative sense of the word). It is one thing to turn thumbs up or thumbs down; it is another thing to explain *why* the thumb is nudged toward the heavens or the opposite. Or someplace in between.

My aim has been to keep things informative and instructive; hence, the discussion is laced with examples from general Broadway history (and my checkered experience on and around Forty-fourth Street). What were the shows like? How were the shows received, by both the critics and the audiences? What other factors contributed to their success or failure?

The discussion of each production is followed by a section of related data, starting with dates and length of run. Performance and preview totals have been compiled using data from the League of American Theatres and Producers. In some cases these differ from the "official" counts appearing elsewhere; I consider the League tabulation—reported week by week, along with the grosses—to be more accurate. Profit/loss information comes from a variety of sources, including the invaluable *Variety*. Shows from nonprofit organizations have been similarly classified where applicable, based on an estimate of surplus income generated by the production. It should be understood that a show that ends its Broadway run with a loss might well make up the difference from post-Broadway income. Conversely, it is not unknown for a show to have recouped its costs but—due to an overextended run or unforeseen touring costs—slip back into a deficit.

Shows that were still running on May 27, 2002—the first day of the 2002–2003 season—are so indicated. (For the sake of completeness, closing dates and performance totals are included for shows that ran into 2002–2003 but closed before this book went to print.) Next comes the critical scorecard, which gives the reader a general idea of the critical reception of each production. The scorecards are based on the opinions of up to ten critics from major newspapers and magazines. The number of reviews varies; not all attractions were covered by all the critics. (One production this season received no reviews, due to extreme circumstances.) The scorecards usually reflect the opinions of critics from the *New York*

Times, the *Daily News*, the *New York Post*, *Newsday*, the *Associated Press*, *Variety*, the *Village Voice*, *USA Today*, and *New York Magazine*, as well as assorted others.

Reviews have been rated in five categories:

Rave   Overwhelmingly positive, enthusiastically indicating that the show should be seen

Favorable   Positive, indicating that the show is good though not outstanding, or that the show is good despite minor flaws

Mixed   Positive and negative aspects are presented, with no overall recommendation; sometimes the reviewer is simply unclear

Unfavorable   Negative, indicating that the show doesn't work— often despite positive elements or good intentions

Pan   Overwhelmingly negative, indicating—often with a hint of annoyance—that the show was downright bad

Quite a few of the reviews fall somewhere between two categories. I have called 'em like I see 'em, although the tenor of some reviews is open to interpretation.

A brief financial section gives the reader an idea of the show's box office performance. Figures, again, have been compiled using information from the League of American Theatres and Producers. Finally, Tony Awards (and nominations) received by the show and its personnel are listed, along with other major awards.

Following the main body of the book are six appendixes that, it is hoped, will prove a useful supplement to the discussion of the season.

And so the curtain rises, as they say, on *Broadway Yearbook 2001– 2002*.

See you at the theatre.

The Shows

A Thousand Clowns

The first new show of the 2000–2001 season was a limited-engagement revival headed by a big-name TV superceleb who had long wanted to star on Broadway in the play, regardless of ability or suitability. Despite a bumpy tryout, it came to town and quickly died.

The first new show of the 2001–2002 season was another limited-engagement revival headed by a big-name TV superceleb. Who had long wanted to star on Broadway in the play. Regardless of ability or suitability. Despite a bumpy tryout, it came to town. And did slightly better, but only slightly.

There were major differences between Kelsey Grammer's *Macbeth* and Tom Selleck's *A Thousand Clowns*. In the first place, Grammer was a current-day Hollywood star, reportedly earning a whopping $1.76 million per episode of *Frasier*. (Per episode, I say; multiply that figure twenty times per season.) Selleck was a former Hollywood star, with eight seasons' worth of the adventure series *Magnum, P.I.*, and film hits like *Three Men and a Baby* on his résumé. Still somewhat bankable, and presumably with lots of cash in the bank. (Selleck: "I know people will laugh at this, but I'm not going to make enough money to pay my mortgage with this.") But Selleck's star, as a star, was relatively faded. That is to say, he wasn't turning down a million a week to appear on Broadway.

It should also be pointed out that *A Thousand Clowns* had been unsuccessfully revived on Broadway less than five years earlier. In an interview with *Playbill*, Selleck said that when he was offered a role in a dif-

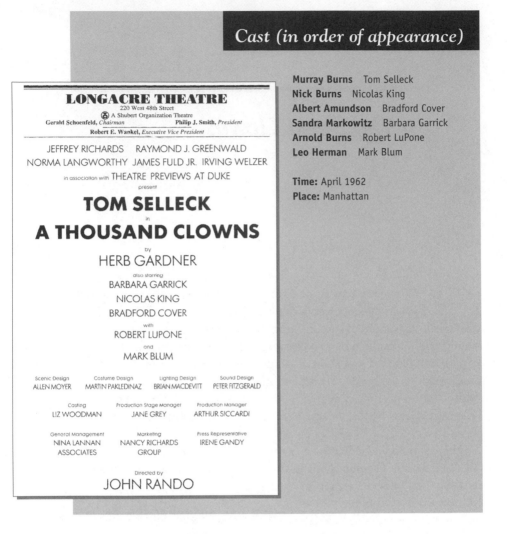

Murray Burns   Tom Selleck
Nick Burns   Nicolas King
Albert Amundson   Bradford Cover
Sandra Markowitz   Barbara Garrick
Arnold Burns   Robert LuPone
Leo Herman   Mark Blum

Time: April 1962
Place: Manhattan

ferent revival—the 2000 production of *The Best Man*, I'd suspect—he replied, "I don't want to do this play, but if you ever want to do A *Thousand Clowns*, I'm your guy." And so he did.

Grammer's attempt was less of a stretch than Selleck's, perhaps. Kelsey was trained at Juilliard, although he dropped out without graduating. He appeared on Broadway in an earlier, almost-as-bad *Macbeth*, and actually played the role when leading man Philip Anglim was indisposed by a bad case of reviews. Selleck, on the other hand, came to town with a charming personality—he was the winner of four People's Choice Awards for Favorite Male Television Performer—but little ammunition, acting-wise. Charm goes a long way, in eccentric comedies at least, and Mr. Selleck was able to get by.

Herb Gardner's A *Thousand Clowns* is not your everyday, forty-year-old

Broadway comedy. To begin with, it's very good; at least, it was when it opened in 1962. Gardner was a professional cartoonist, creator of a strip called *The Nebbishes*. His wife at the time, an aspiring actress, got a role in a small off-Broadway show that showed little promise. "I can write something like that," he reportedly said, and he did. *A Thousand Clowns* was a sizable success, although it ran about forty years less than Rita Gardner's show, *The Fantasticks*.

A *Thousand Clowns* was one of the first of the new breed of offbeat comedies that took the stage in the early 1960s. You note that I don't call them Jewish comedies. Broadway had seen numerous comedies over the years by writers who happened to be Jewish, from George S. Kaufman and Moss Hart to Lillian Hellman and Arthur Laurents. There had also been occasional "Jewish plays" catering to Jewish audiences, usually starring people like Gertrude Berg or Molly Picon. But sophisticated American-Jewish humor suddenly became bankable with the TV popularity of Sid Caesar in the 1950s. Caesar's merry band of writers included Neil Simon, Mel Brooks, Carl Reiner, Larry Gelbart, and Woody Allen, all of whom had a hand in writing the book on late twentieth-century American comedy.

This new type of humor reached Broadway in October 1960, when Mike Nichols and Elaine May brought their act to the Golden in *An Evening with Nichols and May*. *A Thousand Clowns* came next, on April 5, 1962. This was followed by Neil Simon's smash hit *Barefoot in the Park*, which opened in October 1963 and broke the 1,500-performance mark. (Simon's *Come Blow Your Horn* preceded *A Thousand Clowns* into town, but it was of the "Jewish play" category.) By the time Murray Schisgal's *Luv* opened in October 1964, these so-called offbeat comedies had set a new tone for Broadway comedy. Mike Nichols —not coincidentally—was coauthor and star of *An Evening with Mike Nichols and Elaine May*, and director of *Barefoot* and *Luv*.

Herb Gardner had a deliciously offbeat way with words, with a tendency to overwrite; his dialogue was full of flavorable nooks and crannies.

Murray Burns, the unconventional hero of *A Thousand Clowns*, is an unemployed comedy writer. Unemployed by choice. Raising his unconventional twelve-year-old nephew in an unconventional manner, he runs afoul of the child welfare authorities. Scrambling to keep custody of the kid—one of those preteen little-old-men favored by Broadway comedy writers—he beds one of the welfare workers, and even goes back to work for Chuckles the Chipmunk (see below). This ne'er-do-well with child was not an altogether novel situation; Arnold Schulman's *A Hole in the Head*—a comedy hit in 1957, a Frank Sinatra–Frank Capra motion picture in 1959—had pretty much the same setup. But the magic of *A Thousand Clowns* was in the characters, and especially in the text. Gardner turned out to have a deliciously offbeat way with words, with a tendency to overwrite; his dialogue was full of flavorable nooks and crannies.

A Thousand Clowns does not have a Jewish theme, but it seems to be very much about second-generation Jewish-American assimilation. Murray's ex-employer, kiddie show star Leo Herman (aka Chuckles the Chipmunk), is written as a "Jewish" Jew. He wears his ethnicity on his sleeve in the same manner as Sid Caesar or Jackie Mason. Murray's brother, tal-

ent agent Arnold Burns, is the opposite. Dressed in impeccable suits with well-chosen ties and cufflinks, he is as assimilated as can be (for 1962 anyway). Murray himself falls somewhere in between. Like Arnold, he does not show outward signs of his religion. Unlike Arnold, though, he doesn't try to hide it. Murray enthusiastically celebrates Irving R. Feldman's birthday, Irving R. Feldman being the purveyor of Murray's favorite pastrami sandwich. (Arnold would not, under any circumstances, importune his neighbors to celebrate Irving R. Feldman.) Murray does not act like he's Jewish, or like he's non-Jewish; call him American. The

play's love interest, a novice social worker from Queens on her first day of fieldwork, is also presumably Jewish. At least, her name is Sandra Markowitz.

I looked forward to the first Broadway revival of *A Thousand Clowns* when it was announced by the Roundabout for the summer of 1996. Robert Klein, who had done a superb job in *The Sisters Rosensweig*, headed the cast; Gene Saks, director of Simon's *Brighton Beach* trilogy and *Lost in Yonkers*, was at the helm. (Saks, in his acting days, created the role of Chuckles.) I hadn't seen the original *A Thousand Clowns*, having been nine years old at the time, but I was very familiar with the play and the marvelous 1965 screen version that was closely adapted from the Broadway staging. (Fred Coe produced and directed both.) Would the play seem a little dated? a little clunky? a little long?

Yes, indeed. There were extenuating circumstances, though. Klein, his leading lady Jane Addams, and director Saks quit or were fired midway through rehearsals. Judd Hirsch, star of Gardner's *I'm Not Rappaport* (1985), took over the lead, under the direction of Roundabout associate director Scott Ellis. Not surprisingly, the production was a shambles. (Gardner has a reputation for being difficult. His troubled 1974 comedy *Thieves* changed stars, director, and producers during previews.) The Roundabout *A Thousand Clowns* was poorly reviewed; it seemed dated, clunky, and long.

You might think that this reception would dissuade new producers from turning around and mounting a commercial production of the play only five years later. But Tom Selleck wanted to do it. ("When he began his career as an actor," Selleck's *Playbill* bio informed us, "Tom's favorite play was *A Thousand Clowns*; with this appearance he is fulfilling a life-long career ambition.") If you are a producer who believes that Tom Selleck on Broadway is going to sell tickets (at $77.50) like hot knishes, you'll let him do any darn play he wants. Except, maybe, *Macbeth*.

Selleck didn't sell many tickets, it turned out. Certainly not in advance. The plan was to garner good reviews on the road—*A Thousand Clowns* played tryouts in Raleigh/Durham (North Carolina), Chicago, and Boston—and build up a strong Broadway advance. I don't know what kind of advance they ended up with, but they made the highly unusual last-minute decision to cut out a week of previews and move up their Broadway opening. Traditionally, moving up the opening implies that preview business is lousy and the show has run out of money. (The official word was that Gardner was ill, leaving the implication that the producers were afraid he wouldn't make it through the extra week. After which we never heard anything more about Gardner's health.)

Selleck was well matched by his supporting cast, which was less than exemplary. A glance at the 1962 stage and 1965 film casts might prove instructive. Saks appeared in both; so did William Daniels, as Albert.

(Daniels started out as a teenager in *Life with Father*; made an award-winning splash off-Broadway in Edward Albee's *A Zoo Story* in 1960; moved on to the role of John Adams in *1776*; won six Emmys for *St. Elsewhere*; and was elected president of the Screen Actors Guild.) Sandy Dennis, who created Sandra, became a full-fledged Broadway star in 1964 with *Any Wednesday*; her role was undertaken in the film by Barbara Harris. A. Larry Haines was brother Arnold onstage; Martin Balsam played the role on film, and rather astoundingly snagged an Oscar in the role. (In Arnold's big scene, Balsam gave what you might call a primal scream—a startling moment that apparently won him the award.)

True, performers like these might well have made Selleck look like an amateur from Hollywood; but they certainly would have helped the play. Mark Blum, as an ennervating Leo (Chuckles), gave the only performance I would care to see again; he was also good in *The Best Man*, from the same producers. Ten-year-old Nicolas King made an interestingly quirky Nick. Unfortunately, it was difficult to understand much of what he was saying; he talked in paragraphs, as if he had carefully memorized the words but neglected the punctuation. That's often a problem with child actors, especially in a case where they're playing characters who talk like little old (Jewish) men.

The 1996 Broadway revival was dated, clunky, and long. You might think that this would dissuade producers from mounting another only five years later.

Selleck mentioned in interviews that as an acting student, he would do scenes from *A Thousand Clowns* whenever he got the chance. His performance looked it. He was not bad, not bad at all. But there is more to the character than meets the page, and here Selleck was helpless. In acting school, Selleck tells us, the reaction was always "Why are you doing this play? You should be doing *The Rainmaker*. You should be doing Tennessee Williams guys." Murray Burns is a New Yorker with pickle brine in his veins. Selleck is USC all the way. I'm all for casting against type; but the guy you cast against type needs to be able to *act*. Jason Robards was not a New Yorker, either, nor was he Jewish. But he was an actor.

Murray has a speech in the first act about his sister Elaine. Elaine, who stopped by one day with her seven-year-old son and two suitcases; went downstairs to buy a pack of filter-tip cigarettes; and didn't return until six years later. He matter-of-factly explains that the boy's father is not a question of where, but a question of who. "You might call Nick a bastard, or a little bastard, depending on how whimsical you feel at the time."

This speech, to be effective, must be delivered passionlessly, without pity; just the facts, with an occasional joke thrown in. And that's how

Selleck did it. Robards was passionless here, too; but there was pain behind the words. (The play takes place circa 1960, when there was still a
stigma against illegitimacy—especially in what was presumably a middle-
class Jewish family.) With Robards, you felt that Murray Burns had cried
about this, when no one was looking, and forced himself—as a defense—
to adapt the matter-of-fact, sardonic attitude. That was Murray's character, as Robards played him. He casually shrugged off everything that was
important, allowing the audience to recognize what was important by the
way he casually shrugged it off. Selleck just said the words. He said them
very nicely, and he was charming as he said them; but where was Murray?

"You're not a person, Mr. Burns—you're an experience," complains
Albert, the exasperated welfare worker, and that sums things up neatly.
Selleck was nice and charming and more or less lovable; but Murray, in
his characterization, was very much *not* an experience.

Major Barbara

The Roundabout Theatre Company moved to the Broadway-eligible Criterion Center in 1991 and under Todd Haimes's direction quickly became a major force in the New York theatre. While they had been turning out revivals since 1966, Roundabout shook things up with their 1993 revival of Eugene O'Neill's *Anna Christie*. Director David Leveaux took an old-fashioned, seventy-year-old drama, inserted Broadway novices Natasha Richardson and Liam Neeson, and turned it into the steamiest play of the season. This was followed by a delightful revival of Jerry Bock and Sheldon Harnick's *She Loves Me*, which transferred to the Atkinson (for an unsuccessful run); a strong rendition of Harold Pinter's *No Man's Land*, with Christopher Plummer and Jason Robards; and a highly entertaining Brian Bedford-Richard Wilbur exploration of two *Molière Comedies*. The 1995–1996 and 1996–1997 seasons were less notable, although Frank Langella was highly acclaimed for his performance in Strindberg's *The Father*.

But it was the 1997–1998 season that elevated Roundabout into a class with Lincoln Center Theater, Manhattan Theatre Club, and the New York Shakespeare Festival. Revivals of Arthur Miller's *A View from the Bridge* and John Kander and Fred Ebb's *Cabaret* picked up both best revival Tony Awards for that season, along with four of the eight best actor/actress awards. *Side Man* opened after the Tony deadline; it would pick up the Best Play Tony the following year. All three would transfer to open-ended runs; while *Cabaret* proved to be a major hit, both plays struggled and closed at a loss. Still, the sudden burst of artistic success was reminiscent of the glory days of the Shakespeare Festival, with such hits as *That Championship Season* and *A Chorus Line*.

Said success helped Roundabout to acquire and renovate the old Selwyn Theatre, one of those ghost houses on Forty-second Street. That is, the string of successful shows attracted enough benefactors and corporate sponsors to continue underwriting the Roundabout season and fund the theatre project as well. The largest sponsor, apparently, was American Airlines, whose name now graces the Roundabout's main stage.

As fate would have it, the artistic success of the 1997–1998 season proved short-lived. The Roundabout continued to do pretty much what they had been doing in the manner in which they had been doing it. But art is a tricky business. The 1998–1999 season saw only two "Broadway" productions. (The Roundabout also produces a series of "off-Broadway" productions—that is, in a smaller theatre with a lesser set of union scales.) Much was expected from their revival of the Cy Coleman–Dorothy Fields–Neil Simon musical comedy *Little Me*. The show, though, is exceedingly stubborn. It failed, originally, in 1962; it failed when the three authors revised it in 1982; and it was even less successful in the Roundabout's revision, despite the presence of Martin Short and Faith Prince. This was followed by James Goldman's *The Lion in Winter*, one of those not-too-good plays that becomes a well-known title by virtue of its motion picture version (which starred Katharine Hepburn). Stockard Channing and Laurence Fishburne played it at the Roundabout, but it remained not too good.

The 1999–2000 season began with *The Rainmaker*, another one of those not-too-good plays that becomes a well-known title by virtue of its motion picture version (which starred Katharine Hepburn). This one was scuttled by a strange performance by Woody Harrelson; a film and television star, he was a fish out of water as the rainmaker. This was followed by an awkward production of *Uncle Vanya* starring Derek Jacobi, Roger Rees, and Brian Murray. How bad could it be? you wondered, until the truth of the situation smothered you after forty minutes. The season ended with the gala opening of the new American Airlines Theatre and the old Kaufman and Hart rib- **Shaw is always a safe choice for a nonprofit. How can you go wrong? And no royalties to pay!** tickler *The Man Who Came to Dinner*, headed by Nathan Lane (just before donning Max Bialystock's mantle). This production received its share of enthusiastic reviews and did strong business, but it seemed weak at the knees to me. Harold Pinter's *Betrayal* was somewhat less favorably reviewed—by the more "important" critics, anyway—but I found it compelling theatre. I just compiled a list of my top twenty Broadway experiences of the three seasons since *Cabaret*. *Betrayal* is the only entry from the Roundabout.

This was followed by two misbegotten revivals. Noël Coward's *Design for Living* is a difficult vehicle for various reasons, starting with the fact

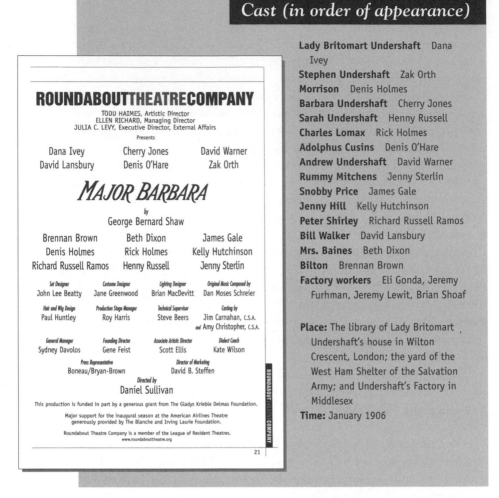

ROUNDABOUTTHEATRECOMPANY

TODD HAIMES, Artistic Director
ELLEN RICHARD, Managing Director
JULIA C. LEVY, Executive Director, External Affairs

Presents

Dana Ivey   Cherry Jones   David Warner
David Lansbury   Denis O'Hare   Zak Orth

MAJOR BARBARA

by
George Bernard Shaw

Brennan Brown   Beth Dixon   James Gale
Denis Holmes   Rick Holmes   Kelly Hutchinson
Richard Russell Ramos   Henny Russell   Jenny Sterlin

Set Designer	Costume Designer	Lighting Designer	Original Music Composed by
John Lee Beatty	Jane Greenwood	Brian MacDevitt	Dan Moses Schreier

Hair and Wig Design	Production Stage Manager	Technical Supervisor	Casting by
Paul Huntley	Roy Harris	Steve Beers	Jim Carnahan, C.S.A. and Amy Christopher, C.S.A.

General Manager	Founding Director	Associate Artistic Director	Dialect Coach
Sydney Davolos	Gene Feist	Scott Ellis	Kate Wilson

Press Representative	Director of Marketing
Boneau/Bryan-Brown	David B. Steffen

Directed by
Daniel Sullivan

This production is funded in part by a generous grant from The Gladys Krieble Delmas Foundation.

Major support for the inaugural season at the American Airlines Theatre
generously provided by The Blanche and Irving Laurie Foundation.

Roundabout Theatre Company is a member of the League of Resident Theatres.
www.roundabouttheatre.org

21

Lady Britomart Undershaft   Dana Ivey
Stephen Undershaft   Zak Orth
Morrison   Denis Holmes
Barbara Undershaft   Cherry Jones
Sarah Undershaft   Henny Russell
Charles Lomax   Rick Holmes
Adolphus Cusins   Denis O'Hare
Andrew Undershaft   David Warner
Rummy Mitchens   Jenny Sterlin
Snobby Price   James Gale
Jenny Hill   Kelly Hutchinson
Peter Shirley   Richard Russell Ramos
Bill Walker   David Lansbury
Mrs. Baines   Beth Dixon
Bilton   Brennan Brown
Factory workers   Eli Gonda, Jeremy Furhman, Jeremy Lewit, Brian Shoaf

Place: The library of Lady Britomart Undershaft's house in Wilton Crescent, London; the yard of the West Ham Shelter of the Salvation Army; and Undershaft's Factory in Middlesex
Time: January 1906

that it was written to order for its original stars, Alfred Lunt and Lynn Fontanne and Coward himself. The Roundabout sensibly assembled an intriguing director (Joe Mantello) and an intriguing pair of newly minted stars (Alan Cumming and Jennifer Ehle), the very same recipe that resulted in the aforementioned *Anna Christie*. There is an inherent danger of attempting a new-style production of an old play. When it works, you're a genius. Otherwise, thud!

And then Roundabout turned to its most highly anticipated production ever, the first Broadway revival of Stephen Sondheim and James Goldman's *Follies*. Another intriguing young director—Matthew Warchus, of *Art* fame—came up with another new take. When it works, as in *Cabaret*, you're a genius. But when you're dealing with a beloved musical with legions of die-hard fans, the thud! is magnified tenfold.

For the opening slot of 2001–2002, Roundabout turned to a safe choice. Shaw is always a safe choice for a nonprofit. Who will attack you? How can you go wrong? And, besides, no royalties to pay! Molière and Rostand and Ibsen and Chekhov all need translations. Unless you're content to trot out an archaic text in the public domain, you either commission a new version or pay to use a recent one; Shaw and Shakespeare are free. Roundabout produced four Shaw plays in their previous ten seasons, *Candida* in 1993 and—on their non-Broadway stages—*Misalliance* (1997), *You Never Can Tell* (1998), and *Arms and the Man* (2000). All four of which were—well, safe choices. None were especially memorable except for the last, which was critically excoriated.

That this *Major Barbara* was not to be just another workmanlike classic became apparent with the announcement of the star and director. Cherry Jones has become one of Broadway's few dependables: dependably good, dependable to return to the stage this year and next year and every other year. (Ms. Jones, at this point in her career, seems to be a modern-day Julie Harris.) Can a production of *Major Barbara* be merely workmanlike with Ms. Jones in the title role? Not likely.

The presence of Daniel Sullivan, too, could only further raise expectations. Sullivan's recent work included *Dinner with Friends* and *Proof*, both of them good plays (and Pulitzer Prize winners). They also happened to be excellently directed. Sullivan also directed Ms. Jones in the 2000 revival of *A Moon for the Misbegotten*; between *Moon for the Misbegotten* and *Major Barbara*, he directed two off-Broadway shows for Lincoln Center Theater, *Spinning into Butter* and *Ten Unknowns*.

Shaw and Sullivan and Jones were well met, with pleasing results. Pleasing, yes; highly pleasing, no. This *Major Barbara* had just about everything you'd wish, except a spark. Jones gave a skillful and enjoyable performance in a role for which she was well suited; one can't expect her to stretch herself every time, can one? After *Pride's Crossing* (at Lincoln Center in 1997) and *Moon for the Misbegotten*, she deserved a role that didn't require superhuman effort for a change. She was well supported by Dana Ivey—who, oddly, received first star billing. Ms. Ivey played Lady Undershaft as if she were the star; she found laughs throughout the text—always valid laughs—which helped move the ninety-year-old, two-and-three-quarter-hour play along.

> Cherry Jones is one of Broadway's few dependables: dependably good, dependable to return to the stage this year and next year and every other year. Can *Major Barbara* be merely workmanlike with Jones in the role?

And then there was the Andrew Undershaft of David Warner. Mr. Warner appeared as if out of nowhere. At the age of twenty-two, he embarked on the fast track to stardom with the Royal Shakespeare Company. He played leading roles in Peter Hall's *War of the Roses* trilogy in 1963 and starred as Richard II in 1964 and Hamlet in 1965. Warner became a movie star in 1966 as the eccentric hero of *Morgan!*, abruptly changing course. He left the stage altogether in 1972, spending the ensuing three decades playing motion picture villains in such films as *The Omen*, *Time after Time*, and *Titanic*. And then he suddenly turned up, at the age of sixty, as the Roundabout's Undershaft. And he was very good; despite his long absence—apparently the result of a numbing case of stage fright— Warner can speak, and he can act. The outspoken Undershaft speaks for Shaw—or, rather, the outspoken Shaw speaks through Undershaft—and Warner's intelligent handling of the role capably transmitted Shaw's ideas. But he never leapt across the footlights at you.

And it helps to have Andrew Undershaft leap across the footlights. A self-described "profiteer in mutilation and murder," Undershaft rails against "Christmas card moralities of peace on earth and goodwill among men." To Undershaft there are two things necessary for salvation: "Money and

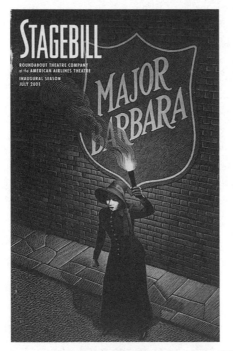

gunpowder." (Adolphus, Undershaft's Greek-speaking prospective son-in-law, notes "that is the general opinion of our governing classes. The novelty is in hearing any man confess it.")

Undershaft jabs away at religion, government, and morality. The seven deadly sins, to him: "Food, clothing, firing, rent, taxes, respectability, and children. Nothing can lift those seven millstones from Man's neck but money; and the spirit cannot soar until the millstones are lifted." Let Lady Undershaft admonish him: "You ought to know better than to go about saying that wrong things are true. What does it matter whether they are true if they are wrong?" Undershaft jabs right back: "What does it matter whether they are wrong if they are true?"

Undershaft shocks moralists by praising alcohol: "It makes life bearable to millions of people who could not endure their existence it they were quite sober. It enables Parliament to do things at eleven at night

Major Barbara
Opened: July 12, 2001
Closed: September 16, 2001
74 performances (and 32 previews)
Profit/Loss: Nonprofit [Loss]
Major Barbara ($65 top) was scaled to a potential gross of
$349,943 at the 740-seat American Airlines Theatre.
Weekly grosses averaged about $243,000, with business
building to $287,000 for the Labor Day week. Total gross
for the fourteen-week run was $3,217,456. Attendance
was about 82 percent, with the box office grossing about
69 percent of dollar-capacity. (These figures are not
indicative, as the potential was calculated at the top
ticket price, but subscribers paid less.)

*Critical
Scorecard*

Rave 4
Favorable 4
Mixed 0
Unfavorable 1
Pan 0

that no sane person would do at eleven in the morning." He really goes
after politicians, casting lances that are curiously sharp ninety-five years
later. "Let six hundred and seventy fools loose in the street, and three policemen can scatter them. But huddle them together in a certain house in
Westminster; and let them go through certain ceremonies and call themselves certain names until at last they get the courage to kill; and your six
hundred and seventy fools become a government." As to the power of the
ballot: "When you vote, you only change the names of the cabinet."

In short, Undershaft is Shaw. *Major Barbara* is deceptively named. Undershaft's daughter is strong-minded and heroic, but she hasn't got a
chance. Shaw gives her good arguments, yes; but only when he's given
Undershaft lines to top her. Undershaft rails against class and government and religion. You don't expect the playwright'll allow himself to be
bested, do you?

In Jones and Warner, Sullivan had two strong and highly capable actors. But where was the struggle between them? Where was the cat-and-
mouse game? Barbara has all the attributes, Undershaft has all the cards.
In this production, Warner simply sat back and waited until Shaw provided gunpowder (in the way of words).

While it is not my place to suggest alternate casting, I can't help but
consider a few men on the Roundabout roster at the beginning of this discussion. Christopher Plummer or Frank Langella, for example. Both have
an onstage presence that allows them to electrify the stage *without* words.
(So do Derek Jacobi and Brian Bedford, who are less likely for the role.)
One can imagine Plummer, especially, stealing the audience's attention
by simply leaning silently against a bookshelf. Picture Plummer and Jones
as Undershaft and Undershaft. While Jones is speaking, you can't help
but constantly shift your eyes toward Plummer; when Chris starts going,

you feel compelled to keep turning to Cherry. This is the sort of thing that keeps theatregoers on the edge of their seats. The only crackling of the evening, from where I was sitting, emanated from Ms. Ivey and Denis O'Hare, who was extremely good in the Roundabout's *Cabaret* (as the black marketeer) and even better as Adolphus.

John Lee Beatty's scenery was memorable, at least his Wilton Crescent library was. (Another Beatty set you'd love to have as your living room.) The dank Salvation Army shelter was suitably poverty-struck, but I wonder what Sullivan and Beatty were up to with the final scene. I would never suggest that director and designer stick slavishly to the playwright's instructions, but Shaw—more than any playwright you can name—was pretty definite in what he intended. He placed the scene in an outdoor section of the factory, on the crest of a scenic slope; punctuated by cannon parts and "several dummy soldiers more or less mutilated, with straw protruding from their gashes. . . . One of them has fallen forward and lies, like a grotesque corpse." Sounds like he was trying to make a point, no? The Salvation Army yard—where the "goodly" go for salvation—is fetid and foul and polluted; the munitions factory, where Undershaft reigns as the Prince of Darkness, is Utopia—complete with clean air.

> **Pleasing, yes; highly pleasing, no.**
> ***Major Barbara* had just about everything you'd wish, except a spark.**

In this production, the scene was played inside a hangar-like factory. Stray from the playwright's vision if you have a reason, boys; the Roundabout's *Design for Living* had ridiculously exaggerated sets, but they served a distinct purpose. Sullivan and Beatty appeared otherwise to stick close by Shaw throughout the evening. I suppose they had a purpose, but from where I was sitting it seemed less effective than Shaw's proscribed locale.

Jones and Sullivan and Shaw's *Major Barbara* had a lot going for it. Not quite enough to cross the line from admirable to memorable, though.

If You Ever Leave Me . . . I'm Going with You!

I magine a Broadway evening with Neil Simon, with a title like *Cut Some Jokes . . . It's Too Damn Funny!* Out he comes, in a comfortable-looking cardigan. After a joke-laced opening monologue, he says: "And now I'll do a scene from *The Odd Couple*." Thirty minutes in, he shows a film clip of himself on the couch with Ed McMahon at the *Tonight Show*, in a line with Mel Brooks, Larry Gelbart, and Imogene Coca. Next he puts on an old man's fright wig and says, "And now, here's one of my favorite moments from *The Sunshine Boys*."

Not your traditional Broadway show, but it sounds good to me.

Now imagine another Broadway evening. Out comes old Doc Simon, and as soon as he's gotten us warmed up, he says, "And now I'll do a scene from *God's Favorite*. . . . And here's one of my favorite moments from *The Curse of Kolchenikov*." And then he shows some videos of his daughters at the pool in Malibu while he plays tennis with Manny Azenberg. Would you pay $66.25 for this?

> **Renée Taylor and Joe Bologna came out to present their greatest hits, the problem being that they don't *have* any greatest hits.**

Which gives you an idea of what we were up against with Renée Taylor and Joe Bologna's *If You Ever Leave Me . . . I'm Going with You!* The stars came out to present their greatest hits, the problem being that they don't *have* any greatest hits. Their stage catalogue consists of two Broadway flops, one off-Broadway flop, and some unproduced flops. The sort of material that you or I or Neil Simon would hide on the top shelf of a dusty bookshelf in the basement, rather than boast about at show-and-tell.

The evening started with a montage of filmed testimonials from peo-

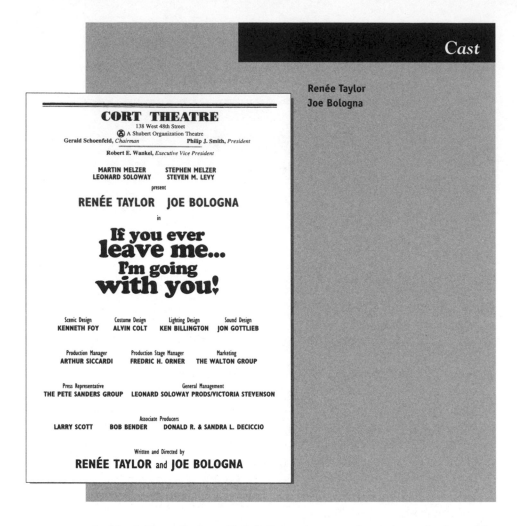

CORT THEATRE
138 West 48th Street
Ⓢ A Shubert Organization Theatre
Gerald Schoenfeld, *Chairman*   Philip J. Smith, *President*

Robert E. Wankel, *Executive Vice President*

MARTIN MELZER   STEPHEN MELZER
LEONARD SOLOWAY   STEVEN M. LEVY

present

RENÉE TAYLOR   JOE BOLOGNA

in

**If you ever
leave me...
I'm going
with you!**

Scenic Design	Costume Design	Lighting Design	Sound Design
KENNETH FOY	ALVIN COLT	KEN BILLINGTON	JON GOTTLIEB

Production Manager	Production Stage Manager	Marketing
ARTHUR SICCARDI	FREDRIC H. ORNER	THE WALTON GROUP

Press Representative   General Management
THE PETE SANDERS GROUP   LEONARD SOLOWAY PRODS/VICTORIA STEVENSON

Associate Producers
LARRY SCOTT   BOB BENDER   DONALD R. & SANDRA L. DECICCIO

Written and Directed by
RENÉE TAYLOR and JOE BOLOGNA

ple like Milton Berle and Sid Caesar, not in their prime, looking like shriveled-up old men. And then the stars entered. Bologna in a purple tuxedo, Taylor in a purple dress. They were both in purple, the sets were purple, everything was purple, apparently on purpose. Taylor waltzed on directly under an open ladder, also apparently on purpose. This was a bad omen, especially since she looked somewhat like a purple tugboat. (I'm allowed to say this, because she continually referred to herself as *zoftig*.)

So what we had were two old people in purple, walking and crawling and otherwise ambulating around the uncomfortable set. They had some funny lines along the way, yes, but the humor was pretty incidental. Most of the jokes came from stage left, where Ms. Taylor spent most of the evening. Taylor and Bologna staged the thing themselves, presumably in their living room, capturing it all on video camera by remote control.

Taylor was a kooky actress in the Elaine May mold. She was discovered by May, actually, when the latter directed the 1964 improvisational off-

Broadway revue *The Third Ear*. May's ex-partner, Mike Nichols, paid a visit; he was looking for an understudy for his new Broadway play, *Luv*, the Murray Schisgal romp that starred Eli Wallach, Anne Jackson, and Alan Arkin. Taylor got the job, and it was off to Broadway. (Understudying the two men was another youngster, Gene Wilder.) Taylor's most visible early role was as Eva Braun, peeling grapes for Dick Shawn in *Springtime for Hitler*, a musical-within-a-movie in some old Mel Brooks film. (*The Producers*, it was called; perhaps you've heard of it?)

Meanwhile, Taylor met Bologna in 1964. ("Bologna" is an Italian word for ersatz ham.) The Jewish Renée married her Italian Joe in 1965, smack-dab on *The Merv Griffin Show*. This was considerably cheaper than hiring a caterer. The gist of *If You Walk Out during Intermission . . . I'm Going with You!* had to do with the trials the pair was forced to endure due to what was then considered a mixed marriage. They never seem to have heard of *Abie's Irish Rose*, the monster hit of 1922 that ran until 1928 and covered the same territory. Neither were they familiar with Eli's Irish Anne, Mel's Italian Anne, or Stiller's Italian Meara, three showbiz marriages that were up and running well before Joe met Renée. Which makes them fourth-rate, by my count.

The pair set down to writing together. The result was *Lovers and Other Strangers*, an evening of four short plays centering on an Italian boy marrying a Jewish girl—which is to say, a fictionalized view of their courtship. The show opened on September 18, 1968, at the Atkinson, with a cast headed by Taylor and Zohra Lampert (but not Bologna) and directed by Charles Grodin. Moderately amusing but spotty, was the verdict. Facing such competition as Neil Simon's *Plaza Suite*, Arthur Miller's *The Price*, and Abe Burrows's *Cactus Flower*,

Lovers and Other Strangers struggled for two months and closed after seventy performances. It was adapted into a successful 1969 film of the same title, with neither Taylor not Bologna on-screen. Richard Castellano, an ethnically Italian actor shaped like an eggplant, made the transfer and received an Oscar nomination for his portrayal of the father of the groom. Castellano's oft-repeated catchphrase—"so what's the story?"—entered the vernacular. For a while, anyway.

Taylor and Bologna came back to Broadway in May 1981 with *It Had to Be You*, a two-character play presenting another fictionalized view of their courtship. This one was even more mirthless—unless, I suppose, you like that sort of thing—and folded after forty-eight performances.

Off they went again, to wherever it is out west that people like Taylor and Bologna go when they are not trying to storm Broadway. They reappeared sixteen years later—this time off-Broadway—with a geriatric sex farce called *The Bermuda Avenue Triangle*. (Bermuda Avenue is in Las Vegas; the third side of the triangle was an embarrassed Nanette Fabray.) This one ground on for five unsuccessful months at the Promenade.

If You Ever Leave Me . . . I'm Going with You! was more or less a spliced-together collection of scenes from *Lovers and Other Strangers*, *It Had to Be You*, and *The Bermuda Avenue Triangle*. Which is to say, Taylor and Bologna's greatest hits. Except they didn't have any hits.

Taylor waltzed on directly under an open ladder, apparently on purpose. This was a bad omen.

From 1993 through 1999, Taylor appeared on the sitcom *The Nanny*, receiving a couple of Emmy Award nominations in the process. The producers of *If You Ever Leave Me* seemed to be banking on Taylor's TV fame to sell tickets. The ads awkwardly exclaimed "TV's *The Nanny*'s Mother on B'way." I can just imagine all those many fans of TV's *The Nanny* throwing down their copies of the *Times* and exclaiming, "Aha! *The Nanny*'s Mother on B'way! Cancel the barbecue, Muriel, it's only one hundred thirty-two fifty a pair, plus service charge."

Me, I never watched TV's *The Nanny*. As I entered the Cort, Taylor and Bologna were—to me—a third-rate copy of Jerry Stiller and Anne

Meara, whom I always placed second to Eli Wallach and Anne Jackson. Nothing I saw in *If You Ever Leave Me . . . I'm Going with You!* changed my opinion.

Fleeing along Forty-eighth Street after the show, I overtook a woman, her daughter, and her daughter's daughter. They had presumably been sitting farther toward the back, as I got out of the theatre quick, let me tell you. The daughter turned to her mother and grandmother and said: "The joke I didn't understand is, what did he mean when he said 'Gentile'?"

"Bologna" is an Italian word for ersatz ham.

I spent the day of the evening I saw *If You Walk Out during Intermission . . . I'm Going With You!* on Centre Street, at the New York State Civil Court. So trust me when I say, *If You Ever Leave Me* was more painful than jury duty.

The Seagull

I've been going to opening nights, when the occasion has presented itself, since 1969, when I attended the premiere of a sorry musical comedy entitled *Come Summer*. (Ray Bolger, Agnes de Mille, nearly three hours without cracking a smile.) I have continued to attend openings whenever tickets came my way. The most memorable opening night, in my experience, was August 12, 2001, when Mike Nichols's star-studded production of *The Seagull* opened at the Delacorte Theatre in Central Park.

There we were: me and Nathan and Matthew and Sarah Jessica and Rosie and Warren and Annette and 1,894 others, standing beneath the narrow overhang outside the four gates leading into the theatre. It had started drizzling as my wife and I passed Balto, the bronze Alaskan sled dog two hundred paces west of Fifth Avenue and Sixty-sixth Street. By the time we reached the Delacorte and picked up our tickets, it was real rain—and plenty of it. But no one was about to leave, seeing as how this was the hottest ticket in memory. Since *The Producers*, anyway. The theatre did not open for seating at 7:30, presumably because they didn't want to seat people in the rain. The Delacorte, home to the New York Shakespeare Festival's Shakespeare in the Park, is an open-air theatre. There is an administration building under the bleachers, containing box office and concession stands and the like, but no other shelter.

So there we were, trying to keep dry under the few feet's worth of overhang ringing the building. The place was packed with familiar faces. While the free-to-the-public *Seagull* tickets were usually distributed on a first-come, first-serve basis, the opening-night audience consisted of some critics; some top-dollar donors; a strong contingency of theatre-business VIPs; and—because it was a Sunday evening, when Broadway shows are dark—just about every star around. Standing under our umbrellas, it seemed as if we were on a little town square. Folks just kind of stopped by to chat with each other, making some odd couples. I mean, where else would you find Nathan Lane hugging Cherry Jones?

The house finally opened at 7:50. We all filed in, took our seats, and raised our umbrellas. It was raining all right, the stage was swamped, but everybody sat tight. (I had gotten a manuscript copy of the playing script from the press agent, the better to write about the performance, and my main problem was keeping it dry through the downpour.) At 8:10 came an announcement that the rain appeared to be letting up and they were determined to get through the performance. (Great cheers.) As soon as the stage was ready, they would start—and please, no umbrellas during the performance.

Out came some Russian peasants with American mops, removing the protective drop cloths from the furniture pieces and swabbing the deck as best they could. When all was set, there came one of those "please turn off your cell phone" warnings. This one was a little different than what you usually hear, as violators were threatened with electrocution. The man's voice—clearly recognizable to fans of the old comedy team of Mike Nichols and Elaine May—asked us to imagine that it was 1895, and we were directly in the flight path of Smolensk Airport. And then, to great applause, the play commenced at 8:19.

Out came a pair of actors playing small roles, Tony Award winner Stephen Spinella and Oscar winner Marcia Gay Harden. They got applause. Within a minute, Ms. Hardin looked around at the rain-soaked stage and said, "I wouldn't be surprised if there's a storm tonight." This got a roar of laughter; that Tom Stoppard is a comic genius, don't you think?

> Under our umbrellas, it seemed as if we were on a little town square. I mean, where else would you find Nathan Lane hugging Cherry Jones?

Stoppard wrote the adaptation of Anton Chekhov's 1896 comedy. The Shakespeare Festival had announced that it would be using a newly commissioned version by Richard Nelson, author of *Two Shakespearean Actors*, *Some Americans Abroad*, and the libretto for *The Dead*. Ms. Streep—who came up with the idea to do the play, asking Nichols if he'd like to join her—was displeased with Nelson's script. They switched to Stoppard, who had adapted the play for Sir Peter Hall's production at the Old Vic in April 1997 (starring Felicity Kendall). Stoppard's 2001 script closely followed the 1997 version in form, although some major speeches were rewritten, and there were numerous word alterations (serving to make references less obscure).

Out loped Christopher Walken, as the heroine's failure-of-a-brother,

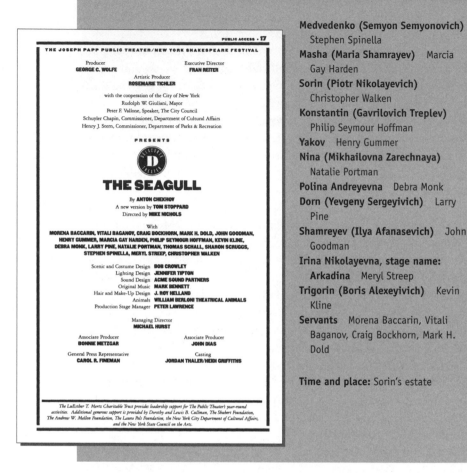

PUBLIC ACCESS · 17

THE JOSEPH PAPP PUBLIC THEATER/NEW YORK SHAKESPEARE FESTIVAL

Producer
GEORGE C. WOLFE

Executive Director
FRAN REITER

Artistic Producer
ROSEMARIE TICHLER

with the cooperation of the City of New York
Rudolph W. Giuliani, Mayor
Peter F. Vallone, Speaker, The City Council
Schuyler Chapin, Commissioner, Department of Cultural Affairs
Henry J. Stern, Commissioner, Department of Parks & Recreation

PRESENTS

D

THE SEAGULL

By ANTON CHEKHOV
A new version by TOM STOPPARD
Directed by MIKE NICHOLS

With
MORENA BACCARIN, VITALI BAGANOV, CRAIG BOCKHORN, MARK H. DOLD, JOHN GOODMAN,
HENRY GUMMER, MARCIA GAY HARDEN, PHILIP SEYMOUR HOFFMAN, KEVIN KLINE,
DEBRA MONK, LARRY PINE, NATALIE PORTMAN, THOMAS SCHALL, SHARON SCRUGGS,
STEPHEN SPINELLA, MERYL STREEP, CHRISTOPHER WALKEN

Scenic and Costume Design   BOB CROWLEY
Lighting Design   JENNIFER TIPTON
Sound Design   ACME SOUND PARTNERS
Original Music   MARK BENNETT
Hair and Make-Up Design   J. ROY HELLAND
Animals   WILLIAM BERLONI THEATRICAL ANIMALS
Production Stage Manager   PETER LAWRENCE

Managing Director
MICHAEL HURST

Associate Producer
BONNIE METZGAR

Associate Producer
JOHN DIAS

General Press Representative
CAROL R. FINEMAN

Casting
JORDAN THALER/HEIDI GRIFFITHS

The LuEsther T. Mertz Charitable Trust provides leadership support for The Public Theater's year-round
activities. Additional generous support is provided by Dorothy and Lewis B. Cullman, The Shubert Foundation,
The Andrew W. Mellon Foundation, The Laura Pels Foundation, the New York City Department of Cultural Affairs,
and the New York State Council on the Arts.

Medvedenko (Semyon Semyonovich)
Stephen Spinella
Masha (Maria Shamrayev)   Marcia
Gay Harden
Sorin (Piotr Nikolayevich)
Christopher Walken
Konstantin (Gavrilovich Treplev)
Philip Seymour Hoffman
Yakov   Henry Gummer
Nina (Mikhailovna Zarechnaya)
Natalie Portman
Polina Andreyevna   Debra Monk
Dorn (Yevgeny Sergeyevich)   Larry
Pine
Shamreyev (Ilya Afanasevich)   John
Goodman
Irina Nikolayevna, stage name:
Arkadina   Meryl Streep
Trigorin (Boris Alexeyivich)   Kevin
Kline
Servants   Morena Baccarin, Vitali
Baganov, Craig Bockhorn, Mark H.
Dold

Time and place: Sorin's estate

and Philip Seymour Hoffman, as the heroine's failure-of-a-son. They chatted for three or four minutes, as the rain got harder and harder. One lady near me, neatly outfitted in designer casual wear and at least four designer face-lifts, got up and walked the long walk to the exit. A few umbrellas were seen shooting up. At 8:31, as Hoffman started describing life with mother, another announcement came over the loudspeakers. "I'm sorry, we're going to have to stop." A collective groan, as out came the Russian peasants to cover the furniture. Walken and Hoffman seemed startled for a moment, then rose to exit. As they turned to the audience, there was a moment of connection, a "we're all in this together" moment, and a rousing cheer. The actors turned to leave the stage, and we suddenly heard a voice shout from the audience: "It stopped!"

And it had. Rain, rain, go away, the saying goes, and it did. The stage manager came right back on the PA and told us that the rain seemed to be stopping. He said that we'd have to wait while the crew mopped up the stage—"for the safety of the actors"—and we'd start again in a few minutes.

The mood of the audience of nineteen hundred strangers turned gleeful through the interlude, everybody—the high and the low—chatting with their neighbor. (I had David Yazbek to the left of me and Julie Hagerty a row back.) There we were, all wet, in the middle of Central Park; a glorious if damp midsummer night's eve, in the most exclusive audience with the hardest-to-get tickets ever. And there was something wonderfully democratic about it; Nathan and Matthew and Sarah Jessica and Rosie and Warren and Annette and Cherry and Mike Myers and Meg Ryan and Marlo Thomas and Rudy Giuliani (with his tabloid-fodder "special friend") were all sitting there too, waiting and dripping. No personal assistants or handlers with umbrellas and towels and bottled water, no special holding areas or luxury trailers, just the same cushionless seats under the same overcast sky. We were all in the same leaky boat, as it were, part of one and the same community.

At 8:42, Walken and Hoffman resumed their places. Applause. Walken, whose impersonation was closer to Groucho than Karl Marx, gave the audience a glint-eyed look and said, "Where wuz we?" Roar. The play resumed. A white horse appeared upstage, which is to say where the Delacorte stage met Belvedere Lake. It was so misty up there that you could barely see the horse or its rider, Natalie Portman. (This pretty much ruined her entrance hand, as she was already speaking when she came into clear view.)

Debra Monk did much better with her entrance, a few minutes later. Ms. Monk is justly celebrated for her way with a line. She was met with a distinct entrance hand; surveyed the audience from side to side, waiting; and then delivered her first line: "It's getting damp." Uproar, applause, cheers.

Unfortunately, it was by now raining again—and how. Harder than before. There was a two-level unit stage left—a summer house, apparently—with what looked to be a wrought iron stairway descending from the second level. Meryl Streep made her entrance from above. (Kevin Kline and John Goodman entered, too, but the audience only had eyes for Meryl.) As the actress descended the stairway, she seemed to be jerked upward as if a marionette on strings. Streep struggled, as her character seemed to continue unaffected; she yanked on her dress, which had been caught on the top

The "cell phone" warning was a little different than what you usually hear, as violators were threatened with electrocution.

of the landing, and then glided down the stairs as if nothing had happened.

Streep got her entrance applause, as well as one of those appreciative ovations. Her heavy gown had an extra-long train, which in its rain-drenched state must have been impossible to maneuver; hence, the struggle on the stairs. If you're Meryl Streep and can earn millions of dollars on a movie whenever you feel like it, you don't really need to stand in the rain for $646 a week (which is what the actors get at the Delacorte). The audience contained hundreds of Broadway actors, who were especially appreciative of this sort of dedication. (Larry Pine, as Dr. Dorn, got a round of applause with his line "there aren't as many outstanding actors nowadays, that's true, but the average level is much higher.") By this point, there were ominous thunderclaps, with all of us sitting in the open air with nothing above us except a steel grid holding electrical lighting equipment.

The cast soon moved into the play-within-the-play, with Ms. Portman's Nina delivering two impenetrable pages of gibberish through the driving rain. This is one of the passages that Stoppard rewrote extensively, filling it with repeated words to great comic effect. "Cold. Cold. Cold! Nothing. Nothing. Nothing! Horror. Horror. Horror." To which Streep responded, "Am I the only one who isn't getting this?"

The play-within-the-play was interrupted, and within a few minutes so was the play proper. The audience groaned, but sat still. The rain got heavier and heavier, so when George C. Wolfe—producer of the New York Shakespeare Festival—hopped on the stage in white pants after five minutes, we knew what he was going to say.

Nathan and Matthew and Sarah Jessica and Rosie and Cherry and Warren and Annette and Myers and Ryan and Rudy and the rest of the dripping playgoers streamed out onto one of the many park pathways leading from the Delacorte to Central Park West. I spilled out of the park right smack-dab into a vacant cab, somehow, which made a lovely U-turn and took us back to the East Side. As for what happened to all those celebrities, smashed among a crush of commoners, in a blinding rain, with their limos and personal assistants not ordered to return for hours—well, to paraphrase Golde in *Fiddler on the Roof*, that's their headache. The gala opening-night party, at the (outdoor) Belvedere Castle overlooking the Delacorte, was necessarily canceled as well, leaving more than one A-lister standing on the curb in a puddle.

All told, the opening-night audience saw thirty minutes of the play. (This was approximately two-thirds of the first of four acts; checking the script, we covered eighteen of seventy-seven pages.) And it was pretty much brilliant. Every moment seemed to register; nothing was wasted, and the frequent laughs made *The Seagull* seem as accessible as you'd like. There are no small actors, only small roles, to paraphrase *Hamlet* (a play that Chekhov continually draws our attention to in *The Seagull*). In Nichols's first act, every subsidiary actor was a star; you could imagine scattered audience members saying, "I once played Medvedenko at the Guthrie, I never realized he was *funny.*"

Based on the partial evening, it was clear that this was a brilliant *Seagull*. There had been talk of a Broadway transfer from the moment the production was announced, and it was clearly warranted. With only twelve more scheduled performances and given the impossibly tight ticket situation, it was unclear whether I'd be able to get back to the Delacorte. I was convinced, though, that this *Seagull* was magnificent. Until the following Friday, that is, when I went back.

The performance began promptly at 8:07, under clear skies. (We felt a few drops as we crossed the park, but they dried up and never returned.) *The Seagull* played like gangbusters through the first act; as before, laughs abounded, and every line by every character landed. Streep, in dry dress, was a comic delight. The play-within-a-play turned out to be about Streep; without the torrents of rain, we saw how the star shifted and turned and gestured her way through Portman's monologue. Streep also managed to make her bench squeak its way through the speech, providing even more laughs. The famous but over-the-hill actress Arkadina is unaccustomed to being out of the spotlight; not surprisingly, she's jealous of the ingenue Nina and determined not to let herself be upstaged. She is also determined to keep Trigorin (Kline) from leaving her for this much younger actress; hence, Streep's much-written-about cartwheel displaying her spryness. After which, she surreptitiously bent down and rubbed her knee, as if she'd done one too many reps at Equinox.

Streep sparkled, totally animating the proceedings. She looked animated, almost, in the pen-and-ink meaning of the word; she wheeled about the stage leading from the neck, gesticulating as if she had springs on her arms that were wired to her fingertips. She had a wonderful habit of starting applause for herself; whenever she let out a joke, she'd hold her palms against her chest and start them flapping until she got her reaction. But after Streep's exit early in act 2, the balloon deflated.

Act 2 belongs to Nina. (*The Seagull* was played at the Delacorte with one intermission, between the second and third acts.) She begins as an observer, making the forty-four-year-old Arkadina look—well, forty-four. She then plays a big scene with Arkadina's son Konstantin (Hoffman), in which he brings on a dead seagull. ("Look at this seagull," Nina says, "a symbol if ever I saw one, but of *what?* I'm sorry, I have no idea.") She then moves into an even bigger scene with Trigorin, in which she begins to seduce him away from Arkadina. Konstantin and Trigorin do most of the talking, but this *Seagull* was scuttled then and there by a Nina who couldn't handle it. Momentum, once lost, was never regained. Good performances from good performers, mostly, but everyone working in a vacuum.

This is not to say that Ms. Portman can't act. She has had great success in motion pictures (including the blockbuster *Star Wars: Episode One*). She also received acclaim for her performance in the title role of the spotty 1997 Broadway revival of *The Diary of Anne Frank*. (I myself was unmoved by performance and production.) Portman, at twenty, presumably has a long career ahead of her; if she keeps appearing with people like Streep and Kline and closely observes their methods, she should turn into quite an actor. But she was out of her element here, effectively capsizing

Streep sparkled, animating the proceedings. She wheeled about the stage leading from the neck, gesticulating as if she had springs on her arms that were wired to her fingertips.

two of the most important scenes of the play. Konstantin's scene was a total loss; Hoffman—who had done such a good job in the 2000 revival of *True West*—needed someone to work against. He seemed interesting in the first act, but his character developed into a whiny sad sack.

Kline, clearly, doesn't need anyone to work against; he can weave theatrical magic on his own, thank you very much. His performance, though, was as awkward as Streep's was wonderful. Trigorin is a reserved character, certainly; a famous writer who is content to sit upstage and fish, and who is tortured by the knowledge that his epitaph will read: "Here lies Trigorin. He was good, but not as good as Turgenev." (Turgenev was so good, in fact, that he ended the season with his own personal Tony nomination. Not bad for a guy who died in 1883.) Nina brings Trigorin to life in the second act, for a spell; at least, she is supposed to. Not here.

Part of the problem might have come from the casting. As written, Arkadina is forty-four. Konstantin is twenty-five. Trigorin is supposed to

The Seagull
Opened: August 14, 2001
Closed: August 26, 2001
12 performances (and 17 previews)
Profit/Loss: Nonprofit
The Seagull charged no admission at the 1,900-seat
    Delacorte Theatre. Attendance was virtually 100 percent.

*Critical
Scorecard*

Rave   3
Favorable   2
Mixed   1
Unfavorable   2
Pan   2

be closer in age to Konstantin than Arkadina; Konstantin describes Trigorin as a "young man" who "only goes for older woman." Kline, in real time, was fifty-four (to Streep's fifty-two). This is not an insurmountable problem, and one under which you'd expect an actor like Kline to flourish. He did not, though; perhaps, again, because he was acting against a beginner.

There is little purpose in citing past productions of plays, especially productions that none of us saw. But the record books tell us that Alfred Lunt and Lynn Fontanne did *The Seagull* for the Theatre Guild at the Shubert back in 1938. Alfred, too, was somewhat overaged for the role, at forty-six. Lynn played Arkadina, Richard Whorf her son, and Sydney Greenstreet her brother. What makes all this relevant is that Lunt and the others played against a Nina even younger than Portman, one who was not even a movie star.

Rather, a German-born, Wisconsin-bred, RADA-trained, totally unknown nineteen-year-old. This girl had not a single Broadway credit to her name, but it turned out she could act. Imagine what Uta Hagen must have brought to the role; imagine how she must have tied Trigorin and Konstantin and Arkadina in knots in the second and third acts, and how poignant it must have been when she dragged herself in—defeated—for her final scene. Hagen's Nina, sixty-three years earlier, made her a star overnight.

We shall not hold Ms. Portman up to the ghost of a performance that we did not see; but her act 2 Nina deflated Nichols's magic, and everything thereafter seemed disjointed. Nina's final scene with Konstantin caps the play, driving him to suicide. At the Delacorte, with a weightless Nina and a Konstantin we really couldn't care about, it all fell flat. As the lights went down, Streep had a wonderful moment as a sense of impending horror lit her face. But that wasn't enough to make us share the horror.

The Seagull appeared a shoo-in to transfer; the word was they would try to work out cast availability—not an easy task, dealing with so many sought-after performers— providing that the reviews were great. As it turned out, Streep was roundly praised for her performance, with plenty of carping about other aspects of the production. Still, a plan to move to the Lyceum in November, with a $100 top, was announced the day after the rained-out opening. Finances would be tight; but it worked on paper, if the producers could get their Central Park cast to commit for a minimum of eight weeks. If the whole scheme sounded unlikely, I was told by a reliable production source that it was set and ready to go—with the million-dollar investment in place—until one of the stars developed a scheduling problem at the last moment.

This *Seagull* will be remembered, mostly, for the ticket crunch. Shakespeare in the Park is free, with tickets distributed on a first-come, first-served basis. Not all tickets, naturally. Some are reserved for the performers and staff; others go to the press; and many are distributed to NYSF subscribers and corporate sponsors, without whose support there would be no Shakespeare Festival in the first place. Still, I would guess this leaves well over one thousand free seats per performance (other than press previews and the celebrity-laden opening night). Tickets are distributed at 1:00 P.M. on the day of the performance; be there, and you're in.

By the end of the run, people were on line at 10:00 P.M. the night before the performance. They stood on line, and slept and ate and cell-phoned, all night and into the day.

That's how it's supposed to work. People who want to be sure of getting seated at the more popular Shakespeare in the Park attractions have learned that you'd better get on line early. Early, meaning 10:00 A.M., or 8:00 A.M. With *The Seagull*, people got on line at 6:00 A.M. As the buzz built, the arrival time got earlier and earlier. Imagine: people who arrived at 3:00 A.M.—ten hours before distribution time—and stood on line through the night, didn't get tickets. By the end of the run, people were on line at 10:00 P.M. the night before the performance; as you left the show, you could see them lurking in the shadows under the trees. They stood on line (and slept and ate and cell-phoned) for fifteen hours; got their two tickets at 1:00 P.M.; and then had seven hours to rest before curtain.

The majority of them weren't all that interested in the play, mind you. Meryl Streep and Kevin Kline and Natalie Portman were the draws; imagine the lines if they were appearing in something more accessible than Chekhov! Crazy New Yorkers standing in Central Park—of all places —through the night, simply to get a theatre ticket. (The park closed in the wee hours, at which point the line would move to Central Park West until dawn. There was a second distribution point downtown at the Public Theatre on Lafayette Street, which attracted similar-sized lines.)

The Seagull ticket saga became a top media story, putting New York theatre on the news pages and telecasts across the nation for the first time since—well, since *The Producers* opened five months earlier. There was much discussion comparing the tightness of tickets for the two shows, with some people going so far as to claim that *The Seagull* was a comparable hit. This was rather silly, as *The Seagull* was a free ticket to a limited engagement. If the producers of *The Producers* gave away hundreds and hundreds of tickets for free every day, the lines would stretch past the Delacorte.

At any rate, I shall remember August 12, 2001, as my most memorable opening night ever. Had I been unable to return after the rainout, the play would have remained equally memorable. Ms. Streep's expert performance made this *Seagull* well worth the visit, unless I'd had to stand on line for fifteen hours for my ticket. And it sure had a great first act.

Mandy Patinkin in Concert

What will we see tonight, and how will it be?

The fair and evenhanded theatre patron takes her or his seat, on any given night or matinee, with an open mind and no preconceived notions. Which brings us to *Mandy Patinkin in Concert*. This one-night engagement, we were told, "marks the launch of his national tour and salutes the release of his new CD *Kidults*." And there you have strikes one and two.

Strike one because Patinkin strikes me adversely. Almost always, I'm afraid. This is not to blame Mr. Patinkin, who is unquestionably a fine artist. He made his Broadway debut in 1977 in *The Shadow Box*, and I found him smarmy. (I didn't much like the play, either, even though it won the Tony and the Pulitzer.) Patinkin made his Broadway musical debut in *Evita*. He was strange, exotic, and over-the-top, as he would be all too frequently over the next two decades. But the role of Che called for an eerie performance, and Patinkin had director Hal Prince to rein him in. (One wonders what Patinkin might have done as the Emcee in Prince's *Cabaret*.)

Evita led to important film work, with roles in *Ragtime* and Barbra Streisand's *Yentl*. Patinkin's subsequent Broadway performances have left me cold, each of them; as the unfeeling George in the title role of Stephen Sondheim's *Sunday in the Park with George* (1984); as the misanthropic Uncle Archie in *The Secret Garden* (1991); and as the altogether hateful Burrs in John LaChiusa and George C. Wolfe's *The Wild Party* (2000).

Patinkin wasn't mediocre in any of these roles, mind you; he was always outstanding, in that he would always stand out. But in a way that hindered—rather than helped—*Sunday*, *Secret Garden*, and *Wild Party*. For me, at least.

During this period, Patinkin performed in numerous films (including, notably, *The Princess Bride* and *Dick Tracy*); made numerous television appearances (including an Emmy-winning stint on the series *Chicago Hope*); filled in as a replacement in the Broadway production of *Falsettos* (1992); and starred as a transsexual in a blue ball gown in Joe Papp's dire 1987 production of David Hare's musical *The Knife*.

Patinkin also made Broadway visits with three concerts: *Dress Casual* (1989), which played the Helen Hayes for sixty-two performances; *Mandy Patinkin in Concert* (1997), which played the Lyceum for fifteen; and the Yiddish-inflected *Mamaloshen* (1998), which played the Belasco for twenty-eight. This performance history made one wonder why *Kidults* was booked for but a single performance. Was Patinkin's Broadway stock at especially low ebb? Rumors and column items abounded about Patinkin's unprofessional and sometimes violent behavior during *The Wild Party*. Biting actors, spitting in their faces, things like that. (Some of these rumors were, apparently, based in fact.)

I haven't enjoyed any evening with Mr. Patinkin ever, other than *Evita* twenty-odd years ago. Which leads me, right or wrong, to be just a wee bit apprehensive when I see his name on the marquee.

And then there was *Kidults*. Patinkin's publicist sent me an advance copy of the CD in mid-August. *Kidults* was aimed at what they called "the kid inside every adult, with delights for parent and progeny alike." This sounded like an attractive idea to me; how far over-the-top could Patinkin possibly get on an album for children? I was in the market for this sort of CD, actually, as I was spending the summer driving through the hills of northwest Connecticut listening to *Mary Poppins* over and over and over again. Here, I thought, was something new for my four-year-old.

> Patinkin commanded that everybody stand and join him in the "Hokey Pokey," in Yiddish. I remained in my seat, while Clive Barnes stood with the rest looking disgruntled and extremely annoyed.

The description of the album—or, perhaps, the inclusion in the song list of two songs from Frank Loesser's *Hans Christian Andersen*—brought to mind Danny Kaye. Kaye was a similarly showy performer with lots of talent and a tendency to overdo it. But I well remember Kaye's specialty album *Mommy, Gimme a Drinka Water* (music and lyrics by Milton Schafer), which was just right for little tykes in the early 1960s. Could Mandy's *Kidults* be descended from Kaye?

I slipped the CD in one midafternoon, and it started out pretty well. Mandy sang "If I Only Had a Brain," growling like Bert Lahr in the Lion's section. "Singin' in the Bathtub," an old novelty song from the 1930 movie musical *Show of Shows*, was a clear winner with my daughter and her two-year-old brother, as they both are always singin' (and battlin') in the bathtub. There followed a rendition of "Soon It's Gonna Rain," Harvey Schmidt and Tom Jones's lovely duet from *The Fantasticks*. Patinkin was joined by Kristen Chenoweth, and the two of them gave as wonderful a rendition of the song as I've ever heard. Until midway, that is, when the sound effects started. Creaky doors; echoes, and echoes of echoes; and thunder. Real thunder, not just the tymp player rattling his sticks. And lots of water, real running water. (In the bathtub?) By the end, all that lovely singing had been pushed aside by sound effects, and it's a shame. Patinkin soon worked his way around to "A Tisket a Tasket," that swinging Van Alexander–Ella Fitzgerald big-band hit. Everything was just fine, again, until Patinkin brought in police sirens and detectives and the whole danged racket squad making a racket. (The lyric is about a lost green-and-yellow basket.) Such a racket, in fact, that my two-year-old yelled, "Charlie no like dis!" and that was the end of *Kidults*.

Now, Mr. Patinkin may sing anything he likes, whenever he likes, in any way he likes. His myriad fans, I suppose, wouldn't have it any other way. But I had a hard time getting through seven tracks of *Kidults*. Which —combined with my prior lack of appreciation of Patinkin on stage— left Mandy two strikes behind when I cautiously filed into the Neil Simon on the evening of September 10.

He entered carrying two baskets of flowers, which he placed next to the sound speakers by the corners of the proscenium. Mandy in black pants with a raspberry-colored V-neck, gray-and-white sneakers, and a noticeably large bald spot. (During the evening he made jokes about the sweater and the bald spot.)

Mandy started to sing. Not a song from *Kidults*; rather, something that was obviously a Sondheim song, although few listeners could have been expected to recognize it. Patinkin didn't identify it, and there was no program listing, but it sounded like something out of *Company*. (The final cadence of the song, actually, was copied into *Company*'s title song.) This turned out to be "If You Can Find Me, I'm Here," from Sondheim's 1966 TV musical *Evening Primrose*; Patinkin had used it previously, in *Dress Casual*.

This was a smart choice for an opening number, as Patinkin's audience was filled with Sondheim fans who perked up their ears and listened hard. This song blended into a medley—a long medley of fourteen minutes—

capped by a highly effective version of Frank Loesser's "The King's New Clothes" intermingled with Sondheim's "Everybody Says Don't" (from *Anyone Can Whistle*). Fourteen continuous minutes of mostly Sondheim got Patinkin his first ovation of the evening.

This was followed by David Rose's "Holiday for Strings," fitted out with a comedy lyric and a comic routine. (Did Danny Kaye do this number? Or was it Jerry Lewis?) Mandy began the song in a sweet-voiced, leisurely tempo. Then up popped a hand puppet—with a Hollywood mogul voice somewhere between Groucho Marx and Mandy Patinkin—complaining, "Stop, you're killing me." (Patinkin explained that the puppet was named Jonathan Schwartz, which was apparently supposed to be a joke.) The puppet started singing, and fast, against Mandy's slower version. This became a duet for one; "You're makin' me puke," said Mandy to Mandy. "Holiday for Strings" did not make me puke, however; it simply neutralized the good impression of the opening medley.

Next on the program was the old standard "The Japanese Sandman," leading into a song called "Cat's in the Cradle" (by Harry Chapin and Sandra Campbell Chapin). Patinkin crooned it gently, in lullaby-like fashion. The song, sung by a father who doesn't have time for his son, just about had me in tears. The lyric is very good, and Patinkin delivered it with pain in his heart. Can any Broadway singer sing so well? This was followed by the aforementioned "Singin' in the Bathtub," in which Mandy Durante went way back over the top.

He then went into a long, long monologue about picking his costume for the evening and courting his wife at the romantic old Black Sheep Inn in the Vil-

> I can understand a talented artist wishing to add something unique. What Patinkin doesn't seem to realize is that his ability to deliver a song— the words as well as the subtext—is in itself unique.

lage. (In the middle of this he turned to his excellent accompanist–musical director, Paul Ford, who was vamping as if he was waiting for a missed cue, and said, "Do whatever you want.") This long, long story finally ended with "Supercalifragilisticexpialidocious" in Yiddish. How and why, I can't for the life of me tell you; but that's what it says in my notes, and I couldn't have made it up. He then commanded that everybody stand and join him in the "Hokey Pokey." Also in Yiddish. (Mr. Patinkin, apparently, does whatever he wants however he wants whenever he wants.) I remained in my seat for this, as I rarely do the "Hokey Pokey" in Yiddish while out for an evening at the theatre. Clive Barnes of the *Post*, two seats down, stood with the rest. He didn't do the "Hokey

Pokey," either; in fact, he looked disgruntled and extremely annoyed. Mandy's fans loved it.

He then went into Rodgers and Hammerstein's "You Are Beautiful," the song working better than I've ever heard it; Mandy-the-singer did a technically impeccable job, and Mandy-the-actor believed the words. This segued into a similarly effective version of Sondheim's "Not a Day Goes By." Such beauty in song, until the end when the lyric goes "I'll die day after day after day after day" and the singer hunched over in pain and started dovenning. (Keening, for our Irish friends.) Again, Mr. Patinkin is welcome to perform any way he sees fit; for me, though, such over-expressive emoting overshadows and warps the music and lyric.

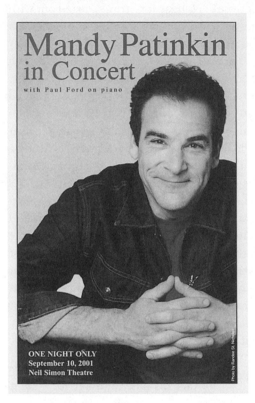

Mandy Patinkin in Concert
with Paul Ford on piano

ONE NIGHT ONLY
September 10, 2001
Neil Simon Theatre

There was now a ring of sweat encroaching on the V of Patinkin's neck. "I could use a nice cold shower now," he volunteered before telling us that he was going to sing a song by the father of Jonathan Schwartz. And then he sang "Growing Pains," a minor number from Arthur Schwartz and Dorothy Fields's long-forgotten *A Tree Grows in Brooklyn*. (This was a worthy failure of a musical that played the Neil Simon stage fifty years earlier, when it was called the Alvin.) The song, in context, is sung by a failed drunkard of a father to his daughter; in Patinkin's hands, it was absolutely breathtaking. "They're not bad," the lyric goes, "just growing pains," and you felt the pain.

Then came a two-minute version of Chopin's "The Minute Waltz," another Danny Kaye–like novelty to little effect—especially since Patinkin had already sung the similar "Holiday for Strings." This was countered by Schwartz and Dietz's "Triplets," that wonderful trio sung so memorably by Fred Astaire, Nanette Fabray, and Jack Buchanan in the

Mandy Patinkin in Concert
Opened: September 10, 2001
Closed: September 10, 2001
1 performance
Profit/Loss: Undetermined
Mandy Patinkin in Concert ($70 top) played the 1,333-seat Neil Simon Theatre. Box
  office figures not available.

film version of *The Bandwagon*. (The song was actually a vanished show tune, written for a quick 1937 failure called *Between the Devil*.) Patinkin did all three parts, with two hand puppets, and it was enchanting. Could anyone else perform "Triplets" so well? He followed this with "Anyone Can Whistle"—quiet, moving, superb—before moving on to "If I Only Had a Brain."

Then came "Trouble"; he was standing on *The Music Man* set, after all. This was another audience participation number, the house standing in for the chorus of townfolk. I didn't mind in this case, though, because Patinkin was as strong a Harold Hill as you could wish. "Trouble" is a songful of words, and Patinkin delivered each and every one of them. He was an early choice for the role in the Susan Stroman production—produced by Michael David and the Dodgers, with whom Patinkin has a long-standing relationship—but he apparently didn't want to commit himself to a long run in a revival.

Excuse me if I seem to be yo-yoing around, folks, but this was *Mandy Patinkin in Concert*. Shining at one moment, searching for a self-expressionistic gimmick the next. He followed his *Music Man* bull's-eye with "Take Me Out to the Ballgame" in Yiddish. And then "God Bless America." Also in Yiddish.

He then went into an exceptional string of Sondheim. "Too Many Mornings" sung as well as you can imagine. (Is Patinkin the actor who could solve the problem of Ben Stone, the hole in the middle of every production of *Follies* I've ever seen?) "Not While I'm Around," from *Sweeney Todd*. "All Things Bright and Beautiful," from *Follies*, perhaps the finest Sondheim song cut from a musical. "Trust me, anything you say, kid," Mandy sang, in such a way that Ben's elusive character was suddenly, momentarily revealed.

Patinkin then did a masterful job on "Losing My Mind." This song has been impeccably performed by others, including Dorothy Collins and

Barbara Cook; but even so. Patinkin followed all this top-drawer Sondheim with "Take the Moment," from the unhappy Rodgers-Sondheim collaboration *Do I Hear a Waltz?* This was a booming ballad for an opera singer slumming on Broadway, presumably intended by Rodgers as a pendant to "Some Enchanted Evening." "Take the Moment" always sounded a bit bombastic, to me anyway, until Patinkin went at it. He removed the boom, if you will, revealing a song of tender beauty.

All in all, it was a mostly up evening with occasional downs. For almost the first time in more than twenty years of Patinkin watching, I was able to get past all that carrying on. I can understand a talented artist wishing to add something unique to his performance; the desire to make it personal rather than just performing the material like everyone else. Patinkin appears to take this as his personal challenge, and that's his prerogative. What he doesn't seem to realize, at least from where I'm sitting, is that his ability to deliver a song—music and lyric, the words as well as the subtext—is in itself unique. A handful of special performers can do this just as well. Barbara Cook springs to mind; but I don't know that anyone does it better. Grafting on gimmicks and funny voices and other eccentricities doesn't enhance the material; it simply detracts from the purity of what Patinkin does best. Which is to express the intent of the authors.

As is customary, Mandy finished his evening with an encore. As chilling an encore as I've ever seen, and I hope never to see again. He prepared the number by placing a music stand before him, at waist level. He put two small, rectangular boxes on either end, placing an Israeli flag on the stage left pedestal and a Palestinian flag on the other. He then launched into "Hatikvah." As he reached the climax of the song, there was a bang on the piano; a flash of red light; and the two towers holding the flags toppled over. He went into "Carefully Taught," to a brusque, martial strain; I wrote in my notes that he barked out the words in what seemed to be a Charlton Heston–Dr. Strangelove voice. He then gently restored the flags and transitioned into "Children Will Listen," Sondheim's stunning anthem from *Into the Woods*.

> Grafting on gimmicks and funny voices and other eccentricities doesn't enhance the material; it simply detracts from the purity of what Patinkin does best. Which is to express the intent of the authors.

Walking home from *Mandy Patinkin in Concert*, I thought to myself; well, I didn't go to the theatre for a political lesson. But Patinkin rented the hall, so I guess he's welcome to make any political pro-

nouncements he wishes. One thing was for sure; it was certainly a stag-
gering moment—a terrifying moment—when he knocked the flags off
their pedestals.

Eleven hours later, before anyone even got around to reviewing Mandy
Patinkin's Monday night concert, the two towers of the World Trade
Center were no more.

Urinetown

In March 2001, I made a quick trip to Paris. I spent my last morning, as always, walking around my favorite neighborhood: along the Rue de la Seine, across le boulevard Saint-Germain, and down to the Jardin du Luxembourg. When the time came to visit the WC, I realized that I was without any change.

Paris abounds with public toilets. They've got some nifty new sidewalk booths here and there, outfitted with a mechanism that scrubs down the facility between uses in the manner of an automatic car wash. But most of *les toilettes* are underground; you take a grimy stairway and stand, waiting, in a dingy tile passageway filled with camera-toting tourists. Through the door you see a little old martinet in dirty apron, rubber gloves, and unbuckled galoshes. She sits there collecting your centimes, or nowadays euros; ask for change, and she gets awful mad. You're inevitably behind some American or German or Japanese tourist who doesn't understand that they are expected to pay; she jabbers away at them in French, they jabber back not in French, and you wait. When you get to the head of the line, she puts up a *fermé* sign and heads off with brush and pail. She then returns, takes your coins, and tells you into which booth you must head.

This wouldn't be so bad, except you never have change. Give Madame DeFarge a five-franc note or a ten-franc note or—Zut, alors!—a twenty-franc note, and she'll spray deprecations on your head. And I mean spray, in French. And then she'll hand you a pocketful of change; imagine presenting a five-dollar bill and being handed back five quarters, twelve dimes, and thirty-seven nickels.

Now I certainly understand the concept behind pay toilets, and I'm all for them. But it's one thing to pay for one of those nifty automated ones; it's quite another to submit to an inquisitionary harpy—for some reason, they're always inquisitionary harpies—and then wind up in what my

four-year-old calls a "stinky toilet." Little did I know as I waited on the
steps of the slimy stairs in that odoriferous fount that this stinky toilet
would serve as the source of a sharp new Broadway musical.

Back in 1995, an underground playwright named Greg Kotis was performing at a theatre festival in Romania. Instead of returning home to
Chicago, he stopped off in Paris with $300. Quickly running through his
francs, he ended up sleeping in the parks. As he told Jesse McKinley of
the *New York Times*, "I found myself choosing between the public amenities, which you had to pay for, and getting a sandwich." Thus was borne
Urinetown, about a mythical metropolis where it is "a privilege to pee,"
and the public amenities are overseen by martinets in dirty aprons, rubber
gloves, and unbuckled galoshes.

Urinetown first appeared at the 1999 New York International Fringe
Festival. Commercial producers eagerly picked it up, but where—exactly—do you take a musical comedy called *Urinetown*? With sixteen actors and five musicians, Broadway was the only place that made economic
sense. How do you take a musical comedy called *Urinetown* to Broadway?

Very carefully.

The decision was made to start off off-Broadway. Way off off-Broad-
way, at something called the American Theatre of Actors on West 54th
Street, a space so rustic that it made the Jane Street Theatre—where
Hedwig displayed her *Angry Inch*—seem like the New Amsterdam. The
American Theatre of Actors was located, actually, within an ancient
night court—a fitting choice, given the nature of the proceedings.

The plan was to allow the show to sneak into town at a low ticket
price; build up great word of mouth; and receive wildly enthusiastic reviews imploring it to move to
Broadway. Far-fetched and highly
unlikely; but not impossible. Back
in 1978, I managed a considerably less interesting show that had
a similarly problematic title (for
the time) and took a similar route, *The Best Little Whorehouse in Texas*. It
raised some eyebrows, but it worked.

> In Paris with only $300, Kotis found
> himself choosing between the public
> amenities, which you had to pay
> for, and getting a sandwich.

Five days after I returned from Paris, I headed to an early preview of
Urinetown. I try not to attend early previews of shows that I expect to review; it's preferable to judge what the authors end up with without seeing how they started. I did not expect to review *Urinetown*, though, as it
seemed an unlikely prospect for transfer to Broadway. I had an old friend
in the cast, my brother had an extra ticket, and so I went.

Walking into the theatre space—dark and dank, behind a set of
bleachers—I heard someone say, "What are you doing here?" When my

THE HENRY MILLER

The Araca Group and Dodger Theatricals
in association with TheaterDreams, Inc. and Lauren Mitchell
present

URINETOWN
THE MUSICAL

Music and Lyrics by
Mark Hollmann

Book and Lyrics by
Greg Kotis

with

David Beach   Jennifer Cody   Rachel Coloff   Rick Crom
John Cullum   John Deyle   Hunter Foster   Victor W. Hawks   Erin Hill
Ken Jennings   Spencer Kayden   Daniel Marcus   Jeff McCarthy
Nancy Opel   Peter Reardon   Don Richard   Lawrence E. Street
Jennifer Laura Thompson   Kay Walbye

Scenic/Environment Design	Costume Design	Lighting Design
Scott Pask	Gregory Gale	Brian MacDevitt
	and	
	Jonathan Bixby	

Sound Design	Wig/Hair Design	Fight Director
Jeff Curtis	Darlene Dannenfelser	Rick Sordelet
and		
Lew Mead		

Orchestrations	Musical Direction	Conductor	Music Coordinator
Bruce Coughlin	Edward Strauss	Ed Goldschneider	John Miller

Production Managers	Casting by	Production Stage Manager
Kai Brothers	Jay Binder, C.S.A.	Julia P. Jones
and	Laura Stanczyk	
Tech Production Services, Inc.	Cindi Rush, C.S.A.	

General Management	Marketing	Press Representative
Dodger Management Group	Dodger Marketing	Boneau/Bryan-Brown

Musical Staging by
John Carrafa

Directed by
John Rando

The Producers wish to thank the Theatre Development Fund for its support of this production.

Officer Lockstock   Jeff McCarthy
Little Sally   Spencer Kayden
Penelope Pennywise   Nancy Opel
Bobby Strong   Hunter Foster
Hope Cladwell   Jennifer Laura Thompson
Mr. McQueen   David Beach
Senator Fipp   John Deyle
Old Man Strong/Hot Blades Harry   Ken Jennings
Tiny Tom/Dr. Billeaux   Rick Crom
Soupy Sue/Cladwell's secretary   Rachel Coloff
Little Becky Two Shoes/Mrs. Millennium   Jennifer Cody
Robbie the Stockfish/business man No. 1   Victor W. Hawks
Billy Boy Bill/business man No. 2   Lawrence E. Street
Old woman/Josephine Strong   Kay Walbye
Officer Barrel   Daniel Marcus
Caldwell B. Cladwell   John Cullum

Place: Urinetown

Original Broadway Cast Album:
RCAVictor 09026-63821

eyes adjusted, I saw that it was Edward Strauss, musical director of numerous shows (including the Jerry Zaks revivals of *Anything Goes* and *Guys and Dolls*). I had known Eddie, casually, for about thirty years, during which we'd worked together once or twice. (I look about thirty years older than when I met him; he still looks twenty-two.)

"We just put in a new number this afternoon, haven't even finished staging it," he apologized. "That's okay," I said, "that's why they call them previews." "Let me know what you think, I'm glad you're here," Eddie said and went to his seat in the top row. (He was musical director, but not conducting.)

I found him at intermission. "Eddie, Eddie, do you realize what this is?" I asked. "This score is wonderful, it's *The Threepenny Opera* for today. And you've made it sound—the band and the singers—like it's Weill or Blitzstein."

"Thanks, that's what we're hoping. Watch what we do in the second act," he said.

As I was waiting around after the performance, along came choreographer John Carrafa, with whom I'd also done a show. "How was it? We just put in a new number this afternoon, didn't have time to finish it really," he apologized.

Carrafa had been a lead dancer for Twyla Tharp for many years. He moved on to choreography back in the 1980s and somehow got pegged as the guy they got when they were doing a play that needed a dance or two. His work had grown more prominent of late, with *Love! Valour! Compassion!* and *Dirty Blonde* conspicuous among his credits. While he had done some musical films, nobody ever entrusted him with a Broadway musical. It turned out that he is extremely creative, with a fine sense of choreographic humor. Even at an early preview, *Urinetown* was highly impressive, and I told him so.

"Thanks," he said. "Oh," he said, grabbing a curly-headed fellow passing by, "you should meet this guy." (Whether I should meet him, or he should meet me, I couldn't tell.) It was Kotis, the librettist-lyricist. I explained to him how remarkable and surprising this show was, even at this early stage. Seeing as how *Urinetown* was something that could get you ridden out of town on a rail, he seemed happy to hear compliments instead of complaints.

Out came Cullum. "Hey, I didn't know you were here tonight." I introduced him to my brother, whom he'd last met as an eleven-year-old at *Shenandoah*. "How did it go?" asked John. "We were winging it, just put in a new number this afternoon."

Cullum is known along Broadway as a singer, since he is (apparently) the last in a line of musical comedy leading men going back to Alfred Drake, John Raitt, and Richard Kiley. What is less apparent is that he is a clever comic, with a strong sense of the ridiculous, as those who saw him in *On the Twentieth Century* might well recall. Here he was gloriously funny—and this was an early preview after a short rehearsal period.

How do you take a musical comedy called *Urinetown* to Broadway? Very carefully.

The point is, I was a fan of *Urinetown* long before it opened on Broadway. I returned in May, when they were officially ready to face the critics; and I went back for the Broadway opening on September 20. (The Broadway opening had originally been scheduled for Thursday, September 13.

It was postponed due to the events of September 11. A week later, everybody was still pretty jittery.)

The score was much the same as at the early preview; the only added number, as far as I could tell, was the jolly new curtain call. But this was a show cram-filled with jokes and sight gags. Over four months of playing and rehearsing, the jokes and gags and actors became more and more assured. Physically, the show lost a little with the change of venue. At the Actors' Theatre you were on bleachers, with the actors directly in front of you or making an entrance alongside your seat. At the Henry Miller, they were onstage, and you were in the theatre. But the Broadway version was that much slicker; every gag was in place, and it worked like clockwork.

As I'd remarked to Eddie after the first act of my first viewing, Kotis and Mark Hollmann (the composer and colyricist) wrote what is in some ways a *Threepenny Opera* for our times. The show started with a prologue that sounds very much like Kurt Weill's—not melodically, but in every other way—and prepared us for what was to follow. The *Threepenny/*Weill flavor continued until midway through the first act, at which point the authors switched to Marc Blitzstein. (*Urinetown's* crusading hero, Bobby Strong, is cousin to Larry Foreman, of *The Cradle Will Rock*.)

As a champion of both Weill and Blitzstein, let me say this: copying these guys is not, in any way, a formula for success. Weill's final four Broadway musicals failed, while Blitzstein's only box office success came with his off-Broadway adaptation of Weill's *Threepenny*. Hollmann and Kotis were successful because they used their models carefully and purposefully. As in the unlikely "It's a Privilege to Pee," a song that needed to get the audience past the novelty of the situation and into the story. The authors were guided by Peachum's "Morning Anthem" (from *Threepenny*), in which the scoundrel cloaks his philosophy in what sounds like an old hymn. In *Urinetown*, the evil keeper of the lavatory keys—a Mrs. Lovett of the slops—is similarly backed by a religious chorale. "The good Lord made us so we'd piss each day," the ensemble sings, and who can argue with that?

The rapid-fire "Cop Song" seemed to spring from Weill's "Army Song" or maybe *Der Silbersee*, while "Follow Your Heart"—the closest thing the show has to a ballad—sounded like something out of Blitzstein's *Reuben, Reuben*; the melody was so tentative and the harmony so dissonant that we knew these lovers were ill-starred. The Act One Finale—which combined *Threepenny* and *Cradle*—was absolutely nifty; sixteen voices interwove four different melodies, singing their collective hearts out about going to the "toilet Judgement seat." (The vocal arrangements—and they are good—were by composer Hollmann.)

Urinetown
Opened: September 20, 2001
Still playing May 27, 2002
284 performances (and 25 previews)
Profit/Loss: To Be Determined
Urinetown ($85 top) was scaled to a potential gross of
$386,346 at the 631-seat Henry Miller Theatre. Weekly
grosses averaged about $283,000, with business in the
small theatre consistently in the $325,000 range until
slipping in the spring (but recovering after the Tony
nominations). Total gross for the thirty-nine-week partial
season was $10,920,312. Attendance was about 81
percent, with the box office grossing about 74 percent of
dollar-capacity.

Critical
Scorecard

Rave 5
Favorable 1
Mixed 1
Unfavorable 0
Pan 3

TONY AWARD NOMINATIONS
Best Musical
Best Book of a Musical: Greg Kotis (WINNER)
Best Original Score: Mark Hollmann (Music and Lyrics), Greg
     Kotis (Lyrics) (WINNER)
Best Performance by a Leading Actor: John Cullum
Best Performance by a Leading Actress: Nancy Opel
Best Performance by a Leading Actress: Jennifer Laura
     Thompson
Best Performance by a Featured Actress: Spencer Kayden
Best Direction of a Musical: John Rando (WINNER)
Best Choreography: John Carrafa
Best Orchestrations: Bruce Coughlin

In the second act, the authors were canny enough to change their
tune; inspiration came from all sides. "What Is Urinetown?" seemed derived from *Fiddler on the Roof*. This led head-on to the irrepressible show-
stopper "Snuff That Girl," a real finger-snapper purloined from *West Side
Story*'s "Cool." ("Bing! Bang! A-bing bang boom!" they sing.) But there
were wonderful numbers throughout. Yes, all this musical theatre short-
hand served as skeletal support; but the music and lyrics themselves were
very good. Here we had a pair of first-time Broadway visitors from fringe
theatre land, and they wrote one of the most impressive new scores in
years. The jokes—not just in the dialogue but in music and lyrics as
well—went by so fast that you could hardly keep up. What was the last
Broadway musical, other than *The Producers*, that kept you laughing?

     Cullum got the juiciest material. Like a luscious ditty about shooting
friendly bunny rabbits, in which he warned that whatever you do, "Don't
Be the Bunny." He also had a crisp introductory number in which he
hailed himself as the "Duke of ducats who brings in bucks by the buckets."
Buckets of what? you might well ask. (See the title.) Cullum has always

known how to deliver a song, and he was at his comic best here, Simon Legree mixed with Snively Whiplash.

Jeff McCarthy—who gave a memorable performance in *Side Show*—served as the tongue-in-cheek narrator, a policeman named Officer Lockstock. (His partner, needless to say, was named Barrel.) McCarthy skillfully straddled the fine line between too much and *way* too much. He was assisted at every turn by Spencer Kayden, who gave a remarkable performance as Little Sally. (Lockstock: "Nothing can kill a show, Little Sally, like too much exposition." Little Sally: "How about bad subject matter? Or a bad title?") Kayden seemed to have wandered in after fifteen seasons in an undernourished bus and truck of *Annie*, wearing her original costume wrapped in a layer of dust.

Nancy Opel displayed a strong voice and good comic sense as the keeper of the latrine; Hunter Foster and Jennifer Laura Thompson played the beset lovers, serious and farcical in turn. The folks in the smaller roles stood out in their solos, most notably Ken Jennings (who led "Snuff That Girl"). Jennings—who like McCarthy is remembered from *Side Show*, where he played the villainous circus owner—is one of the Broadway musical's true eccentrics. He still has the dangerously odd gleam in his eyes that he first displayed as *Sweeney Todd*'s original Tobias. The entire cast was good; *Urinetown* had the best ensemble in town, perhaps because the authors and stagers gave each and every actor a moment (and a gag) in the spotlight.

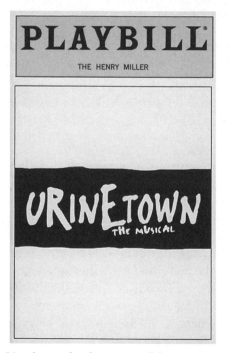

Urinetown was enhanced by dazzling work and clever ideas from all involved. Director John Rando kept things cracking, with sight gags every place you looked. He also took advantage of those comic narrators, using them to sparkplug the action. Choreographer Carrafa shared in the fun, taking his cast of nondancing singers and putting them through ersatz Robbins and Fosse routines. The above-mentioned "Snuff" number was uproarious; so was the revivalist "Run, Freedom, Run," which contained a wickedly funny moment out of *Elmer Gantry*. The score was deliciously and cleverly orchestrated by Bruce Coughlin, who kept up with Hollmann's shifting styles. Eddie Strauss had everything well in hand, balancing the harsh Weill-Blitzstein sound with the cornier musical comedy material; the vocal direction was especially precise, giving full value to the jokey-yet-flavorful lyrics.

Conductor Ed Goldschneider started the show with a joke of his own. As the house lights started to dim, the "policemen" marched him from the balcony boxes across the scaffolding, the short-and-small Goldschneider looking like a 1930s anarchist in one of those black and white Warner Bros. movies. The policemen brought him down to stage level, walked him across to the bandstand in the left wing—and placed him on the bandstand. Big

The jokes—not just in the dialogue but in music and lyrics as well—went by so fast that you could hardly keep up.

laugh, immediately followed by the brass choir opening of the prologue. (This was fully visible off off-Broadway, although sight lines at Henry Miller's caused it to be lost by those seated on the left side of the house.)

The stars of the evening: Kotis and Hollmann. Intriguing and catchy music, matched with brightly clever lyrics, brimming with ideas. *Urinetown* was a Broadway musical almost by accident; the authors say they never imagined that anyone would take it seriously, and I can understand why. Now let's see what they come up with next, knowing what they know now.

Hedda Gabler

One December morn in 1999, a typical Upper West Side soccer mom type walked into breakfast, in her pajamas. Gee, you should play Hedda Gabler, said her husband. Gee, you should play Hedda Gabler, said her mother.

That's all very well and good. Sure, dear, *I* think you're a star.

But this is not such a stab in the dark if your mom happens to run a well-respected summer theatre. Or if your husband runs one of the most prestigious regional theatres in the country. And if your old pal and favorite director has agreed to direct you in *Hedda*, and incidentally runs yet another major theatre, and if the three of them are eager to fit you into their production schedules, then maybe it's time to call Paul Huntley. Your favorite wigmaker.

Kate Burton it was, who was thus approached over the breakfast table. The suggestion of *Hedda* was not, presumably, based on her behavior the evening before; she is the least temperamental person in the ranks of Actors' Equity. (That might be an exaggeration, but not by much.) *Hedda Gabler* opened at husband Michael Ritchie's Williamstown Theatre Festival, in Williamstown, Massachusetts, in the spring of 2000. It moved on to mother Sybil Christopher's Bay Street Theatre, in Sag Harbor, New York, that summer. Finally, it opened at director Nicholas Martin's Huntington Theatre Company, in Boston, in January 2001.

Here's Ben Brantley of the *New York Times*, reporting from the Huntington: "Kate Burton is giving one of those rare benchmark performances that redefine both a classic character and an actress. In daring to be life-size in a traditionally larger-than-life role, Ms. Burton demystifies one of the most formidable heroines of Western drama without sacrificing a shred of the character's fascination."

This is the sort of rave that will propel a regional production to Broadway quicker than you can say *Kentucky Cycle* or *Grapes of Wrath* or *Zoot Suit* or *Texas Trilogy* or—well, you get the picture. *Hedda Gabler* will soon be on Broadway "if fate is merciful," said Mr. Brantley. Eleven or so producers eagerly poured in their money, and Brantley's wish was granted. With, ultimately, mixed results.

For a Norwegian lass from 1890, *Hedda* has been a surprisingly frequent visitor in these parts. She first reached our shores on March 30, 1898, when one Elizabeth Robins essayed the role at the Fifth Avenue Theatre. Mrs. Fiske played it twice at the Manhattan, in 1903 (for 8 performances) and 1904 (for 24 performances). During the latter engagement, over Thanksgiving week in 1904, you could have seen two *Heddas*; Nance O'Neil was playing it as well, at Daly's Theatre.

Then came Broadway's favorite *Hedda*. Alla Nazimova played it for 40 performances in 1906 at the Princess; for another 24 performances in 1907 at the Bijou; and once again —after a world war—for 24 performances in 1918 at the Plymouth. Clare Eames played it for 8 performances in 1924 at the 48th Street. Emily Stevens, Mrs. Elvsted to Mrs. Fiske's 1904 Hedda, played it for 29 performances in 1926 at the Comedy. Eva Le Gallienne undertook the role at her Civic Repertory Theatre in 1928, for 15 performances. The following year, Blanche Yurka did it at the 49th Street for 25 performances.

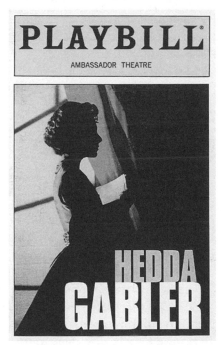

Nazimova, at fifty-seven, returned in 1936 with her fourth and final Broadway *Hedda*, for 32 performances at the Longacre. (This makes Alla the champ, with 120 performances as Hedda on Broadway.) The Greek tragedian Katina Paxinou played it for 12 performances in 1942, also at the Longacre. (She won an Oscar the following year, for *For Whom the Bell Tolls*.) Le Gallienne revived it again in 1948, for 15 performances at the Cort.

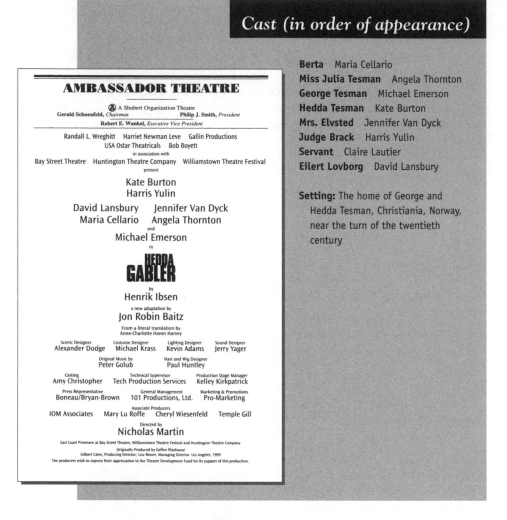

Cast (in order of appearance)

Berta Maria Cellario
Miss Julia Tesman Angela Thornton
George Tesman Michael Emerson
Hedda Tesman Kate Burton
Mrs. Elvsted Jennifer Van Dyck
Judge Brack Harris Yulin
Servant Claire Lautier
Eilert Lovborg David Lansbury

Setting: The home of George and
  Hedda Tesman, Christiania, Norway,
  near the turn of the twentieth
  century

But that was to be the last of the steady parade. The next *Hedda* was
New York's most successful by far, a 1960 off-Broadway production at the
Fourth Street Theatre. Anne Meachum played the lead in Michael Meyer's
then-new translation, for 340 performances.

Another successful *Hedda* came along in 1971 in the person of Claire
Bloom, who played it for 56 performances at the Playhouse in repertory
with *A Doll's House*. The Roundabout gave us Kelly McGillis in a mis-
guided rendition in 1994 at the Criterion, Broadway's only *Hedda* from
1971 until Kate Burton came in thirty years later.

Kate Burton onstage has always been proficient and professional. She
has steadily trod the Broadway boards since graduating from Yale Drama
School in 1982. She immediately joined rehearsals for George C. Scott's
production of Noël Coward's *Present Laughter*. She left during the run to

take the title role in the 1982 revival of Eva Le Gallienne's *Alice in Wonderland*. The Burton name surely helped, initially, but Kate was different enough from Richard to find a place of her own. A highly capable and reliably solid performer, without ever displaying the histrionic fireworks of her famous father. Until *Hedda Gabler*, that is. Chillingly dangerous, she delivered a theatrical knockout of a performance.

Ibsen's Hedda is a terror, to be sure. By camouflaging her behind a facade of measured laughter and steely charm, Burton made her all the more spine-tingling (and contemporary). This Hedda had attacks of the giggles, of all things, but Burton and director Martin made sure that we saw the ice water coursing through her veins. There were several uncanny moments when Burton glanced away from the others and we could actually observe ominous thunderclouds crossing her wide, Welsh forehead. Perhaps the lighting designer Kevin Adams did it, with some pinspots from the balcony rail. But no, I think it was all Kate.

The star was ably abetted by Martin and adapter Jon Robin Baitz. (This version was commissioned for a 1999 production at the Geffen Theatre in Los Angeles, without the involvement of Burton or Martin. Annette Bening starred, under the direction of Dan Sullivan.) Many Ibsen adaptations reek of camphor balls, with musty sensibilities and stilted passions. Baitz—a prolific contemporary playwright with credits including *The End of the Day* and *The Substance of Fire*—brought fresh air to the proceedings. His craft allowed him to examine *Hedda* and figure out what could make her tick, in contemporary terms. His solution, in part, was the dark side of humor: biting sarcasm and fatalistic cynicism. Ibsen, taking an aisle seat at the Ambassador, might not quite understand what his girl was doing. But, then, he didn't speak much English, did he?

> **Burton is highly capable and reliably solid, without ever displaying the histrionic fireworks of her famous father. Until *Hedda Gabler*, that is.**

Burton's castmates were only minimally helpful. Michael Emerson—well remembered in these parts for his Oscar Wilde in the off-Broadway *Gross Indecency*—was best, making an unusual but interesting George Tesman. Rather than the typically dutiful husband whose life is ruined by his bride, this fellow was exceedingly annoying (and somewhat reminiscent of the young Bobby Morse). Hedda, thus, earned sympathy and at least a degree of justification for her actions; maybe she should have just shot Tesman in the second scene and been done with it.

Emerson brought something new, and logically valid, to his role. Harris Yulin's Judge Brack was pretty much what you'd expect. Which is to say, pedestrian; I'm sure that Mr. Yulin has given many fine performances

Hedda Gabler
Opened: October 4, 2001
Closed: January 13, 2002
117 performances (and 17 previews)
Profit/Loss: Loss
Hedda Gabler ($71.25 top) was scaled to a potential gross of
   $504,378 at the 1,085-seat Ambassador Theatre. Weekly
   grosses averaged about $197,000, with business steadily
   below $200,000 but rallying for a $259,000 final week.
   Total gross for the seventeen-week run was $3,297,340.
   Attendance was about 57 percent, with the box office
   grossing about 39 percent of dollar-capacity.

TONY AWARD NOMINATION
Best Performance by a Leading Actress: Kate Burton

*Critical
Scorecard*

Rave 2
Favorable 3
Mixed 0
Unfavorable 1
Pan 4

in his long career, but not for me. David Lansbury's Lovborg was a wee bit
too eccentric, with a wild man of the mountains haircut. The others
were—well, adequate.

Director Martin is a story in himself. Here is a fellow who has been
kicking around Broadway since 1966, when he made his debut as an actor
in the APA-Phoenix company's *School for Scandal*. A protégé of director-
actor Ellis Rabb, Martin didn't start directing professionally until well
into his fifties, when he made a splash with small-scale but artful off-
Broadway plays like *Fully Committed* and Mary Louise Wilson's *Full Gal-
lop*. Martin befriended Burton and Wilson when they appeared together
in 1982 in Le Galliene's *Alice in Wonderland*. Martin, who was the play
reader and artistic adviser to McCann and Nugent Productions (managers of *Alice*), played the Dormouse. Very nicely, too.

Burton had a difficult time with the unwieldy *Alice*; she needed direction and didn't get it. One of the two directors was Le G, who was eighty-
three at the time and not up to the job, especially since she was acting as
well; the other was the producer's husband, who was *not* eighty-three but
who wasn't much of a director (even if his father was Lee Strasberg). Burton got through it fairly well, with moral support—and I expect offstage
coaching—from Martin.

Martin has been in great demand at top regional theatres since the
midnineties, with numerous stints at Williamstown. In 2000 he was
named artistic director of the Huntington Theatre Company in Boston.
With *Hedda*, finally, he made his Broadway directing debut—at the age
of sixty-three. Aspiring artists, take note.

All of which brings us back to Kate Burton. Brack and Lovborg (and
Tesman) found her irresistible, and no wonder; we would, too, if we didn't
know better. (Just watch that girl dance with her pistols.) Ibsen wrote his

play in 1890, but Burton's Hedda was just like someone you or I might have had brunch with last weekend, or next. And that made her performance dangerously fascinating, with icy teeth.

Unfortunately, *Hedda Gabler* came in under a couple of distinct disadvantages. The first was the very thing that propelled this revival to Broadway: Ben Brantley's January rave from Boston. He reiterated his praise in October, but his critical brethren were for the most part distinctly in the minority. Reading through the lines, one detected a distinct sense of "This is *not* the performance of the century, and I don't care what it says in the *Times.*"

The other problem was not the *Times* but the timing. August had seen the arrival of Mike Nichols's star-studded *The Seagull*, with free tickets and scads of publicity. The events of September had, understandably, taken everyone's mind off such mundane things as theatre tickets. And in October, *Hedda* ran up against competition from *Dance of Death.*

Neither Ibsen nor Strindberg was especially well received by the critics; *Hedda*'s reaction was mixed, *Dance of Death* slightly

> There were several uncanny moments when we could actually observe ominous thunderclouds crossing Burton's wide, Welsh forehead.

worse. But the latter, thanks to the presence of Ian McKellen and Helen Mirren, amassed a considerably larger advance sale than the former. Broadway ticket sales all but ceased in mid-September; when they started picking up, musicals (like *Mamma Mia!*) and comedies (like *Noises Off*) were the tonic of choice. Without enough presold seats to guarantee break-even business, *Hedda* never had a chance.

Dance of Death

The first half of the 2001–2002 season was a field day for nineteenth-century, northern European, non-English-speaking, dead playwrights.

Three of them enjoyed major New York productions in short order, before even one Neil Simon came to town. Chekhov, Ibsen, and Strindberg all lived into the twentieth century, but they were alive and kicking back before old Abe Lincoln grew his beard. The plays were written between 1890 and 1901, which puts them over the century mark. All three were well produced; all were well acted; all received plenty of attention, plus mixed reviews; and all were—after the fact—memorable.

What this meant in terms of modern-day, legitimate theatre in America I can't begin to tell you.

Thumbing back through the pages of this book, you'll find that there were actually *four* such productions. George Bernard Shaw, too, was represented. (While Shaw lived until 1950, he was born in 1856—making him older than Chekhov—and thus was very much a product of days gone by.) As previously discussed, the Roundabout's production of *Major Barbara* had a lot going for it, but not quite enough to cross the line from admirable to memorable. *Major Barbara* was forgotten by the time Strindberg opened, but the risk-taking productions of *The Seagull*, *Hedda Gabler*, and *Dance of Death* will be long remembered.

Dance of Death was the least likely of revivals. *The Seagull*, as we saw, came about because Meryl Streep wanted to do it. *Hedda* was a family project, with Kate Burton's mother, husband, and pal each mounting it at their respective regional theatres. *Major Barbara* was a typical offering from the Roundabout, which periodically serves up Shaw. But Strindberg, that melancholy misogynist Swede, is a relatively infrequent visitor to our shores. And for good reason. What's more, *Dance of Death* is not high on the list of his all-time greatest hits.

This production seems to have been born out of *Indiscretions (Les Parents Terribles)*, a Cocteau cocktail that the Shubert Organization imported in 1995. British director Sean Mathias made an impressive Broadway bow, with a production that was striking (although of limited success). Gerald Schoenfeld, chairman of the Shubert Organization, was understandably proud of *Indiscretions*, and duly called on Mathias for more of the same. This time, though, Schoenfeld didn't want an import from the Royal National Theatre; he wanted to produce it, in the old sense of the word, himself.

Mathias went to Sir Ian McKellen, his friend and former companion. McKellen said, in a *Playbill* interview with Harry Haun, "Sean called up and said, 'Gerry Schoenfeld's had a mad idea. He wants to do *Dance of Death* on Broadway.' I said, 'Does he know it's not a musical?'" And that, my friends, was one of the funniest lines of the season.

A translation was commissioned from Richard Greenberg, one of those formerly young playwrights of promise who made a splashy debut in 1989 with a play called *Eastern Standard*. This shuttered prematurely after ninety-two performances, at Schoenfeld's Golden Theatre. Greenberg hadn't been on Broadway since; his nine other produced plays have been barely visible in New York. (As *Dance of Death* opened, Greenberg's play *Everett Beekin* was in rehearsal for a November opening at the Mitzi Newhouse,

> **The first half of the 2001–2002 season was a field day for nineteenth-century, northern European, non-English-speaking, dead playwrights.**

Lincoln Center Theater's off-Broadway venue. By the time this book went to press, Greenberg's smashing 2002 play *Take Me Out* was en route to a February 2003 opening.)

Strindberg's *Dance of Death* is, famously, described as the inspiration for two important American plays: Eugene O'Neill's *Long Day's Journey into Night* and Edward Albee's *Who's Afraid of Virginia Woolf?* The parallels are plain to see: the relationship between the married couples; the general bleakness of the lives being lived; and the way the plays seem to progress through what might be called endless night. O'Neill, though, gives us four fascinating characters in depth, with a real story behind them. Albee, too, gives us four fascinating characters with a real story behind them (and an unreal story, too). And lots of jokes. Strindberg's characters, at least in this translation, are far more sketchy and far less accessible. Perhaps this is due to cultural differences, but I don't think so. *Dance*

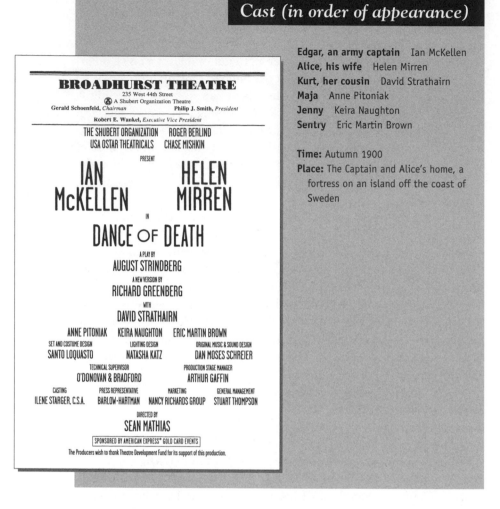

Edgar, an army captain Ian McKellen
Alice, his wife Helen Mirren
Kurt, her cousin David Strathairn
Maja Anne Pitoniak
Jenny Keira Naughton
Sentry Eric Martin Brown

Time: Autumn 1900
Place: The Captain and Alice's home, a
   fortress on an island off the coast of
   Sweden

BROADHURST THEATRE
235 West 44th Street
Ⓢ A Shubert Organization Theatre
Gerald Schoenfeld, *Chairman*   Philip J. Smith, *President*
Robert E. Wankel, *Executive Vice President*

THE SHUBERT ORGANIZATION   ROGER BERLIND
USA OSTAR THEATRICALS   CHASE MISHKIN

PRESENT

IAN McKELLEN   HELEN MIRREN

IN

DANCE OF DEATH

A PLAY BY
AUGUST STRINDBERG

A NEW VERSION BY
RICHARD GREENBERG

WITH
DAVID STRATHAIRN

ANNE PITONIAK   KEIRA NAUGHTON   ERIC MARTIN BROWN

SET AND COSTUME DESIGN   LIGHTING DESIGN   ORIGINAL MUSIC & SOUND DESIGN
SANTO LOQUASTO   NATASHA KATZ   DAN MOSES SCHREIER

TECHNICAL SUPERVISOR   PRODUCTION STAGE MANAGER
O'DONOVAN & BRADFORD   ARTHUR GAFFIN

CASTING   PRESS REPRESENTATIVE   MARKETING   GENERAL MANAGEMENT
ILENE STARGER, C.S.A.   BARLOW-HARTMAN   NANCY RICHARDS GROUP   STUART THOMPSON

DIRECTED BY
SEAN MATHIAS

SPONSORED BY AMERICAN EXPRESS® GOLD CARD EVENTS

The Producers wish to thank Theatre Development Fund for its support of this production.

of Death appears never to have had the impact of the O'Neill or the Albee, even in Strindberg's own time.

Mathias imported two stars from England—Helen Mirren and Sir Ian—but the designers and the rest of the group were all American. This was not an incidental choice. Many of the "class" Broadway attractions of recent years have used British designers. Yes, usually these were imports, which dictated use of the original designs. But more than a few recent American-produced shows have imported British designers (including the very busy—and very good—Bob Crowley); it is almost unheard for West End shows to import American designers. That being said, the producers of *Dance of Death* chose to hire two top American designers, and they came up with a production every bit as striking as, say, *Indiscretions*. Santo Loquasto has done exquisite work over the years, including memorable sets for *That Championship Season* and costumes for *Ragtime*. Natasha Katz is best known for *Aida*, one of the most expert recent lighting designs in recent memory. (Not that the design, itself, was good; it was the stunning visual combination of her lights on Crowley's sets.) Loquasto and Katz came up with as forbidding-but-inviting an ex-prison as you'd want to visit.

The director and his designers combined for some memorably magical moments. The end of the first act, for example. Edgar (McKellen) is ailing and quite possibly won't make it through the night. (Except, what would they have done in the second act without McKellen?) He is lying on a bed center stage, beneath the staircase, tended by Kurt (David Strathairn). There is a lightning flash. Edgar falls asleep, sinking back against his pillow (and thus moving his face out of the light). Kurt leans forward, looking at him. Alice (Mirren) opens the door on the upper level, at the top of the stairs, directly above Edgar and Kurt. She listens carefully, as Kurt brings his fingers to his mouth. He starts to reach for the candle flame, to douse the light. As his fingers approach, Alice starts to slip back out the door. The door closes, the candle simultaneously is extinguished, the stage lights go to black, and the act ends. Director, actors, and designers conspired here to create stage wizardry, but it was otherwise a very long evening.

Dance of Death is, clearly, a vehicle for high-octane star acting. With Olivier and Gielgud and Richardson gone, Ian McKellen is generally ranked high among the greatest English-speaking actors in the world, and he didn't disappoint. His performance was something. The craggy face illuminating Edgar's crotchets and despairs; the weary body bending at every available joint (not all of which were in working order, exactly); the majestical voice blasting cannon shot after cannon shot from the artillery, over the fortress wall.

McKellen was a marvel to watch, all right; but as Shakespeare might say, there's the rub. Because we watched Ian act, fascinated by how he did this and how he accomplished that. He even kicked up his heels in the first act, demonstrating just how "The Entry of the Boyars" should be done. His dance was quite remarkable; he jerked about as if he was a marionette being supported by the shoulder bar, arms and legs swinging every which way until he fell catonic, midway through. This was, indeed, a dance of death impending. (Small print in the back of the program informed us that this was staged by John Carrafa, who prior to *Urinetown* was the guy they got when they were doing a play that needed a dance or two.)

Great acting, yes; except Ian had a frame around him all evening, superimposed with the caption "great acting." This was never Edgar, a low-level captain of the fixed artillery on a small island off the coast of Sweden, living in a circular fortress tower that formerly served as a prison. This was Ian McKellen playing Edgar, and he—McKellen—was always visible.

Those of you with long memories might wish to compare this to McKellen in the 1980 Broadway production of *Amadeus*. Great acting, yes; but from the opening moment, you were completely drawn into the performance. It wasn't until the curtain call that you stopped to consider the actor under the makeup. In *Amadeus*, we watched a decrepit old man named Salieri,

At the end of the first act, McKellen is ailing and quite possibly won't make it through the night. Except, what would they have done in the second act without McKellen?

about to totter over in his wheelchair; in *Dance of Death*, we watched McKellen playing (brilliantly) a decrepit old man.

There is a difference, I contend, between watching a great actor at work and watching a great performance. Still, I shudder to imagine what this production would have been like without McKellen.

Ms. Mirren is a star of major proportions, with a clutch of Emmy Awards and Golden Globe Awards. She is best known for the British TV series *Prime Suspect*. It took but a moment at the Broadhurst to realize that Ms. Mirren, too, is a fine actress; and that she, too, was busy acting. If McKellen and Mirren were acting up a storm, Strathairn—as the third side of the triangle—wasn't. That's for sure. He seemed like a nice fellow who wandered into an open call for American actors because Equity wouldn't let in another Brit.

The other three actors were little more than walk-ons. It was a bit un-settling to discover that the heavily cloaked old peasant woman wander-ing around upstage was Anne Pitoniak, who starred in *'night, Mother* and had more recently played prominent roles in the Roundabout revival of *Picnic* and *Amy's View*. A job, I guess, is a job.

Thanks to a highly impressive-for-Strindberg advance sale, *Dance of Death* did perfectly fine business despite less-than-salutary reviews. Ben Brantley of the *New York Times* praised McKellen to the skies, de-spite reservations about every-thing else (except Ms. Mirren). "Watching Mr. McKellen's cap-tain shooting sparks in the dark mouth of mortality is about as thrilling as theater gets. . . . your only choice is to join the line for tick-ets. That said, it must be admitted that this *Dance of Death* doesn't en-tirely live up to its leading man." For what it's worth, I was seated next to Brantley of the *Times*, who was suffering from a cold and by his own ad-mission "laced with Robitussin."

> We watched Ian act, fascinated by how he did this and how he accomplished that. But there is a difference between watching a great actor at work and watching a great performance.

Dance of Death builds to the moment when Alice's revenge on Edgar backfires. He is leaving her, and she has set wheels in motion that will de-stroy him. It turns out that he isn't leaving, he was simply turning another screw in their game of torture. By destroying his future, Alice has de-stroyed her own as well. As written, Alice's instant of realization should be a moment of horror. As played, we didn't especially care. Or at least, I didn't. I was just sleepy.

Strindberg, having had a jolly old time with *Dance of Death*, sat down and wrote a continuation of the play in which Edgar and Alice's daugh-ter, and Kurt's son, come to join the fun. Let's just be glad we didn't have to sit through another hour's worth of this.

Mamma Mia!

The Producers came tripping into town in April 2001 with spectacular word of mouth, two bonafide ticket-selling stars, and an impressive advance sale reported at somewhere between $13 and $15 million. *Mamma Mia!* came tripping into town six months later with enthusiastic but not-so-spectacular word of mouth, no stars, and an advance sale of $30 million or so. That's right, $30,000,000. Twice as much as Bialystock and Bloom.

The Producers didn't need great reviews, exactly. Audiences loved it, and people would have come even if the critics hadn't anointed the Mel Brooks musical the hit of the century. But the reviews surely helped; they reassured prospective ticket buyers that while the show was a surefire knockout laugh riot, it was also "art."

Mamma Mia! didn't need great reviews, and it's a good thing. The show suffered innumerable slings of critical arrows. Suffered, perhaps, is not the precise word; *Miss Saigon* received the same type of critical reaction on Broadway, and they did okay. (For those who've put the Schönberg-Boublil tearjerker out of mind, at this writing it remains the sixth-longest-running musical in Broadway history. Although it may well be surpassed, in time, by *The Lion King*—and *Mamma Mia!*)

It remains to be seen which show has stronger legs, *The Producers* or *Mamma Mia! Mamma Mia!* seems likely to be the bigger bonanza, as it needs no stars and presumably has a sizably smaller payroll; it is highly suitable for non-English-speaking tourists, a distinct advantage in the sixth, seventh, eighth, ninth, and etcetera years of the run; and producers Judy Craymer, Richard East, and Björn Ulvaeus were already earning *Mamma* millions from the London, Toronto, and Australian productions long before their show got to New York. The Broadway company recouped its $10 million cost in a mere twenty-eight weeks.

It all began with ABBA, the Swedish pop group. Two singers named Benny Andersson and Björn Ulvaeus started writing together back in the late 1960s. In 1972, they formed a quartet with their respective wives, Anni-Frid Lynstad (Andersson) and Agnetha Fältskog (Ulvaeus); the name ABBA was formed from the initials of their surnames. (I suppose they could just have easily been BAAB.) I'm not much of a disco kind of guy, but I seem to recall that ABBA was always sort of a joke, musically speaking. With sales in excess of 350 million units, that's some joke.

At any rate, Benny and Björn divorced Anni-Frid and Agnetha but kept singing with them until 1982, at which point the group disbanded for good (but continued to collect royalties). The boys went on to collaborate with Tim Rice on the 1986 musical *Chess*. Some blamed the show's checkered career on the times; this was a cold war show, opening as the cold war was ending. Others placed blame on the circumstances. This was to be Michael Bennett's comeback hit. Just before departing for rehearsals in London, he became incapacitated (by AIDS) and was forced to withdraw. Trevor Nunn took over, but Bennett's production concept was already set (and Robin Wagner's corresponding set was already built). What was left was a concept musical without its conceptor.

Judy Craymer, Tim Rice's representative at the time, served as the show's executive producer. (Before working for Rice, she had been assistant stage manager on the original London production of *Cats*.) Despite *Chess's* untimely demise, Craymer determined that the old ABBA catalogue could be cobbled into a successful musical comedy. She therefore set out to convince Benny and Björn, and then figure out how to do it. In 1996 Craymer began work in earnest. Her team included Catherine Johnson, a little-known British playwright; and director Phyllida Lloyd, with an impressive list of drama and opera credits but nothing so frivolous as musical comedy on her résumé.

Of course you don't believe the mix of story and song; the creators seemed to be saying: We don't either. But watch how we slip in "Chiquitita"!

What they came up with was a decidedly flimsy and uncomfortably familiar framework, suitable for stuffing with twenty-two ABBA songs. The situation: twenty-one years ago, our feisty heroine was sleeping with three different men at once. Which one is the father of her twenty-year-old daughter? What happens when the three unsuspecting potential dads converge?

What happens? What else? Our heroine panics, sings lots of songs, and finally finds true love.

If this situation sounds familiar, that's because it is. The 1968 film *Buona Sera, Mrs. Campbell* told precisely the same story, with Gina Lol-

WINTER GARDEN

1634 Broadway

Ⓢ A Shubert Organization Theatre

Gerald Schoenfeld, *Chairman*   Philip J. Smith, *President*

Robert E. Wankel, *Executive Vice President*

JUDY CRAYMER, RICHARD EAST AND BJÖRN ULVAEUS
FOR LITTLESTAR IN ASSOCIATION WITH UNIVERSAL

PRESENT

MAMMA MIA!

MUSIC AND LYRICS BY

BENNY ANDERSSON
BJÖRN ULVAEUS

AND SOME SONGS WITH STIG ANDERSON

BOOK BY CATHERINE JOHNSON

PRODUCTION DESIGNED BY
MARK THOMPSON

LIGHTING DESIGNED BY
HOWARD HARRISON

SOUND DESIGNED BY
**ANDREW BRUCE &
BOBBY AITKEN**

MUSICAL SUPERVISOR, ADDITIONAL MATERIAL
& ARRANGEMENTS
MARTIN KOCH

CHOREOGRAPHY
ANTHONY VAN LAAST

DIRECTED BY
PHYLLIDA LLOYD

Sophie Sheridan Tina Maddigan
Ali Sara Inbar
Lisa Tonya Doran
Tanya Karen Mason
Rosie Judy Kaye
Donna Sheridan Louise Pitre
Sky Joe Machota
Pepper Mark Price
Eddie Michael Benjamin Washington
Harry Bright Dean Nolen
Bill Austin Ken Marks
Sam Carmichael David W. Keeley
Father Alexandrios Bill Carmichael
The Ensemble Meredith Akins,
  Stephan Alexander, Kim-E J.
  Balmilero, Robin Baxter, Brent Black,
  Tony Carlin, Bill Carmichael,
  Meghann Dreyfuss, Somer Lee
  Graham, Hollie Howard, Kristin
  McDonald, Adam Monley, Chris
  Prinzo, Peter Matthew Smith, Yuka
  Takara, Marsha Waterbury
Swings Barrett Foa, Jon-Erik
  Goldberg, Janet Rothermel

*On a tiny Greek Island, a wedding is
about to take place . . .*

Act 1: The day before the wedding
Act 2: The day of the wedding

Original London Cast Album: Decca
Broadway 314 543 115

lobrigida as the lusty mama. A 1979 musical comedy, *Carmelina*, covered precisely the same ground. *Mamma Mia!*'s Johnson disavowed any connection between her work and *Mrs. Campbell*; so, oddly enough, had *Carmelina* author Alan Jay Lerner. Apparently the plot sprang from a real-life news story. Both *Mrs. Campbell* and *Carmelina* were set in Italy; *Mamma Mia!* took place in Greece. But why does it have an Italian title?

The not-so-immaculate conception in the Italian versions took place during World War II; the three fathers were American GIs far from home, the mother a poor, orphaned teenager trying to make ends meet. *Mamma Mia!*'s mama, on the other hand, was a free-living disco singer. "I don't care if you slept with hundreds of men, you're my mother," says the love child on the eve of her wedding. Sweet sentiment, no?

In an America that was becoming more and more conservative by the minute, it was curious to see *Mamma Mia!* so wholeheartedly embraced. Here you had a heroine who indulged in—egad!—premarital sex, and with three men simultaneously. A role model for the daughters of the moralists? Apparently so.

There have been any number of attempts at stocking new musical comedies with old songs, although few actually make it to Broadway. Theatre composers are usually the victims; *High Society*, with Cole Porter tunes, was the most recent mishap to hit town. Regionally, Porter was even more recently raided for something called *Roman Holiday*, based on the film of the same title. (This is a wonderful film, but a poor mix of music and locale.) George and Ira Gershwin's catalogue was mined for *They All Laughed*; Jule Styne's for *Three Coins in the Fountain*; and Duke Ellington's music was used for *Play On!*, an adaptation of *Twelfth Night* that had some regional success but was a quick Broadway failure. In the pop music world, Burt Bacharach and Hal David's catalogue was used for *What the World Needs Now*, which failed at the Old Globe in 1998; another Bacharach-David show, *The Look of Love*, has been announced for the Roundabout's 2002–2003 season. And the success of *Mamma Mia!* has, inevitably, jump-started several more projects.

The problem is fairly simple, really. Musical comedy evolved into a form in which the story is told in part by book and in part by song; the lyrics, ideally, are an extension of the character. Good old Professor Henry Higgins is a perfect example. "Why can't the English teach their children how to speak?" he asks in his opening number, using the same vocabulary and searing wit when he *sings* as when he *talks*. The character wears his language like a costume, and I don't suppose any other character in *My Fair Lady*—or any other musical in existence—could sing that particular song.

Theatregoers familiar with the songs—and that encompassed much of the audience—were absolutely loving *Mamma Mia!* It was a game: identify that song!

Imagine Professor Higgins tearing through the Covent Garden flower market and coming out with something written for a World War II musical comedy about navy fliers quarantined in an exclusive girl's boarding school. (Lerner and Loewe had a whole scoreful of slightly used songs of that description, from their first Broadway effort.) Yes, you can construct a musical comedy in such a manner, especially when the fame of the songwriters is the show's main selling point. In some cases the songs will, inevitably, kind of fit the song slots; but neat it isn't.

Mamma Mia! was far from neat; most of the songs were only circumstantially relevant to the proceedings. And a good deal of what passed for plot and characterization was inane. Johnson supplemented her unwed mother with two similarly feisty middle-aged pals, her backup singers from the old days. The twenty-year-old daughter had two twenty-year-old galpals; the daughter's fiancé had two buddies; and there were the three potential fathers as well. That's twelve characters in search of one plot; four characters and eight character sketches, as it turned out. Songs and jokes were distributed with a free hand; characterization was severely rationed, and it was every gal for herself.

There's not one of the twelve characters, by the way, who seemed to be Greek; or in Greece; or who had ever even heard of Greece. The audience knew they were in Greece, though, because the tacky-looking set featured a backdrop of Aegean blue. Also, the program said the action took place "on a tiny Greek Island." And when one of the backup singers arrived on the island, she told us, "I hope I get a chance to get my tongue around a little Greek."

The odd thing is, it didn't matter in the least. Most of these song-catalogue musicals fail due to the uneasy mixture of new characters and old songs. It seems like the more they try to integrate the elements, the more they try to make them appear to fit together, the more strained the results. *Mamma Mia!* was far more haphazard about the whole thing than other attempts, and that seems to have been the key to its success. It wasn't neat, and the creators didn't try to finesse it. They acknowledged it at every turn, and invited the audience in on the joke.

Most of the lyrics didn't make sense, exactly. How could they? People who just met talk about being in love for years, or walking the streets together in Paris—that sort of thing. (In the Paris song, they rhyme "Notre-Dame" with "tourist jam," "Eiffel Tower" with "flower-power," and "the Seine" with "the rain," twice. Maybe that's how they pronounce French in Swedish?) Of course you don't believe the mix of story and song; the creators seemed to be saying: We don't either. But watch how we slip in "Chiquitita"!

And it worked, it worked like gangbusters.

If the score was shoehorned, the book itself was shopworn. The proceedings began with the typical "turn-off-your-cellphone" speech, appended to which was "we would like to warn patrons of nervous disposition that platform shoes and white spandex are used in this production." Clearly the funniest line of the evening.

The humor was of the sort where the runtiest fellow, a character called Pepper, says with a leer: "They call my Peppy." "Why? Because he's hot?" asks one of the girls. "No," says another, "because he gets up your nose."

Is this nostalgia, or what?

Peppy comes on to one of the middle-aged ex-backup girls. "Down

Mamma Mia!
Opened: October 18, 2001
Still playing May 27, 2002
251 performances (and 14 previews)
Profit/Loss: Profit
Mamma Mia! ($100 top) was scaled to a potential gross of
$991,618 at the 1,498-seat Winter Garden Theatre. Weekly
grosses averaged about $964,000, with standing room
frequently pushing the gross over the million-dollar mark.
Total gross for the thirty-four-week partial season was
$31,933,378. Attendance was about 99 percent, with the
box office grossing about 97 percent of dollar-capacity.

TONY AWARD NOMINATIONS
Best Musical
Best Book of a Musical: Catherine Johnson
Best Performance by a Leading Actress: Louise Pitre
Best Performance by a Featured Actress: Judy Kaye
Best Orchestrations: Benny Andersson, Björn Ulvaeus, and
    Martin Koch

*Critical
Scorecard*

Rave 1
Favorable 3
Mixed 1
Unfavorable 1
Pan 4

boy," she says, "I'm old enough to be your mother." "Then you can call me
Oedipus," he responds. Euripides it ain't; but when did Euripides ever gross
a million a week?

The choreography was even less artful, the sort where everybody forms
a line upstage, lifts their arms, and moves down to the apron for a big
finish. There was also a big nightmare sequence in the second act where
the boys are dressed like frogmen in tight-fitting wet suits. Except for the
fiancé, that is; the boys carried him on resplendently outfitted in a full-
blown wedding gown. He looked a little uncomfortable, but then all
those chorus boys were tossing him around like a—well, I suppose there
was some sexual subtext in this, but we'll let that pass. Choreographer
Anthony Van Laast last visited Broadway with the 2000 revival of *Jesus
Christ Superstar*. His work here was of the same quality, although *Mamma
Mia!* seems likely to make him as famous as Gillian Lynne.

The mother was played by a new-to-Broadway Canadian actress named
Louise Pitre, who gave a friendly and attractive performance. Perfectly
satisfactory, but without the sort of star quality that lights up the stage.
Tina Maddigan played the love child, and seemed quite lovely. The problem, though, came when Ms. Maddigan and Ms. Pitre started to sing. The
arrangements were so noisy, and so backed-up by backup voices, that they
seemed canned; you could never tell if they were simply dubbed into the
proceedings.

The heroine's two pals stood out among the others; coincidentally, they were the only Broadway veterans in the lot. Karen Mason has been around a long time, singing in cabarets and onstage, most prominently as the much-utilized standby for the leading ladies of *Sunset Boulevard*. She gave the impression in *Mamma Mia!* that she was coasting along and enjoying the ride, as if to say, "This isn't very demanding, but hey—it's a gig and it's a hit and I've got a big song in the second act, so let's all have a blast."

Judy Kaye has been around even longer than Ms. Mason; she made a leap to Broadway stardom when the late Madeline Kahn hopped off *On the Twentieth Century* in 1978. Kahn, with a clutch of spectacular reviews considerably better than those for the show itself, wanted her schedule reduced to six performances a week. She began missing more and more shows until director Hal Prince got fed up and the producers fired her. Kaye, an understudy with little experience, stepped into Kahn's shoes and proved a more than capable comedienne.

Kaye has given sturdy performances over the years, earning a Featured Actress Tony Award for her Carlotta in the Broadway production of

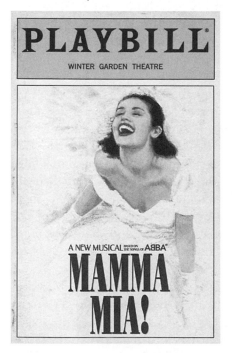

Prince's *Phantom of the Opera*, but she never found another shot at stardom. In *Mamma Mia!*, Kaye was the only person onstage who seemed to be performing in real time, in real life, as if to say, "No, I never did get my big Broadway shot, but I'm standing here in a spotlight on the very same stage where Streisand played *Funny Girl* and I AM GOING TO ENTERTAIN YOU." And Ms. Kaye did.

It was very clear that theatregoers familiar with the songs— and that encompassed much of the audience—were absolutely loving *Mamma Mia!* It was a game: identify that song, from the first notes of the intro if possible, and determine how the song will fit the plot. (In musical theatre, typically, the audience usually has to listen to the words before deciding what the song is about.) Oddly, though, the ABBA fans seemed slightly more entranced at the beginning of the songs than at the end.

This was due to fond memories, no doubt, but it was also a result of the handling of the songs. The creators seemed to slavishly adhere to the old pop arrangements, at the understandable peril of a revolution from the die-hards in the audience. But many of these arrangements built to similar, abrupt endings, suitable for disc or disco. Live theatre is something else again, or should be. Musical numbers, typically, are designed to build to an effective conclusion. In *Mamma Mia!* many of the songs simply seemed to stop.

Call it great or call it poor, one thing was clear: *Mamma Mia!*—the title taken from one of ABBA's greatest hits—was from the first a surefire crowd pleaser. The show opened to instantaneous success at London's Prince Edward Theatre on April 6, 1999; the £3 million ($4.8 million) production cost was recouped within twenty-seven weeks, and *Mamma Mia!* continued to coin pounds through the end of 2001. Then it started earning euros, by the buckets. The Toronto production opened in May 2000, similarly shattering box office records. A United States touring company opened in San Francisco in November 2000, ditto. Same with the Australian company, which opened in June 2001 in Melbourne. And then came Broadway.

None of *Mamma Mia!*'s weaknesses mattered in the least. For the vast majority of theatregoers, anyway, who were awash in a nostalgic love fest of ABBA songs. Some critics went after the show with hatchets; a few—who appear to have grown up listening to the songs—simply accepted the show for what it was. Ben Brantley of the *New York Times* memorably described it as "a giant singing Hostess cupcake."

Quality-wise, I certainly agreed with the naysayers; but as I sat in the Winter Garden, with hundreds of people around me having a fine old time, it seemed that it would be churlish to begrudge them their enjoyment. *Mamma Mia!* was custom-tailored for the ABBA-lovers club, and the ABBA-lovers club appears to be larger than the Sondheim-lovers club and the Jerry Herman–lovers club combined. The songs were old friends, paraded for their pleasure, comfort food for the masses. And what's wrong with that?

> As I sat in the Winter Garden, with hundreds of people around me having a fine old time, it seemed that it would be churlish to begrudge them their enjoyment.

Thou Shalt Not

It would be simple enough to lay *Thou Shalt Not* low with easy jabs at its obvious weaknesses. That's what most all theatre critics did—as in Thou Shalt Not create pretentious musicals, or Thou Shouldst Not Have. But I have not come to bury *Thou Shalt Not*; that was done effectively enough by the assembled creators.

Whenever a high-profile failure explodes on Broadway, the same questions are asked repeatedly: Didn't they know? How *couldn't* they have known? Here you have a show from talented and successful professionals, in this case Susan Stroman, Harry Connick Jr., André Bishop, and Bernard Gersten. How could they have been so wrong?

With the growth of workshops, a new question has entered into the mix: What could they possibly have seen in the workshop to make them think this material would ever—and could ever—work? One can understand how directors and writers might be too self-involved to see the flaws; but what could the money people have been thinking? One assumes that a show like *Thou Shalt Not* could not have looked like a world-beater in workshop, in the same way one assumes that *Contact* probably did. (Look like a world-beater.) How bad does a musical have to be before a producer says thanks, everybody, but let's just go home?

Thou Shalt Not came out of Lincoln Center Theater's musical theatre program, in the same way that *Contact* did (as discussed in *Broadway Yearbook 1999–2000*). Before I proceed, let me point out an omission in that discussion. Yes, Lincoln Center Theater has long been providing facilities and funding for new musicals. What I neglected to cite was that this workshop system originated at Playwrights Horizons, where Bishop served as artistic director before heading to LCT in 1992.

One tends to remember Bishop's years at Playwrights for hits like *Driving Miss Daisy*, *Sister Mary Ignatius Explains It All for You*, and *The Heidi*

Chronicles. One should not overlook the groundbreaking musicals. William Finn was an early Playwrights discovery. In 1978, the theatre workshopped *In Trousers*, the first part of Finn's *Marvin Trilogy*. A full production followed, leading to Playwrights workshops and productions of *March of the Falsettos* and *Falsettoland*. Other Playwrights musicals included Finn's *America Kicks Up Its Heels*; Stephen Sondheim's *Sunday in the Park with George* and *Assassins*; Ahrens and Flaherty's *Lucky Stiff* and *Once on This Island*; and others, including Skip Kennon's *Herringbone* and Wendy Wasserstein's *Miami*.

But let's get back to Lincoln Center and *Thou Shalt Not* and Susan Stroman. For this was Stroman's show; she wrote neither book, lyrics, nor score, but the billing clearly read "a new musical by Susan Stroman, David Thompson and Harry Connick, Jr."

Stroman needs no introduction to readers of this book. She has been on a roll, as they say, since the spring of 1998, when she staged the acclaimed dances for the Royal National Theatre production of *Oklahoma!* (which finally made it to Broadway after *Thou Shalt Not* had come and gone). She followed this by creating and staging Lincoln Center Theater's rapturously received *Contact* in 1999; directing and choreographing the sturdy if not creatively overwhelming 2000 revival of *The Music Man*; and directing and choreographing the hit of the epoch, *The Producers*, in 2001. This gave her an unprecedented four Tony Award nominations (in two categories) in 1999–2000, plus two more in 2000–2001. She won three of the four awards she was eligible for and received an additional nomination in 2002. But not for *Thou Shalt Not*.

This was clearly a magical talent who could do no wrong; or could she? Stroman sprang to attention in March 1991 with her refreshingly enjoyable dances for the off-Broadway revue *And the World Goes Round: The Songs of Kander & Ebb*. This brought her directly to Broadway with the most entertaining dances since the early days of Tommy Tune. *Crazy for You* was the show, in February 1992, a rejuvenation of an old Gershwin musical. So far, so good. This was followed by proficient but unremarkable dances for the Hal Prince revival of *Show Boat* in October 1994; unremarkable dances for the Madison Square Garden version of *A Christmas Carol* in December 1994 (and remounted annually for the Christmas season, to date); unremarkable dances for the ill-assembled musicalization of the film hit *Big* in April 1996; and some highly interesting dances for the ill-conceived *Steel Pier* in April 1997. Choreographers generally have limited power in the creation of a musical—unless they happen to be director as well—and thus deserve little of the blame. But Stroman was the co-conceiver of *Steel Pier* and a key player in the creation of *Big*, two back-to-back, highly anticipated, big-budget flops.

PLYMOUTH THEATRE
236 West 45th Street
Ⓢ A Shubert Organization Theatre
Gerald Schoenfeld, *Chairman*   Philip J. Smith, *President*

Robert E. Wankel, *Executive Vice President*

LINCOLN CENTER THEATER
under the direction of
André Bishop and Bernard Gersten
presents

THOU SHALT NOT
a new musical

by Susan Stroman, David Thompson and Harry Connick, Jr.
based on 'Thérèse Raquin' by Emile Zola

book   *music & lyrics*
David Thompson   Harry Connick, Jr.

Cast (in alphabetical order)

Timothy J. Alex	Dylis Croman	JoAnn M. Hunter	David New
Craig Bierko	Michael Goddard	Cornelius Jones, Jr.	Rachelle Rak
Brad Bradley	James Hadley	Davis Kirby	Kelli Severson
Pam Bradley	Amy Hall	Kate Levering	Patrick Wetzel
Leo Burmester	Ellen Harvey	Ted L. Levy	Kent Zimmerman
Norbert Leo Butz	Amy Heggins	Debra Monk	
	Emily Hsu	J. C. Montgomery	

sets   *costumes*   *lighting*
Thomas Lynch   William Ivey Long   Peter Kaczorowski

sound   *music director*   *orchestrations & arrangements*   *music coordinator*
Scott Lehrer   Phil Reno   Harry Connick, Jr.   John Miller

casting   *production*   *associate director*   *musical theater*
Tara Rubin   *stage manager*   *& choreographer*   *hair & wigs*   *associate producer*
Casting   Peter Wolf   Tara Young   Paul Huntley   Ira Weitzman

general manager   *production manager*   *director of marketing*   *director of development*
Steven C. Callahan   Jeff Hamlin   *& special projects*   Hattie K. Jutagir
                                              Thomas Cott

direction & choreography
Susan Stroman

Leadership support for THOU SHALT NOT is generously provided by The Blanche and Irving Laurie Foundation.

Major support is also provided by AT&T.

Special thanks to The Harold and Mimi Steinberg Charitable Trust for supporting new American plays at LCT.

LCT gratefully acknowledges extraordinary support from The Lila Acheson and DeWitt Wallace Fund for Lincoln Center,
established by the founders of The Reader's Digest Association, and from The Lila Acheson and DeWitt Wallace Endowment Fund.

American Airlines is the official airline of Lincoln Center Theater.

Thanks to the Theatre Development Fund for its support of this production.

The producers and theater management are members of the League of American Theatres and Producers, Inc.

The *Thou Shalt Not* issue of *Lincoln Center Theater Review*
is available at stands located throughout the theater.

Flim Flam   J. C. Montgomery
Papa Jack   Ted L. Levy
Monsignor   Patrick Wetzel
Sass   Rachelle Rak
Sugar Hips   Davis Kirby
Laurent LeClaire   Craig Bierko
Therese Raquin   Kate Levering
Madame Raquin   Debra Monk
Camille Raquin   Norbert Leo Butz
Officer Michaud   Leo Burmester
Oliver   Brad Bradley
Suzanne   JoAnn M. Hunter
Antoine   Patrick Wetzel
Busker   Ted L. Levy
Sanctify Sam   Ted L. Levy
Ensemble   Timothy J. Alex, Brad
   Bradley, Dylis Croman, Michael
   Goddard, Amy Hall, Ellen Harvey,
   Amy Heggins, JoAnn M. Hunter,
   Cornelius Jones Jr., Davis Kirby, Ted
   L. Levy, J. C. Montgomery, Rachelle
   Rak, Kelli Severson, Patrick Wetzel
Swings   Pam Bradley, James Hadley,
   Emily Hsu, Kent Zimmerman

The story takes place in New Orleans,
   in and around the Ninth Ward,
   1946–1947.

Original Broadway Cast Album:
   Papa's—June Music [no catalogue
   number]

In retrospect, it's easy to say that the producers of *Thou Shalt Not* hired the Stroman of *Contact* and *The Producers* but got her wearing her *Steel Pier* hat. Easy to say, but I ask—what would you do? Someone walks in your door with three Broadway musicals running simultaneously, shows that she directed *and* choreographed; two have been rapturously acclaimed, one is a modern phenomenon. What producer would not beg for the right to produce *anything* that said director-choreographer might come up with? Lincoln Center Theater's André Bishop and Bernie Gersten were presumably thrilled to proceed. Even so, as producers of *Contact* they had little choice but to embrace whatever Stroman proffered. Can you imagine the reaction of the Lincoln Center Board if they had let Stroman's next musical get away?

Lincoln Center certainly should have pulled the plug after they saw the workshop, you might well say. But it doesn't work that way. With a traditional book musical, perhaps, you can see flaws more clearly. Bad songs, a hopeless book, or both. (The insolvable flaws on a show like *Big* were clearly visible after the workshop, but the producers decided to plunge ahead nevertheless.) A concept musical succeeds or fails on the vision of the director, though. It's not enough to hear the words and music; it's the overall picture that you need to see, and a director can't paint without scenery, costumes, and lighting.

It's one thing when you have an untried person in charge and the workshop doesn't work. But when you have Jerome Robbins or Hal Prince or Susan Stroman—a comparable talent, at least in 2001 dollars—you simply have to go ahead and let them create. It's one thing to produce a worthy attempt to break new ground that fails; it's quite another to pull the plug on something that could well have been brilliant, and the world will never know.

This was pointed up during the run of *Thou Shalt Not* when a squabble erupted over the status of the show formerly called *Wise Guys*. A set of producers financed a workshop in October 1999 (see *Broadway Yearbook 1999–2000*). The show was at that time clearly not ready to proceed, causing cancellation of the April 2000 Broadway opening. A year later, the authors arranged a subsequent production under different auspices—at which point one of the original producers yelled foul, claiming, in effect, that said production would happen over his dead body. This was all worked out amicably, as they say, and the musical presently called *Gold!* is happily back on course. This story will be picked up, hopefully, in *Broadway Yearbook 2002–2003*.

But let's get back to Lincoln Center and *Thou Shalt Not* and Susan Stroman. Émile Zola's 1867 novel *Thérèse Raquin* presented a pair of characters overwhelmed by uncontrollable passion and thrust into murder. It created quite a scandal in its time, and was resultantly a best-seller. This uncontrollable passion apparently appealed to Stroman as the basis for a theatre piece. She called librettist David Thompson, of the massive international blockbuster *Chicago*.

But let's hold on a minute. Thompson didn't write *Chicago*; he adapted the Fred Ebb–Bob Fosse script for the Encores! concert version, which is to say he whittled down the text in order to accommodate the lack of scenery and production values. (One wonders if Ebb would have done the adaptation himself if he had known that it would ultimately be worth hundreds upon hundreds of thousands of dollars in royalties, rather than the thousand or so that City Center paid.) Thompson's prior main credits were book adaptations of two failed Kander and Ebb musicals, an off

off-Broadway version of *Flora, The Red Menace* in 1987, and a London attempt at *70, Girls, 70* in 1991.

Thompson came to *Thou Shalt Not* with one Broadway musical to his credit, *Steel Pier*. This had a potentially exciting idea, mind you; the show was scuttled mostly by a book that couldn't support it. Not necessarily the librettist's fault; musical theatre in general is, and *Steel Pier* specifically was, a highly collaborative process.

Thou Shalt Not, too, seems to have been similarly scuttled in the early stages. The transformation of Zola's novel, for various reasons, was sure to be difficult; perhaps John Weidman, who worked so well with Stroman on *Contact*, could have gotten somewhere with it. The main problem can be traced to an initial risky choice, transferring the action from mid-nineteenth-century Paris to mid-twentieth-century New Orleans. Let me quote Thompson in an interview with Randy Gener of Broadway.com: "It made sense, since New Orleans is a cousin of Paris."

Well, now, did it? The lazy ol' South is a handy trap for musical theatre folks trying to Americanize properties; there is, naturally, music in the air. This same thinking led to Michael John LaChiusa's 1999 *Marie Christine* (also for Lincoln Center Theater), which transplanted *Medea* to

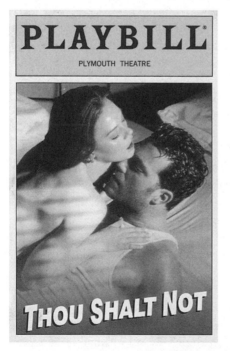

Lake Pontchartrain in the not-so-gay nineties. A few intrepid souls tried a similar exercise back in 1952, transferring *Aida* from wartime Memphis (Egypt) to wartime Memphis (Tennessee), circa 1861. Festooned with the most lavish sets and costumes of its time, *My Darlin' Aida* opened at the end of October and closed at the beginning of January—just like *Thou Shalt Not* did forty seasons later.

Now, I'm not going to tell you that the southern transplantation in itself killed poor *Thérèse Raquin*. Nor will I place blame on the head of composer-lyricist Harry Connick Jr., who seems to have been brought in after the New Orleans decision had been made because he hails from New Orleans. This fellow is very good at what he does, but what he doesn't do is write lyrics for musico-dramatic characters. The choices the creators made in transplanting the characters to the Big Easy took us way too far from Zola, and the results sank in the jambalaya.

Early in the second act, a character we'd never met bounded onstage at Camille's funeral and said, "We send him off the way we send all our musical brothers off." And off they went into a generic New Orleans funeral production number! This reeks of clumsy old musical comedy; I suppose that if the adapters had kept *Thérèse Raquin* in Paris, they'd have taken us up to Montmartre and said, "Zut! Look at zee girls, dancing in zee underwear" and given us a grand old cancan. This sort of thing is not only hazardous to the forward motion of the plot; in this case, it pointed up a main problem of the adaptation. Camille, in *Thou Shalt Not*, was the life of the party. His health, apparently, was wrecked by too many long nights playing jazz and carousing afterward with his musician buddies, so he was duly mourned by every jazz musician and dancer on the stage of the Plymouth Theatre. Camille, in Zola, was just about as anonymous as could be; Laurent wasn't an old friend, merely a vague acquaintance. Even so, he was the closest thing to a friend Camille had ever had. Hence, he was invited into the house and—almost against his will—immediately tore into the fabric of the family.

Zola's tale told of a man and woman seized by uncontrollable passion, leading to betrayal, murder, murderous hatred, and ultimately—with no way out—double suicide. To make his point, Zola created a pair of the dullest, most passionless characters you'd want to meet. Or wouldn't want to meet. Thérèse was a milliner, selling cheap hats and ribbons to low-class shopgirls out of a dusty shop hidden away in a Paris alley; what you might call an indoor girl, drab and sheltered from the sun or a breeze of fresh air. Laurent was a low-level clerk, one of those fellows whose only ambition is to inherit his father's money. Once disowned, he wandered about hoping to find some woman or other to support him. Camille—Thérèse's husband and first cousin—is a childlike invalid, more colorless than even Thérèse or Laurent. The fourth main character, Camille's mother, Mme Raquin, sits in the shop ruling Thérèse's life, an annoying and inert ogre even before she is paralyzed by a stroke. The passion that enflames Thérèse and Laurent is—most of all—*unlikely*. The pair are as ordinary as can be, from all appearances absolutely passionless. This is the foundation on which Zola built his story.

Down in New Orleans, though, this pair was *hot*. Hot and sexy. The new, Americanized Therese was clearly what we might call sexed up; she entered bearing a laundry basket and went right into a touchy-feely ballet, lustily rolling around on the ground in her just-washed bedsheets. The program called this the "I Need to Be in Love Ballet"; to me, it looked more like "The Laundress Has Conniptions." This was followed, fifteen minutes or so later, by the related song. (In musical theatre, we usually sing the song first and *then* do the dance, so that the audience knows what the character is dancing about. But we'll let that pass.) Therese's character-introduction song is called "I Need to Be in Love," and she made this clear the moment she set eyes on Laurent.

But does this character need to be in love? Zola's heroine doesn't know what love is until the moment she is embraced by Laurent; Zola's tale demonstrated how passion—surprisingly and brutally—could seize the least passionate, most unlikely people. Broadway's Laurent came on, too, as a stud on the lookout—which Zola's Laurent was, specifically, not. "Fat and sloppy" is how he is described, at least in the translation I read. "Looking at his big, lumpy body, with apparently no bones or sinews in it, nobody would have dreamed of accusing him of violence or cruelty." When Zola thrust Thérèse and Laurent into uncontrollable passion, his readers were shocked and perhaps shaken; if ordinary people like that can be overtaken, what about moi? The musical demonstrated how passion could seize passionate, oversexed people. No surprise, there.

Didn't they know? How *couldn't* they have known? How could they have been so wrong?

When Stroman and Connick and Thompson tossed them onto a big old bed on a revolving turntable with flashing lights and had Ms. Levering remove her bra during the "Other Hours Ballet," we were not surprised in the least. She carefully wriggled back into that bra, under the sheets, before the "after-sex" scene that followed the ballet—which of course made no sense, in context, and merely looked contrived. She removed the bra at some performances but not at others; 75 percent of the time was the estimate I got from one of the stagehands. But we'll let that pass, too.

The New Orleans setting resulted in other character changes. Camille and Laurent were no longer low-level bureaucratic pencil pushers; they were now jazz pianists, and presumably good ones. (They both tickled the ivories like Harry Connick Jr.) That, in itself, made them *interesting* people—which Zola's nonheroes decidedly were not. Madame Raquin became proprietress of a New Orleans jazz café, where she not only sang risqué ditties but also hopped up to the bandstand and filled in on the drums in a spotlight. A far cry from Zola, don't you think? Madame Raquin was an ogre in the book; here she was a saucy, old good-time gal. (Debra Monk played the role, and her character seemed at least partially derived from the "Everybody's Girl" she played so well in *Steel Pier*.)

Changes of this sort are permissible, certainly, and often necessary; there's no need to stick to the original. But *Thou Shalt Not*'s changes

worked against Zola's theme. Therese and Laurent—that is, Kate Levering and Craig Bierko—were the sexiest people on the Plymouth stage, on
all of Forty-fifth Street in fact. Present us with people who look like us
and act like us—ordinary people—and you'll get a certain reaction. Give
us people who look like movie stars and behave like movie stars and put
them through lust and murder, and we'll think—oh, yes, it's *The Postman
Always Rings Twice* all over again. After *Thou Shalt Not*'s swift demise,
Kathleen Turner moved into Levering's dressing room. Chew on that
one, won't you.

The story seemed familiar, certainly. Shiftless ne'er-do-well with loads
of charm and no undershirt turns up in the backyard of a guy he used to
know—not friends, exactly, merely acquaintances—and is invited to do
chores. He repays the hospitality by seducing his friend's gal under the
steamy mid-America moon, and ruining everything for everybody. The
creators of *Thou Shalt Not* clearly read Zola's *Thérèse Raquin*, but they
seem to have confused it with William Inge's *Picnic*. (Scott Ellis, Stroman
and Thompson's collaborator on *Steel Pier* and two other projects, directed *Picnic* at the Roundabout in 1994, with "musical interludes and
choreography developed by Susan Stroman." Debra Monk was in the cast,
too, in another variation of what became Madame Raquin.)

Elsewhere, the authors had Therese and Laurent go out on the town.
They brought out a park bench and a lamppost and five couples-worth of
"happy people" while the lovers did a tuneful song and dance called "Just
in Time." Wait a minute, that was in *Bells Are Ringing*, the 1956 musical
comedy that was unhappily revived on the very same Plymouth stage six
months earlier. In *Thou Shalt Not*
it was called "Sovereign Lover."
In the middle of the number, out
came some no-named character
in a top hat we'd never seen before—"Busker," he was called in
the program—who engaged in a

**It's one thing to produce a worthy
attempt to break new ground that fails;
it's quite another to pull the plug on
something that could well have been
brilliant, and the world will never know.**

challenge tap dance with Therese. Hold on! Therese Raquin tap dancing!!! Why? Simply because Levering is an expert tap dancer? This is like
asking the star of *Sweeney Todd* to do his famous imitations of Cagney and
Bogey and Jack Nicholson while he's waiting for them to deliver his exe-
cutioner's chair.

The lovers played their impossible parts as well as possible. Bierko was
raffish and rugged, not unlike William Holden in *Picnic*; Levering looked
like Faye Dunaway waiting—and hoping—for something bad to happen
to her. (In a striking moment after her big sex scene with Laurent,
Camille climbed into bed with her and snuggled as she pretended to

sleep. As the scene ended, she opened her eyes with a look of revulsion, as if to scream in horror: "Why oh why oh why did I ever leave *42nd Street?*") The ever-resourceful Ms. Monk had her hands tied, as it were; her character spent the second act as a wheelchair-bound mute paralytic.

Where *Thou Shalt Not* was remarkable was in the performance of a newcomer named Norbert Leo Butz. Not a newcomer, exactly; he'd served as a replacement in *Rent* and a road emcee in *Cabaret*, as well as doing a good job as Jerry in the Roundabout's 2000 off-Broadway production of *Juno and the Paycock*. Just prior to *Thou Shalt Not*, he attracted acclaim in the Chicago premiere of Jason Robert Brown's *The Last Five Years*— which he repeated off-Broadway after *Thou Shalt Not* closed.

Butz displayed a magnetic presence in *Thou Shalt Not*, especially after his character was murdered at the first-act curtain. He had merely to sit there, casting sidelong glances at his wife and his friend, and you felt talent radiating from the stage. Zola's Camille should not be charismatic or attractive or sympathetic, of course; his lack of fire is what drives Thérèse and Laurent together. But when things grow dreary, we'll take what we can get.

Butz was especially delectable in his big second-act number, "Oh! Ain't That Sweet." This sounded like something Frank Sinatra would have sung to a Nelson Riddle arrangement in 1957; it was staged like Ben Vereen's big solo "A New Man" in the 1985 musical *Grind*, a number that appeared out of the blue (and out of context) when Hal Prince asked Bob Fosse to try to salvage that hopelessly bleak mishmash. Butz appeared to have springs in his thighs and mops on his feet; during orchestral fills, he tauntingly snapped his choppers at Bierko like a playfully menacing thirteen-year-old who's too adorable to scold. (Camille bit Laurent on the neck during the murder, causing a wound that refused to heal and eventually drove Laurent nuts. *Thou Shalt Not* was presented in flashback mode, with Laurent telling his musician pals the story after Therese's suicide and just before his own. So why didn't Bierko have the scar in the opening scene???) At any rate, Butz was wonderful, a prime example of why you should never walk out of a musical during intermission.

> The creators of *Thou Shalt Not* read Zola's *Thérèse Raquin*, but they seem to have confused it with William Inge's *Picnic*.

The show did have one effective song, "Tug Boat," which was repeated again and again. The two half notes set to the title actually approximated the sound of a forlorn tugboat—and were thus, perhaps, the only music of the evening that fit the drama. The song accompanied the murder of Camille; Camille sang, "Tugboat, tugboat, push me till I die" moments before Laurent pushed him off the boat till he died. So much for subtlety.

Thou Shalt Not
Opened: October 25, 2001
Closed: January 6, 2002
115 performances (and 33 previews)
Profit/Loss: Nonprofit [Loss]
Thou Shalt Not ($86.25 top) was scaled to a potential gross
of $614,859 at the 1,033-seat Plymouth Theatre. Weekly
grosses averaged about $264,000, with a high of
$320,000 in previews and a low of $175,000 before
Christmas. Total gross for the fifteen-week run was
$3,894,953. Attendance was about 73 percent, with the
box office grossing about 43 percent of dollar-capacity.
(These figures are not indicative, as the potential was
calculated at the top ticket price, but subscribers paid
less.)

TONY AWARD NOMINATIONS
Best Original Score: Harry Connick Jr.
Best Performance by a Featured Actor: Norbert Leo Butz

Critical
Scorecard

Rave 0
Favorable 0
Mixed 1
Unfavorable 1
Pan 8

But enough of this. If *Thou Shalt Not* didn't work—and it clearly didn't
—it was just as clearly full of interesting ideas. The misbegotten scene in
Madame Raquin's Broken Tea Cup Café, for example. (Misbegotten, I say,
because it established the four main characters in the center of an active
world, instead of on the fringes where Zola placed them.) Monk started
by singing what was supposed to be a risqué ditty called "My Little
World"; attention shifted to Laurent, at the piano, singing "While You're
Young"; and Therese broke through in the middle of all this with the
aforementioned "I Need to Be in Love" while a swinging dance number
raged around her, in pantomime. Thus three rather different songs, three
characters expressing their different viewpoints, all happening at once.
This was well conceived, in structure and staging. If only the songs had
suited the material. . . .

Or take the big sex scene, when the bed revolved on the center
turntable while Bierko had to sing some foolishness about Levering being
"all alone in your all night gown." (What, pray tell, is an "all night gown?")
Stroman presented us with a string of black-garbed dancers in suspenders,
with hands in their pockets, who slinked around the lovers while the
orchestra beat out a heartbeat tattoo (which would become a recurring
musical motif). Later in the first act there was a sequence leading to the
Mardi Gras, with the ensemble forming a silhouetted chain upstage
against a blood orange sky. Stunning visuals; Stroman and her *Contact*
team of designers—Thomas Lynch (sets), William Ivey Long (costumes),
and Peter Kaczorowski (lights)—were clearly creating exciting theatre.

It's unfortunate that the material couldn't support it. Still, I'm awfully glad that Lincoln Center Theater gave Stroman the chance to try. I expect that the experiment of *Thou Shalt Not* will pay off in her future work. One thing's for sure. It wasn't boring.

I returned to *Thou Shalt Not* shortly before it closed; I wanted to get a clearer picture of the positive elements, and try to understand where everything went wrong. I was immediately struck by the ensemble (and onstage musicians) in the opening number "It's Good to Be Home." Here it was, a lackluster Wednesday matinee one week before Christmas, three weeks before closing, and four weeks before the unemployment line. And they were full of life, dancing and playing like they were in the hit of the year. That, in itself, was rewarding to see.

Stroman and Connick and Thompson seemed to know what it was that they wanted to do. They were wholly at a loss, though, as to what to do about it.

By Jeeves

Around about 1973, composer Andrew Lloyd Webber and lyricist Tim Rice—newly famous for their *Jesus Christ Superstar*, which jolted Broadway in 1971 and the West End in 1972—decided to write a musical based on P. G. Wodehouse's stories about the butler Jeeves. (Webber and Rice's *Joseph and the Amazing Technicolor Dreamcoat*, written before but produced after *Superstar*, had been considerably less successful.) When Rice opted out of the project, Lloyd Webber approached Alan Ayckbourn, who even then was considered "the British Neil Simon." Ayckbourn already had a string of hits to his name; he had, however, never written a musical, nor written lyrics, nor directed a musical.

Jeeves opened on April 22, 1975, at Her Majesty's Theatre in London and—in the words of Lloyd Webber—was "an outsized turkey." The show was hastily buried and quickly forgotten, except by the authors. Over the years, Lloyd Webber embarked on an unparalleled career in musical theatre with three all-time super-hits: *Evita, Cats,* and *Phantom of the Opera*. While the latter two ran and ran and ran, his post-1986 musicals have all been no-

> "The actors had their hearts set on coming to Broadway, and I couldn't disappoint them," said Lloyd Webber. "So I wrote a check and just kissed it good-bye."

tably unsuccessful: *Aspects of Love, Sunset Boulevard, Whistle Down the Wind,* and *The Beautiful Game*. (Coincidentally or not, Lloyd Webber parted with producer Cameron Mackintosh after *Phantom* and himself served as lead producer on the last four shows.)

Ayckbourn, meanwhile, continued turning out (mostly) hit comedies. Twenty years after *Jeeves*'s initial departure, Lloyd Webber and Ayckbourn decided to give it another go. A newly minted, considerably different mu-

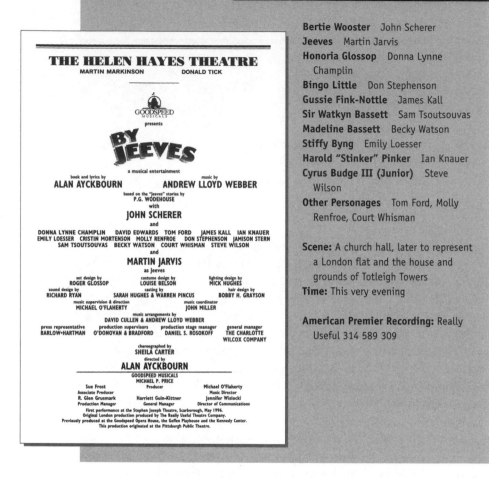

Bertie Wooster John Scherer
Jeeves Martin Jarvis
Honoria Glossop Donna Lynne
  Champlin
Bingo Little Don Stephenson
Gussie Fink-Nottle James Kall
Sir Watkyn Bassett Sam Tsoutsouvas
Madeline Bassett Becky Watson
Stiffy Byng Emily Loesser
Harold "Stinker" Pinker Ian Knauer
Cyrus Budge III (Junior) Steve
  Wilson
Other Personages Tom Ford, Molly
  Renfroe, Court Whisman

Scene: A church hall, later to represent
  a London flat and the house and
  grounds of Totleigh Towers
Time: This very evening

American Premier Recording: Really
  Useful 314 589 309

sical came to life. Under the title *By Jeeves*, it premiered at the Ayckbourn-operated Stephen Joseph Theatre in Scarborough in April 1996, transferring to the Duke of York's Theatre in London in July. Lloyd Webber and Ayckbourn—perhaps sensing that *By Jeeves* might need some tinkering before withstanding the harsh lights of Broadway—arranged for a December 1996 production by the Goodspeed Opera House. Not at the opera house proper, but at the smaller Norma Terris Theatre in Chester, Connecticut. *By Jeeves* was, finally, a well-received hit.

By *Jeeves* did not, as anticipated, come directly into New York. Why compete with Lloyd Webber's other musical of the season, the Hal Prince–directed surefire blockbuster *Whistle Down the Wind*? (Which, as fate would have it, shuttered after its Washington tryout.) *Variety* announced in December 1996 that the Goodspeed production would be remounted at the Geffen Playhouse in Los Angeles in March 1997 (which it was), after which it would play a June engagement at the Terrace Theatre at the Kennedy Center (which it did), after which it would open on Broadway in the fall (which it didn't), probably at the Circle in the Square.

The Kennedy Center engagement was a smash; great reviews, great business, with six weeks extended to thirteen. Lloyd Webber came down in August and announced to the cast that the show would move into Broadway's Booth Theatre in October 1997. Everybody packed their old kit bags, but by Labor Day the Booth had been booked out from under them by David Mamet's *The Old Neighborhood. By Jeeves* went into theatre-jam limbo, with the title resurfacing every so often.

The show lost out on a spring 1999 booking when the owners of the Helen Hayes turned down both *By Jeeves* and *W;t* for an oddity called *Band in Berlin.* Said oddity quickly folded, and *By Jeeves* was duly offered the theatre. It was too late, though; Ayckbourn—who took over as director of *Jeeves* in 1975 when the original director was fired and directed all subsequent productions—was otherwise engaged.

The Goodspeed production was remounted once again, successfully so, at the Pittsburgh Public Theatre in February 2001. The producers tried to grab the Hayes once more, as the *Dirty Blonde* in residence was at this point fraying. *By Jeeves* was halted as before, with the great Andrew Lloyd Webber pushed aside in favor of Hershey Felder and *George Gershwin Alone* (produced, not coincidentally, by the owner of the Hayes). The one-man show, with minimal operating costs, managed to hang on from May through July. At which point, finally, *By Jeeves* had a home.

This is a long time for a fully mounted, fully financed show to

> The score for *By Jeeves* didn't sound much like what one has grown to expect from Lord Andrew. Rather more fun than usual, with a lightheartedly jazzy feel.

be kept waiting in the wings. Which in itself is not a reflection of the production's quality or lack thereof; still, it is a clear statement that no theatre owner with a suitably intimate house thought they would make money with it. It is especially curious that the Shuberts, landlords of *Cats* and *Phantom of the Opera*, neglected to make space at one of their smaller venues. The Shuberts lost a bundle—two bundles—on the pre-Broadway tryouts of *Sunset Boulevard* and *Whistle Down the Wind*, but that's another story.

So *By Jeeves* finally made it to Broadway, five years after the London opening (and twenty-six years after the premiere of *Jeeves*). But not without yet another obstacle. Following the World Trade Center disaster, understandably skittish investors pulled out half of the show's capitalization.

Goodspeed, which was producing the Broadway engagement, was forced to call the whole thing off. Two days later, Lloyd Webber—and what he at first described to the press as "friends"—took up the slack and sent along the missing $800,000. After the opening but before the closing, Lloyd Webber told Michael Reidel of the *New York Post* "the actors had their hearts set on coming to Broadway, and I couldn't disappoint them. So I wrote a check and just kissed it good-bye."

Kissed it good-bye, indeed.

The most remarkable thing about *By Jeeves*, to me, was how amateurish it seemed. Yes, I know that within the conceit of the show they were supposed to appear to be a provincial British church group attempting to

play upper-class twits; but they were flouncing around like the real thing, and I found it desperately unfunny. For comparison, consider *Noises Off*, the revival of which opened four days later. This is another play-within-a-play, in which the actors are asked to play not-very-good actors (and not-very-good actors playing British twits). Playwright Michael Frayn had an attitude about his characters, though, which made them doubly funny; Ayckbourn and Lloyd Webber's dramatis personae simply seemed on the stupid side of silly. This is odd, as Ayckbourn is typically expert at this sort of thing. *By Jeeves* was a successful crowd pleaser at Goodspeed, at the Kennedy Center, and in Pittsburgh. But not at the Hayes, it wasn't.

They lost me early on. Show me characters named "Honoria Glossop" and "Harold Stinker Pinker," and I'm ready to head for the doors. Bertie Wooster, the erstwhile hero, came out onstage, looking embarrassed; it turned out he should have been. "I will entertain you, never fear, tonight," he sang; I think not. Poor John Scherer, who seemed a likably pleasant performer, was mired in the Wodehousian treacle. "I staggered back, appalled," he tells us, illustrating this with enough comic business to open a Halloween costume rental shop. No reaction from the audience. "My knees all but gave way before me." And they did; his knees, that is. No reaction. Painful, and it was only 8:20.

By Jeeves

Opened: October 28, 2001

Closed: December 30, 2001

73 performances (and 15 previews)

Profit/Loss: Loss

By Jeeves ($86.25 top) was scaled to a potential gross of
$369,280 at the 577-seat Helen Hayes Theatre. Weekly
grosses averaged about $190,000, hitting the $200,000
mark in only three weeks. Total gross for the eleven-week
run was $2,090,954. Attendance was about 71 percent,
with the box office grossing about 51 percent of dollar-
capacity.

Critical Scorecard

Rave 0

Favorable 2

Mixed 3

Unfavorable 0

Pan 4

Intermission didn't come for another fifty minutes, at which point
Jeeves said to Bertie, "Let's see if they're still here when we come back."
Act 2 started where they left off. Bertie: "Still here." Jeeves (disdainfully):
"Most of them." Which was a bit of an exaggeration. I brought a friend
with me, the sort of chap who'd rather be rollerblading or hang-gliding or
climbing the rock wall at Chelsea Piers. "You're kidding me," he said as he
fled up the aisle. "Andrew Lloyd Webber didn't write *this*."

Now, I'll readily confess that I'm not the world's biggest Lloyd Webber
fan; tell me that something doesn't sound like Lloyd Webber and I might
take that as a compliment. The score for *By Jeeves* certainly didn't sound
much like what one has grown to expect from Lord Andrew. Rather more
fun than usual, with a lightheartedly jazzy feel. Few of the songs fit their
slots, though; it seemed that the characters would simply start singing
whenever the fellow in the video monitor started waving a stick at them.
(That is, the conductor, who was stage right on an upper-level veranda.)
One song stood out, a boy-girl ballad with a straightforward melody called
"Half a Moment." This was quite nice; it stood out, too, as sounding different in style from the other songs.

Which were awkward. Take "By Jeeves," for example. This is the sort
of list song that Cole Porter seemed to effortlessly turn out in half an
hour. But Sir Alan isn't Cole Porter. To wit, or lack thereof: "By mar-
malade, by bowler hat / By toothpaste tube, by Burmese cat / By baby
newts, by autumn leaves / By George, by Jove, by Jeeves." And this, folks,
was the big comedy number.

The thing is, Wodehouse himself was a wonderful lyricist. With Jerome
Kern and Guy Bolton, he more or less revolutionized the American musical theatre with a series of entertainments fondly referred to as the
Princess Theatre shows (although only two were actually produced at the
Princess, on West Thirty-ninth Street). Without going into a lot of history, let us simply say that the four Kern-Bolton-Wodehouse musical
comedies written between 1916 and 1918 directly influenced a whole
generation of writers. Prominent among whom were a couple of teenaged

composers named George Gershwin and Richard Rodgers, and a couple of budding lyricists named Ira Gershwin and Lorenz Hart.

The lyrics for Wodehouse's ballads sound a bit old-fashioned to today's ears, but his comedy songs—like "Nesting Time in Flatbush," "Cleopatterer," "Sir Galahad," "Bungalow in Quogue," "Bongo on the Congo," and "Tulip Time in Sing-Sing"—still pack a punch. One wouldn't expect such craftsmanship from a nonlyricist like Ayckbourn, but it seems odd to pay homage to Wodehouse with flat-footed lyrics.

The whole thing ended with the entire company singing something called "Banjo Boy," standing around in costumes intended to represent third-rate approximations of the familiar figures from the 1939 motion picture version of *The Wizard of Oz*. (Wodehouse wrote his first "Jeeves" stories prior to World War I.) Why *The Wizard of Oz*, pray tell? All I know is that the actors looked mighty embarrassed.

One of the actors looked not only embarrassed but also very much pregnant; the love interest, no less, insofar as *By Jeeves* had a love interest. Emily Loesser, who was playing Stiffy Byng and who sang the best song in the show, had been waiting around for *Jeeves* to reach Broadway since 1996. Her condition was not overwhelmingly noticeable, as Loesser is normally a wisp of a thing; to those who know her, though, she appeared to be very pregnant. Which I suppose made her the first ingenue in Broadway history to give birth within a month of opening night. (Loesser's husband, Don Stephenson, was also in the cast, although not as her onstage lover.) While we don't necessarily cite such events in *Broadway Yearbook*, the grandchild of the great Frank Loesser and his wife, Jo Sullivan, rates a mention. Ah, what Frank might have done with the lyrics for *Jeeves*.

> **Wodehouse himself was a wonderful lyricist. It seemed odd to pay homage to him with flat-footed lyrics.**

Standing on the sidewalk in front of the exit doors on Forty-forth Street before the performance were two out-of-work actors wearing *By Jeeves* baseball caps, offering patrons and passersby a cuppa tea and biscuits. Better they should have passed out something considerably stronger, at least to theatre critics.

Noises Off

A n avalanche of hilarity erupted during the second act of the 2001 revival of Michael Frayn's *Noises Off*. (The first scene of the second act, as on this occasion they combined the second and third into one.)

The first act takes place during the final tech rehearsal of a provincial tour of a sex farce called *Nothing On*. The action is continually interrupted by missed lines; missed cues; missed props; inoperable doors; lost contact lenses; and the long-suffering director running interference.

The second act takes place one month later, backstage, before and during a Wednesday matinee performance of the first act of *Nothing On*. By this point, the star is battling with her lover, the juvenile; the lover is jealous of a middle-aged actor in the cast; the director is romancing both the ditsy ingenue and the (female) stage manager; and the over-the-hill old-timer is hot in pursuit of any bottle he can find. Playwright Frayn combines the "onstage" lines with offstage pantomime; we see the actors exiting (to make their entrances) and entering (as they exit). We know the business, from watching it in the first act, and we can see key parts of the "onstage" action through the windows and doors. (This being British farce, the set is full of slamming doors and what is supposed to be split-second timing.)

Thus, we see one actor sneaking up on another—who is about to make an entrance—and tie the laces of his shoes together. This fellow opens the door to make his entrance, takes a step, and falls headlong onto what we know is the balcony of the onstage set. Laugh. He says his next line out of sight, while we're trying to stop laughing. He then "bounces" across the balcony—we see him bobbing along, through the "window" in the set. Once he is out of sight, someone else speaks onstage; we know the line, but we're still laughing. We then hear—but do not see—him tum-

⋙N⋘ BROOKS ATKINSON THEATRE
UNDER THE DIRECTION OF THE MESSRS. NEDERLANDER

AMBASSADOR THEATRE GROUP and ACT PRODUCTIONS
WAXMAN WILLIAMS ENTERTAINMENT, D. HARRIS/M. SWINSKY,
USA OSTAR THEATRICALS and NEDERLANDER PRESENTATIONS, INC.

Present

PATTI LUPONE PETER GALLAGHER
RICHARD EASTON

In
THE ROYAL NATIONAL THEATRE PRODUCTION OF

NOISES OFF

By
MICHAEL FRAYN

With

KATIE FINNERAN	T.R. KNIGHT	THOMAS McCARTHY	ROBIN WEIGERT

Also Starring
FAITH PRINCE
and
EDWARD HIBBERT

Sets & Costumes by **ROBERT JONES**	*Lighting by* **TIM MITCHELL**	*Sound by* **FERGUS O'HARE** *for Aura*
Casting by **JIM CARNAHAN**	*Technical Supervision* **UNITECH**	*Production Stage Manager* **DAVID O'BRIEN**
Press Representative **BARLOW•HARTMAN** *public relations*	*Marketing* **TMG** **THE MARKETING GROUP**	*General Management* **101 PRODUCTIONS, LTD.**

Associate Producers
PRE-EMINENCE INCIDENTAL COLMAN TOD CURTIS/JOHNSON

Directed by
JEREMY SAMS

The producers wish to express their appreciation to the Theatre Development Fund for its support of this production.

Dotty Otley   Patti LuPone
Lloyd Dallas   Peter Gallagher
Garry Lejeune   Thomas McCarthy
Brooke Ashton   Katie Finneran
Poppy Norton-Taylor   Robin Weigert
Belinda Blair   Faith Prince
Frederick Fellowes   Edward Hibbert
Tim Allgood   T. R. Knight
Selsdon Mowbray   Richard Easton

Time and Place:
Act I   The living room of the Brent's
   country home, Wednesday afternoon
   (Grand Theatre, Weston-super-Mare,
   Monday, January 14)
Act II   The living room of the Brent's
   country home, Wednesday afternoon
   (Theatre Royal, Ashton-under-Lyne,
   Wednesday matinee, February 13)
Act III   The living room of the Brent's
   country home, Wednesday afternoon
   (Municipal Theatre, Stockton-on Tees,
   Saturday, April 6)

bling down the stairs. By orchestrating what's happening, what's supposed to be happening, and what isn't happening, Frayn designed a perfect puzzle that can't fail to produce hilarity. And this second act erupted, as mentioned above, into what were the funniest moments in the district since Bialystock and Bloom invaded Forty-fourth Street.

This was all very well and good. Very funny, too, and more than satisfying enough to make the evening a delight. But there was a slight problem. The original Broadway production—presented on the very same stage, in 1983—was this funny throughout the first act, too.

It is unfair and unwise and unnecessary to compare today's show with yesterday's show. An old play—*Noises Off, The Women, Hedda Gabler,* or even *Hamlet*—is new to someone who has never before seen it or read it. A considerable segment of the audience with which I attended this *Noises*

Off had clearly seen a prior production, and the show was clearly inferior to a considerable segment of the segment.

Still, the play was new to most of the audience. Could they tell what they were missing? The first act was received somewhat tentatively; yes, it was very funny, but something seemed not to be clicking. That's how my wife put it, during intermission. A first-timer, she "liked it a lot" and thought it was "very funny." But she felt that something wasn't "clicking"; it seemed to her like it should have been funnier than it was. When the actors started to do their second-act relay race—with one chasing another with a fire ax, a third ducking away from a fourth brandishing a brandy bottle, and a fifth discovering the bottle in midair like manna from heaven and heading for a dark corner—I turned to my wife (while gasping for breath between laughs) and said, "That's how the whole thing should play."

Observing the pandemonium, Tim Allgood (the Company Manager-within-the-play, and well played by T. R. Knight) notes, "This is getting farcical." An accurate assessment, but therein lay the problem; the ideal *Noises Off* should be wildly farcical long before 9:15.

Why the difference between 1983 and 2001? And did it matter?

Let us start with Michael Blakemore. He's the fellow who won twin directing Tonys in 1999–2000, for the musical *Kiss Me, Kate* and the play *Copenhagen*. Blakemore has directed eight plays by Frayn, including the original London and New York productions of *Noises Off*. The pair seem to complement each other, professionally. They worked wonders for each other on *Noises Off* and *Copenhagen*; that is, Blakemore brought out layers of laughter (from one) and meaning (from the other), to the extent that one couldn't tell precisely what came from the au-

An avalanche of hilarity erupted during the second act of the revival. But the original production was this funny throughout the first act, too.

thor and what from the director. And that's not so simple as it seems; look at Neil Simon's *45 Seconds from Broadway*, discussed a dozen pages from here, where directorial gags and "business" were clearly evident.

Blakemore was not on board for the new *Noises Off*, and understandably so; I suppose he directed at least a half dozen casts and replacement casts last time round, and it can be stultifying to start all over again once more. The directorial reins for this revival—which originated at the Royal National Theatre in October 2000—were handed over to Jeremy Sams; his staging, to say the least, compared unfavorably to Blakemore's.

I have never seen Sams's work as a director; the *Playbill* credits him with nine prior London productions, none of which made it to New York. What did make it to Broadway are three of his translations and/or adaptations. *Indiscretions (Les Parents Terrible)* was a succès d'estime back in 1995 under the direction of Sean Mathias. Sams's translation of Jean Anouilh's *The Rehearsal*, at the Roundabout in 1996, was dreary. Reading his bio during intermission, I felt that something was missing; I knew that I had seen something of his more recently, and I had a strong feeling that whatever it was, I didn't like it. I realized after the fact that the missing credit was *Waiting in the Wings*, Noël Coward's geriatric exercise that played the Kerr in 1999. "Revisited by Jeremy Sams," went his billing, whatever that meant. This credit was omitted from his *Noises Off* bio, and not without reason.

Here I am, apologizing for a crowd-pleasing hit. One that I, myself, enjoyed in the theatre. This seems contradictory, I admit, but that is how the production struck me. What we had was laugh after laugh after laugh; but at too many times, in the first act and parts of the third, the laughs were separated. What was wanted—and what Blakemore provided back in 1983—was laugh on top of laugh on top of laugh. Laughs overlapping, so that you couldn't keep up and were simply too busy laughing to care. And that's not what we had at the Atkinson, not this time.

> **What we had was laugh after laugh after laugh, but the laughs were separated. What was wanted was laugh on top of laugh on top of laugh, laughs overlapping.**

Prior to the performance, the *Noises Off* logo was projected onto the house curtain in a decidedly non-hi-tech manner; some of the letters were blurry. This was probably intentional, as *Nothing On*—the play-within-the-play—is meant to be a third-rate, provincial tour. But the play itself—that is, the Broadway revival of *Noises Off*—was just as hazily out of focus.

The cast, too, seemed capable and comic but at times ineffective. *Noises Off*—the play—is a well-oiled machine, construction-wise; this combination of actors didn't quite get it. The easy answer is, "Well, of course not; you can't expect American actors to be trained in English farce." But the 1983 cast was only partially British. Most important, the star—an extremely British role—was played by Broadway's own Dorothy Loudon.

Dorothy Loudon, Patti LuPone; same thing, right? That is, both are distinctive, idiosyncratic musical comedy stars with voracious talent and a penchant to grab hold of an audience and not let go. But there is a difference, as was apparent within two minutes after beginners (or places, as Americans would say).

LuPone played British TV star Dotty Otley in *Noises Off*, who played Mrs. Clackett—the resident housekeeper—in *Nothing On*. Let me quote the bio in the program for the play-within-the-play: "Dotty Otley makes a welcome return to the stage to create the role of Mrs. Clackett after playing Mrs. Hackett, Britain's most famous lollipop lady (Ooh, I can't 'ardly 'old me lolly up!) in over 320 episodes of TV's *On the Zebras.*"

In other words, Dotty is one of those overly exposed TV stars who has typecast herself out of any possible career and is reduced to shoestring tours of the provinces in third-rate farces. Financed by herself.

Now, an actress doesn't need to be an ex-TV star to play "Britain's most famous lollipop lady." (A lollipop lady is a school crossing guard, although you wouldn't know it from the proceedings.) Nor does she have to be British. What she must be, though, is a clown. She must be able to get a laugh by merely standing up. Or merely sitting down. Or merely doing nothing. Or glaring at an actor, or a sardine, or at a telephone that is ringing. (Or a telephone that is *not* ringing.)

Dorothy Loudon had a history of doing just that; a talent developed from years of appearing in poorly written musicals where it was survival of the fittest, and she was it. (Among her catastrophes was a 1971 musicalization of *Lolita*, in which she played the nymphet's mother. Charlotte necessarily dies at the end of the first act; otherwise Humbert can't run off with Lolita, can he? The moment Loudon's character was offstage for good, *Lolita, My Love*—as it was called—died too.)

Transplanted Briton Carole Shelley had the comic sensibility as well; she replaced Loudon when the original cast headed west for the Los Angeles engagement. Carol Burnett might seem ideal casting for the role; she starred in Peter Bogdanovich's odd 1992 film version, which was Americanized to ill effect. Watching Burnett in the 1995 Broadway farce *Moon over Buffalo*—one of those baldly unfunny farces that quickly sink into desperation—I couldn't help but think, if only they were doing *Noises Off* instead. (For what it's worth: Lynn Redgrave—who replaced Burnett in *Buffalo*—was heading the West End revival of *Noises Off* when the Patti LuPone production opened in New York.)

Which brings us to Ms. LuPone. She is a highly distinctive singer with a flair for comedy; she has the ability to grab her audience, with song, and hold them. What she is not prepared to do, however, is stand onstage milking laughter in droopy drawers. (Padded flesh-colored tights, actually. While LuPone has passed the fifty-year mark in calendar years, she very much looked like a glamorous "young" person in a fat suit with a frumpy wig.) LuPone is far better in musical comedy—and musical drama—than Lucille Ball, say; but *Noises Off* cries out for a clown who can milk laughter in droopy drawers. Although as I've noted in past editions of *Broadway Yearbook*: don't blame the actor for accepting the role offered to her. And this is not to say that LuPone was unsatisfactory in the part. Yes, she was funny, as was the entire enterprise. She—and it—just wasn't rip-roaring.

While the 1983 cast wasn't all British, it did contain performances from two Broadway regulars from across the sea. Brian Murray, who has been at home on our shores since playing Rosencrantz in *Rosencrantz and Guildenstern Are Dead* in 1967, was director Lloyd Dallas; Paxton Whitehead, who replaced Jonathan Miller in 1963 in the American production of *Beyond the Fringe*, played middle-aged Frederick Fellowes. Both of these gentlemen are accomplished and well-rounded actors who have proven themselves time and again in various enterprises of differing nationalities and accents.

But *Noises Off* is British sex farce, the kind of dry, slow-burning comedy that comes naturally to British hams. The roles in the Broadway revival fell to two perfectly respectable American actors, Peter Gallagher (who was starred) and Edward Hibbert. (The latter is Anglo-American, having been born in New York while his British father was appearing in the original Broadway production of *The Boy Friend*.) Gallagher and Hibbert both did everything well, but neither had the added sensibility provided by Murray and Whitehead. Richard Easton did somewhat better as the hard-of-hearing old soak Selsdon Mowbray, creating an eccentric-but-lovable (and kindly drawn) coot. Easton spent thirty years toiling in regional theatre anonymity before calmly walking into the Broadway spotlight with his performance in Tom Stoppard's *The Invention of Love*, winning the 2001 Tony Award for Best Actor. Said award apparently resulted in his receiving star billing, despite his appearing in the smallest role.

Noises Off **is still the best farce I've ever seen. But I can't imagine I would say that based on this revival.**

What this *Noises Off* did have, and how, was a knockout performance by Katie Finneran in the role of the sex-crazed, lingerie-clad, contact-lensed Brooke Ashton. Finneran didn't act, so much; she reacted. She re-

Noises Off
Opened: November 1, 2001
Closed: September 1, 2002
348 performances (and 20 previews)
Profit/Loss: Profit
Noises Off ($75 top) was scaled to a potential gross of
$522,566 at the 1,051-seat Brooks Atkinson Theatre.
Weekly grosses averaged about $319,000, going above
$400,000 early in the run (including capacity business in
the Thanksgiving and New Year's weeks) but sliding down
into the $200,000s when the spring competition arrived.
Total gross for the forty-six-week run was $14,678,125.
Attendance was about 77 percent, with the box office
grossing about 61 percent of dollar-capacity.

TONY AWARD NOMINATIONS
Best Revival of a Play
Best Performance by a Featured Actress: Katie Finneran
(WINNER)

DRAMA DESK AWARD
Outstanding Featured Actress: Katie Finneran (WINNER)

Critical Scorecard

Rave 5
Favorable 3
Mixed 0
Unfavorable 1
Pan 1

acted in a grand sweep, with her head swinging from shoulder to shoulder
like a rag doll with a spring in its neck. And she reacted on cue. That is,
her character reacted on a delayed cue. Ask Vicki (her character in *Nothing On*) a question, and you got a blank response; it seemed to take a moment for Brooke (her character in *Noises Off*) to remember what role she
was playing. She would compensate by answering with her whole being.
Vicki's body language was extreme, seductively shifting her torso or drap-
ing herself along the balcony railing like a *Playboy* bunny when the photographer shouts "hold it!" at a photo shoot. At one point, when Vicki
was supposed to be startled by a mysteriously disappearing tote bag, Finneran did what I can only describe as a sextuple-take (which is to say,
three double-takes in one). This was the funniest moment of the evening,
and one which Finneran obligingly reprised in the final act. Ms. Finneran
was memorably funny as someone-or-other's girlfriend in the 1997 Neil
Simon play, *Proposals*. More recently, she played Mrs. Elvsted in the tryout of Kate Burton's *Hedda Gabler* and Molly in the tryout of *Smell of the
Kill*. Finneran seems to have opted out of *Hedda* and *Smell* to take *Noises
Off*, which turned out to be a brilliant career move.

Finneran's excellence served as a constant reminder of the heights of
hilarity otherwise missing. One of the not-very-many present-day American actors who might have given Dotty Otley the missing zest was, oddly
enough, up there onstage wrestling with LuPone. Faith Prince undertook

the supporting role of Belinda Blair; I suppose she simply felt the need to keep working after the disappointingly short run of the 2001 revival of *Bells Are Ringing*. Prince, like LuPone, is a musical comedy girl; but she is also a natural comedienne, as we learned when she chewed up the scenery as Adelaide in the 1992 revival of *Guys and Dolls*. Prince had relatively little to do in *Noises Off*, but as she tiptoed around the backstage set in the second act, one could sense a manic intensity lacking in the other performances (excepting Finneran).

In *Broadway Yearbook 1999–2000*, while discussing Frayn's *Copenhagen*, I said: "I won't say that *Noises Off* is the best farce of the last sixty years, as I have not seen every farce of the last sixty years. It is the best new farce I've ever seen, though."

I am still glad to pronounce *Noises Off* the best farce I've ever seen. But I can't imagine I would say that based on this revival.

The Women

C lare Boothe Luce was, by all accounts, one of the more re-markable personages of the mid–twentieth century. She was born, illegitimate, in 1903; her father was a manufacturer-turned-violinist, her mother what might be euphemistically termed a chorus girl. Her father walked out when she was nine, leaving her mother to support herself on her charms, as it were. Luce began her career in a paper factory, earning $18 a week. She became involved in the women's suffrage move-ment, coming under the wing of society multimillionairess Alva Vander-bilt Belmont, founder of the National Woman's Party. This led Boothe to an abusive alcoholic millionaire playboy named George Brokaw; they married in 1923—the wedding was the top society event of the year—and divorced in 1929, leaving Boothe with a stunning alimony settle-ment in the amount of $425,000.

Boothe nevertheless chose to work, taking a job writing captions at *Vogue*. She moved on to *Vanity Fair*, bewitching editor Frank Crownin-shield and replacing him as man-aging editor when he died (a jeal-ous suicide?) in 1933. In 1935 she married Henry Luce, founder of the *Time* magazine empire. That same year she turned playwright, with four Broadway plays in five

In 1936, the critics blushed, uncom-fortable at being let in on the secret manifestations of the opposite sex. Women, on the other hand, relished the merciless exposure of their kind.

years. She became a war correspondent for Luce's *Life* and *Time* in 1940; a two-term Republican congresswoman from Connecticut, starting in 1942; an Oscar nominee for best original story in 1950 for *Come to the Stable*; and the American ambassador to Italy from 1953–1957. She turned ultraconservative in 1964, alienating herself from the Republican Party and being forced into retirement (although Ronald Reagan brought her

Jane Heather Matarazzo
Sylvia (Mrs. Howard Fowler) Kristen Johnston
Nancy Blake Lisa Emery
Peggy (Mrs. John Blake) Amy Ryan
Edith (Mrs. Phelps Potter) Jennifer Coolidge
Mary (Mrs. Stephen Haines) Cynthia Nixon
Mrs. Wagstaff Barbara Marineau
Olga Jennifer Butt
First Hairdresser Gayton Scott
Second Hairdresser Roxanna Hope
Pedicurist Cheryl Stern
Mud Mask Julie Halston
Euphie Adina Porter
Miss Fordyce Jane Cronin
Little Mary Hallie Kate Eisenberg
Mrs. Morehead Mary Louise Wilson

First Salesgirl Ann Talman
Second Salesgirl Barbara Marineau
Miss Shapiro Cheryl Stern
First Saleswoman Julie Halston
Second Saleswoman Susan Bruce
Miss Myrtle (a model) Adina Porter
Crystal Allen Jennifer Tilly
First Model (negligee) Jen Davis
Second Model (corset) Kelly Mares
A Fitter Jennifer Butt
Princess Tamara Roxanna Hope
Exercise Instructress Gayton Scott
Maggie Mary Bond Davis
Miss Watts Susan Bruce
Miss Trimmerback Ann Talman
A Nurse Adina Porter
Lucy Julie Halston
Countess de Lage Rue McClanahan
Miriam Aarons Lynn Collins
Helene Roxanna Hope
First Girl Jennifer Butt
Second Girl Gayton Scott
First Woman Julie Halston
Second Woman Susan Bruce
Sadie Cheryl Stern
Cigarette Girl Adina Porter
Dowager Barbara Marineau
Debutante Roxanna Hope
Girl in distress Ann Talman

ACT 1
Scene 1 Mary Haines's living room
Scene 2 Hairdressing booth at Michael's a few days later
Scene 3 Mary's boudoir an hour later
Scene 4 A dressmaker's shop two months later
Scene 5 Exercise room at Elizabeth Arden's two weeks later
Scene 6 Mary's pantry a few days later
Scene 7 Mary's living room a month later

ACT 2
Scene 1 A hospital room a month later
Scene 2 Mary's living room in a Reno hotel weeks later
Scene 3 Crystal's bathroom one evening two years later
Scene 4 Mary's bedroom, 11:00 the same night
Scene 5 Powder room at the Casino Roof later that night

ROUNDABOUTTHEATRECOMPANY

TODD HAIMES, Artistic Director
ELLEN RICHARD, Managing Director
JULIA C. LEVY, Executive Director, External Affairs

Presents

Kristen Johnston Rue McClanahan Cynthia Nixon Jennifer Tilly Mary Louise Wilson
Lynn Collins Jennifer Coolidge Hallie Kate Eisenberg Lisa Emery Amy Ryan

THE WOMEN

by
Clare Boothe Luce

Susan Bruce Jennifer Butt Jane Cronin Jen Davis Mary Bond Davis
Julie Halston Roxanna Hope Kelly Mares Barbara Marineau Heather Matarazzo
Adina Porter Gayton Scott Cheryl Stern Ann Talman

Set Designer	*Costume Designer*	*Lighting Designer*	*Musical Arrangements and Sound Designer*
Derek McLane	Isaac Mizrahi	Brian MacDevitt	Douglas J. Cuomo

Dialect Coach	*Production Stage Manager*	*Technical Supervisor*	*Casting by*
Stephen Gabis	Peter Hanson	Steve Beers	Jim Carnahan, C.S.A.

General Manager	*Founding Director*	*Associate Artistic Director*
Sydney Davolos	Gene Feist	Scott Ellis

Press Representative	*Director of Marketing*
Boneau/Bryan-Brown	David B. Steffen

Directed by
Scott Elliott

Support for this production generously provided by **W·e**

Roundabout Theatre Company is a member of the League of Resident Theatres.
www.roundabouttheatre.org

21

back to Washington in 1981 to serve on the President's Foreign Intelligence Advisory Board). She died there, in 1987.

With such a personal history, it was perhaps understandable that she established her own facts; Boothe self-invented herself, over and over again, during her many careers. This is a woman who credited herself with inventing the term "New Deal"—a claim that might not have been all that far-fetched. Prior to setting her sights on Luce, she was mistress to the presidential adviser and all-influential power broker Bernard Baruch. (When Boothe wrote *The Women*, she didn't go pounding doors to find an agent; she simply had Baruch call up Max Gordon, a top Broadway producer of the day, and say he was sending the script over.)

The Women, Boothe's second play, opened at the Ethel Barrymore Theatre in 1936 on the day after Christmas. (Although she was already famously known as Clare Boothe Luce, the play was originally produced under the name Clare Boothe—presumably to avoid confusion with actress Claire Luce, who starred opposite Fred Astaire in the stage version of Cole Porter's *Gay Divorce*.) The show received mixed reviews and little enthusiasm. A contemporary view, from producer Gordon himself: "Some said the critics blushed, that men in general were uncomfortable at being let in on some of the more secret manifestations of the opposite sex. Indeed, Mrs. Luce pulled few punches as she removed not only the stage's so-called fourth wall but also the partitions that hide bathrooms, powder rooms and maternity wards. Women, on the other hand, relished the merciless exposure of their kind." Business started out weak, but within a month the matinees were packed with—well, with women. "Soon the evening performances were doing as well—gentlemen friends, sweethearts and husbands having been persuaded to submerge their inhibitions." The highly favorable word of mouth allowed the show to build into a long-running hit with 657 performances. This, in the depths of the Great Depression.

> The Park Avenue wives of *The Women* are all of a piece, products of their time and their class. It is this class that was missing from the revival.

As with many hit comedies of the time, the script received some doctoring—in this case, from George S. Kaufman (who was one of Gordon's silent partners). GSK provided jokes throughout and wrote most of the pantry scene between the cook and the maid—which included one of the show's biggest laughs, about "that prize in Sweden." *The Women* is full of highly effective jokes, which is not the case with Boothe's other plays. Her first, *Abide with Me*—about an abusive alcoholic husband—lasted a month, in 1935. (Boothe married Luce two days after it opened.) Her third and fourth plays, the comedy *Kiss the Boys Good-Bye* (in 1938) and the satirical Nazi melodrama *Margin for Error* (in 1939), were moderately successful, with six-month runs. Her final play, the religious drama *Child of the Morning*—in which child star Margaret O'Brien made her stage debut, as an angelic girl who is brutally raped and murdered—closed during its Boston tryout in 1951.

The original production of *The Women* featured some thirty-three of them; while some of the players were well known at the time, most are forgotten. Atop the cast were Margalo Gillmore—Mrs. Darling, to those who saw Mary Martin's *Peter Pan*—as the heroine Mary and Ilka Chase as the tart-tongued Sylvia; making her Broadway debut, as the model called Princess Tamara, was Arlene Francis. With its large cast, endless costumes, and eleven sets, the show was apparently quite something to see. And funny! The play moved to near-legendary status when it was turned into a film in 1939. This was from M-G-M, home of "all the stars that are in heaven," and they certainly applied a liberal sprinkling. George Cukor directed a cast that included Norma Shearer (as Mary), Joan Crawford (as home-wrecker Crystal), Rosalind Russell (as Sylvia), Mary Boland (as the much-married Countess), Paulette Goddard (as the musical comedy star Miriam Aarons), and Joan Fontaine (as the mousy Peggy). Phyllis Povah and Marjorie Main re-created their stage roles, as the much-married Edith and the outspoken Nevada hostess Lucy.

The large scale of *The Women* has limited its stage life. There was one Broadway revival, which opened April 25, 1973, at the 46th Street Theatre (now the Richard Rodgers). This was intended to be the last word in style; Morton Da Costa, who had directed the glamorous *Auntie Mame* on stage and screen, was at the helm. (That was part of the problem. *Auntie Mame* was in 1956, Da Costa peaked the following year with *The Music Man*, and he was long washed up when *The Women* came knocking at his door.) The cast was deep in ex–movie stars, led by Myrna Loy (as Mary's mother, Mrs. Morehead), Alexis Smith (as Sylvia), and Rhonda Fleming (as Miriam). Also prominent were Kim Hunter (as Mary), Dorothy Loudon (as Edith), and Jan Miner (as the Countess). The revival came at the height of Broadway's nostalgia craze; in fact, it helped kill off Broadway's nostalgia craze, expiring unmourned within two months.

> Imagine yourself a respected professional who has spent twenty-five or thirty years working at your craft. And they force you to parade in front of the audience in a bra?

The Women is a high-class soap opera, really. The leading character is somewhat too bland to hold our interest, and the plot goes through too many characters and short scenes for comfort. Still, it is more than entertaining enough to get by. This was, apparently, the reaction in 1936;

and it was the case in 2001. The production had its weaknesses, but it made for an entertaining and amusing evening in the theatre. The Roundabout went out on a financial limb to produce it, what with the large physical production and cast (which—with extensive doubling—was cut from thirty-three to twenty-four). Thanks to generally favorable reviews and good word of mouth, *The Women* did extremely well by nonprofit standards. That is, it sold most of its nonsubscriber tickets; and it was able to extend its eleven-week engagement to fourteen, which was as long as the theatre was available.

The Roundabout was unable to come up with the star power of the 1973 production; but said star power didn't count for much in 1973, did it? Cynthia Nixon played the central character, Mary; Jennifer Tilly played the shopgirl Crystal; Kristen Johnston played Sylvia; Rue Mc-Clanahan hammed it up as the Countess; and Mary Louise Wilson played Mrs. Morehead. (Wilson also appeared in the 1973 revival, as Nancy, the mannish writer.) Each gave an interesting performance, in her own way; but the overall tone of the performances was all over the scale.

Here is Ms. Boothe: "*The Women* is a satirical play about a numerically small group of ladies native to the Park Avenues of America," she wrote in 1936, adding that "the title, which embraces half the human species, is therefore rather too roomy." That is to say, the play is not supposed to be about all women; Ms. Boothe warned that the viewer who "claims to discover in it a portrait of *all* womankind, is obviously bound to experience the paradoxical discomfort which ensues to the wearer when the shoe unexpectedly fits."

Which is to say: *The Women* is about a certain class of women, who could be found (at the time) on Park Avenue. Boothe knew these women well; she was an outsider who stormed the citadel, "stole" husbands, and used her innate charm and keen mind to amass fame, respect, and millions of dollars. But she was still an outsider—a bastard, no less—and in some respects remained self-conscious about her upbringing and lack of education. Crystal, the shopgirl in the play who stormed the citadel and stole Mary's husband, was more Boothe's style, and probably not coinci-

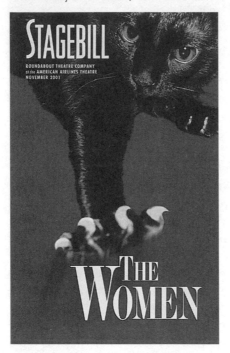

dentally; Crystal Allen translates fairly easily to Ann Clare, which was Boothe's given name. (Boothe's mother—a sometime shopgirl—was also named Ann Clare.)

The wives of *The Women* are all of a piece, products of their time, their environment, and their class. It is this class that was totally missing from the 2001 revival. At no time, in any way, did you feel that these characters—however different one might be from the other—sprang from the same society, or attended the same exclusive (and restricted) schools and dances and parties and country clubs. They seemed to come from different worlds; any sense of style or touch of class was random. (To see how this aura can be captured in the current-day world, pop Whit Stillman's 1990 film *Metropolitan* into your VCR.)

This was somewhat surprising, in that director Scott Elliott otherwise seemed to do quite well; there were very many deft directorial touches, punctuating the laughs and helping along some of the more obscure jokes. Elliott's management of the production—with all those characters and all those sets—was similarly impressive. The characterization work, alas, was weak. One glimpse at the marvelous Mary Louise Wilson was enough to show you what was otherwise missing. Ms. Wilson—typically a larger-than-life comedienne—simply exuded class. Even when she was sitting quietly, merely listening to the others, she simply controlled the stage. I couldn't take my eyes off her, and I suppose that's because almost nothing else was going on, acting-wise. Ms. Nixon did well, given the passive nature of her role; and Kristen Johnston continually picked up the pacing with her Sylvia. (Her second-act catfight with Lynn Collins was quite an event, and surely the most realistic battle seen on Broadway for a long while.) Otherwise, it was everyone for herself. Heather Matarazzo, for example, understood what she was doing. In the tiny role of Jane, Mary's maid, she had little to do but watch her betters behave. But she did so with an attitude that said more about class than anything else in the evening. When Mary noted that her young daughter "doesn't want to be a woman," Jane said, "Who does?" Matarazzo made this two-word speech one of the most telling of the evening.

And then there were the costumes. High-fashion designer Isaac Mizrahi made his Broadway debut with scads of thirties-deco costumes. Some were stylish and quite wonderful; others were singularly unattractive and unbecoming. Couture, I suppose, is in the eyes of the couturier. Director and designer combined for what I thought was an appalling choice: let's force them all to take their curtain calls in underwear. Lingerie, yes, and some of it stylish; but curtain calls are the actors' personal, out-of-character moment with the audience. Some of the cast clearly didn't mind this, and might well have actually enjoyed it; but imagine yourself a respected professional who has spent twenty-five or thirty or even forty years working at your craft. And they force you to parade in front of the audience in a bra? Perhaps I overreact, but I found this distasteful and demeaning. Imagine the reaction if they had sent out the cast of *Invention of Love* in their underpants. Why, pray tell, was it acceptable to do so with the women of *The Women*.

45 Seconds from Broadway

N eil Simon's first Broadway play opened in 1961, when he was thirty-three. *45 Seconds from Broadway* marked his thirty-second visit to Broadway in forty years, not including numerous revivals.

Simon spent his formative days as a television comedy writer and has also written some twenty screenplays; but his heart, apparently, belongs to Broadway. He transplanted himself to California years ago, and it must be a chore for him to keep coming back to attend to the numerous details of play production. (In the case of *45 Seconds to Broadway*, he was hospitalized with a herniated disc following the first few previews and shipped back to the Coast prior to the opening.) At a time when others might be concentrating on their golf scores or Rorschach-shaped watercolors or simply gone fishin', Simon keeps stepping up to the plate.

At this point in time, the man has nothing to prove; he has no superego to satisfy; and he clearly doesn't need the money. After a string of embarrassing failures in the midnineties, Simon threatened to traverse Broadway's byways no more. But writing plays for Broadway is what he does, and apparently what he must.

While his overall list of credits remains highly impressive, it is hard to exaggerate the extent of his early success. Simon hit his stride in 1963 with *Barefoot in the Park*, which was followed by *The Odd Couple*: two outright comic blockbusters, and very funny, too. He saw twelve shows produced between 1963 and 1972. *Ten* of them were hits, most with highly profitable road tours; they not only sold tickets but also were economical and relatively non-star-dependent. All but two were made into motion pictures, as well.

Mind you, nobody in the history of the world—the Broadway world, that is—ever wrote ten-hits-out-of-twelve. It's hard to think of any other

American playwright with ten Broadway hits ever, period. Philip Barry? Robert Sherwood? Lillian Hellman? Moss Hart? O'Neill? Miller? Williams? Albee? None of them. George S. Kaufman, yes. (My tenth-floor window overlooks the garden of the townhouse on East Sixty-second Street where Simon wrote his greatest hits and the garden of the townhouse on Sixty-third Street where Kaufman wrote *his* greatest hits.) George Abbott had numerous hits, as well. But the two Georges were, for most of their careers, highly-in-demand directors; as expert play doctors, they often received coauthor credit on projects they "improved" rather than originated. Simon worked alone, except on his five musicals; on these, he accepted songwriters as necessary evils.

Yes, Simon's record is unmatchable. Eighteen hits and fourteen flops, all told. His post-1972 stats are not quite so impressive, twelve failures to eight hits. But, again, how many playwrights do you know who have written eight hits—shows that paid off their investment, that is—*ever*? So there is no reason whatsoever to feel sorry for Neil Simon. But I do, I do.

The poor guy keeps earnestly typing away, and he seems such a decent fellow. His plays are still met with high expectations; after all, he *is* Neil Simon. And every one of them, nowadays, disappoints. The last decade has brought forth the muddled *Jake's Women*; the disastrous *Goodbye Girl*; the mirthless *Laughter on the 23rd Floor*; the pedestrian *London Suite*; the moody *Proposals*; and the sour *Dinner Party*.

> At last, I thought, a sure-fire, old-fashioned Neil Simon hit! Or what sounded like it must be a sure-fire Neil Simon hit.

When it was announced in the fall of 2000 that the playwright would return with a play about the goings-on at the so-called Polish Tea Room, this Simon admirer felt almost giddy. At last, a surefire, old-fashioned Neil Simon hit! Or what sounded like it must be a surefire Neil Simon hit.

Sounded like it must be, because Simon's strength is writing funny. His early plays had strong, comic starting points; the resulting hilarity was almost automatic. In 1973 he got serious, or seriocomic, anyway. (It was at this point that his first wife, Joan, died of cancer.) He started alternating between typical Neil Simon stuff and darker efforts, like adaptations of Chekhov and parables from the Book of Job. His most satisfying later work—the *Brighton Beach* trilogy and *Lost in Yonkers*—successfully combined the old and new Simon, but just about everything else has failed to amuse.

Laughter on the 23rd Floor, which opened at the Richard Rodgers in 1993, was an especially strange case. Here was a play set in the writers' room at the old Sid Caesar show, peopled with facsimiles of Simon and

RICHARD RODGERS THEATRE

UNDER THE DIRECTION OF THE MESSRS. NEDERLANDER

Emanuel Azenberg   Ira Pittelman

James Nederlander   Scott Nederlander   Kevin McCollum

present

Neil Simon's
45 Seconds From Broadway

Starring

Lewis J. Stadlen

Louis Zorich   Rebecca Schull

with

David Margulies
Lynda Gravátt

Kevin Carroll   Dennis Creaghan   Julie Lund   Bill Moor

and

Judith Blazer   Alix Korey

also starring

Marian Seldes

Scenic Design	Costume Design	Lighting Design
John Lee Beatty	William Ivey Long	Paul Gallo

Sound Design	Special Effects	Wig and Hair Design
Peter J. Fitzgerald	Gregory Meeh	Paul Huntley

Technical Supervision		Production Supervisor
Brian Lynch		Steven Beckler
Neil A. Mazzella		

Casting by	Media Advisor	Press Representative
Jay Binder, C.S.A.	Alan Bernhard	Bill Evans & Associates

Associate Producer		General Manager
Ginger Montel		Abbie M. Strassler

Directed by

Jerry Zaks

Mickey Fox   Lewis J. Stadlen
Andrew Duncan   Dennis Creaghan
Bernie   Louis Zorich
Solomon Mantutu   Kevin Carroll
Megan Woods   Julie Lund
Arleen   Alix Korey
Cindy   Judith Blazer
Rayleen   Marian Seldes
Charles W. Browning III   Bill Moor
Zelda   Rebecca Schull
Bessie James   Lynda Gravátt
Harry Fox   David Margulies

Place: A coffee shop in New York
Act 1: Summer; Fall
Act 2: Winter; Spring

Mel Brooks and Larry Gelbart and King Sid himself. With Nathan Lane as Caesar, and golden-boy director Jerry Zaks at Simon's side, how could *Laughter* help but be hysterical?

But it wasn't. It was as unfunny as could be, considering the presence of Simon and Lane and Zaks; one of the most disappointing Broadway plays of the decade. (Simon's *The Goodbye Girl*, the 1993 musicalization of his 1977 original screenplay—with a score by Marvin Hamlisch and David Zippel, and a cast headed by Bernadette Peters and Martin Short—was one of the most disappointing Broadway musicals of the decade.) *45 Seconds from Broadway*, promising that old Simon touch, was *Laughter* all over again.

In a preopening *New York Times* piece, Simon described the play's genesis. "It happened to me as my wife, Elaine, and I were walking past the

Edison Café on our way to see a new play. Suddenly, I stopped and looked in the window, staring for a few minutes. 'Who are you looking at?' Elaine asked. 'A play,' I answered. 'I see one in there.' "

(Elaine is Elaine Joyce, who played the Marilyn Monroe role in the 1972 stage musicalization of *Some Like It Hot. Sugar*, it was called; the show, which Simon doctored, wasn't too good, but Joyce was.)

Manny Azenberg, Simon's steady partner-producer since 1972, described this somewhat differently in a *Playbill* interview. Back in 1996, he was sitting with Simon at the Edison, the pair's usual lunchtime haunt when the playwright is in town. Suddenly Simon turned to his producer and said, "This is a play."

A word of explanation. The Edison, a popular Broadway tourist hotel, has been operating continuously since 1931. The Café Edison is located in the ground-floor space on the Forty-seventh Street side of the hotel. The space was at one point far grander than it is today; the delicate molding around the ceiling, despite untold layers of paint, hints at a former life as a ballroom. In the early seventies, a Polish-American couple named Harry and Frances Edelstein took over the premises and opened a typical tourist-hotel diner. Typical except for the inclusion in the menu of Polish and Jewish specialties.

In the early eighties, the Edison began to attract the Broadway in-crowd. For several reasons. First, it was right next door to the Theatre Guild building, which housed the offices of the League of New York Theatres (as the producers' and theatre owners' trade organization was then called). As a younger generation of producers became powerful, the League was transformed from a gentlemen's club to a working organization. The new generation of manager-producers would stop in at the League for business; where do you think they would go to eat, with the Gaiety no longer downstairs? The Edison next door, featuring not only sandwiches and omelets but also such ethnic delights as matzo ball soup and borscht and blintzes. It was fast and cheap, and homey, too. You could stop by at half hour and wolf down a brisket sandwich; or you could escape the office phones and sit at a booth for a couple of hours and negotiate a deal. (There were no cell phones in those days, lest you get the wrong impression.) Manny Azenberg, I'd guess, helped start the parade; but soon a core group of managers and producers was ever present.

By the late eighties, lunchtime on nonmatinee days began to resemble a meeting of the managers and press agents union. Azenberg, at the time, was a constant producing partner of the Shuberts. In 1989, Manny and the Shuberts—that is, Bernie Jacobs and Gerry Schoenfeld—produced a show called *Jerome Robbins' Broadway*. The Edison was their home away from the theatre; if I recall correctly, they even took over the premises for their opening night party. Around about then, the northwest corner of the restaurant was officially roped off for VIPs. That is, Manny (and his guests) and the Shuberts (and their guests). Oh, and Jimmy Nederlander as well; the Edelsteins couldn't afford to play favorites.

As the century turned, Bernie was gone. (Jacobs died in 1996; Simon named the Edelstein character in his play Bernie.) Manny was now wedded to the Nederlanders, having had a falling out with his former associates; but the autographed *Jerome Robbins' Broadway* window card remained in a place of honor on the wall, and the Café Edison has remained ever the same.

Oh, and one more thing. Nobody ever called it the Café Edison. It's *in* the Edison, but it has always been known along the street as the Polish Tea Room. That is, not the ritzy Russian Tea Room just to the right of Carnegie Hall; rather, the tea room of the common folk. It's said that the name was coined by legendary Broadway press agent Harvey Sabinson, who at the time ran the League, and it does sound like something Harvey would have come up with. There are times when I'd think that the Yiddish Tea Room might be more apt. But still, stop in for a bowl of matzo ball soup and a slice of streudel or rice pudding sometime, why don't you?

And since nobody asked, the title 45 *Seconds from Broadway* was borrowed from George M. Cohan's *Forty-five Minutes from Broadway*, although I wonder how many people caught the reference. This was a 1906 musical comedy; the still-familiar "Mary's a Grand Old Name" was the hit of the show. It took place in New Rochelle; in the title song, star Victor Moore complained that the locale was a hick burg despite the fact that it was only "forty-five minutes from Broadway."

But let us return to Neil Simon, ninety years later, staring in the Edison window. What did he see? Jackie Mason, that's for sure. My impressions of Jackie Mason's impressions were discussed at length in *Broadway Yearbook 1999–2000*, and there is no reason to discuss him once more simply because Neil Simon chose to borrow his persona for the central character of 45 *Seconds*. Let it be said that, yes, Jackie Mason has been known to populate the Polish Tea Room; he could be spotted there frequently, especially when he was playing *The World According to Me* at the Atkinson down the block in 1987. Mason would not sit in the VIP section, nor would he sit in the booths along the western wall where the producers and managers usually sit. Mason would be right smack-dab in the center of the tourist section, along the Forty-seventh Street windows. Whenever I saw him at the Edison, he was dining alone, swiveling his head from side to side, trying to make eye contact with anyone who might recognize him.

Simon's version of Jackie Mason was named Mickey Fox, a loud-mouthed, objectionable, overly ethnic, egocentric stand-up genius (just ask him). In other words, a mild and humane version of the real thing. Simon also saw, in the window, stand-ins for the Edelsteins. How closely he drew the couple, I can't tell you. I've been in the Edison hundreds of times and never got more than a "hello, how are you" from the proprietor; he presumably is more chummy with Manny and Neil and the Shuberts, and with reason. The character in the play is one of those slightly crusty septuagenarians revealed to have a heart of gold, the sort of character someone like Louis Zorich plays all the time. Louis Zorich played the

part. As for his wife, she had a bigger part in the play than she does at the restaurant, where she is only barely visible puttering in the background (and I imagine cracking a whip in the kitchen). Simon's version was harder-hearted than her husband, but he gave her a big "Holocaust survivor" speech.

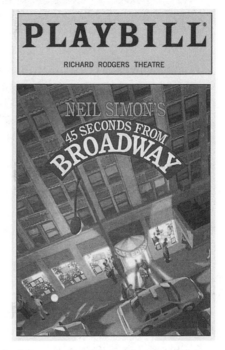

If there was some semblance to reality in these three, the rest of the characters were straight out of comedy-writer land. There is an aspiring playwright from South Africa named Soloman Mantutu. The play opens with this fellow finishing a meal he can't pay for. Bernie, needless to say, takes pity and hires him as a waiter. Mantutu goes back to South Africa during intermission and turns up at the overly contrived final curtain. There is also a young aspiring actress just off the bus from Ohio; Bernie also puts her to work.

(I've been dining at the Edison for more than fifteen years, and I've never seen a waiter or waitress under forty. Further, I have never seen an African-American employee in the place; Hispanic busboys, yes, but that's it. Neither have I seen many non-Caucasian patrons, other than August Wilson, who sometimes sits by the window in writerly reverie.)

There is additionally an African-American singer type who seems patterned on Carol Woods, who did a protean job as a singing landlady breathing life into Simon's *The Goodbye Girl*. Cast in the role was Carol Woods—until the final week of rehearsals, when she departed for reasons unknown. (Veteran actress Joan Copeland, who was playing the propri-

45 Seconds from Broadway
Opened: November 11, 2001
Closed: January 13, 2002
73 performances (and 31 previews)
Profit/Loss: Loss
45 Seconds from Broadway ($70 top) was scaled to a
    potential gross of $628,953 at the 1,380-seat Richard
    Rodgers Theatre. Weekly grosses averaged about
    $295,000, with business remaining steadily over
    $300,000 until the discounted advance sale ran out in
    mid-December. Total gross for the thirteen-week run was
    $3,839,871. Attendance was about 67 percent, with the
    box office grossing about 47 percent of dollar-capacity.

Critical
Scorecard

Rave   0
Favorable   3
Mixed   1
Unfavorable 2
Pan   4

etress and happens to be Arthur Miller's sister, simultaneously quit or was fired. Woods and Copeland were replaced by their understudies, who were merely functional.) The Woods character is called Bessie James, the name intended to provide two jokes. The first was a play on Jesse James; the second had Mickey entering and saying, "Hello, Bessie. I just saw Porgy. He's looking everywhere for you."

Andrew Duncan is an elderly British producer type who wants to present Fox in a West End revival of *Fiddler on the Roof*. ("If I did Tevye," Fox demurs, "they'd think I was pushing the Jewish thing too much.") There is a stationer from Philadelphia who happens to be the estranged brother of Mickey Fox, and who has the only dramatic scene in the play. (This might be a reflection of Simon and his brother Danny. Imagine the life of a comedy writer who taught his kid brother everything he knows, and the kid brother turns out to be Neil Simon.) There is a pair of know-it-all know-nothings from New Jersey, what we in the trade call "matinee ladies," who provide a running commentary on Broadway. ("I didn't say it wasn't funny," one explains to the other. "It was extremely funny. But it was stupid. I enjoyed it, but I didn't like it.")

Finally, there is a pair of eccentrics or perhaps lunatics, take your pick. The lady, with the unlikely name Rayleen, is like nobody you've ever seen unless you've ever seen Marian Seldes sweeping along the street minding her own business. Marian Seldes played the part. Her husband is the silent type, henpecked into what appears to be senility; he doesn't say a word until late in the evening, when he does what they call "a reversal" in Introduction to Playwriting. Simon desperately needed to start tying up loose ends at this point, and characterization went out the window.

Bernie has sold the restaurant to a mysterious buyer, without telling his wife. Why? To provide a semblance of a plot. The British producer returns

to hire Fox not for a big-money gig but for a small role in a fringe production in a ninety-seat theatre outside London that pays nothing. Fox,
needless to say, accepts. The author of the play, it turns out, is Solomon
Mantutu. And to make everybody happy, the purchaser of the restaurant
cancels the deal because "I don't think anyone can run it as well as you."
And get this kicker-of-a-curtain-line: the purchaser, it turns out, was
Marian Seldes's comatose husband.

Lewis J. Stadlen did quite a job as Jackie Mason, managing to be every
bit as abrasive as the real thing but somehow sympathetic. Stadlen started
out on Broadway with a splash, as the young Groucho Marx in *Minnie's
Boys*. He followed this with fine performances in Simon's *The Sunshine
Boys* and Hal Prince's version of *Candide*. His performances began to grow
repetitive over the years, but his recent work has been highly impressive,
in the Manhattan Theatre Club's *Mizlansky/Zilinsky* and the Roundabout's *The Man Who Came to Dinner* (in which he played a mixture of
Harpo Marx and Jimmy Durante). Stadlen comes naturally by his mim-
ickry; his father, Allen Swift, was Popeye. (That is, he was "the man of a
thousand voices," king of the cartoons.) A four-time second banana to
Nathan Lane, Stadlen finally received star billing on Broadway in *45 Seconds*, single-handedly keeping the flimsy enterprise afloat. Stadlen was
overlooked come Tony time, but his performance nabbed him Lane's role
in the first touring company of *The Producers*.

Marian Seldes was suitably outlandish in an outlandish part, sort of a
Times Square Norma Desmond. Simon appears to have written the role
to order, giving Seldes ample opportunity to pose and gesture. He also gave
her one hell of a coat, which got
the most laughs of the evening.
The playwright described it in his
stage direction as seeming to be
"made of pieces of fur from every
animal ever found. Strips of mink,
squirrel, white cat, gray dog and

**Simon's version of Jackie Mason was a
loud-mouthed, objectionable, overly
ethnic, egocentric stand-up genius (just
ask him). In other words, a mild and
humane version of the real thing.**

maybe a pinto horse." William Ivey Long, Broadway's wildest costume designer since Raoul Pene duBois traded in his scissors, came up with just
the thing; Mickey Fox posited that "maybe it's not fur. It could be the
toupees of all her former lovers." Whatever it was, Seldes wore the coat
with flair, and it had more life than most of the evening.

Bill Moor had a certain dignity as Seldes's silent husband. (One of the
scenes takes place during a snowstorm, at which point Moor entered un-
kempt, uncombed, wearing one of those warm-up jackets you see around
town and looking exactly like Manny Azenberg. Azenberg's photo was
prominently placed on the wall of the set, too. Inside jokes, I guess.) Oth-

erwise, nobody had much to do. Special mention should be made of Judith Blazer and Alix Korey, two highly talented but underutilized singing comediennes. As the matinee ladies, they simply sat around expertly delivering Neil Simon one-liners; but, hey, it's a living.

And what was Jerry Zaks doing through all this? The aforementioned two Georges—Kaufman and Abbott—under such circumstances would have been doctoring and fixing and rewriting and doing anything for a joke. So, presumably, would Mike Nichols (who directed Simon's earliest superhits). Zaks seemed to be directing the traffic —that is, the separate pairs of actors having conversations—and doing a professional job of it. But what do you do when your play is little more than a string of jokes that aren't working, and your playwright is flat on his back a coast away with sciatica? Which takes us back to poor Neil Simon.

What do you do when your play is little more than a string of jokes that aren't working, and your playwright is flat on his back a coast away?

45 Seconds from Broadway opened November 11 to the same sort of dismal reception as *The Dinner Party* had a year earlier. Well, a slightly better reception than *The Dinner Party*. *The Dinner Party*, though, had two TV star-celebrities, a passel of out-of-town raves, and a resultantly large advance sale. *45 Seconds* had none of the above, and it was gone in two months.

On Thanksgiving Day 2002, the Polish Tea Room was open between shows for holiday dinner. Soup of your choice, salad, roast turkey with all the trimmings, dessert, and beverage; all for $16.95, plus tax and tip (but no restoration charge). The Richard Rodgers was serving turkey for Thanksgiving, too: $70 a head—without strudel—and not a quarter as tasty as what you could get at the Edison.

QED

A lan Alda and *QED*—a biographical play about a quantum physicist—faced a stern task. It was preceded on Broadway with three, count 'em, better plays of high intellect. At the same time, *QED* fared well, audience-wise; Alda's presence allowed Lincoln Center Theater to virtually presell their entire run prior to facing said reviewers.

Yes, I can understand reasons for critical carping. *QED* was slight, contrived, and quirky. True. But *QED*—and most especially Mr. Alda—was highly entertaining, if only moderately enlightening. Coming on the heels of such mirthless attractions as *A Thousand Clowns*, *If You Ever Leave Me*, *Dance of Death*, *Thou Shalt Not*, *By Jeeves*, and *45 Seconds from Broadway*, *QED* was OK by me.

Michael Frayn's *Copenhagen* was imported from London to Broadway in April 2000. It addressed fission and fusion and the quantum theory, centering on a historical but much disputed 1941 meeting between physicists Niels Bohr and Werner Heisenberg. David Auburn's *Proof* transferred to Broadway from the Manhattan Theatre Club in October 2000. It was an insightful psychological drama, built on mathematical proofs and madness. Tom Stoppard's *Invention of Love* was mounted on Broadway by Lincoln Center Theater in March 2001 (although it premiered in London in 1997). It dealt with matters literary rather than scientific, but it—too—probed the unfathomable cobwebs of the mind of an intellectual, the poet and classicist A. E. Housman.

Yes, the play was slight and contrived. But *QED*—and most especially Mr. Alda—was highly entertaining, if only moderately enlightening.

Like *Copenhagen* and *Invention of Love*, *QED* was biographical in nature. Richard Feynman was a bongo-playing, safe-cracking, liquor-

**LINCOLN CENTER THEATER
AT THE VIVIAN BEAUMONT**

under the direction of
André Bishop and Bernard Gersten
presents
the Mark Taper Forum production of

"QED"

a new play by
Peter Parnell

inspired by the writings of Richard Feynman
and Ralph Leighton's *Tuva or Bust!*

with
Alan Alda
and
Kellie Overbey

creative consultant Ralph Leighton

sets Ralph Funicello   costumes Marianna Elliott   lighting D Martyn Bookwalter

sound Jon Gottlieb   stage manager Robin Veith   casting Daniel Swee

director of development Hattie K. Jutagir   director of marketing/special projects Thomas Cott

general manager Steven C. Callahan   production manager Jeff Hamlin

directed by
Gordon Davidson

Special thanks to The Harold and Mimi Steinberg Charitable Trust
for supporting new American plays at Lincoln Center Theater.

"QED" is supported by a generous grant from the Henry Nias Foundation.

Lincoln Center Theater's New Works Fund is sponsored by Philip Morris Companies Inc.

American Airlines is the official airline of Lincoln Center Theater.

"QED" was commissioned by and had its world premiere at the Mark Taper Forum.

swilling nutty professor who taught at Caltech. Feynman crossed paths with Bohr, actually, when they both worked on the creation of the atomic bomb; Feynman, the character, relates his firsthand experience at Los Alamos. (Bohr, Heisenberg, and Feynman each won the Nobel Prize for Physics, in 1922, 1932, and 1965, respectively.)

QED was far more biographically reliable than *Copenhagen* and *Invention of Love*. Frayn and Stoppard, renowned workers of intricate literary traps, provided their own interpretations of their real-life character's meanings and motivations. QED was drawn from three principal sources: Feynman's books *Surely You're Joking, Mr. Feynman! (Adventures of a Curious Character)* and *What Do You Care What Other People Think? (Further Adventures of a Curious Character)*; and *Tuva or Bust! Richard Feynman's Last Journey* by Ralph Leighton, published in 1991 (after Feynman's death in 1988). Leighton, Feynman's friend and colleague, was the "as told to" author of *What Do You Care What Other People Think?* Thus, much of *QED* (which was written in the form of a lecture) was composed of Feynman's own words.

QED was world's apart—dramatically speaking—from the other plays, and that was fitting. The others were playwright-driven; that is to say, the authors used the characters and situations as a vehicle to express ideas deep from within. *QED* was Alda's baby, a self-designed actor's vehicle. Alda—who by this point in his career could afford to do anything he wished—has a deep-seated fascination in science. Since 1994 he has hosted the PBS series *Scientific American Frontiers.* From PBS publicity material: "Whenever I think of how much pleasure I have interviewing scientists, I remember that they're having the real fun in actually being able to *do* the science."

Feynman—a brilliant scientist with showbiz flair, or what you might call a quirky man with a quark—intrigued Alda. (QED, for those of you who simply need to know these things, is quantum electrodynamics. Feynman, apparently, disproved part of the then-existing theory and re-jiggered the field.) In 1998, Alda brought the idea to Gordon Davidson, artistic director and producer of the Mark Taper Forum and the Ahmanson Theatre in Los Angeles. Davidson enlisted Peter Parnell, author of *The Cider House Rules* (which was just then playing at the Taper). Alda, Parnell, and Davidson combined to create *QED*, which opened a sold-out six-week engagement at the Taper on March 25, 2002.

Lincoln Center Theater booked the play into the Vivian Beaumont for eighteen performances over nine weeks, on *Contact's* dark nights. The engagement quickly sold out prior to the opening. (Alda did not sell especially well when he first returned to Broadway after achieving TV fame, in 1992 with Neil Simon's *Jake's Women.*) With no tickets available, the reviews for *QED*—favorable for Alda but in most cases lukewarm for the play—were be-

Feynman was a brilliant scientist with showbiz flair, or what you might call a quirky man with a quark.

side the point. Ticket demand was such that Alda and *QED* were invited to return to the Beaumont in February for another thirteen two-performance weeks.

Alda had a typical (?) American upbringing. Alphonso D'Abruzzo was born in New York in the heart of the Depression, on January 28, 1936. His father, Alphonso Giuseppe Giovanni Roberto D'Abruzzo, was a radio singer. When young Alphonso was nine, his father suddenly became a movie star; under the name Robert Alda, he played George Gershwin in the pseudo-biographical *Rhapsody in Blue.* When Alan was fourteen, his dad came to Broadway in the landmark musical *Guys and Dolls*; he won the Best Actor Tony Award for his Sky Masterson, beating out Sam Levene's Nathan Detroit.

Robert Alda had darkly handsome good looks and a strong singing voice. (He introduced the classic "Luck Be a Lady.") Alan Alda had neither; but he had a keen comic sense and a sensitive manner, which was to make him a perfect symbol of the socially and politically liberal male, circa 1970.

He began his stage career playing Abbott and Costello sketches opposite his father at the Hollywood Canteen. Robert, a onetime straight man in burlesque, played Abbott; the teenaged Alan played Costello, the funny one. While attending Fordham University, Alan made his theatre

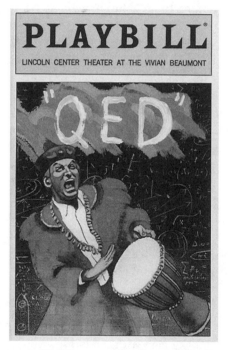

debut in 1953 as Jack Chesney in a summer stock production of *Charley's Aunt*. He also played Leo Davis—the young playwright from the sticks—in the farce *Room Service*. (This at the Teatro del 'Eliseo in Rome, in 1955, while Alda was spending his junior year abroad. Robert Alda was starring at the del 'Eliseo that season, in an Italian musical.)

Alan came to Broadway in 1956 as Don Murray's understudy in the baseball comedy *The Hot Corner*. How Alda got the job I don't know, but the play was coauthored by John Boretz (of *Room Service*) and directed by Sam Levene (who also starred). The comedy closed after three days, on Alda's twentieth birthday. What did you do on your twentieth birthday?

He then spent a few seasons in stock, including his first musical role as a twenty-three-year-old Sky Masterson. Alda finally appeared on Broadway in November 1959, playing a telephone installer in Jerome Lawrence and Robert E. Lee's comedy *Only in America*. This lasted only a month, but Alda was on a fast track to stardom. Next came more forays in stock, including a stint as the title character in *Li'l Abner* (which sounds like wonderfully offbeat casting). Off-Broadway, he wrote and appeared in the

QED

Opened: November 18, 2001
Closed: June 16, 2002
40 performances (and 7 previews)
Profit/Loss: Nonprofit [profit]
QED ($55 top) was scaled to a potential gross of $112,010
(for a two-performance week) at the 1,067-seat Vivian
Beaumont Theater. The show went on hiatus December 17,
reopening February 17, 2002 (at a $60 top). Weekly
grosses averaged about $91,000, with virtual sellout
business. Total gross for the run was $2,128,818.
Attendance was about 93 percent, with the box office
grossing about 81 percent of dollar-capacity. (These
figures are not indicative, as the potential was calculated
at the top ticket price, but subscribers paid less.)

Critical Scorecard

Rave 2
Favorable 3
Mixed 1
Unfavorable 3
Pan 0

1960 revue *Darwin's Theories*, which lasted two performances at the Madison Avenue Playhouse.

Alda had his first important role in Ossie Davis's 1961 comedy, *Purlie Victorious*. This was a sharply satirical jab at race relations, about a "newfangled preacher man" tussling with the bigoted "Ol' Cap'n." Alda played Charlie Cotchipee, the decidedly liberal son of the villain; he made his film debut in 1963, when the play was filmed under the title *Gone Are the Days*.

There were a couple more bumps in Alda's early career. A dismal off-Broadway comedy called *A Whisper in God's Ear*, which lasted three weeks in 1962. The 1963 pre-Broadway tryout of *Memo*, starring Macdonald Carey. Alda returned to the main stem in February 1964 in the comedy *Fair Game for Lovers*. This was one of those horrid comedies, which Howard Taubman of the *Times* called "a naughty play without a trace of wit or humor." But Alda made quite an impression, and not only because he set his bathrobe on fire during his second scene on opening night. Norman Nadel of the *World-Telegram & Sun*: "It occurred to me that there are easier ways to get out of a bad play. . . . Alda is quite an actor, who appeared to be carrying the play almost single-handedly." This brief engagement won Alda a Theatre World Award for Promising Personalities.

He quickly rebounded two months later, in the musical *Cafe Crown* (starring—yet again—Sam Levene). This lasted two days, giving Alda ten performances in two different Broadway shows in two months. Here's Walter Kerr, in the *Herald Tribune*: "For the second time this season, and for the second time in a disaster, special mention must be made of Alan Alda. Mr. Alda plays a dentist from Buffalo who is gradually learning that there is no difference between chopped liver and chopped herring if you chop it fine enough (that's about as good a line as Mr. Levene ever gets), and Mr. Alda remains alert enough to land a genuine laugh of his own. Mr. Alda should be noted by people who have better shows in mind."

Philip Rose, producer of *Cafe Crown*, did have better shows in mind. Phil had a knack for discovering and launching talent; Diana Sands, Godfrey Cambridge, Michele Lee, Al Pacino, Cleavon Little, Melba Moore, Sherman Hemsley, and Penelope Milford all came out of the Rose showshop. And Alan Alda, from Rose's *Purlie Victorious*.

Rose came across a play about a shy writer and an outspoken prostitute called *The Owl and the Pussycat*. Kim Stanley was set to star, under the management of Alexander H. Cohen. Stanley withdrew, Cohen dropped it, Rose picked up the option and cast the two most suitable people he could think of: Diana Sands and Alan Alda. This was controversial casting at the time, which was 1964, and apparently a bit of a surprise to author Bill Manhoff. (After losing Kim Stanley and Alex Cohen and the prospects of a "class" Broadway production, Manhoff wasn't about to turn down Rose's interracial cast.) *The Owl and the Pussycat* opened that November and was a hit, running a full year.

Alda next starred in the 1966 musical *The Apple Tree*, from Jerry Bock, Sheldon Harnick, and Mike Nichols. He left Broadway for his first major film role, as writer George Plimpton in the 1968 feature *Paper Lion*. Four films and five years later, Alda undertook the role of Hawkeye Pierce in the sitcom version of the motion picture M*A*S*H. Alda, the intelligent theatre actor, became a major television celebrity. M*A*S*H ran eleven seasons, bringing Alda five Emmy Awards and making him the only person, as far as I can tell, to win TV's top award as actor, director, and writer.

Alda made quite an impression in his first major Broadway role in 1964, and not only because he set his bathrobe on fire during his second scene on opening night.

Over the years Alda made more than forty films, mostly in starring roles. He also wrote and directed some of his starring vehicles, including *The Four Seasons* and *Betsy's Wedding*. Alda was absent from Broadway for a full quarter of a century until he appeared in 1992 in the muddled *Jake's Women*. He returned in the 1996 New York production of the international hit *Art*, giving a fine comic performance.

And then he called Gordon Davidson about Richard Feynman, which ultimately brought him back to Broadway in *QED*. Alda was, once again, very good; this was possibly his finest stage performance ever. Watching him lope around the stage of the Beaumont, I couldn't help but think that he might have been a top musical comedy star. Imagine Alda in *Sweet Charity* or *Promises! Promises!* or *On the Twentieth Century* or *They're Playing Our Song*. Broadway's loss was pop culture's gain. Still, it was nice to have Alda back on the boards, and happily so, in *QED*.

Sexaholix . . . a love story

John Leguizamo bounded onto the stage in *Sexaholix*, exploding through space doing what I'd have to describe as backward hip-hop shuffle aerobics. Upstage was a "wall" consisting of strands of lightbulbs wired in strings. Each vertical strand lit up as Leguizamo sped by backward, a visually arresting start for a show with no scenery.

"Wassup Manhattan?" he brayed to his fans. "Talk to me, lemme feeeeeel you." The crowd roared. "We're gonna get real raw tonight . . . we're gonna get funky, get nasty."

Leguizamo, from his very entrance, had his audience where he wanted them. But, then, he has elicited dynamic audience response with each of his four off-color autobiographical onstage therapy sessions.

He still bounds onstage like a ghetto kid, but he is a kid no longer; he turned thirty-seven during his *Sexaholix* tryout tour. Ten days prior to the originally scheduled November 4 opening, Leguizamo rushed his preshow warmup and tore a hamstring. He continued performing through his injury—hey, business was good—and opened on December 2, after the press had returned from the Thanksgiving holiday.

> "Wassup Manhattan?" Leguizamo brayed to his fans. "Talk to me, lemme feeeeeel you." The crowd roared.

Born in 1964 in Bogotá to a Colombian mother and Puerto Rican father, Leguizamo grew up in Queens, where his father was a waiter. He majored in drama at (but did not graduate from) New York University, as well as taking classes at the HB Studio; but traditional stage acting is not where he found his niche. His first solo show, *Mambo Mouth*, opened on November 8, 1990, at the American Place Theatre. Leguizamo was hailed by the critics as an important new voice. The off off-Broadway engagement was extended to 107 performances, with an off-Broadway transfer to the Orpheum the following June (where it played 80 additional performances). Leguizamo won an Obie Award, and *Mambo Mouth* was subsequently telecast on HBO.

His second show, *Spic-O-Rama*, was similarly successful. It opened October 9, 1992, at the off-Broadway Westside Theatre for a limited engagement of 86 performances. This, too, won the actor acclaim and awards and another HBO telecast. It also led to a mainstream movie career, with his first major performance being as the endearingly lovable Chi Chi Rodriguez in *To Wong Foo, Thanks for Everything, Love Julie Newmar*.

Next came *Freak*, "a demi-semi-quasi-pseudo autobiography" that was developed off off-Broadway at the Atlantic Theatre in September 1997 (for 35 performances). *Freak* brought Leguizamo to Broadway's Cort Theatre on February 12, 1998; a surprise hit, it enjoyed a moneymaking 145-performance run and garnered Leguizamo well-earned Tony nominations as playwright and actor.

The HBO version of *Freak*, under the direction of Spike Lee, earned Leguizamo an Emmy. He then went on to star in Lee's 1999 film *Summer of Sam*. His film career continued with a prominent turn as Toulouse-Lautrec in Baz Luhrmann's 2001 hit, *Moulin Rouge*.

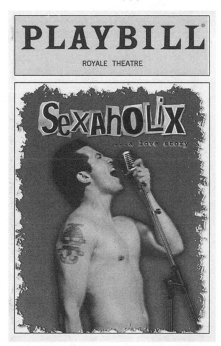

All of which is pretty good for a skinny, foul-mouthed Hispanic kid from Queens. Leguizamo has a secret, though, which is still kept pretty much in the shadows. He is not a skinny, foul-mouthed Hispanic kid from Queens; he is an actor. And a good one. During the opening moments of the second act of *Sexaholix*, as he was dancing in the aisle a few feet from my elbow with a girl plucked from the audience, I was struck by the fact that he reminded me —at one and the same moment —of both the skinny Marlon Brando in *A Streetcar Named Desire* and Matthew Broderick's Leo Bloom in *The Producers*. *Cat on a Hat Tin Roof* next?

Maybe Leguizamo will turn to acting; dramatic acting, that is. He went

John Leguizamo

Cast Album: RCAVictor 07863-68090
(excerpts, entitled *John Leguizamo Live*)

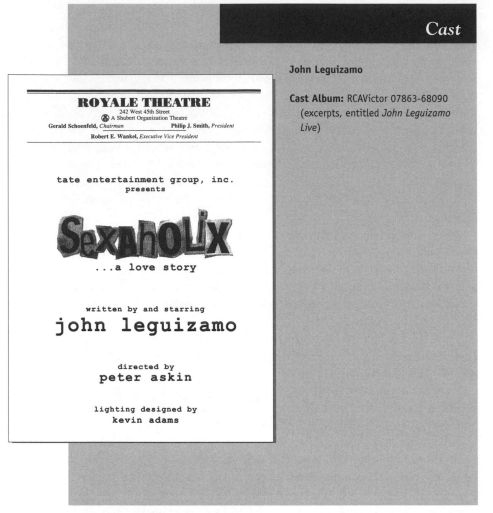

ROYALE THEATRE
242 West 45th Street
Ⓢ A Shubert Organization Theatre
Gerald Schoenfeld, *Chairman*   Philip J. Smith, *President*
Robert E. Wankel, *Executive Vice President*

tate entertainment group, inc.
presents

Sexaholix

...a love story

written by and starring
john leguizamo

directed by
peter askin

lighting designed by
kevin adams

out of his way to announce that *Sexaholix* would be his final one-man show, although I wouldn't exactly bet on it. A successful one-man show, written by yourself, is far more profitable than pulling down an actor's salary; even a "star" salary. In any event, this guy is good.

Sexaholix . . . a love story (as it was officially titled) followed the path of the author's growth to emotional maturity. Or immaturity. Take your pick; the stage Leguizamo would probably opt for the latter. (In a humorous interview-with-himself for the *Sunday Times*, he noted that "underneath this scrawny exterior is an insecure, self-absorbed workaholic with the emotional maturity of a 12-year-old. With the help of my therapist, 13 here I come.")

He took us, in turn, through his parents' marriage and divorce; puberty at his grandparents' house; coming of age in high school; his early romances; his first, unhappy marriage; and his present blissful relationship with the mother of his two infants. Sex is strewn through the many wrecked relationships, romantic and familial. Love—note that subtitle—finally conquers all; at least for now. The love in question, incidentally, turned out to be not Leguizamo's love for his so-called soul mate Teeny, but the love of a man for his two-year-old daughter and one-year-old son.

This last development is identical to the one in Spalding Gray's *Morning, Noon and Night* (discussed in *Broadway Yearbook 1999–2000*). Which makes for an interesting comparison. Both superegoed men appear to have been radically transformed by fatherhood. That is, as self-dramatized and presented on the Broadway stage. Gray, in *Morning, Noon and Night*, appeared to be somewhat awestruck by his boys (a five-year-old and a two-year-old who, in his telling, sounded like little old Borscht Belt gagmen).

Leguizamo, in *Sexaholix*, appeared to be less tamed by his new charges; the immature "popi" was still alive and kicking. "We don't need kids," he complains to his beloved, "we got me." And after the usual toddler-related complaints about lack of time and lack of sleep, he confesses, "That's why I wrote this show—to get out of the house." Gray talked a better game— he's a verbalist, after all—but Leguizamo seemed far more genuine.

Some readers might recall my comments about Gray's carefully measured sips of water; they were supposed to appear casual but were seemingly preprogramed for use when he couldn't think of any other way to get from one acting moment to the other. When Leguizamo needed some water, he found a glassful, gulped it down, and enthused, "Ah, vodka!" Planned and rehearsed, no doubt; but as refreshing as a cold sip of—well, vodka.

Leguizamo's audience was rocking throughout, literally. At one point, he launched into a discussion of the older woman who taught him the ropes, a fortyish gum-chewing feminist named Penny (who seemed to be a character out of Lily Tomlin). "Higher, slower, to the right," she directed him. The audience literally exploded; the actress sitting in front of me bounced so high in her seat that the cushion groaned. (She looked like an actress; I'm pretty sure it was Alice Ripley.)

> **Leguizamo has a secret. He is not a skinny, foul-mouthed Hispanic kid from Queens; he is an actor. And a good one.**

If the audience was rockin', I wasn't (rockin'). But I was with him all the way. Yes, he had a slightly offputting attitude, a sort of ghetto-bred, streetwise bravura. Still, the man could carry it off—and with a reassuringly warm smile, too. As the evening progressed, anything he wanted to

Sexaholix . . . a love story
Opened: December 2, 2001
Closed: February 10, 2002
67 performances (and 53 previews)
Profit/Loss: Profit
Sexaholix ($76.25 top) was scaled to a potential gross of
$394,793 (for a seven-performance week) at the 1,074-
seat Royale Theatre. Weekly grosses averaged about
$311,000, with a high of $376,000 in the final week.
Total gross for the eighteen-week run was $5,337,342.
Attendance was about 86 percent, with the box office
grossing about 79 percent of dollar-capacity.

TONY AWARD NOMINATION
Special Theatrical Event

*Critical
Scorecard*

Rave 2
Favorable 5
Mixed 1
Unfavorable 0
Pan 2

say was okay with me. *Sexaholix* was raw and funky, as promised in the opening monologue, although I found it more endearing than nasty. Vulgar, yes, but highly likable. (The show was well directed by Peter Askin—of *Mambo Mouth*, *Spic-O-Rama*, and *Hedwig and the Angry Inch*—and sharply lit by Kevin Adams.) Artful, too, and exceedingly funny. How funny?

Leguizamo set the tone early on, talking about his mom. "My mother wanted to get an abortion, but it was too late. I was already in college." There was another abortion joke at the end of the first act, when his girlfriend at the time gets one. "It's not fair to kill the fetus," she threatens, "and let the father live." The actor's father was no gem, either. "We were poor, but my father was cheap, too. He put the funk in dysfunctional."

He told us about his two-week vacation as a "ghetto prize" with a rich family of WASPs in Vermont, courtesy of the Fresh Air Fund. "It was so great to find out that white people were f****d up, too." His beloved grandfather taught him that "life is about pain, failure, misery, and Budweiser." He went to a city public school where gang recruiters stood outside the door; Leguizamo tells us that he flunked the drug test, testing only barely positive from Flintstones and Midol. (Flintstones is a children's multivitamin, and Midol is—well, never mind.) Hence the show's title; Leguizamo and his nerd buddies, unable to join one of the big, bad gangs, formed their own hapless band, the Sexaholix.

He told us about his budding film career. "I'd like to see you in a snuff picture," said supportive dad. He told us about his failed marriage. "You're supposed to love me no matter what," he told his wife. "You must be confusing me with Jesus," she replied. He finds true love—or at least workable love—with a Jewish girl he calls Teeny (name in real life, Justine).

Everything is fine, because "she's messed up, too." That is, until she tells him "my clock is ticking." "Well," he responds, "just put it on snooze."

But they have kids, half Latin and half Jewish. ("They'll be able to dance and balance their checkbooks.") Leguizamo gave virtuosic renditions of his two natural childbirth experiences, with the tiny heads peering out through the womb. Holding his newborn daughter, he came to a startling realization: "No matter what I did, I was going to f*** her up." The newly reformed dad found himself spinning bedtime stories. Like a fairy tale about "a boy who had all these monsters, and he had to tame them."

If the audience was rockin', I wasn't. But I was with him all the way. Yes, he had a slightly offputting attitude, but he could carry it off.

He did tame them, and became a Broadway star, too.

Barbara Cook:
Mostly Sondheim

Y ou either got it, or you ain't. And boys—I got it."

Those lyrics by Sondheim did not appear in *Mostly Sondheim*, nor are they likely to be heard in any Sondheim anthology revue you're likely to come across.

But Barbara Cook? Well, "you either have it—or you've had it." And Ms. Cook, at seventy-four, has it. And how.

Hers is an atypical tale of tawdry Broadway.

Twenty-year-old Georgia peach, pretty as a picture with a voice like a bell, boards a train with mama and heads to New York back in 1948. Takes lessons, works as a typist; gets a singing job at the Blue Angel nightclub in 1950; gets stage experience at Tamiment, one of those summer-camps-for-adults in the Poconos. The hard work pays off in 1951, when at the age of twenty-three she's cast as the ingenue in a big new Broadway musical. From Cheryl Crawford, cofounder of the Actors' Studio and innovative producer of the magical *Brigadoon*; and Yip Harburg, the hypertalented author of the brilliantly caustic *Finian's Rainbow*. But *Flahooley*, alas, is a terrible failure; five weeks and out. (John Chapman of the *Daily News* gave Cook her first good Broadway review, singling her out as "sweet.")

Back to auditions. *Oklahoma!* was the *Cats* of its day, only much bigger. The first national company, after nine and a half years in the hinterlands, was booked into New York's City Center for a five-week return engagement in the fall of 1953. Rodgers and Hammerstein, who had three other musicals playing on Broadway at the time, spruced up the cast for the occasion and added a new Ado Annie: Barbara Cook. (Florence Henderson played Laurey.) Walter Kerr of the *Herald Tribune* found Cook "suitably flighty"; Robert Coleman of the *Daily Mirror* found her "cute"; and William Hawkins of the *World-Telegram & Sun* found her "pretty and spirited as Ado Annie, with the voice and energy to take fine care of her immortal numbers." Then Cook hit the road, until *Oklahoma!* closed in May 1954. Cook was back at City Center in June for a ten-week run as Carrie in *Carousel*. (Jo Sullivan played Julie.) At this point, Cook got a new singing coach named Robert Kobin, whom she still praises almost fifty years later. Given the results, he must have done something right.

The *Carousel* gig led to Cook being cast in a not-dissimilar part in *Plain and Fancy*, an Amish-themed musical that opened in January 1955. She played the sixth-most-prominent role, with only two solos, but she made her mark. "Barbara Cook, right off a blue and white Dutch plate, is delicious all the time, but especially when she perches on a trunk, savors her first worthwhile kiss, and melts into the melody of 'This Is All Very New to Me.' " This from the aforementioned Kerr, who appreciated Cook from the very beginning, while her fan Hawkins said that "outstanding credit goes to Barbara Cook, who flings her own heart over the footlights with whatever she does, and sings and dances her way into the hearts of the audience."

You either got it, or you ain't. And boys—Cook has got it.

"Flings her own heart over the footlights with whatever she does"; that's a good way of describing Ms. Cook then and—a half century later—now. *Plain and Fancy* was only moderately successful, but Cook was on her way. Her appearance nabbed her a Theatre World Award for promising personalities, in company with two actors named Chris Plummer and Tony Perkins, and an English lass called Julie Andrews.

And then, in December 1956, came Cook's biggest break. Leonard Bernstein and Lillian Hellman undertook a musicalization of Voltaire's *Candide*. Cook was given the role of Cunegonde, one of musical comedy's most sorely beset ingenues. "Miss Cook tears down the house with a coloratura on a song called 'Glitter and Be Gay,' lustily achieving the trill beyond the trill beyond the trill," said Tom Donnelly in the *World-Telegram & Sun*. Brooks Atkinson in the *Times* noted not only that she was "a lustrous singer" but also that "her acting portrait of a lyrical maiden who quickly learns how to connive with the world is sketched with skill, spirit, and humor."

Candide was famously troubled, with the composer, librettist, and director all working at cross-purposes. The show lasted a mere nine weeks, but Cook's performance was memorialized on the original cast album. "Glitter and Be Gay" has since been sung by numerous theatre singers

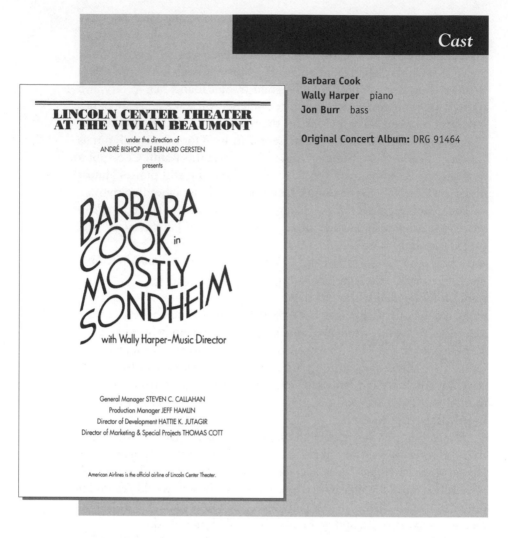

Barbara Cook
Wally Harper piano
Jon Burr bass

Original Concert Album: DRG 91464

LINCOLN CENTER THEATER
AT THE VIVIAN BEAUMONT

under the direction of
ANDRÉ BISHOP and BERNARD GERSTEN

presents

BARBARA
COOK in
MOSTLY
SONDHEIM

with Wally Harper–Music Director

General Manager STEVEN C. CALLAHAN
Production Manager JEFF HAMLIN
Director of Development HATTIE K. JUTAGIR
Director of Marketing & Special Projects THOMAS COTT

American Airlines is the official airline of Lincoln Center Theater.

and opera singers, but Cook's rendition remains unsurpassed. Yes, she poured musicality into every last note; ah, but underneath there was a saucy comedienne poking fun at comic operettas in general, and coloratura arias in specific.

In 1957, just after she turned thirty, Cook was cast as Robert Preston's leading lady in *The Music Man.* No one along Broadway was surprised when she turned in a first-rate singing-and-acting performance as that sadder-but-wiser girl, Marian the Librarian. By now, her excellence was a given: she was the "unfailing" Barbara Cook, a "beguiling," "delectable" "doll." This brought Cook a Featured Actress Tony Award, eligibility in those days being determined by whether your name was above or below the title.

In 1960 she returned to City Center in yet another Rodgers and Hammerstein musical, *The King and I*. Cook was a full twenty years younger than Gertrude Lawrence had been when she created the role (only nine years earlier). This difference—which caused some to dub the production "The Son of the King and I"—made a strong impression. Mr. Atkinson: "In the past, Barbara Cook has been playing provincial maidens—playing them especially well. As Anna, the English woman who flounces into nineteenth-century Siam, she is now playing a cultivated woman of maturity. It is the best performance of her career. Her voice has not only purity, it also has a weight that gives musical importance [to Anna's solos]. As an actress, Miss Cook's familiar candor also gives Anna a cool dignity that adds a little more stature to the part than it has had before."

This was followed in 1961 by Cook's first bona fide starring role, with her name finally above the title. *The Gay Life* was the show, a musicalization of Schnitzler's giddy Viennese roundelay *Anatol*. But what was intended to be a Sacher torte of a musical fell flat; Kerr complained that it was "approximately as continental as a box of Cracker-Jack." He singled out our darling, nevertheless: "As she lifts her sweet, precise voice and opens her earnest child's eyes, all of the atmosphere that has been lying in wait, unused, now wraps itself around her. Whatever those other people are in, Miss Cook is in a success, her head and our hearts are high."

Three months work, then a year's wait until her next show—and her best role. Jerry Bock and Sheldon Harnick's 1963 musical *She Loves Me* had what might have been the finest score of the decade. The show nevertheless failed, one of those affairs that most everybody liked but too few loved. Here's Norman Nadel of the *World-Telegram & Sun*: "The expression 'sings her heart out' certainly applies to Miss Cook, who has both the heart and voice to do it. Her clear soprano is not only one of the finest vocal instruments in the contemporary musical theatre, but it conveys all the vitality, brightness, and strength of her feminine young personality, which is plenty." Nadel was one of the more music-conscious critics of the time; he was the only major critic, a year later, who lavished excited praise on Sondheim's otherwise embattled *Anyone Can Whistle*.

The demise of *She Loves Me*, after a disappointing run of less than a year, signaled the turning point in Cook's professional career (and, apparently, her personal life as well). In the summer of 1964 she went off on a stock tour of a minor musical, *The Unsinkable Molly Brown*, before returning to Broadway in November with something called *Something More!* This came from a set of authors who didn't know any better and a producer named Jule Styne, who should have known better than to hire himself as a director. (He also ended up ghostwriting a significant part of the score, including a couple of winning tunes for the star.) Here's the lady's champion on the aisle once more, Walter Kerr: "Miss Cook just turns front and lets the phrases of a simple Sammy Fain tune float toward us without fuss, without selling, without winking or blinking or having to stamp her pretty foot. The sweetness is direct, personal, and should be packaged as a substitute for honey, no matter how many bees are thereby put out of business. Miss Cook is one of the true treasures of our musical comedy theatre."

Something More! shuttered in two weeks. Cook soon moved into Sandy Dennis's role in the long-running comedy *Any Wednesday*, but her musical misadventures had taken a toll. Since her Broadway debut in 1951, audiences and critics had been praising her voice, her beauty, her sweetness, and more; life offstage, though, wasn't so positive. Cook had a husband named David LeGrant. He has been described, in different places, as a comedian and an acting teacher. While leafing through Cook's early reviews, I found yet another description of him. It turns out that he played Ali Hakim, the traveling salesman who tangles with Ado Annie, in Cook's *Oklahoma!* Here's our man Kerr's take: "David LeGrant is waving a stick pretty frantically at the already broad antics of Ali Hakim, and some of the show's comedy takes fright and disappears under the thrashing."

Cook and LeGrant were married in 1952, before she joined *Oklahoma!*; they had a child, Adam, in 1960, just after her *King and I*. They divorced in 1965, at which point Cook descended into a deep depression. A deep depression fed by alcohol and, over the course of time, food. "I drank every day," she recalled in a Sunday *Times* interview with Anthony Tommasini. "Not on the days I worked, usually, which were not many. But otherwise, come five o'clock, I'd start drinking and keep drinking until I fell into bed."

She kept performing as opportunities presented themselves. A 1966 Music Theater of Lincoln Center revival of *Show Boat*, produced by Dick Rodgers; a new Broadway comedy from cartoonist Jules Feiffer, *Little Murders*, which opened in 1967 and closed after seven performances; a summer stock tour of Styne's *Funny Girl*. She resurfaced in 1971 for one last Broadway musical, *The Grass Harp*, which also shuttered after seven performances. Cook gave her usual fine performance, with that same amazing voice filling the Martin Beck, but her physical appearance was startlingly altered; the pert and trim ingenue was gone. True, she was forty-three, but musical comedy heroines aren't expected to age like normal beings.

Cook next went into an exceedingly strange 1972 musical called *Halloween*, from *Man of La Mancha*'s Mitch Leigh. She appeared with David Wayne and Dick Shawn in the initial tryout at Florida State University but withdrew before the pre-Broadway tryout opened (and closed) in Bucks

County, Pennsylvania. In November 1972, she appeared in Ellis Rabb's production of Gorky's *Enemies*, for the Repertory Theatre of Lincoln Center. As Cook related thirty years later in *Mostly Sondheim*, John Simon wrote, "Now that she can't sing anymore, she's decided to try to act." Simon's quote provided Cook with an enormous laugh in 2002, although I don't suppose she was laughing at the time.

In the summer of 1973, I was doing publicity for a shoestring stock operation that booked cheesy touring packages. Vivian Blaine and Robert Alda in *Follies*, Patty Duke and John Astin in *A Shot in the Dark*, that sort of thing. Oh, and Milton Berle in *Norman, Is That You?* Which was quite an experience; place yourself in Milton Berle's small-town hotel suite at midnight, eating Kentucky Fried Chicken while the onetime king of comedy expounded outdated philosophies to an audience of one. At any rate, one of the packages was an exceedingly sad thing called *The Gershwin Years* (or something of the sort). There they were, four washed-up-but-unquestionably-still-talented musical comedy stars who couldn't get arrested, sitting on bar stools in spotlights. Helen Gallagher, Julie Wilson, Larry Kert, and an enormous Barbara Cook.

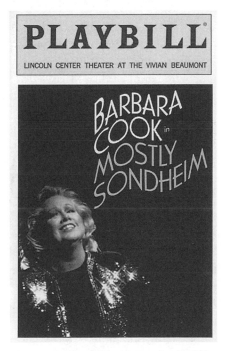

And then came Wally. Wally Harper, that is, a musical director and arranger with a vast store of musical theatre knowledge; his most prominent credit at the time was as dance arranger for Sondheim's 1970 musical *Company*. Harper almost hit it big that year as composer of *Sensations*, an off-Broadway musicalization of *Romeo and Juliet* that received a good deal of attention (in part because of its interracial, nude love scene). The show failed, though, and appears to be Harper's only full score; he was to contribute material over the years to musicals as diverse as the Debbie Reynolds revival of *Irene* and Tommy Tune's *Grand Hotel*.

Cook and Harper got together and started to work. They played a successful 1974 engagement at the nightclub Brothers and Sisters. This led to a 1975 concert at Carnegie Hall, with a recording—*Barbara Cook at Carnegie Hall*—celebrating the occasion. Cook was reborn with a new ca-

Barbara Cook: Mostly Sondheim
Opened: January 14, 2002
Closed: August 26, 2002
26 performances (and 5 previews)
Profit/Loss: Nonprofit [profit]
Barbara Cook: Mostly Sondheim ($60 top) was scaled to a
    potential gross of $112,010 (for a two-performance week)
    at the 1,067-seat Vivian Beaumont Theater. The show
    went on hiatus February 11, reopening June 23. Weekly
    grosses averaged about $78,000, with business falling off
    slightly during the summer return engagement. Total gross
    for the run was $1,202,355. Attendance was about 86
    percent, with the box office grossing about 69 percent of
    dollar-capacity. (These figures are not indicative, as the
    potential was calculated at the top ticket price, but
    subscribers paid less.)

TONY AWARD NOMINATION
Special Theatrical Event

Critical Scorecard

Rave	8
Favorable	2
Mixed	0
Unfavorable	0
Pan	0

reer as a concert and nightclub singer. She was in no shape, physically, to appear in a musical, but the voice remained inviolate. She returned to Carnegie Hall in 1980 with another concert. This one featured "It's Better with a Band," one of several songs written by Harper with up-and-coming young lyricist David Zippel. Life became a succession of concert tours and recordings. She made it back to Broadway in April 1987, when *Barbara Cook: A Concert for the Theatre* played thirteen performances at the Ambassador.

Cook made a couple of brief returns to the gaze of theatergoers. In September 1985, she sang Sally Durant in two concert performances of *Follies* with the New York Philharmonic. One can only wonder about Cook's absence from the original production. Her name appears on an official "preliminary casting list," for the roles of both Phyllis and Sally. *Follies* definitely needed all the star power they could muster, and director-producer Hal Prince was presumably happy with her work in *She Loves Me*. Could it have been her physical appearance when she showed up to audition?

She tried one more theatre piece, the infamous 1988 musical *Carrie*. This was produced by the Royal Shakespeare Company in Stratford-upon-Avon. Cook bailed out after the three-week Stratford run, thus avoiding the show's even more catastrophic Broadway engagement. And it was back to concerts and nightclubs.

Casting about for a theme on which to hang her November 2000 cabaret act at the New York supper club Feinstein's, Harper came up with the idea of combining songs by Sondheim with songs on Sondheim's list of "songs I wish I'd written (at least in part)." This was compiled by the master in connection with the "Stephen Sondheim 70th Birthday Concert" on May 22, 2000, at the Library of Congress in Washington, D.C. It received nationwide distribution in Frank Rich's birthday valentine of a profile in the *New York Times Sunday Magazine*.

Barbara Cook: In Good Company turned out to be a very good idea. Cook and Harper played it here and there, refining it as they went, and brought it to Carnegie Hall for Valentine's Day 2001 under the title *Mostly Sondheim* (with Malcolm Gets singing a good deal of the Sondheim material). A live recording of said concert was released in 2001, and Cook, Harper, and *Mostly Sondheim* hit the road (including a highly acclaimed run at the Donmar Warehouse in the summer of 2001). The show was also booked for a three-week appearance at Kennedy Center's Sondheim Celebration in the summer of 2002.

Lincoln Center Theater, meanwhile, booked Alan Alda and *QED* into the Vivian Beaumont for two performances a week on *Contact*'s dark nights. *QED* was an immediate sellout. Alda was unable to extend immediately, but he could return later in the season. This left open seven Sundays and Mondays, just perfect for *Mostly Sondheim*. Cook, too, proved an immediate sell-out, so Lincoln Center Theater booked a return engagement in June.

Barbara Cook's *Mostly Sondheim* was quite a feast. "You either got it, or you ain't." Sondheim's list gave Cook the perfect excuse to sing some exceptional songs, including two stunners by Harold Arlen and Johnny Mercer, "I Wonder What Became of Me" and "I Had Myself a True Love." (The remnants of Cook's Georgia accent brought added flavor and an unexpected authenticity to Mercer's lyrics.) These were as close to definitive as you need to get, as was Cook's rendition of Arlen and Harburg's "The Eagle and Me" from *Bloomer Girl*. Cook also sang her signature song, "Ice Cream," from *She Loves Me*. She introduced this by saying it was "what I think is one of the best musical comedy songs ever written," and I think I agree.

By 1957, her excellence was a given: she was the "unfailing" Barbara Cook, a "beguiling," "delectable" "doll."

Equally breathtaking, on the Sondheim side, were "In Buddy's Eyes," "Happiness," "Send in the Clowns," "Not a Day Goes By," "Losing My Mind," and "Anyone Can Whistle." Ten or so absolutely amazing renditions, as good as you'd ever hope to hear, in ninety minutes. Pretty good for a seventy-four-year old.

But Cook has a secret, a secret she has apparently always had. She can sing. She sings as naturally as most people can talk. (More naturally, actually.) When most singers sing, they are singing. When Cook sings, you feel like the notes themselves are a given; this frees her to concentrate on the words. Cook sings like she breathes, even at an age when such a gift might well be expected to have diminished.

Looking through my notes, I find that I kept writing phrases like "expresses the pain" and "feels the pain" and "the pain comes through" and "true pain." So many of these songs—as sung by Cook—were searingly beautiful, but with an unmistakable undercurrent of hurt and sorrow. In preparing this chapter, I stumbled across Ms. Cook's Web site, and there it was:

"When somebody can really communicate, boy, it resonates out there to the ends of the earth."

"On stage, safety lies in the very thing that seems most dangerous. And that is: Your vulnerability, your ability to allow people to see the pain and all the life stuff. But very few have been given the gift to communicate. And when somebody can really communicate, boy, it resonates out there to the ends of the earth."

Barbara Cook's voice. It resonates out there to the ends of the earth.

An Almost Holy Picture

The Roundabout Theatre Company began their 2001–2002 Broadway season with Clare Boothe Luce's comedy *The Women* on November 8. (*Major Barbara*, starring Cherry Jones, was technically the final offering of the Roundabout's 2000–2001 subscription season.) Next up was the long-awaited Broadway debut of Stephen Sondheim and John Weidman's *Assassins*, scheduled to open on November 29. Back in 1991, it played a limited off off-Broadway engagement at Playwrights Horizons, but unexpectedly failed to transfer. Ten years later, tickets were on sale, publicity was in full swing, scenery was under construction, and a cast had been signed.

Joe Mantello, who directed *Love! Valour! Compassion!* and the Roundabout's 2001 *Design for Living*, was at the helm; John Carrafa, of *Urinetown*, was the choreographer. Douglas Sills, who had managed to turn himself into something of a star with only one Broadway appearance in one underbaked musical, *The Scarlet Pimpernel*, was to head the cast as that most famous of all assassins, John Wilkes Booth. Also on board was Neil Patrick Harris, a former TV star (from the *Doogie Howser, MD*, series); he had made a strong showing as Tobias in the 1999 Los Angeles and 2000 New York concert versions of Sondheim's *Sweeney Todd*. The cast also included two up-and-coming actors, Denis Hare (who had done so well in Roundabout's *Cabaret* and *Major Barbara*) and Raul Esparza (who had created a stir off-Broadway in Jonathan Larson's *tick, tick . . . BOOM!* and as a replacement in *Cabaret*).

Rehearsals were scheduled for September 17, 2001, with previews to

With the cancellation of *Assassins*, Roundabout had two holes to fill in their season and little time to fill them.

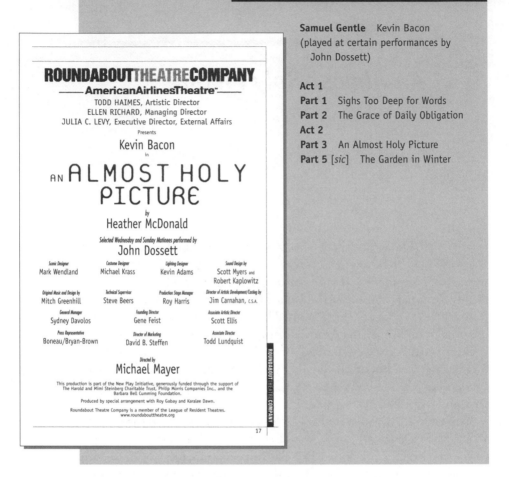

Samuel Gentle   Kevin Bacon
(played at certain performances by
John Dossett)

Act 1
Part 1   Sighs Too Deep for Words
Part 2   The Grace of Daily Obligation
Act 2
Part 3   An Almost Holy Picture
Part 5 [*sic*]   The Garden in Winter

start November 1 at the Music Box (which offered a larger gross potential than the Roundabout's home base at the American Airlines Theatre). And then came the events of September 11. The authors issued a statement: "*Assassins* is a show which asks audiences to think critically about various aspects of the American experience. In light of Tuesday's murderous assault on our nation and on the most fundamental things in which we all believe, we, the Roundabout, and director Joe Mantello believe this is not an appropriate time to present a show which makes such a demand."

This left the Roundabout with a hole in their season, and little time to fill it. They had offered subscribers a season of four Broadway shows: *The Women*, *Assassins*, a revival of Rodgers and Hart's *The Boys from Syracuse*, and "an additional play to be announced." With the cancellation of *As-*

sassins, this left two slots to be filled. This is not an uncommon occurrence in subscription theatre–land; two of the shows on Roundabout's 2000–2001 season also went missing, O'Neill's *Desire under the Elms* (replaced by Pinter's *Betrayal*) and Brian Friel's *The Faith Healer* (replaced by Shaw's *Major Barbara*).

Needless to say, there are plenty of shows around hoping to be scooped up and produced on Broadway; one of these, the Williamstown Theatre Festival's 2000 production of Arthur Miller's *The Man Who Had All the Luck*, was selected as the original "additional play to be announced." But it takes time to find a play and find a director and cast it and build a set; and in this case, they needed a director and cast who were available almost immediately.

Roundabout also produces an off-Broadway season, at the time at the 477-seat Gramercy Theatre. Among the plays on that schedule was Heather McDonald's *An Almost Holy Picture*. This wasn't a new play, exactly; it was initially produced at the La Jolla Playhouse in September 1995. Michael Mayer, resident director of the Roundabout, directed it, with David Morse (of *How I Learned to Drive*) in the leading and only role. McDonald, Mayer, and Morse also took the play to the McCarter Theatre in Princeton; other productions played at the Berkeley Repertory Theatre, Center Stage, and the Indiana Repertory Theatre. It took an awfully long time for the play to make it to New York. Not without reason, as it turned out.

An Almost Holy Picture was already announced for the Gramercy, it was ready, and the Roundabout was able to entice a bona fide movie star to sign on, thus giving the show an added measure of ticket-selling credibility. Kevin Bacon, an intense stage actor who made his name in such films as *Diner* and *Footloose*, had been offered the play when it was scheduled for the Gramercy. He was interested, but not interested enough; the character is very much alone in the universe, and Bacon thought it would be more effective with him stranded on a vaster, Broadway stage. When the cancellation of *Assassins* left Roundabout in sudden need of another Broadway subscription offering, Bacon came in to do a reading. He was pleased, the Roundabout was pleased, everybody was pleased. And so a play that almost surely didn't belong on Broadway was suddenly on Broadway.

> "I am glad she has a guardian angel who smokes and wears tuxedos because who am I but that man in the linen cloth running silent naked alone in the dark." Now there's a curtain line to entice you back for the second act.

This was all understandable, under the extreme circumstances. But *An Almost Holy Picture* was an odd play. Very odd.

I did not read the program notes before the show began; I generally prefer to let the story unfold on its own, unless it's a play by Tom Stoppard. I already knew that this was a one-character show, but with Alan Alda and John Leguizamo and Barbara Cook in recent memory, this could be looked at as an asset. If I had glanced at the cast

It is not a good sign when in the course of a mystically theological drama you start thinking nostalgically of bad, thirty-year-old musicals.

listing page, I would have learned that the two parts of act 1 were subtitled "Sighs Too Deep for Words" and "The Grace of Daily Obligation," and I would have worried. What's more, I would have seen three quotations that the playwright presumably wanted me to have on my mind as the curtain rose. One was from the Bible; one was from good old Anonymous; and the other was from Pablo Neruda.

You know, Pablo Neruda. The Chilean poet, whose real name was Neftalí Ricardo Reyes Basoalto. (Isn't the Internet wonderful for stuff like this?) I must confess, I get a little queasy when they quote poems in the program by Pablo Neruda. But then, that's me.

And there was that poem from Anonymous, who had presumably studied punctuation with e. e. cummings:

> light travels as mystery travels
> on the edge of faith
> severing in its path
> dark corners of memory
> tragic consequence
> and the taste of death

Reading this before the curtain rose, I suppose, would have frozen me in terror at what was to come. As it was, it took eleven minutes before I knew what I was in for. Samuel Gentle, a gentle former minister with horn-rim glasses, approached and started talking. He took us from a cranberry bog in Truro (on Cape Cod) to the Cebolletta Mountains (near Acoma, outside Albuquerque) with Jesus and Moses and Jeremiah and the apostle Paul on the Damascus road and sacks of beans and garlic and jars of salsa verde and a blur on the road that was not a rabbit but a seven-year-old girl whose hair had caught fire in a kitchen and nine dead native children in a shallow ditch in a culvert and Ernesto Yah-Tah-Hey with chicken pox and a one-eyed champion javelin thrower named Cervantes. In the eleventh minute—I looked at my watch here—our hero told us about his wife's three miscarriages, at which point I calculated that there were roughly ninety-five minutes to go. With time off for good behavior, otherwise known as intermission.

The much-awaited interval came at 9:02, but not until Mr. Gentle told us, "I am glad she has a guardian angel who smokes and wears tuxedos because who am I but that man in the linen cloth running silent naked alone in the dark." Now there's a curtain line to entice you back for the second act.

The second act, it turned out, was far more interesting (and shorter) than the first. McDonald concentrated here on Gentle's daughter Ariel, who was born with a disease that McDonald calls lanugo. As I understand it, lanugo is actually the fine, peach-fuzz-like hair that grows on the skin of a fetus for the last four months of a pregnancy. It is often visible at birth, especially in premature children, but almost always disappears within weeks. (Isn't the Internet wonderful for stuff like this?)

Congenital hypertrichosis lanuginosa, however, is an extremely rare condition in which the hair continues to grow into adulthood. Hair, everywhere. In the case of Ariel, the hair was light and downy, almost angelic; in olden days, many people so afflicted over the centuries were relegated to carnival sideshows. (Modern-day theory has it that so-called apemen and werewolves of yore were possibly CHL sufferers.)

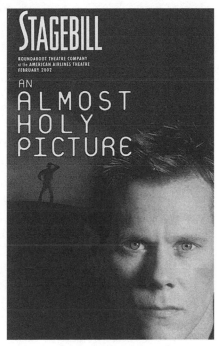

At any rate, the playwright acknowledges Pamela Ward's story "The Hairy Little Girl" as a source. Her point in all this was—I don't know. Poor Samuel Gentle was sorely beset from the beginning; long before his daughter was born, he was in that bus crash in New Mexico. And from the beginning, we knew we were in for a play in which bad things would happen, and Mr. Gentle would talk and talk and talk about said bad things and God and religion and beans.

We knew about beans because the set was full of them. It was a mound of dirt, actually, with five lopsided wooden chairs partially buried in said dirt. Along stage left, there was a pyramid of jars filled with beans; a stack of sacks of beans; and stalks of garlic. Some crazy lady in New Mexico, who was driving that fatal school bus, kept sending the stuff to him, along with lots of salsa.

As if Gentle didn't have enough problems, he had the set to contend with. A nice-looking set, actually, designed by Mark Wendland (and effectively lit by Kevin Adams). But the mound was raked; that is to say, the playing surface slanted up from the stage floor. You try walking around on a mound of diagonal dirt for two hours; it must be treacherous. (Bacon played only seven performances a week, with "selected Wednesday and Sunday matinees" played by John Dossett, who had been signed by the Roundabout to play Leon Czolgosz in *Assassins*.)

Kevin Bacon, mind you, was quite good; he did everything you could reasonably expect, other than breathing life into the play (which you couldn't reasonably expect). But he said the lines and made the moves, he was sympathetic and touching. Hopefully, he will stick around; he was a good and an intelligent actor before he left for Hollywood, and he remains so. I don't know how that "Six Degrees of Kevin Bacon" game works, but I worked on Bacon's first show—Marsha Norman's powerful *Getting Out*, back in 1979—and I also did a show with someone who acted with the great Duse. That should be good for a few degrees, anyway.

And then there was the dirt. In the play's final scene Gentle dug a ditch, burying some beans and intending to toss in some illicit photographs that showed his daughter's deformity. One of the photos—"where Ariel dances by the sea, the scarf billows in the wind behind her, and she is surrounded by a shimmering halo"—is, he realized, "an almost holy picture." Curtain.

Watching Bacon digging, with the smell of soil wafting across the footlights and lodging itself in the hapless theatregoers' nostrils, a sense of déjà vu took me back to 1972. *Dude*, it was called; a real fiasco of a musical, from two of the three authors of *Hair*. The Shuberts allowed them to tear apart the Broadway Theatre, transforming it into an environmental theatre-in-the-round, with a dirt-filled central platform serving as the stage area.

It is not a good sign when in the course of a mystically theological drama you start thinking nostalgically of bad, thirty-year-old musicals. *Dude* was strange; but, then, so was *An Almost Holy Picture*.

Carnival

City Center Encores! started its ninth season with *Carnival*, a fondly remembered musical from 1961. Fondly remembered for its highly theatrical staging, rather than for the score and book.

Carnival is one of those long-ago hits strewn through the annals of the Broadway musical. Not a classic, not a blockbuster; simply a musical of some distinction, but not too much distinction. It enthralled audiences in its day, turned a substantial profit, remained a well-cherished memory to some, and by 2000 was unknown to most. Encores! executive director Judith Daykin and artistic director Jack Viertel gave *Carnival* a somewhat grander physical mounting than is customary for Encores!, a decision that paid off with one of the most charming and entertaining evenings of the series.

How successful was the original *Carnival*? Substantially so; when it closed, it was producer David Merrick's second-most-profitable show. It opened on April 13, 1961, and ran 719 performances (three months shy of two years). Merrick voluntarily cut the run short, vacating the Imperial on December 15, 1962, so that he could have the house for *Oliver! Carnival* was still strong enough to warrant a move for the holidays to the Winter Garden, which was suddenly vacant (due to the quick failure of *Nowhere to Go but Up*). *Carnival* closed there, on January 5, 1963. The cumulative box office gross was $7,432,461, with a gross profit of slightly over $1 million on a $250,000 investment.

To put this in perspective, Merrick's *Gypsy* (1959) had a larger overall profit, of about $1,200,000; but the payback ratio was less, as it had been capitalized at $350,000. Third on Merrick's list was *Fanny* with an $850,000 profit on a $275,000 investment. It should be added that *Gypsy* and *Fanny* both benefited from motion picture sales; *Carnival* had no movie rights to sell, as it was adapted from a film in the first place.

Merrick produced his first musical, *Fanny*, in 1954. He opened three shows on Broadway in October 1957—an unprecedented act, further unprecedented in that they were all hits. He quickly realized that he could make his mark on the theatre, and remake the industry, by embarking on mass production. In February 1958 he had four shows running simultaneously—all on one block—causing West Forty-fifth Street to be temporarily dubbed Merrick Parkway.

This sort of production schedule called for an unlimited pipeline. Merrick began optioning properties left and right; many of them remained unproduced, some were ultimately produced by others. Among his many projects was a musicalization of the hit 1953 movie *Lili*. Leslie Caron and Mel Ferrer were starred; the Oscar-winning background score included the song hit "Hi-Lili, Hi-Lo," by Bronislau Kaper and Helen Deutsch.

Screenwriter Deutsch was a onetime Theatre Guild press agent. She went to Hollywood to become a screenwriter in 1944. (Her first hit was the Elizabeth Taylor vehicle *National Velvet*, which Merrick also optioned but never produced.) Merrick put Deutsch to work adapting *Lili* for the stage, pairing her with composer-lyricist Bob Merrill.

Why is *Carnival* virtually forgotten, while two harshly received shows of the year—*Camelot* and *The Unsinkable Molly Brown*—have proven more durable?

Merrill had one of the odder careers among successful Broadway songwriters. He started in Hollywood, working in radio before moving into films as a dialogue director. Merrill wrote pop songs as a sideline, composing songs like "How Much Is that Doggie in the Window?" on a toy xylophone. While at M-G-M, he worked on a proposed Doris Day movie musical, *A Saint She Ain't* (based on Eugene O'Neill's *Anna Christie*). When the project was dropped, George Abbott took it over, wrote a new book, and brought Merrill to Broadway with *New Girl in Town* (1957).

Merrick already held the musical rights for O'Neill's gentle comedy *Ah, Wilderness!* With *New Girl* a hit (albeit a minor one), Merrick signed up Merrill for *Take Me Along* (1959). This show only barely broke even and is best remembered for the massive battles between the producer and star Jackie Gleason. Merrick and Merrill hit it off, though, so the producer put the songwriter on the musical that became *Carnival*.

Work began in the winter of 1959–1960. The unheralded sleeper hit *Bye Bye Birdie* opened in April 1960, introducing to Broadway an innovative new director-choreographer. Gower Champion was a well-known nightclub and television performer, but his refreshingly creative work for *Birdie* garnered a quick call from Merrick. The pair became close associates and, simultaneously, bitter enemies; their seven musicals together in-

Cast (in order of appearance)

Jacquot David Costabile
B. F. Schlegel David Margulies
The Incomparable Rosalie Debbie Gravitte
Marco the Magnificent Douglas Sills
Lili Anne Hathaway
Grobert Philip LeStrange
Paul Berthalet Brian Stokes Mitchell
Dr. Glass Peter Jacobson
Roustabouts Lloyd Culbreath, Angelo Fraboni, Peter Gregus, Julio Monge
Bluebird Girls Sara Gettelfinger, Liz McCartney, Cynthia Sophiea, Rebecca Spencer
Carnival People Timothy Robert Blevins, Enrique Brown, Jessica Leigh Brown, Sara Gettelfinger, Blake Hammond, Emily Hsu, Kevin Ligon, Liz McCartney, Carol Lee Meadows, Tina Ou, Andrew Pacho, William Ryall, Cynthia Sophiea, Rebecca Spencer
Puppeteers Stephanie D'Abruzzo, John Tartaglia

Place: The outskirts of a town in southern Europe

cluded five hits—including two of the biggest blockbusters ever—as well as two enormous failures.

Champion set to work with Merrill and Deutsch; the first announcement I can find of *Carrot Top*, as it was then called, came in September 1960. At some point thereafter, it was determined that Deutsch—who had never written for the stage—had to go. (Hence, the ambiguous billing "based on material by Helen Deutsch," in size equivalent to that of the other authors.) Michael Stewart, Champion's librettist for *Bye Bye Birdie*, was brought in; reportedly, he was given only thirty days to write a new libretto.

Stewart came up with a compact and fast-moving book, although in later years he expressed little enthusiasm for the show, finding it emotionally false. His biggest contribution, and one he had to fight for, was to keep the puppets offstage for as long as possible; he knew they were gold, and he wanted to keep them in reserve. It is not until the end of the first act that the puppets speak; when Lili is driven to suicide, Carrot Top appears out of nowhere and distracts her from the attempt. They then have an extended sequence—five consecutive songs—at the top of the second act.

Carnival appears to have been the most financially successful production of the 1960–1961 season. Why is it virtually forgotten, while two harshly received shows of the year—*Camelot* and *The Unsinkable Molly Brown*—have proven more durable?

Three reasons. The lack of a movie sale, which helps broaden a musical's potential afterlife; the inaccessibility of the score, which contains only one near-standard; and—most important—the fact that magic is ephemeral, and *Carnival* was founded on magic. Actual magic, as in magical effects; illusory magic, as in the puppets who took on a life of their own; and stage wizardry, courtesy of Gower Champion.

The score fell into three almost equal parts. Composer-lyricist Bob Merrill was at his best with the charm material written for his waif-of-a-heroine Lili and her four puppet friends. The gentle waltz "Love Makes the World Go 'Round" served as the theme song, and fit perfectly; this was a crucial success on Merrill's part. The first act ended with Lili singing the song to the puppets, and audiences were so enchanted that they didn't miss "Hi-Lili, Hi-Lo." "Yes, My Heart" was soaringly pleasing; "Mira" was touchingly fragile; and the songs for the second-act puppet showcase—especially "Beautiful Candy"—were pure charm.

Then, there were a bunch of operetta-like songs, mostly for the puppeteer Paul. A once-great dancer crippled while fighting for the French Resistance, he is bitter; so much so, that he sings to florid, melodramatic music. The songs—with titles like "I've Got to Find a Reason" ("for living on this earth")—aren't poor, mind you. With Brian Stokes Mitchell singing them at Encores!, they were mesmerizing. But they are certainly—well, melodramatic. Lili had a similar number, "I Hate Him."

The third section of the score was musical comedy, and—like much of Merrill's other work as a composer—ranged from ordinary to crass. One of the songs worked very well, a production number called "Grand Impérial Cirque de Paris" that built and built and built until the house fell down. That is, it got the biggest ovation, night after night, in 1961 and—the night I was at Encores!—the biggest ovation in 2002. The other musical comedy songs—including a flamenco-ish dance specialty called "A Sword and a Rose and a Cape," the extraneous duet "Humming," and the novelty "Always, Always You"—are mediocre. This last provides an effective scene, in that it is sung while the magician-roué is plunging swords into his leading lady. The song itself, though, is uninspiring.

But the score hardly mattered in 1961. *Carnival* was pure magic from the very opening. Imagine this. There was no overture, no show curtain. The arriving audience saw a bare stage, a vacant lot, a gray sky on the backdrop with a scrawny tree painted on. Before the house lights went down, a scamp of a man entered and seated himself on a little bench jutting out from the stage left proscenium. He sat there quietly, whittling (if I remember correctly). As the show was about to begin, even before the house lights went down, he picked up a little melodeon—an accordion-like squeezebox—and started to play. Just one little man, playing the melody of "Love Makes the World Go 'Round."

The audience, realizing the show had started, quickly hushed. Eight measures in, the house lights went down. After another eight, the celeste joined the melodeon; then the trumpets came in, and then the trombones, and finally the rest of the orchestra. Four roustabouts—circus workers—came on, carrying a large tent pole, and inserted it in the deck. They came back with pieces of canvas; more actors came on with carnival flags and other props. As the number continued and the full orchestra played, the ensemble combined their bits and pieces to form a circus tent. This got the first ovation of the evening. (The opening sequence is significantly longer than the version included on the original cast album.) The number built and built until the full company paraded on to sing "Direct from Vienna."

Had any Broadway musical ever started in plain view, without a curtain? Possibly, but not that I know of. Had any musical started with the house lights on, or with a solitary instrument playing for sixteen measures, or with no apparent scenery? Had anyone ever seen a Broadway musical in which the cast constructed the set and moved the scenery, in plain vision, with the lights on? Probably not. Were audiences astounded by the sheer wizardry? Absolutely. Gower worked like a painter on holiday, trailing his brush through a rainbow palette. *Hello, Dolly!* (his next musical) and *42nd Street* (his last) were far more successful, but in my opinion *Carnival* was Gower at his creative best. Pure magic.

Which was totally lacking in *Carnival*'s last major production, in December 1968. On the very same City Center stage. Only six years after the original closed, *Carnival* looked tired, wispy, faded, and ready for mothballs. This despite the presence of Champion's choreography (glumly re-created by an assistant) and the original puppets, but with a new director and different scenery. Thankfully, the irrepressible Karen Morrow was on hand as The Incomparable Rosalie; but the production was so bad that it proved the final nail in the long-faltering City Center Light Opera Company.

Carnival sat dormant for many years; I have continually recommended it to producers looking for properties to revive. Jack O'Brien of the Old Globe had expressed interest but ran into problems. He wanted to revise the book, as he did for his 1994 revival of *Damn Yankees*; Francine Pascal, who as Mike Stewart's sister controls the rights, demurred. In 2000, the

folks at Disney Theatricals took an option on what would have been their first Broadway revival. They produced a February 2001 workshop of the piece, with Peter Gallagher, Sarah Uriarte Berry, and Michele Pawk playing major roles. But Disney decided against proceeding; they were apparently dissuaded, in part, when they tracked down the original source material. In Paul Gallico's novella *Love of Seven Dolls*, the Lili character is an ex-stripper who is raped by the Paul character—an embarrassing provenance for a Disney heroine.

This left *Carnival* not only back on the shelf but also with a black mark against it. Disney, with its vast resources and built-in audience, didn't want it, so who else was going to pick it up? The folks at City Center Encores!, and it proved an exceptionally happy choice.

Kathleen Marshall, the Encores! director-in-residence, knows the ins and outs of the format. Her choreography for the 1998 concert version of *Li'l Abner* was remarkable, considering time and space restrictions; and she did especially fine work on *Babes in Arms* (1999) and *Wonderful Town* (2000). Marshall used charm and enchantment to replace Gower's wizardry. A tall order, but well calculated and positively endearing.

Carnival's score benefited greatly from the concert setup. Phil Lang (of *Take Me Along*, *New Girl in Town*, and *Hello, Dolly!*) provided an uncharacteristically delicate set of orchestrations. Featured are the accordion, mandolin, celeste, and harp, instruments that benefited from being out in the open (as opposed to hidden away in the orchestra pit). Supported by a strong string section, musical director Rob Fisher created the musical equivalent of an impressionistic wash; the orchestra, surrounding the players, became part of the overall atmosphere. The whole thing sounded perfectly lovely, with Brian Stokes Mitchell adding several degrees of distinction to the ballads.

The two leads were especially good, among the finest in recent Encores! memory. Lili was performed by Anne Hathaway, a nineteen-year-old Vassar freshman best known for her appearance opposite Julie Andrews in the 2001 Disney movie *The Princess Diaries*. Here, though, she was standing on a Broadway stage surrounded by veterans, facing an informed and demanding audience. And she was lovely. Charming, sympathetic, sweet voiced, and with a smile that could lighten up a 2,700-seat auditorium. When she sang Merrill's string of puppet songs early in act 2, she wasn't an actress singing with puppets; she seemed to be one of them, an equal in their world of enchantment.

Brian Stokes Mitchell gave a masterful performance in the difficult part of Paul, the cranky curmudgeon who is able to express his humanity only through puppets. Jerry Orbach, who created this role in 1961, was equally strong in a very different portrayal. Orbach was an outsider; Mitchell—as Paul—seemed to dominate the others in an almost Machiavellian manner. Mitchell also dominated the evening with his singing. At the performance I attended, all four of his songs stopped the show cold. The songs are somewhat florid, as previously noted, but little matter.

Magic is ephemeral, and *Carnival* was founded on magic. Actual magic, as in magical effects; illusory magic, as in the puppets who took on a life of their own; and stage wizardry, courtesy of Gower Champion.

We have grown so unaccustomed to this sort of raw power—and complete control—on the musical comedy stage that Mitchell simply electrified the house.

Douglas Sills, he of *The Scarlet Pimpernel*, was somewhat less successful as Marco the Magnificent. I wonder if the role itself was the culprit; the character stands around preening with a self-satisfied gaze, behaving in an egotistical way that is nowadays hard to take. Debbie Gravitte did far better as Rosalie; she made her grand entrance, singing "Direct from Vienna," as if she was a tigress leaping out of a hat. She was able to sustain that impression, despite some decidedly lukewarm material.

David Costabile played Jacquot, the gentle soul of the piece, and garnered the evening's biggest ovation with the aforementioned "Grand Impérial Cirque de Paris." Costabile also appeared in a September 2001 concert version of Cole Porter's 1941 musical *Let's Face It*. Under the direction of Ian Marshall Fisher of London's Lost Musicals, this was an off off-Broadway, piano-only affair, and thus not included in *Broadway Yearbook*. Costabile didn't even mention it in his *Playbill* bio, but let it be said

Carnival
Opened: February 7, 2002
Closed: February 10, 2002
5 performances (and 0 previews)
Profit/Loss: Nonprofit
Carnival ($80 top) played the 2,753-seat City Center. Total
   gross for the engagement was about $673,000.

*Critical
Scorecard*

Rave 3
Favorable 3
Mixed 1
Unfavorable 1
Pan 0

that he stole the show with his irrepressibly outlandish rendition of "A Little Rumba Numba."

Hidden away among the ensemble was a rotund fellow named Blake Hammond, who enjoyed a moment in the spotlight twirling a baton and tossing it high in the flies, over the heads of cringing onstage violinists. This fellow has recently turned up in *Kiss Me, Kate*, where he garnered laughs when he got stuck in front of the curtain during a crossover; and in *The Music Man*, where he was the high tenor in the barbershop quartet. Hammond always seems to get explosive laughs. One of these days someone will give him a real part.

Despite the generally laudatory tone of the reviews, the show was roundly criticized for placing a childlike young heroine in the path of considerably older men. (The other male lead, Marco, is very clearly a rake approaching middle age.) This was not a question of writing but merely a coincidence of casting. Mitchell was, indeed, forty-four, more than double the age of Ms. Hathaway. But since when has age—or looks, for that matter—mattered in a concert version? You want, foremost, people who can sing (and hopefully act) the roles. Mitchell did both with great distinction. The age question is not inherent in the piece. Orbach was only six months older than Anna Maria Alberghetti, who created the role of Lili; when the show opened, he was twenty-five, and she was twenty-four. The road company was headed by Susan Watson (at twenty-three) and Ed Ames (at thirty-two). So carping about the age difference is a non-issue, or at least should be.

And then there were the puppets. *Carnival* revolves around Carrot Top (a gentle little puppet boy) and Horrible Henry (a lovable seal), with support from Marguerite (a grand opera singer whose favorite role is Barbara of Seville) and Renaldo (a fox who does a mean fox-trot). Lili relates to the puppets as equals, not comprehending that they are extensions of their creator, Paul. The Encores! folk decided to go with a set of puppets from the "Jim Henson Company NY Muppet Workshop." The results worked extremely well; the puppets were immense crowd pleasers, highly professional, and impeccably handled.

I must admit a prejudice in favor of the original puppets, though, which were created to Gower's specifications by a wizard from Tennessee named Tom Tichenor. I saw *Carnival* shortly after it opened, when I was eight, and I fell in love with these puppets. Seventeen years later, when Merrick cleared out his warehouse space, I was given Carrot Top and Henry as an incredibly special birthday present.

Mind you, the original puppets were presumably unavailable to Encores! There are perhaps three or four sets still in existence. (There were at least three companies of the show, and I'd guess each had two sets.) I don't suppose any of them are durable enough for stage use; my Henry could probably get through a performance or two, although the formerly vibrant green has turned the color of pea soup. Carrot Top's face is worn through, and he needs major reconstructive surgery.

The 2002 puppets looked quite different, naturally, and they were certainly the best that money could fabricate. But one of the charms of the originals was that they looked like they had been built in somebody's basement. Carrot Top has teardrops sewn on—a lyric describes his smile as being "painted with shellac"—and the buttons on his tunic are attached with safety pins. Henry's skin is a shaggy blanket, his nose is off a pool-table, and his tusks are crooked cylinders of cotton-stuffed felt.

Anne Hathaway was charming, sympathetic, and sweet voiced, with a smile that could lighten up a 2,700-seat auditorium. Brian Stokes Mitchell simply electrified the house, stopping the show cold.

The new puppets were Muppets; professional, lovable, and ready for prime time. They were also more complex than the originals. Stokes and Costabile surely didn't have time on the Encores! rehearsal schedule to learn to operate the puppets, but I don't suppose they could have in any case. The originals were simple hand puppets; these Muppets were larger, with arms operated by rods. Still, the puppets were perfect for the over-sized City Center, which is twice the size of the Imperial and most Broadway houses. If *Carnival* had transferred, as was immediately discussed, I'm sure the Muppets would have gone along and done very well. Still, there was something raffish about the rough-hewn originals; or maybe this is just misplaced sentiment.

In addition to being one of Encores! finest outings ever, press releases touted the fact that *Carnival* was the most successful, grossing almost

$675,000 over five performances. This is only a slightly helpful statistic; Encores! never previously publicized its figures for earlier shows, nor did they mention that *Carnival* was their first show at an $80 top. Still, *Carnival* looked perfectly enchanting, and a good time was had by all, myself included.

Bea Arthur on Broadway: Just between Friends

Bea Arthur spent a good quarter of a century kicking around musical comedy before turning to greener pastures in TV land. Much greener, by the millions. But before there was *Maude*, Bea was a Broadway baby, and she was very good at what she did. But roles were hard to come by; she was what you might call an abrasive Amazonian character comedienne.

Born in New York, she moved with her family to the Eastern Shore of Maryland during the Depression. (Her father ran a clothing store.) Arthur attended college and became a medical lab technician—imagine that, now, will you—before throwing down her test tubes and moving back to New York in 1947 to study with Erwin Piscator at the Dramatic Workshop of the New School in 1947. (The same school that Elaine Stritch attended.)

Arthur made her professional debut in *The Dog beneath the Skin* by W. H. Auden and Christopher Isherwood, in July 1947 at the Cherry Lane Theatre. Also in the cast was another Dramatic Workshop student, one Jean Saks, doubling as a vicar and a poet. The two were married in 1950, by which point he had changed his name to Gene. Arthur had changed her name as well, from Bernice Frankel. Bea came, presumably, as homage to the great Bea Lillie; Arthur came from her first husband, Robert Alan Aurthur. (After their divorce, Aurthur became a playwright-producer in the days of live TV. He was librettist for the 1961 Broadway musical *Kwamina* and won two 1979 Oscars as producer and coauthor of *All That Jazz*.)

Arthur spent the summer of 1953 as a comic cutup at the Pennsylvania summer-camp-for-adults Tamiment. (The same place that Barbara Cook worked.) Arthur's first notable appearance occurred the following spring, when she played Lucy Brown in Marc Blitzstein's landmark adaptation of Weill and Brecht's *The Threepenny Opera*. *Threepenny* opened off-Broadway at the Theatre de Lys in March 1954 for a limited engagement and then returned in September 1955 for a record-breaking six-and-a-half-year run. In February 1955, during the hiatus, Arthur attracted positive attention in the off-Broadway *Shoestring Revue*, where she sang a torch song by a young composer-lyricist named Sheldon Harnick. "Garbage," it was called, with the despondent chanteuse complaining that she was "calm and cool and collected." ("If I am garbage—then take me away.") She made her Broadway debut that May, when she was rushed into the tryout of a lame musical called *Seventh Heaven* **Bea was a Broadway baby, but roles were hard to come by; she was what you might call an abrasive Amazonian character comedienne.** (based on the 1927 tearjerker of the same name). Arthur replaced the middle-aged French-Canadian cocotte Fifi D'Orsay as a tart-tongued madame of a madam; one of her girls was Chita Rivera.

Arthur went back to *Threepenny*, then in April 1956 detoured to Boston with *The Ziegfeld Follies of 1956*. This was not the real *Ziegfeld Follies*, mind you; the Great Glorifier died in 1932. Rather, this was a crass revue attempting to cash in on its distinguished title, with Tallulah Bankhead as the unlikely headliner (and an even-more-unlikely Bea Arthur as Tallulah's understudy). She returned to Broadway in a small role in Herman Wouk's *Nature's Way*, which opened in October 1957 at the Coronet (now the Eugene O'Neill) and quickly closed.

More notable was her next off-Broadway role—again as a madam—in Burgess Meredith's remarkable 1958 production of *Ulysses in Nighttown*. Zero Mostel starred as Leo Bloom; joining Arthur in support were John Astin (from *Threepenny*), Carroll O'Connor, Anne Meara, and Swen Swenson (who, eight years after his death, was to contribute one of the funniest jokes to *Bea Arthur on Broadway: Just Between Friends*).

TV producer-director Norman Lear brought Arthur to Hollywood in 1958 as a regular on *The George Gobel Show*. (*Elaine Stritch at Liberty* quotes Gobel, on drinking onstage.) Arthur lasted two episodes, then it was back to more off-Broadway flops. Listen to Walter Kerr, though, discussing a May 1959, six-performance horror called *Chic*: "Beatrice Arthur, a landslide of a soubrette who has been here before in a fugitive revue or two, has a very firm, haughty way of informing you that the next line—no matter what it says—is going to be funny. Others may read lines hopefully, wistfully, or noncommittally—Miss Arthur sets her lips, adjusts her eyes so that you can't quite avoid them, and oozes comic com-

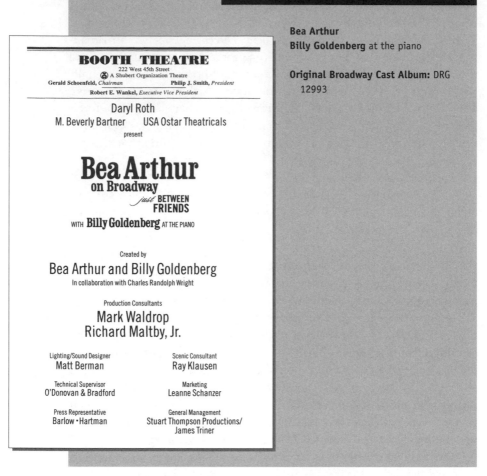

Bea Arthur
Billy Goldenberg at the piano

Original Broadway Cast Album: DRG
12993

BOOTH THEATRE
222 West 45th Street
Ⓢ A Shubert Organization Theatre
Gerald Schoenfeld, *Chairman*   Philip J. Smith, *President*
Robert E. Wankel, *Executive Vice President*

Daryl Roth
M. Beverly Bartner   USA Ostar Theatricals
present

Bea Arthur
on Broadway
just BETWEEN
FRIENDS
WITH **Billy Goldenberg** AT THE PIANO

Created by
Bea Arthur and Billy Goldenberg
In collaboration with Charles Randolph Wright

Production Consultants
Mark Waldrop
Richard Maltby, Jr.

Lighting/Sound Designer   Scenic Consultant
Matt Berman   Ray Klausen

Technical Supervisor   Marketing
O'Donovan & Bradford   Leanne Schanzer

Press Representative   General Management
Barlow • Hartman   Stuart Thompson Productions/
                                 James Triner

mand." She sure does, Mr. Kerr; that review could just as well have been written anytime between then and now.

Arthur reached what might well have been the end of her career in 1962 with Nichols and May in *A Matter of Position*, which folded in Philadelphia. (For the grisly details, see *Taller Than a Dwarf* in *Broadway Yearbook 1999–2000*.) Gene Saks, meanwhile, had become more and more prominent. Starting with a long-term replacement job in *South Pacific*, he had moved up to important character roles. In 1959 he was featured in Paddy Chayefsky's *The Tenth Man*; in 1961 he supported Julie Harris and Walter Matthau—another Dramatic Workshop classmate—in *A Shot in the Dark*. In 1962 he created the inimitable Chuckles the Chipmunk in Herb Gardner's *A Thousand Clowns*. As *A Matter of Position* faltered, Saks moved into directing with the comedy *Enter Laughing*, adapted by Joseph Stein from Carl Reiner's autobiography.

Arthur and Saks adopted a child in 1961; they adopted a second son in 1964. With Arthur nearing forty and Saks earning an increasingly good living, she started to ease out of performing. However, Joe Stein (of *Enter Laughing*) and Sheldon Harnick (of "Garbage") were writing a new musical. Fred Coe was producing; he had also produced *A Thousand Clowns* and *A Matter of Position* (which was written by Harnick's wife at the time, Elaine May). They all, apparently, decided that Bea needed to play Yente the Matchmaker in *Fiddler on the Roof*. Right? Of course right.

Arthur's role was considerably shortened by the time the show reached Broadway in September 1964, but she made a strong impression. This led to her first (and last) major role on Broadway, as Vera Charles—bosom buddy to the star—in the 1966 musical *Mame*. Arthur was devastatingly funny and won a featured Tony Award for her efforts. (The show was directed by Saks, but Arthur more than pulled her own weight.) Ready for full-fledged stardom Arthur was given the title role in the 1968 musical *A Mother's Kisses* (also directed by Saks). This one was a disaster, closing —once again—prior to Broadway. That was, effectively, the end of Arthur's theatre career.

Fortunately for Arthur and a vast audience of future fans, Norman Lear—of *The George Gobel Show*—called. He was doing a little sitcom called *All in the Family*, which had revolutionized popular entertainment and made household names out of Bea's former colleagues Carroll O'Connor (from *Ulysses in Nighttown*) and Jean Stapleton. Would Bea come out to the coast to do a guest shot?

She did, for a September 1971 episode in which she played the role of Stapleton's liberal cousin

> Arthur told us how she would love to do *Gypsy*; but she sang "Some People," with a heap of acting thrown in, and you thought—my God, this would be excruciating.

Maude. Her battle with O'Connor's Archie Bunker resulted, overnight, in the commissioning of a new series. *Maude* went on the air in 1972, and Arthur—after twenty-five nearly anonymous years in the New York theatre—was an instant celebrity. After six years (and an Emmy Award) for *Maude*, Arthur went on to seven years (and another Emmy Award) for *The Golden Girls*.

Arthur's second hit series went off the air in 1992, leaving her with enormous fame, gobs of money, the kids out of the house, and a husband long gone. (Saks walked out for a younger woman in 1978.) If the theatre is in your blood—and despite all those years in Hollywood, Arthur was first and foremost a stage performer—you eventually head back to Broadway.

Arthur made numerous appearances at charity benefits throughout the 1980s and 1990s, working with pianist Billy Goldenberg. A twenty-minute stint at an AIDS benefit in 2000 convinced them to extend their act to a full evening. *And Then There's Bea*—the title suggested by the theme song from *Maude*—got off to a rocky start when it opened in April 2001 at the Guthrie Theatre in Minneapolis; Arthur literally fell from the stage, injuring her ankle. (She worked this into the act, as an explanation of why she was doing the show barefoot.) The show embarked on a tour of thirty cities, to moderate business, before they brought it to Broadway with a new and unwieldy title.

Sad to say, it wasn't very good. Ms. Arthur is a dedicated performer and a talented clown, and you'd like to see her efforts pay off. But the

evening was pointless. The proceedings began with the star entering—shoeless—and reciting a lamb recipe. That is, a recipe for cooking lamb. ("I start by removing all the fat, and you know that thin filament that sort of covers the whole thing? And then I whip up this mayonnaise-like mixture of olive oil, Dijon mustard, ground ginger, garlic and either rosemary or basil.") Why? I don't know. She soon called out Goldenberg, a little old character man-type with concave shoulders from decades and decades of shrugging, no doubt.

"Billy, I'd like to sing a song," she said, and she did. "Fun to Be Fooled," a jaunty old ditty by Harold Arlen, Ira Gershwin, and Yip Harburg. A good job of it, too; light and cheery and professional. Arthur moved on to some negligible patter, then into a suggestive novelty song called "What Can You Get a Nudist for Her Birthday?" (by Alan Leclerq). Amusing, but what was the point?

She then went on to stories about her early years as an actor, in hit-or-miss fashion. She talked about her hapless, early auditions. She told us, repeatedly, about her "long brown hair and enormous breasts." When she got around to *Fiddler on the Roof*, she told us about working with that genius Jerry Robbins. ("He was really a dreadful human being.")

Then she gave us another *Fiddler* story. About Pia Zadora. Not Zero Mostel, or Hal Prince, or one of the authors; but Pia Zadora, a cast replacement in a minor role. It wasn't even a remembered anecdote, really;

Bea Arthur on Broadway: Just between Friends
Opened: February 17, 2002
Closed: April 14, 2002
65 performances (and 23 previews)
Profit/Loss: Profit
Bea Arthur on Broadway ($66.25 top) was scaled to a
   potential gross of $362,923 at the 781-seat Booth
   Theatre. Weekly grosses averaged about $156,000, hitting
   $238,000 the week after the opening but quickly
   plummeting below $100,000 (with a $49,000 week
   impelling the producers to cancel the announced
   extension). Total gross for the eleven-week run was
   $1,715,877. Attendance was about 54 percent, with the
   box office grossing about 43 percent of dollar-capacity.

TONY AWARD NOMINATION
Special Theatrical Event

Critical Scorecard

Rave 0
Favorable 4
Mixed 1
Unfavorable 1
Pan 4

just an overripe joke of the personal insult variety. Why Pia Zadora, you might ask? Was it in some way important to Arthur, personally, to ridicule Pia Zadora? Arthur simply sounded vindictive, in an ugly sort of way.

We learned that Angela Lansbury has a mouth like a longshoreman, and that some unnamed Broadway actress Arthur worked with had terrible body odor. She also told several extended jokes that some might consider off-color. The one about the boy and his boyfriend and his mother and a silver soup ladle; another about a taxi driver and a nun named Ken. Funny, perhaps; but what do they have to do with Bea Arthur, just between friends? The star described her evening as "a collection of songs and stories that I've saved up over the years that mean a lot to me, that I would like to share with you." One certainly hopes that these stories do not represent the peaks of her experience.

The material had several sets of thumbprints on it. Arthur and Goldenberg received "created by" billing. Charles Randolph Wright—author of *Blue*, which received a 2001 off-Broadway production by the Roundabout—was given "in collaboration with" billing, in type smaller than that afforded the marketing person. Mark Waldrop and Richard Maltby Jr. received duo billing—in type larger than that of the producers—as production consultants. Waldrop and Maltby are not a team, mind you. This billing stream indicates numerous creative types passing through a revolving door, displeasing the star, and being sent packing (but retaining billing and a small royalty). It might well begin to explain why the evening seemed to meander vaguely. After eighty-five minutes Arthur returned to her lamb recipe, suitably framing the evening but pointing up its pointlessness.

Still, Arthur was very sharp. Not in her singing, but in her line readings; Walter Kerr had it right, back in 1959.

The evening's high point came about a third of the way through.
Arthur gave a chilling rendition of "Pirate Jenny" from *The Threepenny
Opera*. Close to spellbinding, it was, but the evening went downhill from
there. Most of the songs were unsuited to Arthur, at least in 2002 at the
age of seventy-eight. She simply couldn't hit too many of the notes, and
those she hit she couldn't sustain; so she just talked and rushed her way
through. (With her gruff, low tones and rushed delivery, she sounded un-
cannily like composer Billy Finn.) Arthur told us how she would love to
do *Gypsy*; but she sang "Some People," with a heap of acting thrown in,
and you thought—my God, this would be excruciating. She also tried to
sing "Fifty Percent"—from Gold-
enberg's only Broadway musical
as a composer, *Ballroom* (lyric by
Marilyn and Alan Bergman)—but it lacked power. Arthur simply couldn't
sustain the notes. Goldenberg was very good for Arthur; he followed her
erratic tempos and knew when she needed support with the melody. This
was a performance not for the ages but for the aged.

**This was a performance not for the ages
but for the aged.**

It is unfair and unfortunate that Ms. Arthur was compared with her
contemporaries Barbara Cook and Elaine Stritch; but there they were,
three septuagenarians in search of an audience, all on Broadway at the
very same time. As Neil Simon once said, that's the way things crumble,
cookie-wise. Cook's *Mostly Sondheim* was not just a cabaret song recital; it
was a work of art in itself. The same can be said, even more so, for *Elaine
Stritch at Liberty*. (Stritch opened on Broadway four nights later, but most
critics and hard-core musical comedy fans had seen her sold-out off-
Broadway engagement.)

Consider the material itself. Stritch built to "The Ladies Who Lunch."
Cook built to "Ice Cream." Bea Arthur built to "The Man in the Moon
Is a Lady." And that was the difference between these three one-person
shows. *Bea Arthur on Broadway* was for fans, and for fans only.

Elaine Stritch at Liberty

E laine Stritch stormed onto Broadway in *At Liberty*, receiving just about the best set of critical love letters since Lena Horne did much the same thing with *The Lady and Her Music* in 1981. Fitting company. Stritch strode on, a star down to her fingertips, and—like poor Johnny One-Note, of Rodgers and Hart fame—"sang out with gusto and just overlorded the place." I never knew, precisely, what "overlorded" meant. Until I saw *Elaine Stritch at Liberty*.

Stritch came at the end of an unprecedented string of five one-person shows. John Leguizamo opened his *Sexaholix* in December; Barbara Cook brought *Mostly Sondheim* to Lincoln Center in January; and February saw Kevin Bacon in *An Almost Holy Picture*; *Bea Arthur on Broadway: Just between Friends*; and finally Elaine. (The Messrs. Leguizamo and Bacon were spry youngsters of thirty-seven and forty-three, respectively; the ladies, as previously mentioned, ranged from seventy-four to seventy-eight.)

This was not only five one-person shows in a season, mind you; this was five in a row. And a sixth, *The Mystery of Charles Dickens*, was on the way. (I don't include Alan Alda and *QED* in the mix, although I suppose I could; there was a second character flitting around the edges of that play, but she had less to do than Barbara's Wally Harper or Bea's Billy Goldenberg.) One might carp about pro-

> **An unforgettably extraordinary, gut-wrenchingly exhilarating tour de force which proved that a one-person show on a bare stage can be as pertinent and entertaining as the biggest extravaganza on Broadway.**

ducers trying to foist off simplistic entertainments with low production costs at outrageously high ticket prices (Cook, $60; Bacon, $65; Arthur, $66.25; Leguizamo, $76.25; Stritch, $85). But three of these attractions were easily among the season's finest Broadway experiences, and four of

Elaine Stritch

Original Broadway Cast Album: DRG
12994

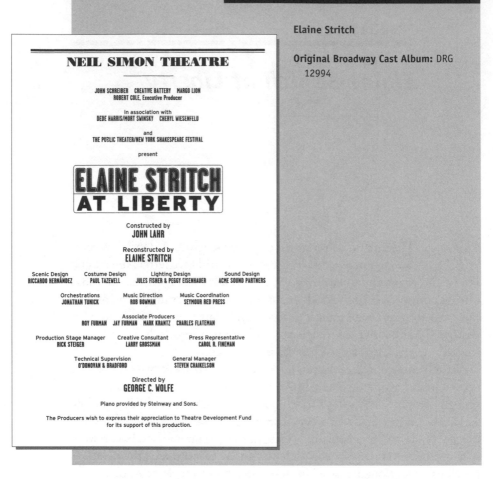

NEIL SIMON THEATRE

JOHN SCHREIBER   CREATIVE BATTERY   MARGO LION
ROBERT COLE, Executive Producer

in association with
DEDE HARRIS/MORT SWINSKY   CHERYL WIESENFELD

and
THE PUBLIC THEATER/NEW YORK SHAKESPEARE FESTIVAL

present

**ELAINE STRITCH
AT LIBERTY**

Constructed by
JOHN LAHR

Reconstructed by
ELAINE STRITCH

Scenic Design	Costume Design	Lighting Design	Sound Design
RICCARDO HERNÁNDEZ	PAUL TAZEWELL	JULES FISHER & PEGGY EISENHAUER	ACME SOUND PARTNERS

Orchestrations	Music Direction	Music Coordination
JONATHAN TUNICK	ROB BOWMAN	SEYMOUR RED PRESS

Associate Producers
ROY FURMAN   JAY FURMAN   MARK KRANTZ   CHARLES FLATEMAN

Production Stage Manager	Creative Consultant	Press Representative
RICK STEIGER	LARRY GROSSMAN	CAROL R. FINEMAN

Technical Supervision	General Manager
O'DONOVAN & BRADFORD	STEVEN CHAIKELSON

Directed by
GEORGE C. WOLFE

Piano provided by Steinway and Sons.

The Producers wish to express their appreciation to Theatre Development Fund
for its support of this production.

---

them were commercial successes. Give me *Liberty*, *Sondheim*, and Legui-zamo, I'll cheerily forgo *A Thousand Clowns*, *By Jeeves*, and *45 Seconds from Broadway*.

According to the calendar, Stritch was the last to come along; in fact, she preceded them all. *Elaine Stritch at Liberty* originated off-Broadway, at the New York Shakespeare Festival's Newman Theatre. The November 7 opening was greeted with the same type of response that *A Chorus Line* received in the same space twenty-six years earlier, resulting in an immediately sold-out engagement. Thus, the critics viewed John and Barbara and Kevin and Bea with the incomparable Elaine, who had not yet opened on Broadway, as a yardstick. When they finally saw Stritch in her new digs, they welcomed her back with even better reviews than she had received downtown.

Was *Elaine Stritch at Liberty* that good? Yes, it was. An unforgettably ex-traordinary, gut-wrenchingly exhilarating tour de force. An evening with Elaine Stritch proved, among other things, that a one-person show on a bare stage with no props or costumes can be as pertinent and entertaining as the biggest extravaganza on Broadway.

Well, there was a costume. Stritch appeared in a pair of black tights, an oversized white shirt (untucked), and some white pearls. Nothing up her sleeve, just talent. And there was a prop, one prop. A bar stool. Stritch carried it on at the top of the show and lugged it into place even before she turned to acknowledge the tidal wave of entrance applause.

This was a keen touch, one of the many that the lady and author John Lahr and director George C. Wolfe displayed in the course of the evening. Here was a show about life, liberty, and the pursuit of musical comedy; but we saw, at the start, that it was *work*. Hard work. Stritch was not only pro-viding the entertainment for two and a half hours, as she had been doing for fifty-five years. She was doing the heavy lifting as well, as she had been doing onstage—and offstage—for even longer. Effortless entertaining = gruelingly hard work + heavy lifting = Elaine Stritch.

A word about John Lahr. Drama critic, novelist, and playwright, he has always specialized in insightful studies of high-strung theatrical types. He has written many perceptive profiles for the *New Yorker*, as well as full-length biographies of Joe Orton (*Prick Up Your Ears*) and Bert Lahr (*Notes on a Cowardly Lion*). The latter, of course, was John Lahr's enor-mously talented and famously neurotic father; an even harder nut to crack, if you will, than Elaine Stritch.

The billing page read "constructed by John Lahr, reconstructed by Elaine Stritch." We can take that to mean that Stritch dictated her mem-oirs, Lahr came up with the format and wrote a script, then Stritch re-worked it all. And then Wolfe, who is himself keenly talented, wrapped it up and focused it. The billing page, on Broadway but not at the Public, also credited Larry Grossman—Stritch's neighbor, and the composer of *Grind* and *A Doll's Life*—as "creative consultant."

One skinny lady on one big stage, work and sweat and stardust. Star-dom is in the eyes of the beholder, of course; and those who beheld Stritch were uniformly smitten. Oddly enough, the record doesn't support the label. Elaine Stritch, musical comedy star? Not precisely. They wrote musicals for her once, once upon a time; twice upon a time, technically. But her last vehicle closed in 1962.

Stritch made her first New York performance in 1944 at the age of nineteen, playing a tiger and a cow in *Bobino*, a children's show at the Adelphi Theatre on West Fifty-fourth Street (later the George Abbott). She had her first real Broadway role in *Loco*, which opened in October

1946 and ran a month. Stritch discussed much of her career in *At Liberty*, but she didn't mention this comedy, produced and directed by the infamously maniacal Jed Harris. She went directly into a replacement job in another negligible comedy, *Made in Heaven*, which opened a week after *Loco* and ran ten weeks.

Stritch's first major role came in April 1947, when she played one of the title characters in *Three Indelicate Ladies*. But this turkey—which starred Bela Lugosi, of all people—shuttered after the first week of the tryout. Stritch attracted favorable attention that December, when she opened in the revue *Angel in the Wings*. She played comedy sketches, mostly—including a deft impersonation of the then-famous singer Hildegarde—but she also had a

song, the irrepressible novelty number "Civilization." ("Bongo, bongo, bongo, I don't want to leave the Congo," it goes.) This was included in *At Liberty*, with Stritch essaying what she told us was the original choreography. I didn't see her do "Civilization" in 1947, as I was unborn at the time, but it was quite something in 2002. Most remarkably, her performance in 2002 seemed to be that of a twenty-two-year-old soubrette.

Angels kept Stritch gainfully employed for its nine-month run. She spent the 1948–1949 season absent from Broadway. In August 1949, she landed the ingenue lead in the Johnny Mercer musical *Texas, L'il Darlin'*; by the time it reached Broadway in November, though, she had been replaced. She finished the decade in William Douglas Hume's comedy *Yes, M'Lord*; a big hit in London, a ten-week flop in New York. Mind you, Stritch was not, as of yet, knocking them dead. Most critics who bothered to mention her in these shows described her as frenetic, overly energetic, and way too broad. In his review of *Yes, M'Lord*, Robert Garland (of the *Journal-American*) memorably stated that Elaine Stritch and Hugh Kelly—who played her fiancé—"don't act up to their coiffures."

Stritch landed a major hit in 1950, when she was hired as standby for Ethel Merman in *Call Me Madam*. No stage time, but a steady paycheck.

She came into her own singing the pseudo-striptease "Zip" in the January 1952 revival of Rodgers and Hart's *Pal Joey*. (*At Liberty* contained a lengthy set piece about how Stritch shuttled between New York and New Haven so that she could hold both jobs. This contained a logistical error; she told us six times that she waited until 7:30—a half hour before curtain—to make sure that Merman was safely in her dressing room. The Broadway curtain time in those days, though, was 8:40. A very small inaccuracy, but one that she kept repeating so many times per performance that you'd have thought somebody would catch it.)

Stritch's *Pal Joey* role was brief, with only one scene and one song, but she received enthusiastic personal notices all around. No Tony Award, though; it went to Helen Gallagher, who was more prominently featured in the same *Pal Joey*. Stritch quickly left the show to take Merman's role in the road company of *Call Me Madam*. Stritch played Merman for ten months—the one and only successful starring role of her musical comedy career. Until 2002, fifty years later.

Stritch returned to Broadway in October 1954 in a featured role in a short-lived revival of Rodgers and Hart's *On Your Toes*. (Rodgers reached into his songbook to interpolate "You Took Advantage of Me" for her, and she slayed 'em.) She returned to Broadway in March 1955 in a featured role in a major award-winning hit: William Inge's *Bus Stop*. Stritch earned a Tony nomination; she lost, to Una Merkle for *The Ponder Heart*. Her next Broadway show was the comedy *The Sin of Pat Muldoon*, a one-week flop in March 1957. Stritch finally got her big break in 1958. Walter Kerr—even then one of Broadway's finest critics—wrote and directed a musical satire of the silent picture era, and Stritch got the lead. But the show, *Goldilocks*, was no good. They fired one of the two stars during the tryout—not Stritch, the other one. The show was a quick failure, nevertheless, closing after twenty weeks.

Noël Coward paid Stritch a visit during the out-of-town tryout. "Take heart, Stritchie," he said consolingly (as related in *At Liberty*). "Anyone who doesn't do a double take when she's asked to dance with a nine-foot bear is my kind of actress." So he wrote Stritch a new vehicle, three years later. But the show, *Sail Away*, was no good. They fired one of the two stars during the tryout—not Stritch, the other one. Still, the show was a quick failure, closing after twenty-one weeks. Stritch earned another Tony nomination; she lost, to Anna Maria Alberghetti and Diahann Carroll (who tied for *Carnival* and *No Strings*). And that was Stritch's second and final star vehicle.

She was back on Broadway in April 1963, as Martha in Edward Albee's *Who's Afraid of Virginia Woolf?* (Uta Hagen played six performances a week; Stritch was the second of three actresses who played the matinees.)

She left Albee for *The Time of the Barracudas*, an October 1963 play that closed during the tryout.

In the forty years since Stritch left *Virginia Woolf*, she has made only three Broadway appearances, with only a single appearance in a new musical. But it was an important one: *Company*, in 1970. Stephen Sondheim provided Stritch with the searing "Ladies Who Lunch"; the combination of song and singer is near legendary. Was it a starring role? No. This was an ensemble piece. (Stritch had two solos.) She did receive special billing; Dean Jones, who played the hero, was listed first, followed by Barbara Barrie (in the same size), then eleven other actors, in a smaller type. At the bottom of the column, in the same size as Jones and Barrie, came "and Elaine Stritch." Her agent, presumably, insisted that she get better billing than the others, as the only cast member who had ever starred on Broadway.

Stritch received a Tony nomination again; she lost, to Helen Gallagher again. This was a year with the strangest Tony Award eligibility jumble ever. Stritch was nominated as best actress, as was Susan Browning, one of the clustered names in the middle of the *Company* billing list. Gallagher starred in the 1971 revival of *No, No, Nanette*—clearly, on both the billing page and the stage—and deserved the award. Would Stritch have won in the supporting category? Nominees Barbara Barrie and Pamela Myers—another two of the *Company* ladies—probably wouldn't have bested Stritch. It would have been a close race against Patsy Kelly, a sixty-one-year-old, tough-as-nails comedienne with as much baggage as Stritch, who won for *Nanette*.

Stritch left *Company* in 1971 to take the show to London and was not back on Broadway for more than twenty years, an absence caused, in part, by her continued alcoholic unreliability (as discussed, at length, in *At Liberty*). She made a number of films over the years, twenty or so; she also paid occasional visits to TV land, including the Roz Russell role in the 1960 sitcom *My Sister Eileen*. But Stritch was principally a creature of the stage, and the fates decreed that she spend most of her career out of the follow spot.

> **Stritch appeared in a pair of black tights and an oversized white shirt. Nothing up her sleeve, just talent.**

She returned to Broadway in a virtually nonsinging role in the 1994 revival of *Show Boat*, directed by *Company*'s Hal Prince. Her only subsequent Broadway appearance was in the 1996 revival of *A Delicate Balance*, in which she gave a striking dramatic performance. Stritch earned another Tony nomination; she lost, to Zoe Caldwell for *Master Class*.

So, yes, Stritch was clearly a Broadway musical comedy star, and could rationally be described as such even before *At Liberty* made that question moot. But a star, technically, without the billing.

Elaine Stritch at Liberty
Opened: February 21, 2002
Closed: May 26, 2002
69 performances (and 11 previews)
Profit/Loss: Profit
Elaine Stritch at Liberty ($85 top) was scaled to a potential
    gross of $425,379 (for a five-performance week) at the
    1,328-seat Neil Simon Theatre. Weekly grosses averaged
    about $313,000, falling below $300,000 midway through
    the run but building to $398,000 in the final week. Total
    gross for the sixteen-week run was $5,000,248.
    Attendance was about 80 percent, with the box office
    grossing about 73 percent of dollar-capacity.

TONY AWARD NOMINATION
Special Theatrical Event (WINNER)

NEW YORK DRAMA CRITICS CIRCLE AWARD
Special Citation (WINNER)

DRAMA DESK AWARDS
Outstanding Solo Performance: Elaine Stritch (WINNER)
Outstanding Book of a Musical: John Lahr and Elaine
    Stritch (WINNER)

*Critical
Scorecard*

Rave 9
Favorable 1
Mixed 0
Unfavorable 0
Pan 0

If Lena Horne's aforementioned show was entitled *The Lady and Her Music*, Stritch's could well be called *The Lady and Her Bottle*. She told us, early on, how she discovered whisky sours when she was thirteen. One drink, and she dominated the dinner table. She tells us how she tingled and glowed, explaining it with the song "This Is All Very New to Me," from *Plain and Fancy*. (A song introduced by—guess who?—Barbara Cook.) Stritch used the song to describe the wonder of her newfound love—the bottle—but she sang it with the tentative innocence of a teenager. You could see it in her face, and it was uncanny; the cares, the weathered lines, seemed to disappear. She next delivered "I Want a Long Time Daddy," a risqué novelty song, with the air of a sixteen-year-old who knew the lines were shocking but didn't know why. (Jonathan Tunick—who was an unseen star of the evening—gave this a wild orchestration, as if it came out of the score of *Gypsy*.) Stritch sang Sondheim's "Broadway Baby" as if she was a twenty-year-old kid walking off her tired feet pounding Forty-second Street.

Stritch was always in the moment, delivering the material in the context of her story; that was the inner secret of the show. This was not some seventy-six-year-old woman up there, singing her heart out. (Except when she got to "I'm Still Here." This contained a great touch from Wolfe and lighting wizards Jules Fisher and Peggy Eisenhauer. Stritch stood framed by the inner proscenium of tarnished gold, flanked by twin silhouettes from crisscrossed lights hidden in the upstage wings.)

At *Liberty* made clear the problem with Stritch's career. She always did the best she could with the material she had; but she never had good material, except for one song in *Company*. For most of her fifty-odd years in show business, she simply did the best she could with subpar parts. (Compare this with Barbara Cook, who had *Candide* and *The Music Man* and *She Loves Me*.) What Stritch needed, and didn't have, and finally found in *Elaine Stritch at Liberty*, was a character to play; a well-conceived, well-constructed character that you could actually believe in. The character was herself, as it happened. Happily, she had the art and the stamina to play it.

Act 2 unraveled somewhat; but, then, so did Stritch's career at that point in the narrative. But it didn't much matter. After more than two treasurable hours, Stritch dragged her bar stool downstage.

Here was a show about life, liberty, and the pursuit of musical comedy; but we saw, at the start, that it was *work*. Hard work. Stritch was doing the heavy lifting.

"So what's this all been about, then? This existential problem in tights?" (This line, parenthetically, sounded less like the real Elaine Stritch and more like the real John Lahr.) The answer: "I've been reclaiming parts of my life that I wasn't there for." That's some life, and aren't we fortunate that she did the reclaiming in the spotlight? This resulted in the most entertaining show since *The Producers*, and the most exhilarating theatrical event since— well, since I don't know when.

During her opening salvo, Stritch told us: "Good news—I have a terrific acceptance speech for the Tonys. The bad news, I have had it for forty-five years." This was five minutes into the show, in February, but it was already very clear that she would be needing that speech come June. At which point the speech would be cut off midstream by the gods of the network control booth. But let's leave *Elaine Stritch at Liberty* on a triumphant note. And fittingly so.

Metamorphoses

There is life, theatrically speaking, outside of New York, and there always has been. I'm talking artists, here; accomplished directors and producers who have established themselves beyond question but—due to chance, circumstance, or choice—were infrequent visitors to Broadway. Margo Jones, for example, who pioneered the regional theatre movement in Dallas and was happy to remain in Texas. (She did visit Broadway to direct three early plays by her discovery Tennessee Williams, including *The Glass Menagerie*). Zelda Fichhandler, founder of Washington's Arena Stage. Nikos Psacharopoulos, of Williamstown Theater Festival. Jon Jory of the Actors Theatre of Louisville.

Add Mary Zimmerman to the list. Born in Lincoln, Nebraska, she went to Northwestern University in Evanston, Illinois, as an undergraduate; stayed on as a graduate student; and became an assistant professor of performance studies. (Frank Galati, Zimmerman's mentor, was also on the faculty.) Zimmerman is also an Artistic Associate of **There is life, theatrically speaking, outside of New York.** both the Goodman Theatre (in Chicago) and the Seattle Repertory Theatre. She burst on the avant-garde theatre scene in 1992 with her adaptation of *Tales from the Arabian Nights* at the Lookingglass Theatre in Chicago. This was followed by *The Notebooks of Leonardo da Vinci*; *Journey to the West*, a Chinese-Buddhist tale; *Mirror of the Invisible World*, from a twelfth-century Persian poem; *Eleven Rooms of Proust*; *S/M*, based on the life of the Marquis de Sade; and a successful adaptation of *The Odyssey*.

Two of her early plays made brief visits to New York in 1994. *Arabian Nights* played forty-eight performances at Manhattan Theatre Club's Stage II; *Leonardo da Vinci* played four performances at the John Jay The-

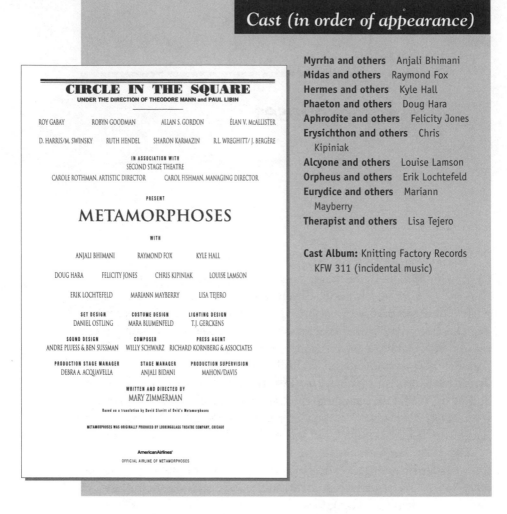

atre as part of Lincoln Center's Serious Fun festival. Neither made much of a mark, nor did her two visits to Shakespeare in the Park, with *Henry VIII* (in 1997, the final production in the Public's ten-year Shakespeare Marathon) and *Measure for Measure* (in 2001, starring Billy Crudup and Joe Morton).

But Zimmerman's work was highly acclaimed elsewhere. So much so that she won a MacArthur Fellowship in 1998. That's the so-called genius award, unrestricted cash grants to "talented individuals who have shown extraordinary originality and dedication in their creative pursuits, and a marked capacity for self-direction." The MacArthur clearly makes a difference financially; a major drawback with being a great theatre director outside of Broadway is that you live in a world of relatively small fees, with little if any royalties. Zimmerman's MacArthur Fellowship carried an award of $240,000 (paid over five years). This gives the creator financial freedom to create.

Metamorphoses predated the MacArthur. It was first staged for two weekends in 1996 as a student production at Northwestern, under the title *Six Myths*. (Ultimately it was expanded to nine myths, with a tenth included in a brief pantomime.) Zimmerman started with tales from the ancient Roman poet Ovid (43 B.C.–A.D. 17), as translated by David Slavitt. Her concept, from the beginning, was to place her work in a pool of water. The pool proved to be the coup de théatrè that elevated *Metamorphoses* to unlikely heights.

Zimmerman brought the piece to Chicago's Lookingglass Theatre Company, of which she is an ensemble member. Lookingglass—which had already produced four of her works—mounted the first professional production of *Metamorphoses* at the Ivanhoe Theatre in 1998. Wildly successful, the limited engagement was extended to eight months. Further productions were staged at Berkeley Repertory Theatre (in California); Seattle Repertory Theatre; and in April 2000 at the Mark Taper Forum, where it won five Los Angeles Drama Critics Circle Awards.

The continued success of *Metamorphoses* brought it to New York, with the Second Stage Company producing it at their off-Broadway house on October 9, 2001. The play was rapturously received by theatregoers still numbed by the events of the prior month, with many critics specifically citing the play's sudden relevance. ("Though Ms. Zimmerman produced the play in 1998 in Chicago," said Ben Brantley in the *New York Times*, "it could surely never have had the resonance it acquired in the aftermath of Sept. 11.") The run was extended through year's end, and a commercial transfer

> **Metamorphoses was rapturously received by theatregoers still numbed by the events of the last month, with many critics specifically citing the play's sudden relevance.**

was arranged to the Circle in the Square. As is typically the case nowadays, ten producers and $1.7 million were needed to finance this ten-character, one-set—or, rather, one-swimming-pool—play.

The central stage area of the Circle in the Square was overtaken by water, a thirty-foot wading pool. The depth ranged from several inches to a foot and a half, allowing the performers different depths for different effects. The watery rectangle was bordered by a pool deck, surrounded on three sides by the front row of seats. (Poolside ticket buyers were warned, with towels provided by the management.) Along the upstage wall of the space were a large set of wooden entrance doors on one side and a multipurpose platform for the gods on the other.

The unusually shaped theatre always proved difficult, scenery-wise, during the decades when it was operated by the nonprofit Circle in the Square. A companion to the group's off-Broadway home base on Bleecker Street, it opened in 1972 as the Circle in the Square–Joseph E. Levine Theatre; Colleen Dewhurst starred in a memorable revival of Eugene O'Neill's *Mourning Becomes Electra*. Since the company went bankrupt in 1996, the problematic thrust stage has become the theatre's greatest asset. The most recent bookings—*Not about Nightingales, True West, The Rocky Horror Show*, and *Metamorphoses*—had inventive designers who took advantage of the space. Here you can do things, scenically, that would be impossible at any other Broadway theatre.

Metamorphoses displayed flashes of remarkable theatricality. Take the fifth myth, for example. The fourth myth—that of the musician Orpheus—ended with a music stand upturned in the pool. As at the end of

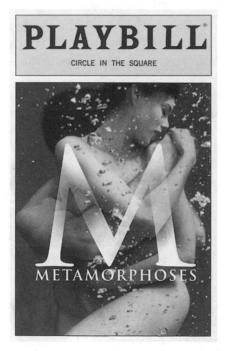

the previous myths, cast members entered to clear the old props and set the new. One of the actors—a puckish fellow named Doug Hara—grabbed hold of the music stand and climbed out of the pool. As he did so, he caught sight of something in the water. He stood, stooped over like a crane, at the side of the pool. He stood and stared, and stared and stared and stared at —what? His reflection? He remained, mesmerized, for what must have been a full ninety seconds. As time passed, clumps of theatregoers started to laugh as they got the joke; eventually, applause broke out (with the actor still staring in the pool). Finally another actor came on with a potted plant—a narcissus, naturally—as Hara exited and Zimmerman rolled on seamlessly into the tale of the incestuous Myrrha.

The seventh myth, too, was especially refreshing in its mixture of olden tale with modern sensibility. Out came Mr. Hara again, wearing sunglasses and bright yellow swim trunks, floating on a bright yellow raft. With a Jungian therapist at poolside, this fellow complained about parental neglect. "I went to an expensive school and there were a lot of boys there who were, you know, sons of the rich and famous. One day we were all on the playground and this one kid, Epaphus, he goes to me, 'So Phaeton blah blah who's your father, what does he do? blah blah' you know. And I say my father is the sun and he says 'Tell me another' and I say 'He's the sun, he's Phoebus Apollo' and he just basically trampled me, just basically beat the s*** out of me. Like I was lying."

Apollo offers his son one wish, to make amends. "There's only one thing I want, I mean it's obvious, right? I say, 'give me the keys to your car.' " Phaeton climbs into the chariot and, inevitably, sets the earth on fire.

Hara appears to be quite a talent. A member of Lookingglass since 1991, he looked like a twenty-something version of Theodore Cleaver (aka "the Beaver") mixed with Matthew Broderick. He was the only cast member, in my view, who connected directly with the audience; even when he was playing Eros (Cupid), dressed solely in a pair of white wings. (It must have gotten mighty cold for these actors, jumping in and out of the pool all night.)

The other performers, like Hara, were longtime associates of Ms. Zimmerman; three of them had joined the piece as college students at Northwestern in 1996. "Because of the way I work, it requires that I collaborate with the people I've already worked with," Zimmerman told Robert Simonson of *Playbill*. (Zimmerman goes into rehearsals without a script, allowing the action and text to develop improvisationally.) There are advantages to this approach, but it tends to make the actors vehicles of the director's vision rather than interpretive performers. This resulted in an overall sense of sameness, from everyone except Mr. Hara.

Most of the text seemed merely functional narration. There was at least one lovely stretch of dialogue, for the two narrators of the Eros and Psyche dream.

> ANSWERER   The soul wanders in the dark, until it finds love. And so, wherever our love goes, there we find our soul.
>
> QUESTIONER   It always happens?
>
> ANSWERER   If we're lucky. And if we let ourselves be blind.
>
> QUESTIONER   Instead of watching out?
>
> ANSWERER   Instead of always watching out.

As for the rest of the evening? Well, I was impressed but not especially moved. Call me cynical, but "story theatre"–type improvisation—actors turning themselves into birds and trees and stone statues while other actors narrate and provide simplistic effects—rarely holds my attention for more than fifteen minutes at a time. The Narcissus and Phaeton segments were arresting enough to intrigue me; most of the rest of the evening did

not. The Alcyon and Ceyx dream, for example, in which King Ceyx goes
to sea despite his wife's misgivings and is drowned in a tempestuous storm
(which doused a fair number of people in the front row). At the height
of the storm came a roar of thunder and a flash of lightning—coming
from a crystal chandelier (!) hanging above the pool. Moments like this
perked me up, but I spent too much of the evening watching actors in
cloaks narrating ancient tales while others waded through the water.

But don't go by me. I wasn't keen on *Paul Sills' Story Theatre*, Broadway's last dose of the stuff. (Can it be more than thirty years ago!) Sills
was another one of those innovative Chicago theatre folk, cofounder of
Compass Players and The Second City and author of *Improvisation for the
Theatre*. *Story Theatre* reinterpreted tales mostly from the Brothers Grimm,
providing an enchanting program for children and (some) adults. (The
tales, in actuality, hid an anti-Vietnam agenda; Sills began to develop the
idea with his group The Body Politic, formed in 1968, during the turmoil
of that year's Democratic National Convention in Chicago.)

Story Theatre reached Broadway's Ambassador Theatre on October 26,
1970, where it received some incredibly enthusiastic reviews. (Clive
Barnes in the *New York Times*: "Great, unequivocally great.") It was enhanced by a fine cast of standouts, including Paul Sand (who won a

Tony), Valerie Harper, and Richard Libertini. But it was perceived as a show for children, which resulted in lots of discounted school groups but weak full-price sales. As business wound down, the producers decided to alternate *Story Theatre* with a second story theatre show: *Ovid's Metamorphoses*, which opened on April 22, 1971. Nobody went, though, and the twin bill shuttered on July 3, after 270 performances of *Story Theatre* and 35 of *Metamorphoses*.

Zimmerman's *Metamorphoses* did far better than Paul Sills's, and on the Wednesday before the Tony Awards they announced that they had recouped their production costs within three months of the opening. Impressive. On Tony Award Sunday, Zimmerman won the Tony Award as best director of a play.

On the Sunday following Tony Award Sunday, *Metamorphoses* ran a quarter-page ad in the *Arts and Leisure* section of the *New York Times*, announcing that it had won the Tony Award for Best Play. *The Goat, or Who Is Sylvia?* also ran an ad announcing that it had won the Best Play Tony. (The Arts and Leisure deadline is on Monday afternoon, so ads with varying copy are necessarily made up in advance. Somebody at the advertising agency or at the *Times* chose the wrong ad, and nobody double-checked it. Oops!) I suppose that the *Metamorphoses* ad sold more tickets than the *Goat* ad; but the goof generated a good deal of press, which only served to publicize the fact that *The Goat* was the best play of the season—per the Tony voters—and *Metamorphoses* wasn't.

Metamorphoses ran a quarter-page ad in the *Times*, announcing that it had won the Tony Award for Best Play. Which it hadn't.

But *Metamorphoses* was already in the hit column, while the worthy *Goat* was fated to financial failure.

One Mo' Time

Musical shows have traveled to Broadway via unlikely routes, heaven knows, but *One Mo' Time* marked an especially unusual path to the so-called Great White Way.

Vernel Bagneris was, and is, a remarkable, eccentric dancer with legs like toothpicks. In 1978, he put together a little, one-night-only revue at a movie house on Toulouse Street in New Orleans. The idea was to present a nostalgic remembrance of the type of vaudeville acts that played the old Lyric Theatre in the French Quarter. This was the local stop on the segregated TOBA circuit; the acronym stood for Theatre Owners Booking Agency, but it was more popularly known among the talent as Tough on Black Asses. Here it was that people like Ethel Waters, Bessie Smith, Bill Robinson, and Bert Williams played before they crossed over to the big time.

The Lyric burned down in 1927. (A rumor started that the proprietors set it ablaze so that they wouldn't have to pay the performers that week.) Half a century later, Bagneris's little revue—presenting what one of the characters calls "the best in *common* entertainment"—proved highly popular and became a local tourist attraction. Off-Broadway producer Art D'Lugoff caught the show, packed up the physical production (in a couple of cardboard suitcases, presumably), and brought it north to his theatre in Greenwich Village. The Village Gate was a grungy cabaret on Bleecker Street—right down the block from *The Fantasticks*—with a postage stamp–sized stage and greasy hamburgers on paper plates. The Gate is best remembered, by

The original production's success could be ascribed to its small-scale nature and lack of pretension. *One Mo' Time* looked woefully out of place in an eleven-hundred-seat Broadway theatre.

me, anyway, as the home of the long-running 1968 hit *Jacques Brel Is Alive and Well and Living in Paris*.

One Mo' Time opened at the Gate on October 22, 1979, and ran 1,372 performances. It was a profitable venture, on a moderate level. The show was produced on a shoestring, and looked it. I seem to recall that they lived on discounted group business, but that proved sufficient; D'Lugoff thrived on food and liquor sales. Other companies of *One Mo' Time* sprang up, but it was no *Ain't Misbehavin'*. Bagneris returned to the Gate in 1990 with a sequel, entitled *Further Mo'*. But by then there was no place for a ragtag vaudeville, not in an era of *Sophisticated Ladies* and *Black and Blue*, and there was no further Mo' after 174 performances.

And that, presumably, would have been that, but for the follow spot operator back in 1979. Not a follow spot operator, really; just a twenty-year-old college kid who came to New York to get a job in the theatre. He landed at *One Mo' Time*, running the spot for seventy dollars a week. In 1981 he became a stage manager, for the Circle in the Square; in 1988 he moved on to Lincoln Center Theater. He became a stage manager for the prestigious Williamstown Theatre Festival, in Williamstown, Massachusetts, in 1990 and moved up to the top spot in 1996.

Scheduling his sixth season, for the summer of 2001, Michael Ritchie thought—why not *One Mo' Time*? It is his prerogative to select shows; Williamstown offers a wide variety of attractions; and Ritchie had done a fine job in his six years at the helm. Three of his productions transferred to Broadway during the 1999–2000 season: revivals of N. Richard Nash's *The Rainmaker* and Arthur Miller's *The Price*, as well as Miller's new-to-Broadway *The Ride Down Mt. Morgan*. Another three would come to Broadway in 2001–2002: *Hedda Gabler* (starring Kate Burton, who happens to be Ritchie's wife), *One Mo' Time*, and Miller's *The Man Who Had All the Luck*.

One Mo' Time, with Bagneris re-creating his original performance and

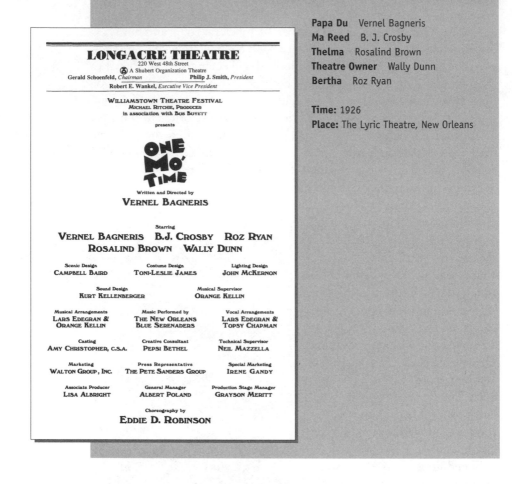

Papa Du   Vernel Bagneris
Ma Reed   B. J. Crosby
Thelma   Rosalind Brown
Theatre Owner   Wally Dunn
Bertha   Roz Ryan

Time: 1926
Place: The Lyric Theatre, New Orleans

LONGACRE THEATRE
220 West 48th Street
Ⓢ A Shubert Organization Theatre
Gerald Schoenfeld, *Chairman*   Philip J. Smith, *President*
Robert E. Wankel, *Executive Vice President*

WILLIAMSTOWN THEATRE FESTIVAL
MICHAEL RITCHIE, PRODUCER
in association with BOB BOYETT

presents

ONE MO' TIME

Written and Directed by
VERNEL BAGNERIS

Starring

VERNEL BAGNERIS   B.J. CROSBY   ROZ RYAN
ROSALIND BROWN   WALLY DUNN

Scenic Design	Costume Design	Lighting Design
CAMPBELL BAIRD	TONI-LESLIE JAMES	JOHN McKERNON

Sound Design		Musical Supervisor
KURT KELLENBERGER		ORANGE KELLIN

Musical Arrangements	Music Performed by	Vocal Arrangements
LARS EDEGRAN & ORANGE KELLIN	THE NEW ORLEANS BLUE SERENADERS	LARS EDEGRAN & TOPSY CHAPMAN

Casting	Creative Consultant	Technical Supervisor
AMY CHRISTOPHER, C.S.A.	PEPSI BETHEL	NEIL MAZZELLA

Marketing	Press Representative	Special Marketing
WALTON GROUP, INC.	THE PETE SANDERS GROUP	IRENE GANDY

Associate Producer	General Manager	Production Stage Manager
LISA ALBRIGHT	ALBERT POLAND	GRAYSON MERITT

Choreography by
EDDIE D. ROBINSON

direction, was a popular hit at Williamstown (which generally presents somewhat loftier fare). An enthusiastic donor offered backing, so Williamstown decided to try *One Mo' Time* on Broadway—thereby giving us one of the more unlikely Broadway musicals in recent memory. It was, at heart, a shoestring revue; people sing songs, people deliver jokes, and then they sing more songs. The songs were all authentic, and they were all old, and most of them tended to sound the same after a while.

The original production's success in 1979 could be ascribed, in part, to its small-scale nature and lack of pretension. *Bubbling Brown Sugar* and *Eubie*, similar revues with similar material, looked mighty flimsy when magnified to Broadway scale. That's precisely what happened to *One Mo' Time* in 2002; it looked woefully out of place in an eleven-hundred-seat

Broadway theatre. This was triply apparent to theatregoers who saw the irrepressible *Ain't Misbehavin'* early in its run, on the very same Longacre stage. The Fats Waller revue had dazzling energy, interrelated material, and knockout performances, three elements lacking in the friendly but haphazard *One Mo' Time*.

As in 1979, Bagneris was a marvel. The man is a human string bean, a loose-limbed scarecrow with toothpick legs. He made it look effortless, gliding along the stage as if magically supported by marionette strings from above. At one point, while doing a hip-gyrating step during "Hop Scop Blues," he lobbed across the footlights the fact that "I like this myself." And when he formed a mini–chorus line with the girls, his high-kick seemed way higher than anatomically possible. There's a problem with specialty performers, though; repeat the specialty three or four or six times, and it starts to look merely skillful.

Bagneris was joined by a trio of singing actresses. Roz Ryan played Bertha, the "star" of the troupe with a large frame and an ego to match. She got to sing such racy ditties as "Kitchen Man" and "You've Got the Right Key but the Wrong Keyhole," but she had a little too much oomph for my comfort. Rosalind Brown was somewhat better as the youngest member of the group, doing nicely on "He's Funny That Way." B. J. Crosby, as the jaded-but-reliable Ma Reed, came off best of all, despite some thankless material. She can sing, and she managed to hold her own with dialogue like "I got an uncle in heaven and an aunt in hell and a twin in prison—and if you don't pay me, we're both gonna visit one of them tonight!"

It should be mentioned that the show started like a house afire, courtesy of the band. The five-man New Orleans Blue Serenaders launched into "Darktown Strutter's Ball," and they were hot. Every so often they had a solo spot—"Tiger Rag," "Weary Blues," and the entr'acte "Muskrat Ramble"—and you felt that the joint was, as they say, jumpin'. But those were the only times the joint was jumpin'. Otherwise, it was simply lazin' around. Conductor Orange Kellin—a holdover from 1979—played a mean clarinet. (This fellow, a Norwegian by birth, sported bright orange hair.) Trumpeter Mark Braud had an amazing set of chops, percussionist Kenneth Sara was really cooking, and tuba player Walter Payton let that "Tiger" really rip.

> **Bagneris was a human string bean, a loose-limbed scarecrow with toothpick legs. There's a problem with specialty performers, though; repeat the specialty three or four times, and it starts to look merely skillful.**

One Mo' Time
Opened: March 6, 2002
Closed: March 24, 2002
21 performances (and 16 previews)
Profit/Loss: Loss
One Mo' Time ($76.25 top) was scaled to a potential gross of
    $328,892 at the 1,095-seat Longacre Theatre. Weekly
    grosses averaged about $111,000, with inconsequential
    business throughout the run. Total gross for the five-week
    run was $514,302. Attendance was about 32 percent, with
    the box office grossing about 31 percent of dollar-
    capacity.

Critical Scorecard

Rave 2
Favorable 3
Mixed 0
Unfavorable 3
Pan 1

But by 8:40, *One Mo' Time* had become a succession of similar songs, separated by similar chunks of backstage chatter and/or double entendres. And how many times can you expect to land the same sort of material, especially when none of it is extraordinary? *One Mo' Time* bored me silly in 1979. This made me apprehensive about seeing it one mo' time, an apprehension that proved well placed.

The Crucible

Reading Arthur Miller's *The Crucible* prior to the premiere of Richard Eyre's 2002 revival, I was somewhat surprised to find the 1953 play considerably more engrossing than I remembered it. I had a vague recollection of a meandering tract, with the characters patiently plodding through endless discussion before getting around to the gripping parts. As I read it again, Miller seemed to be patiently constructing a platform from which to hang his arguments.

Back on the stage, away from the page, the 2002 *Crucible* meandered once more. Sitting in the Virginia, observing a significant portion of the audience glaze over before the first hour of earnest speechifying had passed, I couldn't quite understand why the play seemed so much less involving than it had when I read it a month before. The dialect formulated by Miller to suggest olden times was part of the problem, perhaps, though it was an understandable choice; all those awkward tenses and double negatives succeeded in separating the 1692 witch-hunt from the one in progress when the play was written.

Sitting in your living room you can read between the lines; Miller, in the published script, actually *wrote* between the lines.

But the overflowing cascade of words, in the theatre, did not allow the audience to read between the lines. Sitting in your living room with script in hand, you definitely could read between the lines; Miller, in the published version of the play, actually *wrote* between the lines. And I'm not just talking about stage directions. The playscript is punctuated by paragraphs and—at times—pages full of information from the playwright. Even before the first line of dialogue, in between the traditional description of the set and the first stage direction, come five full pages of background material.

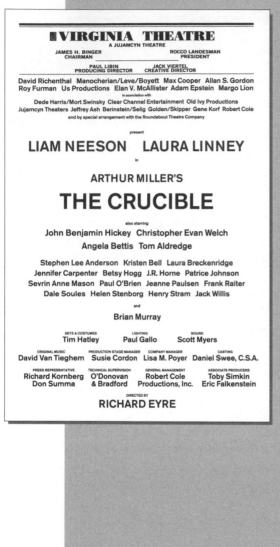

▌VIRGINIA THEATRE
A JUJAMCYN THEATRE

JAMES H. BINGER
CHAIRMAN

ROCCO LANDESMAN
PRESIDENT

PAUL LIBIN
PRODUCING DIRECTOR

JACK VIERTEL
CREATIVE DIRECTOR

David Richenthal Manocherian/Leve/Boyett Max Cooper Allan S. Gordon
Roy Furman Us Productions Elan V. McAllister Adam Epstein Margo Lion

in association with

Dede Harris/Mort Swinsky Clear Channel Entertainment Old Ivy Productions
Jujamcyn Theaters Jeffrey Ash Berinstein/Selig Golden/Skipper Gene Korf Robert Cole

and by special arrangement with the Roundabout Theatre Company

present

LIAM NEESON LAURA LINNEY

in

ARTHUR MILLER'S

THE CRUCIBLE

also starring

John Benjamin Hickey Christopher Evan Welch

Angela Bettis Tom Aldredge

Stephen Lee Anderson Kristen Bell Laura Breckenridge
Jennifer Carpenter Betsy Hogg J.R. Horne Patrice Johnson
Severin Anne Mason Paul O'Brien Jeanne Paulsen Frank Raiter
Dale Soules Helen Stenborg Henry Stram Jack Willis

and

Brian Murray

SETS & COSTUMES
Tim Hatley

LIGHTING
Paul Gallo

SOUND
Scott Myers

ORIGINAL MUSIC
David Van Tieghem

PRODUCTION STAGE MANAGER
Susie Cordon

COMPANY MANAGER
Lisa M. Poyer

CASTING
Daniel Swee, C.S.A.

PRESS REPRESENTATIVE
Richard Kornberg
Don Summa

TECHNICAL SUPERVISION
O'Donovan
& Bradford

GENERAL MANAGEMENT
Robert Cole
Productions, Inc.

ASSOCIATE PRODUCERS
Toby Simkin
Eric Falkenstein

DIRECTED BY

RICHARD EYRE

Reverend Parris Christopher Evan Welch
Betty Parris Betsy Hogg
Tituba Patrice Johnson
Abigail Williams Angela Bettis
Susanna Walcott Kristen Bell
Mrs. Ann Putnam Jeanne Paulsen
Thomas Putnam Paul O'Brien
Mercy Lewis Severin Anne Mason
Mary Warren Jennifer Carpenter
John Proctor Liam Neeson
Rebecca Nurse Helen Stenborg
Giles Corey Tom Aldredge
Reverend John Hale John Benjamin Hickey
Elizabeth Proctor Laura Linney
Francis Nurse Frank Raiter
Ezekiel Cheever Henry Stram
Marshal Herrick Jack Willis
Hopkins Stephen Lee Anderson
Judge Hathorne J. R. Horne
Voice of Martha Corey Dale Soules
Deputy Governor Danforth Brian Murray
Girl in courtroom Laura Breckenridge
Sarah Goode Dale Soules

Act 1: A small upper bedroom in the home of Reverend Samuel Parris, Salem, Massachusetts, in the spring of the year 1692

Act 2: The common room of John Proctor's house

Act 3: The vestry room of the Salem Meeting House, now serving as the anteroom of the General Court

Act 4: A cell in the Salem jail, that fall

This production is dedicated to Inge Morath (1924–2002).

And interesting material it is, too. Miller describes the town of Salem and its inhabitants, and their inability to convert the heathen Indians; thus, the forest on the edge of the wilderness became the Devil's preserve and a place of evil. Uprooting the tribes and seizing their land, in some lights, could be seen as a godly act.

The need for protection from outside forces resulted in a paradox, from which the witch-hunt arose: "For good purposes, even high purposes, the people of Salem developed a theocracy, a combine of state and religious power whose function was to keep the community together, and to prevent any kind of scrutiny that might open it to destruction by material or ideological enemies." Miller added, pointedly, "It is a paradox in whose grip we still live, and there is no prospect yet that we will discover its resolution."

Thus, the witch-hunt in Salem—and in Washington—was a struggle between society rule and individual freedom. "It was also, and as importantly, a long overdue opportunity for everyone so inclined to express publicly his guilt and sins, under the cover of accusations against the victims."

All this came before the very first line of dialogue, placing readers in a considerably different mind-set than folks whose only admonition before the curtain rose was to turn off their cell phones. Miller's instructions to readers continued throughout the text. Consider the entrance of the goodly Rebecca Nurse, the highly respected Salem matriarch who is the symbol of all that is good—and who three hours later lifts her aged head and nobly marches to the scaffold rather than confess to a crime she did not commit. (Miller's youngest child—born in 1962—was named Rebecca.) To theatregoers, Rebecca Nurse simply seems to be a goodly (and obviously nurturing) woman. Putnam and his wife, Ann, we learn, have lost seven children in childbirth; Rebecca Nurse, who nursed the children, is arrested and convicted for "the marvelous and supernatural murder of Goody Putnam's babies."

Miller tells readers considerably more. Nurse's husband had amassed an estate of three hundred acres, arousing jealousy from neighbors who over the course of decades had been impelled to sell Nurse their land. One of these neighbors was this same Putnam, the chief accuser of evil in the play. The son of the richest landowner in the village, he felt slighted by everyone in town. Among his many grievances was that his brother-in-law had been rejected for the position of minister of Salem—with resistance led by the husband of Rebecca Nurse.

This background has enormous bearing on the action of the play. Miller tells us that "long-held hatreds of neighbors could now be openly expressed, and vengeance taken, despite the Bible's charitable injunctions. Land-lust which had been expressed before by constant bickering over boundaries and deeds could now be elevated to the arena of morality; one could cry witch against one's neighbor and feel perfectly justified in the bargain. Old scores could be settled on a plane of heavenly combat between Lucifer and the Lord."

This information is key to our understanding of *The Crucible*; among other things, it informs us of the author's views on witch-hunts other than the one in Salem. But Miller tells this to readers only; the theatregoer cannot read between the lines, because these lines of text are not spoken from the stage. This lack of background, motivation, and justification in the play as performed makes the characters—other than Miller's hero John Proctor—little more than poppets.

Poppets serve as a critical plot point in the play; Elizabeth Proctor, wife of the play's main character, is accused of practicing witchcraft with a poppet. These are heathenish representations of beings that are controlled by others; we know them, today, as puppets. The characters of *The Crucible* are as poppets, made to act and speak by the author in order to make his many political and humanitarian points. Points which a theatregoer then and now might well agree with and support, but which smack less of dramaturgy than propaganda. What the playgoer gets is a bunch of characters—twenty characters, an enormous cast for a nonmusical—provided with plenty of ideas but little emotional pull.

We have seen recent New York revivals of four other Miller plays: *All My Sons*, *Death of a Salesman*, *A View from the Bridge*, and *The Price*. (These, with *The Crucible*, can reasonably be termed his major plays, and the only ones that met with Broadway success.) Miller was in each case addressing larger issues than might be apparent in a plot synopsis; but the characters and the stories were gripping and human. Not so much in *The Price*, perhaps, which was ultimately underdeveloped, but certainly in the other plays. Joe Keller (in *All My Sons*) is a tragic figure, a proud munitions manufacturer whose faulty product inevitably killed his beloved son—and "all my sons." Salesman Willy Loman is—well, you know the story. Eddie Carbone (of *A View from the Bridge*), too, is swept to tragedy. These characters are hard to love and morally flawed; but we feel for them, as the author crashes the world down on their heads. Each of the plays has its own inner reality, with a clutch of supporting characters that are equally memorable.

The Crucible, too, has a flawed being at its center. John Proctor is a man fighting over principle—fighting for his life, literally. Flawed but decent, striving to do right but knowing all too well his weaknesses. In Miller's words, between the lines: "He is a sinner, a sinner not only against the moral fashion of the time, but against his own vision of decent conduct." A man with a "sharp and biting way with hypocrites."

Which might well describe the playwright himself.

Liam Neeson did fairly well in the role, which is to say that he effectively relayed Proctor's moral dilemma and held our interest. Was this a great performance? Was his an overpowering presence, commanding our unwavering attention and bringing us into the jailhouse with him as he grappled with his final decision of whether to lie and live or speak the truth and die? No, not for me. Neeson demonstrated such power when he made his Broadway debut in the 1993 Roundabout revival of *Anna Christie*; his Matt was so powerful that it leapt over the footlights. In Salem, he was safely on the other side of the footlights. Proficient, and far more effective than anyone else onstage, but that was all.

Nobody else came close. The most perplexing element of the evening, perhaps, was Beatrice Straight as Elizabeth Proctor. Well, no. She didn't play Elizabeth Proctor, Laura Linney did. Ms. Straight died, in fact, in April 2001. What puzzled me, though, was what Straight's performance must have been to earn her a Tony Award, over competition from Kim Stanley and Eileen Heckart (from the Pulitzer Prize–winning *Picnic*) and the critically embraced Broadway debuts of Rosemary Harris (in *The Climate of Eden*) and Geraldine Page (in *Mid-Summer*).

Linney, last seen locally in the Roundabout's tame 2000 production of *Uncle Vanya*, was billed over the title; thus, she was eligible for a Leading Actress Tony (rather than the featured award Straight received). But the character seemed unaffecting in Linney's hands, and it's hard to see how it could have been otherwise. Elizabeth, the character, is absent in the first act, restrained in the second, and can only come alive upon her entrance at the end of the third-act trial. Beatrice Straight must have done something incredible up there. Linney didn't, at least from where I was sitting.

(Late in the run, I spoke to a fellow critic—whose opinion I respect—who had raved about Linney's performance. He described, in detail, her work in a section of the trial scene, work I didn't see. In comparing notes, we realized that I was sitting house right, between the aisle and the wall, in D 8; he was on the opposite side of the theatre, in F 1. Could it be that I missed Linney's great moment because of poor staging, her body turned away from my side of the house?)

The Crucible
Opened: March 7, 2002
Closed: June 9, 2002
101 performances (and 19 previews)
Profit/Loss: Loss
The Crucible ($85 top) was scaled to a potential gross of
$737,356 at the 1,255-seat Virginia Theatre. Weekly
grosses averaged about $479,000, with the show
alternating between seven- and eight-performance weeks.
Grosses remained over $500,000 for the first month of the
run, after which they started to slip, although rarely
falling below $400,000; still, this was almost but not
quite enough to recoup the relatively steep production
costs. Total gross for the sixteen-week run was
$7,657,715. Attendance was about 77 percent, with the
box office grossing about 69 percent of dollar-capacity.

TONY AWARD NOMINATIONS
Best Revival of a Play
Best Performance by a Leading Actor: Liam Neeson
Best Performance by a Leading Actress: Laura Linney
Best Performance by a Featured Actor: Brian Murray
Best Direction of a Play: Richard Eyre
Best Lighting Design: Paul Gallo

Critical Scorecard

Rave 2
Favorable 1
Mixed 3
Unfavorable 2
Pan 2

Brian Murray was third billed, on a separate line below the two groups of featured actors. (This was one of those ambiguous cases were you couldn't quite tell which billing was supposed to be better; in such cases, the "Who's Who in the Cast" order tells the tale.) Murray, who costarred with Linney in that disappointing *Uncle Vanya*, played Deputy Governor Danforth, and I don't think this was a good idea. Danforth is "a grave man in his sixties, of some humor and sophistication that does not, however, interfere with an exact loyalty to his position and his cause." Murray is a man in his sixties of some humor and sophistication, and a skilled actor as well; gravity, though, is not what one expects from him. Things perked up slightly at his first appearance, as is customarily the case with Mr. Murray, but his was a charming presence where a threateningly imposing one was needed.

Tom Aldredge, like Murray, has become such a familiar presence that he often seems to bring the same character along with him from job to job. Here he portrayed Giles Corey, yet another crusty, eccentric old-timer; he was last seen in these parts at the end of the 2000–2001 season as Muff Potter in *The Adventures of Tom Sawyer*. (*Tom Sawyer*'s Becky Thatcher was in Salem as well, as one of the hysterical girls and under-study to Mary Warren.) Aldredge surprised us in *The Crucible*, avoiding all his familiar tricks and making Corey the only character on the Virginia stage—other than Neeson's Proctor—that seemed human. Otherwise, there was a lot of shrieking.

As for the production by the noted British director Richard Eyre, it was dark and stuffy. Yes, this is somewhat indicated by the text; but it sure made things sleepy.

In addition to all the helpful authorial explanations, the published version of *The Crucible* contains something else that was not included in the 2002 revival. Miller voluntarily deleted act 2, scene 2 after the closing of the original production. (The play was written in four acts; it was performed in 2002 with one intermission, between acts 2 and 3.) This scene disappeared from the play until Miller reinstated it—in print, if not in performance—in 1971.

Elizabeth Proctor has been arrested, along with sixteen other good women of Salem. John Proctor ends the first scene of act 2 in a violent confrontation with Mary Warren, impelling her to turn against Abigail Williams and admit the truth. ("My wife will never die for me! I will bring your guts into your mouth but that goodness will not die for me!") Mary counters by revealing Proctor's secret shame: his affair with Abigail. Proctor determines to publicly reveal himself as a sinner, and thereby clear his wife.

We then go straight to intermission, followed by the trial scene in the Salem vestry house. Miller originally took us to a forest glade for a ten-minute, midnight meeting between Proctor and Abigail. (In her nightgown, with her hair down.) Pleading with her to recant the accusations and tell the truth, Proctor suddenly realizes that she *believes* the accusations; he sees her madness, per Miller's explicit stage direction. "Oh, John, I will make you such a wife when the world is white again!" Abigail says, kissing his hand as he recoils in horror.

One can understand why Miller made the cut. With this scene, he is clearly stating that the accusations were false; without the scene, this is only inferred (although strongly inferred). I suppose that pro-McCarthy audiences in 1953 wanted to believe that the accused were indeed guilty, and the courts justified in sentencing them to their death. Either way, it was a risky stance to take. The third and

> John Proctor is "a sinner not only against the moral fashion of the time, but against his own vision of decent conduct." A man with "a sharp and biting way with hypocrites." Which might well describe the playwright himself.

fourth acts might well play better without the truth of what happened in the forest glade. But it does make a powerful scene, and it does make a difference in the way one perceives the play.

The Crucible was, in many ways, a product of its time. Miller addressed the original reaction to the play in a 1983 interview with Matthew C. Roudané: "There was a fear of fear. Once they caught on to what *The Crucible* was about, a coat of ice formed over the audience because they felt they were being called upon to believe something which the reigning powers at the time told them they were not to believe. . . . I stood in the back of that theatre after opening night and I saw people come by me whom I'd known for years—and wouldn't say hello to me. They were in dread that they would be identified with me. Because what I was saying in the play was that a species of hysteria had overtaken the United States and would end up killing people if it weren't recognized."

Miller was there, so I suppose his is an accurate reading of the initial reception. I read the original reviews from the major critics, though, and they seem reasonably appreciative and not especially skittish. The original *Crucible*, too, was financially profitable. So perhaps this legend of the play's struggle for respect is a bit exaggerated.

Or perhaps the author is slightly self-conscious about a troublesome flaw at the play's center. Despite the accusations and charges and wrung-out confessions, one assumes that very few residents of the time and place actually signed their name in the Devil's book. There were accusations and charges and wrung-out confessions in Miller's place and time, too; the difference, though, is that some of the accused did, indeed, sign their name. Not in blood in the Devil's book, but on Communist Party membership cards. This is not to equate the enormity of one sin (consorting with the Devil) with the other (consorting with Communists). But none of the accused in 1692 Salem, presumably, actually signed on the proverbial dotted line. At least some of those in 1952 America certainly did.

> There's a troublesome flaw at the play's center. None of the accused in 1692 Salem, presumably, actually signed their name (in the Devil's book). At least some of those in 1952 America did.

The Goat, or Who Is Sylvia?

Edward Albee's *The Goat, or Who Is Sylvia?* was nothing new. Just the same old story.

Middle-aged man. Highly successful, professionally; happily married, with well-adjusted family; respected by all; and rich. The man who has everything. But something is missing. What could it be? And so he falls in love—unsuitably in love—and ruins it all.

In the 1920s, he fell in love with a chorus girl. In the 1940s, he fell in love with a free-spirited poetess. In the 1960s, he fell in love with a black woman. In the 1980s, he fell in love with a white boy. How, in the twenty-first century, is a playwright to put a new spin on the tale that will get our attention?

Leave it to Albee to find a way. He certainly did, bringing a new element to this same old plot. An unthinkable one, and scandalously controversial. I wonder, though, how much more controversial this was than the first play in which the middle-aged father ran off with a black girl, or a boy in bell-bottomed trousers.

Albee claimed that he was "testing the tolerance of the audience," and his outlandish musings certainly got our attention. Martin is the man of the family, the youngest person to win the Pritzker Prize, "architecture's version of the Nobel." As he turns fifty, he is very much in love with his wife, Stevie, and very understanding of his eighteen-year-old-son, Billy—who, as he tells us, is a "real cute kid, bright as you'd ever want, gay as the nineties."

But there's a hitch. Martin confesses to a malaise, "the sense that everything going right is a sure sign that everything's going wrong." It isn't

> How much more controversial was *The Goat* than the first play in which the middle-aged father ran off with a black girl, or a boy in bell-bottomed trousers?

Cast *(in order of appearance)*

Stevie Mercedes Ruehl
Martin Bill Pullman
Ross Stephen Rowe
Billy Jeffrey Carlson

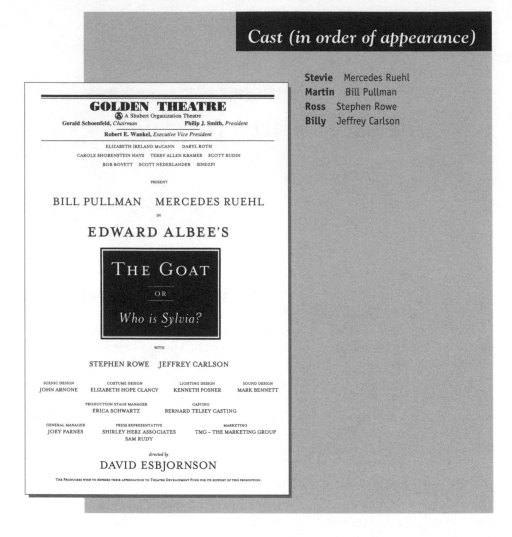

GOLDEN THEATRE
Ⓢ A Shubert Organization Theatre
Gerald Schoenfeld, *Chairman*   Philip J. Smith, *President*

Robert E. Wankel, *Executive Vice President*

ELIZABETH IRELAND McCANN   DARYL ROTH

CAROLE SHORENSTEIN HAYS   TERRY ALLEN KRAMER   SCOTT RUDIN

BOB BOYETT   SCOTT NEDERLANDER   SINE/ZPI

PRESENT

BILL PULLMAN   MERCEDES RUEHL

IN

EDWARD ALBEE'S

THE GOAT

OR

Who is Sylvia?

WITH

STEPHEN ROWE   JEFFREY CARLSON

SCENIC DESIGN	COSTUME DESIGN	LIGHTING DESIGN	SOUND DESIGN
JOHN ARNONE	ELIZABETH HOPE CLANCY	KENNETH POSNER	MARK BENNETT

PRODUCTION STAGE MANAGER   CASTING
ERICA SCHWARTZ   BERNARD TELSEY CASTING

GENERAL MANAGER   PRESS REPRESENTATIVE   MARKETING
JOEY PARNES   SHIRLEY HERZ ASSOCIATES   TMG – THE MARKETING GROUP
SAM RUDY

directed by
DAVID ESBJORNSON

THE PRODUCERS WISH TO EXPRESS THEIR APPRECIATION TO THEATRE DEVELOPMENT FUND FOR ITS SUPPORT OF THIS PRODUCTION.

long before Albee spills the problem of his problem play. As Stevie puts it, her husband is "a decent, liberal, right-thinking, talented, famous, gentle man who right now would appear to be f*****g a goat." (Forgive my use of all those asterisks. Albee doesn't use them, but I do.)

Far be it from me to discern Albee's intentions; the playwright has gone to great lengths, over the years, to keep his meanings to himself. I don't in the least think that he was talking about bestiality, though; sending his hero into the stall with a goat called Sylvia was a way to get us to prick up our ears, to borrow a phrase from one of Albee's British contemporaries.

And there was plenty for our ears to catch. Albee dialogue, typically, resembles a game of Ping-Pong with firecrackers mixed in among the ammunition. (Ammunition among the Ping-Pong balls, that is.) Typically, the rat-tat-tat-tat is liberally sprinkled with four- and seven-letter words. This has always made Albee's work notoriously difficult for some audiences; the Pulitzer committee made no award in 1963 rather than give the prize to Albee's outspoken *Who's Afraid of Virginia Woolf?* (The citation at the time was for "the original American play performed in New York which shall best represent the educational value and power of the stage in raising the standard of good morals and good manners." The 2002 Pulitzer went to Suzan-Lori Parks's *Topdog/Underdog*.)

The repeated use of such language has a numbing effect, at least for a significant segment of the audience; after a while, it simply becomes part of the fabric of the play's vocabulary. Albee made playful use of it, too. In the first scene of *The Goat*, Martin complains to his friend Ross, "You say 'f**k' a lot." Ross responds, "You say 'fine' a lot." And they both laugh. (Martin also points out that Ross—the "normal" one of the characters, in that he cheats on his wife with prostitutes—peppers his language with the words "sick" and "Jesus.")

The 1960 off-Broadway one-act *Zoo Story* brought Albee acclaim; the groundbreaking *Who's Afraid of Virginia Woolf?* (1962; 644 performances) brought him notoriety, fame, and—to date—his only long-running moneymaker. *Ballad of the Sad Café* (1963; 125 performances), *Tiny Alice* (1964; 167 performances), and *Malcolm* (1966; 7 performances) brought even more controversy, while *A Delicate Balance* (1966; 132 performances) brought him a Pulitzer Prize. But the promise of *Virginia Woolf*—commercially, anyway—went unfulfilled.

Then came twenty-five years or so of even worse fortune on Broadway: a salvage job on the musical *Breakfast at Tiffany's* (1966; closed during previews); *Everything in the Garden* (1968; 84 performances); *All Over* (1971; 42 performances); and *Seascape* (1975; 63 performances), which brought Albee his second Pulitzer. But to little avail. Albee was now dead on Broadway. His next three plays each folded within two weeks: *The Lady from Dubuque* (1980; 12 performances), *Lolita* (1981; 12 performances), and *The Man Who Had Three Arms* (1983; 16 performances).

Albee's first Broadway play ran 644 performances. His next eleven Broadway plays ran 654 performances combined.

Albee's first Broadway play ran 644 performances, approximately nineteen months. His next eleven Broadway plays, up to but not including *The Goat*, ran 654 performances combined.

Albee's next major play headed off-Broadway. *Three Tall Women* (1994; 582 performances) was a major hit, only the second of Albee's career. It won the playwright his third Pulitzer and had a highly successful London run (starring Maggie Smith). *The Play about the Baby* (2001; 263

performances), too, went off-Broadway, meeting a mixed reception but enjoying a moderately successful run. *The Goat* was Albee's first new work to reach Broadway in nineteen years. Happily, he took up where he had left off, with a stimulating, provocative, and controversial play. Of questionable commerciality, alas; but the combination of author and subject matter almost guaranteed a problematic reception.

As in previous works, Albee engaged in word games. He can't help it, which is to say his characters can't help it; that's part of what defines them, even in the middle of a crisis. Martin, Stevie, and Billy, that is; Ross, Martin's best friend, is obliviously out of the circle. When Ross holds up a snapshot and says "this is Sylvia, who you're f*****g," Martin can't help but respond "Don't say that. *Whom.*"

These are people who pride themselves on their intellect. "We see the deep and awful humor of things go over the heads of most people; we see what's hideously wrong in what most people accept as normal," Stevie tells us. In a situation such as the tragedy of *The Goat*, they realize, this is a weakness. Stevie (to Martin): "God, I wish you were stupid." Martin: "Yes! I wish you were stupid, too." Ignorance equals invulnerability to the piercing tortures of the intellect.

Martin: "Why aren't you crying?" Stevie: "Because this is too serious." And later, Martin: "Be serious!" Stevie: "No! It's too serious for that."

The words came fast and furious, even in the heat of battle. Especially in the heat of battle. Billy (yelling at his father): "Now shut the f**k up! Semanticist!" Martin: "Very good. Where did you learn that?" Billy: "I go to a good school." Martin: "Yes, but still . . ." This scene ends with Billy collapsing in tears in his father's arms and hugging him; this is then converted into a "deep, sobbing, sexual kiss." (Albee named the goat-lover's son Billy.) Ross walks in on this and is, naturally, repulsed. ("Jesus. You're sick!" he says.) Billy admits that he gets confused between sex and love: "I probably do want to sleep with him. I want to sleep with everyone." Pause, and then to Ross: "Except you."

But once the audience—or at least most of the audience—was acclimated to the language and the subject matter, the writing was very real, and very affecting, and very humanly funny. As for Martin, Albee had him say, a dozen times over the course of the evening, "you don't understand." To Stevie, to Billy, to Ross; but it is Martin, himself, who most seemed not to understand.

Albee also slipped in at least two inside jokes. There was discussion of a prostitute named Large Alice (ref. Albee's *Tiny Alice*), which was roundly saluted by the critics and got a knowing laugh from the audience. Another exchange seemed to go over everyone's head. Billy: "Oh, dad!" Martin: "Poor dad!" Billy: "What?" Martin: "Nothing." This, presumably, referred to the Arthur Kopit–Jerome Robbins–Barbara Harris hit *Oh Dad, Poor Dad, Mamma's Hung You in the Closet and I'm Feeling So Sad* (1962), the outlandishly absurdist off-Broadway farce that in some ways prepared audiences for the opening of *Virginia Woolf?* eight months later.

Mr. Albee split the critics—which, given his track record, seemed a better reception than usual. (To quote the playwright: "The only time I'll get good reviews is if I kill myself.") Bill Pullman and Mercedes Ruehl gave two performances of the very highest caliber. Ruehl was nominated for a Tony Award, and deservedly so. Her sudden, piercing shriek of anguish in the second scene—breaking through her character's otherwise icily controlled handling of the situation—will long be remembered. Chilling!

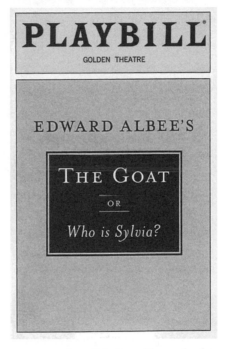

Pullman, somehow or other, was overlooked by the Tony nominators; this was a season overloaded with impressive performances by male stars in plays. And when was the last time that happened? Even without a Tony Award or nomination, Pullman gave a magnificent and unforgettable performance. "Does nobody understand what happened?" he asked in the play's final moment. "Why can't anyone understand this? That I am alone. All alone." In Pullman's hands, this intentionally incomprehensible character was real and believable and, ultimately, sympathetic.

Director David Esbjornson made his third interesting showing in three seasons, the others being *The Play about the Baby* and Arthur Miller's *The Ride Down Mt. Morgan* (2000). And let us not overlook the setting by John Arnone. This was a grand, oblong living room composed of architecturally angled rectangles and squares, even down to the lamps and sconces, softened only by an abundant collection of rounded crockery. (Said crockery, inevitably, got smashed by Stevie in the revelation scene.) The set was provocatively skewed off-center, threatening to spill into the first rows of the Golden. Costume designer Elizabeth Hope Clancy had relatively little to do, but she was canny enough to place Ms. Ruehl in a brown leather outfit suitable for the goat song. ("Tragedy" comes from the

Greek *tragoidia*, which is to say *tragos* [goat] + *oide* [ode]. Why, exactly, no-body seems to know.)

The Goat had a controversial preview period. No question about it; people loved this play, or they hated this play, but they *talked* about it. There were some problems with the ending, in which the title charac-ter—of necessity—made an appearance. This was not a live goat, as in-dicated by the large family portrait showcased in the Golden Theatre's window box just outside the box office entrance. Rather, it was a (realis-tic-looking) white, blood-stained prop goat with its throat slit.

Originally, Ruehl carried the bloody goat in her arms, in a Pietà-like pose. Said staging elicited a gale of howls from that portion of the audi-ence that disliked the play, utterly ruining the dramatic impact of the mo-ment. This sort of thing is devastating for actors, especially when they are dealing with such difficult material. (The actress appealed for emergency help at a note session. Albee reportedly responded, "Well, you know, the character can't hear the laughter." *Not* reassuring.) Esbjornson dutifully worked on the problem; Ruehl was soon carrying the goat in a sack, with its bloody head sticking out. Finally, she simply dragged in the sack. Again, this was staggeringly powerful for people who were caught up in the play, but a source of ridicule for those who were insulted or enraged. One thing you can say for Albee; nobody at *The Goat* was bored.

As was only natural. Albee was "testing the tolerance of the audience," as he told Jerry Tallmer in a *Playbill* interview. "I suppose some people will be offended and outraged. I hope more people will find it informing and involving."

During the week that *The Goat* opened, a mother in Texas was convicted of murdering her five small children. In the Middle East, a teenaged girl carried out a suicide bombing. The Archdiocese of Boston announced that it anticipated the need to sell off church property to finance a settlement agreement—estimated at $15 to $30 million—in a sexual abuse lawsuit. Within a month, similar cases were uncovered across the country, embroiling the Vatican and bringing the scandal to front-page prominence around the world.

> **Albee split the critics—which, given his track record, seemed a better reception than usual. To quote the playwright: "The only time I'll get good reviews is if I kill myself."**

And in jolly old England, a twenty-three-year-old man was sentenced to six months in jail after pleading guilty to "buggery with an animal." Seems that a commuter train slogged through a field at an inopportune moment, catching the poor fellow—and the poor goat—in the act (as they say).

Just how horrible and morally repugnant, I couldn't help but wonder, was the unspeakable crime at the center of *The Goat*?

Sweet Smell of Success

The first rule of Broadway musicalizations of motion picture hits is—or should be—if you can't enhance the experience of the original, don't do it. As, for instance, the legendary 1966 fiasco *Breakfast at Tiffany's*. Or *Gone with the Wind*, an American musical that began in Tokyo, improved in London, but flopped en route to Broadway in 1973.

Broadway has its own graveyard of musical versions of great films: the mausoleum includes titles like *Nothing's Sacred*; *Destry Rides Again*; *Hail, the Conquering Hero*; *The Yearling*; *The Blue Angel*; *La Strada*; and *Some Like It Hot*. Musicalizations of memorable, though less-than-classic, films have failed as well: *The Quiet Man*; *Miracle on 34th Street*; *Never on Sunday*; *Zorbá the Greek*; *Georgy Girl*; *Lilies of the Field*; *The Baker's Wife*; *King of Hearts*; *Woman of the Year*; and *The Goodbye Girl*.

Most recently, *Sunset Boulevard* and *Big*—thud!—failed to measure up to their cinematic predecessors. There have been exceptions, including *Promises! Promises!* and *The Full Monty*. But a whole lot of money has been lost on surefire Broadway stabs at film favorites.

And then came *The Producers*, the Mel Brooks monster hit that rewrote Broadway history. *The Producers*, though, had a secret weapon that wasn't available to *Breakfast at Tiffany's*, *Gone with the Wind* and the others: Mel Brooks, himself, to write the thing. It's not enough to keep the best jokes and write new material in between; *The Producers* works, in part, because the new jokes (and plot developments) came from the same warped sense of humor as the old.

The highly awaited, long-in-gestation *Sweet Smell of Success* seemed poised to follow the success of *The Producers*. At least, it came from two of the main *Producers* producers and followed that show's pre-Broadway route through Chicago. Like *The Producers*, the *Sweet Smell* tryout was a hot ticket; Windy City theatregoers who lost out on Bialystock and Bloom weren't about to be embarrassed again. They didn't laugh this time, though; audiences and critics quickly learned that *Sweet Smell* was not quite so—well, sweet. *The Producers*, it turned out, was a mere exception to Broadway's Hollywood flop parade. Or maybe not; as *Sweet Smell* soured, *Hairspray* approached.

The 1957 film *Sweet Smell of Success* was written by Clifford Odets (of *Awake and Sing* and *Golden Boy*) and Ernest Lehman, from Lehman's 1950 novella. It was directed by Alexander Mackendrick, the acclaimed British director of such films as *The Man in the White Suit* (1951) and *The Ladykillers* (1955). *Sweet Smell* is an explosively vibrant glimpse at the seamy underside of a small portion of the world. Since that portion of the world was located within a twenty-block square—with the epicenter being the Brill Building, at Broadway between Forty-ninth and Fiftieth Street—the film has long been a favorite of theatrical types.

The film was unsuccessful upon its release, meeting with poor business and not even a single Oscar nomination in the year of *The Bridge on the River Kwai*. But no matter; it's a wonderful movie. The main characters are monumental creations, both in the writing and in the playing of Burt Lancaster and Tony Curtis; the dialogue is memorably spicy, in a Broadwayese slang too perfect to be authentic; the jazz-influenced background score (by Elmer Bernstein) and the cinematography (by James Wong Howe) envelop the film in twin atmospheres so evocative that you can almost smell the smoke-filled nightclubs and sweetly slick printer's ink.

Impossible to transfer to the stage, no? Well, maybe. That's the magic of Broadway, folks; the likeliest musicals seem to fail, while the hardest-seeming ones to pull off—like *West Side Story* and *Fiddler on the Roof*—sometimes beat the odds. But achieving a successful adaptation of something that is well-nigh perfect demands a mixture of talent (skill), vision (artistic), and luck (plain). The several creators

The first rule of Broadway musicalizations of motion picture hits is if you can't enhance the experience of the original, don't do it.

of the musical *Sweet Smell of Success* possessed varying degrees of talent, vision, and luck, but not necessarily of the helpful variety.

I suppose that we need to lay a great deal of blame at the feet of composer Marvin Hamlisch. Not because his work ruined the show; the major problems were, perhaps, elsewhere. But *Sweet Smell* (the film) takes place in a world of music, and not only atmospherically. The characters work and live in nightclubs and bars, which in those days featured live music

■ MARTIN BECK THEATRE
A JUJAMCYN THEATRE

JAMES H. BINGER
CHAIRMAN

ROCCO LANDESMAN
PRESIDENT

PAUL LIBIN
PRODUCING DIRECTOR

JACK VIERTEL
CREATIVE DIRECTOR

Clear Channel Entertainment   David Brown   Ernest Lehman
Marty Bell   Martin Richards   Roy Furman   Joan Cullman
Bob Boyett   East of Doheny   Bob and Harvey Weinstein

present

John Lithgow

in

Sweet Smell of Success

A New Musical

MUSIC BY **Marvin Hamlisch**

LYRICS BY **Craig Carnelia**

BOOK BY **John Guare**

Based on the novella by Ernest Lehman and the MGM/United Artists motion picture
with a screenplay by Clifford Odets and Ernest Lehman

ALSO STARRING **Brian d'Arcy James**

FEATURING **Kelli O'Hara   Jack Noseworthy   Stacey Logan**

SCENIC & COSTUME DESIGN BY **Bob Crowley**

LIGHTING DESIGN BY **Natasha Katz**

SOUND DESIGN BY **Tony Meola**

HAIR DESIGN BY **David Brian Brown**

ORCHESTRATIONS BY **William David Brohn**

MUSICAL DIRECTOR	ASSISTANT DIRECTOR	ASSOCIATE CHOREOGRAPHER	PRODUCTION MANAGEMENT
Jeffrey Huard	Drew Barr	Jodi Moccia	Juniper Street Productions
PRODUCTION SUPERVISOR	MUSIC COORDINATOR	CASTING	MARKETING SERVICES
Peter von Mayrhauser	Michael Keller	Mark Simon CSA	TMG–The Marketing Group
EXECUTIVE PRODUCERS	PRODUCED IN ASSOCIATION WITH	PRESS REPRESENTATIVE	GENERAL MANAGEMENT
Beth Williams &	The Producer Circle Co. &	Barlow - Hartman	Alan Wasser Associates
East Egg Entertainment	Allen Spivak and Larry Magid	Public Relations	Allan Williams

CHOREOGRAPHED BY **Christopher Wheeldon**

DIRECTED BY **Nicholas Hytner**

ORIGINAL BROADWAY CAST RECORDING AVAILABLE ON SONY CLASSICAL

J. J. Hunsecker   John Lithgow
Sidney   Brian d'Arcy James
Susan   Kelli O'Hara
Dallas   Jack Noseworthy
Rita   Stacey Logan
Madge   Joanna Glushak
Abigail Barclay   Elena L. Shaddow
Tony   Frank Vlastnik
Billy Van Cleve   Michael Paternostro
Pregnant woman   Jamie Chandler-Torns
Pepper White's escort   Eric Sciotto
Charlotte Von Habsburg   Michelle Kittrell
Otis Elwell   Eric Michael Gillett
Lester   Steven Ochoa
Kello   David Brummel
Club Zanzibar singer   Bernard Dotson
Cathedral soloist   Kate Coffman-Lloyd
Senator   Allen Fitzpatrick
Senator's girlfriend   Jill Nicklaus
J. J.'s vaudeville partner   Jennie Ford
Press agent   Timothy J. Alex
Swings   Mark Arvin, Lisa Gajda, Laura Griffith, Drew Taylor

Location: New York City
Time: 1952

Original Broadway Cast Album: Sony Classical SK89922

(as opposed to jukeboxes and disc jockeys). One of the main characters is a jazz musician, who necessarily performs on camera.

The soundtrack makes extensive use of the Chico Hamilton Quartet, an innovative jazz group at the time. For the film, the quartet became a quintet, led by guitarist Steve Dallas (the character who has fallen in love with the sister of gossip columnist J. J. Hunsecker, to his doom). Hamilton, the actual leader of the combo, is on the drums.

Hamlisch apparently tried to emulate Bernstein—Elmer, not Lenny —by providing the same type of jazzy and seemingly never-ending musical texture. Like the film, the stage version was highly underscored; but the stage characters keep interrupting, to sing to us. (The score was reformatted for the cast album, giving a much clearer idea of what composer Marvin Hamlisch and lyricist Craig Carnelia were trying to do than was evident in the theatre.)

Music, yes, but a different type of music. Place an actor in a spotlight so he can spend three minutes explaining his motivations and illuminating his aspirations, and the pressure is off. Imagine *Sweet Smell of Success* without pressure, and—well, that's what they had at the Beck. The authors chose to spread out the show's time span by adding exposition; they also expanded the presence of two characters, Susan and Dallas, who serve as pawns in the film. This was done, presumably, to allow Hamlisch and Carnelia to write love songs—which, again, stopped everything cold. And not in a good way.

Only one song truly worked in the context of the show: the young anti-hero's solo "At the Fountain." This took us in the wrong direction, perhaps, humanizing and creating sympathy for a character who in the movie was chillingly inhuman and unsympathetic. Be that as it may, the song was strong and effective. Too many of the others weren't; several seemed to come from another score altogether, and not a good one. Prime examples: "Rita's Tune" and "Don't Look Now." Others were a case of right song–wrong show, like "Dirt" (out of *Chicago*'s "All That Jazz.")

A stronger score wouldn't have solved *Sweet Smell*'s problems, but it would have given theatregoers something to hang on to. Somewhere around nine o'clock, while I was trying to figure out why nothing whatsoever was working, I touched upon what might well have been the problem. Was Hamlisch trying to write *City of Angels*? That's the nifty Hollywood-noir musical that Cy Coleman, David Zippel, and Larry Gelbart combined for back in 1989. Coleman overstuffed his score with music, too, filling it with themes and underscoring in Broadway-jazz style. But *City of Angels* had tunes, highly melodic tunes, to spare. It also had dazzling lyrics and a knockout comedy book, yes; but the show developed from song to song to song.

There's little purpose in comparing Hamlisch with Coleman; Marvin, certainly, has the hits and awards and money that have evaded Cy throughout his career. But the musical style called for in both *City of Angels* and *Sweet Smell of Success* comes naturally to Cy, who started as a fifties jazz pianist. Marvin was presumably trying to write his own jazz score, but in places—"Rita's Tune" and "Don't Know Where You Leave Off," for example—you could almost hear him lusting after *City of Angels*.

Hamlisch was an interesting choice for the assignment. The man became an instant celebrity on Oscar night in 1974, when he picked up three statuettes for his work on *The Sting* and *The Way We Were*. Michael Bennett was just then embarking on an innovative musical about Broadway dancers. He didn't want a traditional score; rather, music built to order for a choreographer who knew what he wanted. So he called Hamlisch, who had done dance arrangements for the early Bennett musical *Henry, Sweet Henry*. (The other dance arranger on this 1967 flop was Billy Goldenberg, who came to Broadway in 2002 as Bea Arthur's accompanist. Bennett must have liked the dance arrangements for *Henry*; he used Hamlisch on *A Chorus Line* and Goldenberg on his next musical, the 1978 *Ballroom*).

A *Chorus Line* made Hamlisch even more famous, adding a Tony and a Pulitzer to his Oscars (and making him tremendously rich in the process). But *A Chorus Line* is an odd score; parts of it are excellent, including delicious musical comedy songs like "Nothing" and "Dance: Ten, Looks: Three," and musical scenes like "At the Ballet." Much of it, though, is merely effective, while other sections seem to be more arranged than composed (which was presumably Bennett's goal).

Hamlisch has written more than forty movie scores, but his sights have apparently remained on Broadway. His second musical was the Neil Simon hit *They're Playing Our Song* (1979), which succeeded solely on its joke book; the title song was catchy, the rest of the score instantly forgettable. Hamlisch's subsequent musicals have been nothing but trouble. *Jean Seberg* was a "musical tragedy" that premiered with great fanfare in 1983 at London's Royal National Theatre but was such a fiasco that it was quickly pulled. *Smile* (1986) was another one of those let's-adapt-a-hit-movie musicals. It seemed to mold itself—fatally—on the still-running *A Chorus Line*, with a bunch of beauty pageant contestants standing on the line. *The Goodbye Girl* (1993) was yet another one of those let's-adapt-a-hit-movie musicals, and perhaps the worst of Hamlisch's shows. This one featured a handful of major Broadway names, headed by Neil Simon. They turned out to be poison-pen collaborators, though, and a good time was had by none.

The *Sweet Smell* team sounded interesting, at least. The serious-themed subject matter was perhaps a stretch for Hamlisch, but the fifties-jazz milieu seemed like it might be a good match. (This turned out not to be the case.) Librettist John Guare has amply demonstrated his talents in the past, with such plays as *The House of Blue Leaves* and *Six Degrees of Separation* and his screenplay for *Atlantic City*. He was also lyricist-librettist for the 1971 hit *Two Gentlemen of Verona*, a Vietnam protest piece of great charm (although it dated quickly). *Sweet Smell* needed a thinking-man's librettist, someone whose dialogue could match the acerbic sharpness of the screenplay, and Guare appeared to be a major asset to the project. (This turned out not to be the case.)

Craig Carnelia was more of a question. A "promising" composer-lyricist, he has been on the verge of success since 1975 or so. He contributed four songs—two of them extremely good—to the 1978 failure *Working*; he wrote one complete Broadway score, for the 1982 failure *Is There Life after High School?* Frequently heard in cabaret settings, Carnelia has remained promising for almost a quarter of a century. While he always writes his own music, a big-league shot at the sweet smell of success was powerful enough to get him to work as lyricist only.

It should be noted, incidentally, that Hamlisch has written six produced musicals with six different lyricists. Seven lyricists, actually; the original score for *Smile*, with lyrics by Carolyn Leigh, was discarded. Howard Ashman then entered the project, writing book and lyrics *and* directing (all ineffectively). Hamlisch's other theatre lyricists were Ed Kleban on *A Chorus Line*, Carole Bayer Sager on *They're Playing Our Song*, Christopher Adler (son of Richard) on *Jean Seberg*, and David Zippel on *The Goodbye Girl*. The purpose of this paragraph is to point to a truth. Show me a successful composer who switches lyricists with every project, and you're quite possibly looking at a guy who is not only difficult to work with but also unable to share credit with others (rooted in a hidden insecurity about his own talent). *A Class Act*, the 2001 musical based on the life of Kleban, painted an especially unflattering (though humorous) por-

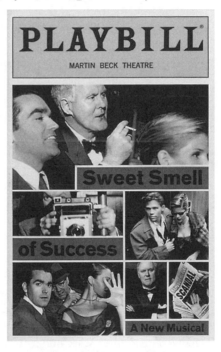

trait of Hamlisch. Interestingly enough, Marty Bell, one of the main producers of *Sweet Smell*, originated *A Class Act* as well.

Joining Hamlisch, Carnelia, and Guare was British director Nicholas Hytner. He is a man with impressive dramatic credits, including the London productions of *The Madness of King George III*, *The Lady in the Van*, and *Mother Clap's Molly House*. (During the *Sweet Smell* tryout, he was appointed the new director of the National Theatre, effective 2003.)

Hytner's musical work is somewhat more questionable. His revival of *Carousel* was stunning in London in 1992 (and somewhat less so at Lincoln Center in 1994); but there, he started with a near-perfect score and script. *Miss Saigon* was a major international hit, so I suppose it's late in the day to consider its quality. It seemed a muddled, noisy, disorganized affair to me, though; I rather liked Hytner's staging, but I'm one of those people who believe the director is also supposed to edit the writers and help clarify the material. When you sit down and watch *Oklahoma!* or *Carousel* or *Porgy and Bess*, you rightfully marvel at the work of Rodgers and Hammerstein and Gershwin and Heyward. There was a guy sitting in the room with them, though, a cranky Russian named Rouben Mamoulian. He advised and cajoled and fought and guided them, playing a major part in the finished project. (His name no longer appears in the credits, but only because his lawyer didn't insist that he get a cut of future productions.) *Sweet Smell of Success* by its very nature needed a director—or someone—to help the authors mold the material. Nobody apparently served as guide, and failure was inevitable. Even designer Bob Crowley—who has done such wizardly work on shows as varied as *Les Liaisons Dangereuses*, *The Capeman*, and *Aida*—seemed uninspired. Natasha Katz provided some artful lighting, anyway.

The cast didn't help matters, although one doubts whether Lancaster and Curtis together again live in person could have set *Sweet Smell* coming up roses. John Lithgow is a real actor; by that, I mean that he spent many years on Broadway before going off to Hollywood to make feature films and become an Emmy Award–winning TV star.

> How, you might ask, does J. J. Hunsecker *sing*? He doesn't; he can't, unless you have Stephen Sondheim in the house. (Think *Sweeney Todd*.)

Lithgow's stage work has been varied and consistently impressive, since his 1973 debut in *The Changing Room* (in which he had to play a gripping dramatic scene in the nude, winning a Tony Award in the process). He was similarly memorable in José Quintero's production of *Anna Christie*, opposite Liv Ullman, and David Henry Hwang's *M. Butterfly*.

But what could Lithgow possibly do with the role of J. J. Hunsecker? Modeled on Walter Winchell, this fellow personifies evil. Lancaster, who played the role in the film (which he also coproduced), made the fellow as gruff and morose and creepily unattractive as possible. How, you might ask, does such a character *sing*? He doesn't; he can't, unless you have Stephen Sondheim in the house. (Think *Sweeney Todd*.) But I wonder if Sondheim would have gone near *Sweet Smell*, as he is no doubt aware of the first rule of Broadway adaptations of motion picture hits. To repeat: if you can't enhance the experience of the original, don't do it.

Hunsecker was forced to sing because you can't write a musical in which the star doesn't sing. Pardon me, you *can* write a musical in which the star doesn't sing, but not a *good* musical. Hollywood character man Thomas Mitchell won a Best Actor Tony Award in 1953 for *Hazel Flagg*, which as far as I can tell was the first of those bad let's-adapt-a-hit-movie musicals.

So here was Lithgow, acting the Machiavellian monster but interrupting himself on cue to sing. Singing in order to express feelings that he can't express in words; singing to reveal himself and his inner motivations; and—in a particularly ill-conceived vaudeville segment—singing, apparently, in an attempt to get the audience to like him. (The authors seemed to remember the "Tap Your Troubles Away" number in *Mack & Mabel*, wherein one character led a big production-number-of-a-cheer-up song while off on the side the heroine overdosed on heroin.) A sympathetic Hunsecker; is it any wonder that *Sweet Smell* didn't work? But I wouldn't for a moment blame Lithgow for his performance; look to the material. Lithgow gave it his all, and won a Tony Award as consolation prize.

Brian d'Arcy James, in the role of the pimpish press agent Sidney Falco, had similar problems to contend with. Tony Curtis was so memorably fascinating, in part, because the character was so vile and the actor was allowed to be; thus, a close-up of a lizard as he wheedles and cringes. How do you make this fellow sing? Singing, again, can only add humanity to a hard character and soften the edges. D'Arcy James is a talented and sympathetic performer who was impressive in *Titanic* and the Manhattan Theatre Club *Wild Party*, and—in the summer of 2001—gave an acclaimed performance off-Broadway in the one-character play *The Good Thief*. His was an imposing presence in *Sweet Smell*, and he did well under the circumstances. But just what did the creators want us to feel?

Nor were the other three main characters helpfully reconceived for the stage. J. J.'s sister Susan had considerably more character than her film counterpart, though to little avail. Steve Dallas was changed from a guitar-playing member of the jazz quintet to a piano-playing singer named Dallas Cochran; this being a musical, I suppose they figured that they might as well have a character who can sing a couple of songs without having to justify why he's singing. Steve is the good guy in the film, a noble fellow with principles who is the innocent victim of Hunsecker's poison. Making him smarmy, and removing his nobility, didn't help matters. And why that name change, from Steve Dallas to Dallas Cochran? I suppose the creators had their reasons. Maybe their astrologer made them do it?

Rita was the most puzzling of the alterations. In the film, Sidney had a long-suffering secretary named Sally, a wallflower presumably in love with (and available to) her boss. There was also a dumb-blonde cigarette girl named Rita, who was a casual acquaintance (and occasional fling) of Sidney's. In a key plot development of the film, Rita invites herself up to

Sidney's place after closing. As the events of the night transpire, Sidney
needs a favor from a minor columnist named Otis Elwell. His solution:
forcing Rita to service Elwell. This provides one of the most poignant
moments of the film.

In the musical, the authors saw fit to combine Sally and Rita. Thus,
the new Rita is Sidney's girlfriend, a mundane waitress in a blue-collar
diner. J. J., in a show of power as he courts Sidney to become his hatchet
man, gets Rita the job of cigarette girl at a fancy nightclub. Under these
circumstances, Sidney's pimping of Rita (now his girlfriend, rather than
a friendly bimbo) has a whole different connotation. To make matters
worse—*much* worse—the new Rita was given one of those "gosh, gee, my
boyfriend's about to come home" songs, the aforementioned "Rita's
Tune," which was as phony as a torn three-dollar bill in the mud (as Hunsecker might say). False moments like this make whole rows of theatregoers stare at their *Playbill* in the dark, counting how many more songs
they have to sit through.

One last, telling observation. The columnist Elwell was left pretty
much unaltered in the musical; no transformation, no song, simply the

same guy Odets and Lehman wrote in the first place. For my money, Elwell
—as played by Eric Michael Gillett—was the only character from the
screenplay who made the transfer to the stage undiluted.

Sweet Smell of Success was, in a way, the last dying gasp of the unla-
mented Livent. This was one of two intriguing musicals in development
when Garth Drabinsky's Toronto-based house of cards folded in 1999.
SFX picked up the remains at a fire sale, which included the valuable
Ford Center for the Performing Arts and the rights to *Seussical* and *Sweet
Smell of Success*. SFX (which changed its name to Clear Channel Entertainment in July 2001) struggled on with both, with similarly dire results.
Sweet Smell had eleven producers billed over the title, in type double the
size of screenwriters Clifford Odets and Ernest Lehman. So many producers, signifying money-raising troubles, that there was room for only five
(of twenty-five) actors on the title page of the *Playbill*. The producers included Roy Furman, the financier who dumped money into Livent in
1998 only to see it drown in the quicksand; and Marty Bell, former head
of creative affairs for Livent. Drabrinsky never did get to see his *Sweet
Smell*; with a U.S. arrest warrant hanging over his head, he remained
north of the border.

The critical reception of *Sweet Smell* ranged from rough to savage, with
the major critics pretty much divided between unfavorables and pans—
with one startling exception.

Clive Barnes of the *New York Post* gave the show a rave. A slightly
qualified rave, if read at length, but nevertheless wholly enthusiastic, calling the show "a stunningly good idea" and "a must-see for anyone interested in musical theatre." This enabled the producers to run their daily
ABC ad with the quote "Brilliant and wondrous! A must-see!" I suppose
that one or two unsuspecting tourists read the ad, thought, well, that
looks good, and actually plunked down $95 (plus $1 restoration fee) for
tickets. As J. J. Hunsecker would say, caveat emptor.

This is not to say that a critic who violently disagrees with his or her
colleagues on a particular show is necessarily wrong, mind you. I wouldn't
even mention Clive's review had he not gone to the extreme length of
writing a Sunday column in the *Post* the following weekend, trying to justify his opinion. The situation had been exacerbated by his similar rave
for Broadway's next musical, *Oklahoma!*, which he found to be "spanking
new and gleaming" and "both a reinvention and a discovery" while most
everyone else found it considerably less to their liking.

"It's worth noting I have disagreed with almost all of my colleagues,"
said Clive. "The critics all agreed that the new musical *Sweet Smell of Success* stinks—everyone, that is, but me. I joyously labeled it a 'must-see.' "
He went on to explain himself, in extraordinary terms: "I could hear just

as well as anyone that Marvin Hamlisch's unmemorable and mediocre music and Craig Carnelia's pedestrian lyrics would never strut on any hit parade. But for me they provided adequate support to what I found was a fascinating musical noir."

Meanwhile, the *New York Times* had scheduled a symposium called "Behind the Scenes with *Sweet Smell of Success*," to be held on April 7, 2002. This was part of their "*Times* Talks" series, with columnist Jesse McKinley interviewing Hamlisch, Guare, and Lithgow. The week after the opening, the producers took a hundred-thousand-dollar-plus full-page ad in the *Sunday Times*. Opening the paper, they found yet another devastating pan—this one from *Times* critic Margo Jefferson—entitled "Why *Sweet Smell of Success* Went Sour on Stage." The *Sweet Smell* participants pulled out of the *Times* symposium, due to "scheduling conflicts." And I ask, can you blame them?

> The *Times* symposium "Behind the Scenes with *Sweet Smell of Success*" was cancelled due to "scheduling conflicts" after the *Times* ran a second pan entitled "Why *Sweet Smell of Success* Went Sour on Stage."

Just after the *Sweet Smell* bloodbath, it was announced that Broadway Inner Circle—the organization selling prime seats for *The Producers* for $480 apiece—added *The Crucible* to their list (for $250). A friend of mine, who was too closely involved with some of the *Sweet Smell* people for me to use his name, e-mailed me a supposed press release in Hunsecker style: "*Sweet Smell* following trend set by *The Producers* . . . selling prime Inner Circle seats . . . $15."

Oklahoma!

B ack in the summer of 1998, word filtered through Times Square about miraculous doings on the windswept plains of *Oklahoma!* This from London's Royal National Theatre, of all places.

Trevor Nunn, director of the RNT and director of the new production, joined the Royal Shakespeare Company in 1964; he became artistic director in 1968, at the age of twenty-eight. Nunn built his career and reputation on plays, classic and contemporary. In his spare time, as it were, he amassed a handful of musical theatre credentials. His work was restricted to modern-day spectacle musicals like *Cats* and *Les Misérables* (which rank atop the most successful productions in theatrical history), along with other high-profile but checkered works like *Starlight Express*, *Chess*, *Aspects of Love*, and *Sunset Boulevard*. Nunn's one major traditional book musical, a 1989 stab at fixing Stephen Schwartz's *The Baker's Wife*, was a quick flop in London. While we need not cry for Mr. Nunn, all his musicals—including *Cats* and *Les Misérables*—received generally mixed reviews or worse, in New York at least. *Cats* and *Les Misérables* are the only ones to have shown a profit on Broadway; but what a profit!

If Nunn seemed like an odd match for Rodgers and Hammerstein, the choice of the 1943 classic *Oklahoma!* was not unprecedented. RNT had produced a highly acclaimed revival of the team's *Carousel* in 1992, directed by Nicholas Hytner. (Hytner, who had received international acclaim for his direction of the RNT's *Madness of King George III* in 1991, succeeded Nunn as director of the National in 2003.) Producer Cameron Mackintosh moved the National into musical theatre in 1990 with a £1 million contribution to help finance a series of classic musicals, beginning with *Carousel* and continuing with *Sweeney Todd*, *A Little Night Music*, and *Lady in the Dark*. When Nunn became director of the National

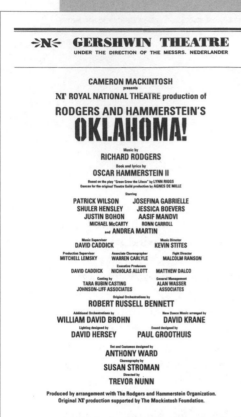

⇥N⇤ GERSHWIN THEATRE

UNDER THE DIRECTION OF THE MESSRS. NEDERLANDER

CAMERON MACKINTOSH
presents

NT ROYAL NATIONAL THEATRE production of

RODGERS AND HAMMERSTEIN'S

OKLAHOMA!

Music by
RICHARD RODGERS

Book and lyrics by
OSCAR HAMMERSTEIN II

Based on the play "Green Grow the Lilacs" by LYNN RIGGS
Dances for the original Theatre Guild production by AGNES DE MILLE

Starring

PATRICK WILSON   JOSEFINA GABRIELLE
SHULER HENSLEY   JESSICA BOEVERS
JUSTIN BOHON   AASIF MANDVI
MICHAEL McCARTY   RONN CARROLL
and ANDREA MARTIN

Music Supervisor
DAVID CADDICK

Music Director
KEVIN STITES

Production Supervisor
MITCHELL LEMSKY

Associate Choreographer
WARREN CARLYLE

Fight Director
MALCOLM RANSON

Executive Producers
DAVID CADDICK   NICHOLAS ALLOTT   MATTHEW DALCO

Casting by
TARA RUBIN CASTING
JOHNSON-LIFF ASSOCIATES

General Management
ALAN WASSER
ASSOCIATES

Original Orchestrations by
ROBERT RUSSELL BENNETT

Additional Orchestrations by
WILLIAM DAVID BROHN

New Dance Music arranged by
DAVID KRANE

Lighting designed by
DAVID HERSEY

Sound designed by
PAUL GROOTHUIS

Set and Costumes designed by
ANTHONY WARD

Choreography by
SUSAN STROMAN

Directed by
TREVOR NUNN

Produced by arrangement with The Rodgers and Hammerstein Organization.
Original NT production supported by The Mackintosh Foundation.

Aunt Eller Andrea Martin
Curly Patrick Wilson
Laurey Josefina Gabrielle
Ike Skidmore Ronn Carroll
Will Parker Justin Bohon
Jud Fry Shuler Hensley
Ado Annie Carnes Jessica Boevers
Ali Hakim Aasif Mandvi
Gertie Cummings Mia Price
Andrew Carnes Michael McCarty
Cord Elam Michael X. Martin

Ensemble

Corky Matt Allen
Jess Clyde Alves
Susie Bradley Benjamin
Slim Kevin Bernard
Aggie Amy Bodnar
Joe Stephen R. Buntrock
Sam Nicolas Dromard
Chalmers Merwin Foard
Ellen Rosena M. Hill
Jake Chris Holly
Mike Michael Thomas Holmes
Kate Elizabeth Loyacano
Armina Audrie Neenan
Rosie Rachelle Rak
Tom Jermaine R. Rembert
Vivian Laura Shoop
Emily Sarah Spradlin-Bonomo
Fred Greg Stone
Sylvie Kathy Voytko
Lucy Catherine Wreford

Children

Lil' Titch Julianna Rose Mauriello
Travis Stephen Scott Scarpulla
Desiree Lauren Ullrich
Maverick William Ullrich
Swings Dylis Croman, Rommy Sandhu,
Jennifer West, Tony Yazbeck

Time: Just after the turn of the century
Place: Indian Territory (now Oklahoma)

Original London Cast Album: First
Night Loud 1790

in October 1997, he chose *Oklahoma!* to be the first musical revival of his reign.

Joining Nunn in the project was American choreographer Susan Stroman. Yes, you've heard of her, but at that point she was just a choreographer. (After *Oklahoma!* opened at the National, she began her directing career with the developmental workshop of *Contact*.) Just a choreographer, but a distinctive one—which signified radically different plans for *Oklahoma!* While musical theatre choreography is usually rethought from production to production, Agnes de Mille's groundbreaking work for *Oklahoma!* has been, until now, understandably retained for most major productions. Understandable in that Rodgers and Hammerstein incorporated a full-fledged ballet to help propel their plot. De Mille's work has been re-created, again and again, in major *Oklahoma!* productions; it was also memorialized in the 1955 motion picture version.

The replacement of de Mille's work made clear that this was going to be a new and different *Oklahoma!* Still, a rethinking of the fifty-five-year-old show was bound to happen at some point; who better to oversee such changes, in today's world of theatre, than respected theatre artists like Nunn and Stroman?

Early word of mouth was highly enthusiastic, signifying that something spectacular was happening on the South Bank of the Thames. *Oklahoma!* opened at the Olivier on July 15, 1998, to wild acclaim from theatergoers and critics. ("This *Oklahoma!* is the best we are ever likely to see in the rest of all our lifetimes," said Sheridan Morley in the *International Herald Tribune*.) Superlatives continued to hurtle across the Atlantic, with top Broadway critics making the pilgrimage overseas. Their response was as radiant as that fabled bright golden haze on the meadow. "A triumphant, miraculously fresh-feeling production," said Ben Brantley of the *New York Times*. "Oh what a beautiful evenin'! I fell madly in love with *Oklahoma!* all over again," said Clive Barnes of the *New York Post*.

This calls for a Broadway transfer, critics and audiences and New York theatre owners said. The great Cameron Mackintosh worldwide producing machine—which had waged similar campaigns with *Cats*, *Les Misérables*, *The Phantom of the Opera*, and *Miss Saigon*—oiled its wheels and started gearing up. The three-month run at the Olivier was a quick sellout. Plans were made to transfer the production to London's Lyceum Theatre, in January 1999, for a five-month run (at which point the theatre needed to be vacated for the incoming *Lion King*). Everybody would then pack up their grip and head for Broadway, with previews slated for September 1999. *Oklahoma!* opened to torrid business at the Lyceum in January as scheduled, but it hit a snag in February. Jes' hold yer horses, said Actors' Equity.

Actors' Equity Association, the American actors union, that is (as opposed to British Equity). This was a sticky business. The production contract between Actors' Equity Association (AEA) and the League of American Theatres and Producers goes on at length about the importation of alien actors. (Four full pages; comparatively, it includes one page about onstage nudity and two paragraphs about blacklisting.) This is not only a matter to be worked out with AEA; the producer must also apply to the U.S. Immigration and Naturalization Service (INS) for work permits, which is especially tricky to swing over the objection of AEA. And we all know how diligent the INS is. There have been protracted battles over the use of so-called alien actors in the past, most notably the one waged and won by Mackintosh in support of Jonathan Pryce in *Miss Saigon*; but it is mighty hard to get around Actors' Equity.

The concern of the union is not unreasonable; if you are going to produce a show on Broadway (or elsewhere within the jurisdiction), they want you to use dues-paying AEA actors. When permission to allow aliens is granted, it is usually under the condition that dues-paying AEA members be hired as understudies and replacements (should the show run that long).

Exceptions are regularly granted to major box office stars, whose applications need be backed up by "documents testifying to the current widespread acclaim and international recognition accorded to the alien, receipt of internationally recognized prizes, or awards for excellence." This is often a clear-cut decision; Ian McKellen in *Dance of Death* or Liam Neeson in *The Crucible* or Alan Bates in *Fortune's Fool*, for example. It is sometimes less obvious, with stars in Britain who are not especially well-known here, like Helen Mirren in that same *Dance of Death*.

I always assumed that the magic of the London *Oklahoma!* would be transplanted and reproduced. But it's a Barnum and Bailey world, and shows are not reproduced so easily as shoes.

There are three other categories under which producers can apply for permission to import aliens. One is for an actor who "will be providing unique services which cannot be performed by any current member of Equity," providing further "that there is no citizen of the United States or resident alien domiciled in the U.S. capable of performing such services." This is a judgment call; Conleth Hill and Séan Campion were presumably approved for *Stones in His Pockets* under this classification, as I suppose were two young Australians who showed up off-Broadway in the fall of 2001 with a show featuring body-part origami.

The next classification is for what is called a "unit company." This is an existing group transplanted from an overseas repertory organization, which is supposed to perform at least two shows in repertory. The only such company I can think of in the last thirty years with two shows in repertory on Broadway—giving each show the same number of performances, as technically required under the rule—was the Royal Shakespeare Company's twin productions of *Cyrano de Bergerac* and *Much Ado about Nothing* in 1984. I served as American company manager of this production—there was a British company manager as well, along with British and American stage managers—and, believe me, the labor costs of alternating from one set to the other every week were so prohibitively high that it couldn't have possibly worked were it not for the strength of Derek Jacobi's name at the box office.

The final provision comes under the catchall heading of "companies and plays of special character." This can be interpreted to mean just about anything; ask any writer or producer or director or actor, *they'll* tell you they're a special character. The rub, though, is that "the determination shall be entirely within the discretion of the Council of Actors' Equity Association, such determination to be final and binding."

The underlying purposes of all this are twofold. More jobs for foreign actors mean less jobs for American actors, obviously; but there also seems to be an extreme sensitivity about the lack of reciprocity. Throughout the latter half of the twentieth century, a parade of British actors appeared on Broadway. Relatively few Americans were invited to make the reverse trip. For years there was indeed a qualitative difference, due to the better training available in England, and that still seems to rankle. This, actually, is spelled out in writing. "It is the purpose of this rule that a balance be maintained so that in each country where English is spoken, the number of non-resident aliens from each such country admitted to perform under this Rule shall not exceed the number of United States citizens employed in the theatre in such foreign country." It says United States citizens, but it clearly means United States citizens who are also dues-paying Equity members.

I am all for this in principle. I have managed three Royal Shakespeare Company productions imported to Broadway, including one directed by Nunn; I have produced an American musical imported to the West End with the original AEA cast, with the permission of British Equity. I am also, as it happens, a member (inactive) of AEA, as well as two other Broadway unions. Truly outstanding performances don't come along every day; I say, let the audience see them, regardless of the color of a performer's passport. Some may argue that such-and-such a performance isn't really outstanding, and the producer is merely trying to get away with something. The reality is that an imported performer is going to cost a producer far more than a domestic union member. There might be a savings on rehearsal costs, but use of foreign actors necessitates transportation and housing and immigration costs that you wouldn't have with an actor who

> **Ben Brantley went from "a triumphant, miraculously fresh-feeling production" to "audiences who didn't see the London version may wonder what the fuss was about."**

lives on the Upper West Side. (While West End pay scales are lower than those of Broadway, actors imported with the permission of AEA receive at least AEA minimums).

Ultimately, it comes down to economics; if the outstanding performances—real or merely hyped—don't sell tickets on Broadway, the producers lose their money. The only ones who gain are the American stagehands, musicians, wardrobe personnel, managers, and press agents employed by the show during its run.

Mackintosh—who with *Cats*, *Les Misérables*, *The Phantom of the Opera*, and *Miss Saigon* must be the largest single employer of AEA members since Lee Shubert died in 1953—showed up before the Equity Council with his London reviews, including his raves from American critics. Nunn and Mary Rodgers (daughter of *Oklahoma!* composer Richard) also appeared, pleading their case. The extenuating circumstance: while *Oklahoma!* could, in fact, be recast with Americans, Nunn and his choreographer Susan Stroman were unavailable to rehearse new actors in the foreseeable future. Thus, Broadway might never see this acclaimed *Oklahoma!* unless the already rehearsed RNT cast be allowed.

No go, said the Council of Actors' Equity Association, and that's final. "We're all disappointed but resigned to it," said Mackintosh, canceling his Broadway plans in February 1999. "The fact that Equity feels they can't allow this leaves us nowhere else to go."

At the time, I wrote: "Properly launched, this *Oklahoma!* could run for years and years on Broadway and the great American road. While I'm all for supporting the work rights of American actors, it seems to me that permitting the English in for four months can ultimately result in tens of thousands of workweeks for American Equity members. Let us remember that the Royal National's equally admirable *Carousel*—which was remounted on Broadway in 1994, after a delay, with an American cast—was far less effective here than in London, resulting in a disappointing ten-month run. Count the potential work weeks, Equity."

The experience of the RNT *Carousel* was—or should have been—cautionary. I went to London to see it in 1992 and found it mesmerizing. The Broadway remounting—with only one of the London leads, Michael Hayden (an American)—was merely quite good, creating little of the excitement of the London production. Had *Carousel* transferred with the RNT cast, would it have done better in America?

My comments brought a few words of displeasure from a friend of mine who was a former Council member. American actors need jobs, he explained; and American actors are just as good as British actors, especially in American musicals. Reasonable statements, with which I wholeheartedly agree. But let us consider starting a show on Broadway with the sort of momentum that *Carousel* or *Oklahoma!* had in London. What do you pick up in the way of presumably guaranteed rave reviews from critics who loved the show overseas? What do you pick up in the way of word of mouth? The show will, within six months or so, switch to an American cast; AEA will write that into the bargain.

A $12 million advance is nice, but it only goes so far when your theatre is scaled to a million a week.

Suppose *Carousel* had been a multiyear hit, like the 1996 revival of *Chicago* or the 1998 revival of *Cabaret* (both of which ran into the 2002–2003 season). Let's imagine that *Carousel* had run for four and a half years. That would represent four years of Broadway wages for *Carousel's* forty-two AEA members, after an initial six months with no AEA members employed. At the same time, there would be four and a half years of paychecks for another sixty or so American musicians and stagehands and wardrobe workers. The cost to AEA: "lost" salaries for the first six months.

Toting it up on the back of a ticket envelope, we find that *Carousel's* Broadway run of 322 performances—plus rehearsals and previews—resulted in approximately 2,100 workweeks for AEA members (fifty weeks for forty-two actors and stage managers), plus 2,500 workweeks for other American union members. Had the show been as strong as *Chicago* or *Cabaret*, this would work out to approximately 9,800 workweeks for AEA members, plus 13,000 workweeks for other American union members. And these figures don't consider an additional couple of years of a

road tour, with all-American personnel. So who came out ahead on
Carousel?

With the fall 1999 opening of *Oklahoma!* canceled, Nunn and Stroman gathered their laurels and went on to other business. For Sir Trevor,
that meant running the National as well as directing two additional major musical revivals in 2001: Lerner and Loewe's *My Fair Lady*, which was
well received (though not as well as *Oklahoma!*) and happily transferred
to Theatre Royal, Drury Lane; and a disappointing mounting of Rodgers
and Hammerstein's *South Pacific*. Stroman, within three years, directed
and choreographed *Contact*; the 2000 revival of *The Music Man*; *The Producers*; and *Thou Shalt Not*.

The Broadway *Oklahoma!*, Americanized as mandated by AEA, was
rescheduled for a December 7, 2000, opening at the Ford Center. This
was postponed in July 2000, due to scheduling conflicts—which is to say,
The Producers. Following that show's phenomenal opening, Mackintosh
announced his new opening date of March 21, 2002, at the Gershwin.
And so, finally, it came to pass.

For all the carryings-on, I always felt sure that *Oklahoma!* would eventually make it way to Broadway. I further assumed that with Trevor Nunn and Susan Stroman at the helm, the magic of the production—whatever that might have been—would be carefully transplanted and reproduced. But it's a Barnum and Bailey world, and shows are not reproduced so easily as shoes.

There clearly appeared to be a qualitative difference between the London *Oklahoma!* and the one that opened at the Gershwin. This is something I can't begin to adequately discuss, not having seen the 1998 version. Let's take Mr. Brantley's word for it; he went from "a triumphant, miraculously fresh-feeling production" to "audiences who didn't see the London version may wonder what the fuss was about. . . . This *Oklahoma!*, while eminently agreeable, is only occasionally transporting."

Oklahoma! opened on Broadway with an advance of $12 million, which is quite healthy. (Advance sales figures are notoriously unreliable, but here are reported opening-night advances of some recent shows: *Sweet Smell of Success*, $4 million; *The Graduate* $5 million; *The Producers*, $15 million; *Saturday Night Fever*, $16 million; *Mamma Mia*, $30 million.) Twelve million is nice, but it only goes so far when your theatre is scaled to a million a week. A cushy place to start, but you need to keep selling tickets.

At this writing, it's too early to judge the ultimate fate of this *Oklahoma!*; it might well prove impervious to the lackadaisical Broadway reception. *Miss Saigon* received significantly worse reviews when it opened at the Broadway in 1991, and Mackintosh got ten years out of it.

And mind you, the Broadway *Oklahoma!* was not bad by any stretch of the imagination. It was highly competent, with some very nice touches. Had Nunn and Stroman mounted this production initially on Broadway—without the huzzahs from London—I suppose that it might have been warmly received. But it certainly had the feeling of a museum piece, even if it was not in an Agnes de Mille display.

Is this the best we can expect from revivals of old musicals? Certainly not. The 1999–2000 season saw revivals of *Kiss Me, Kate* (from 1948) and *The Music Man* (from 1957) that, at least intermittently, caught fire in a manner that the 2002 *Oklahoma!* (from 1943) never did. Theatregoers had only to leave the Gershwin at intermission and hightail it up to Fifty-fourth Street or down to Forty-fourth to catch the second act of *Cabaret* or *Chicago* to see how vibrant a revival can be. By all reports, that's the kind of excitement Nunn and Stroman's *Oklahoma!* generated in London. Not here, it didn't.

Golden Boy

Stubbornly unworkable, I guess you can say.

"A hard-fisted piece of work about a prizefighter whose personal ambition turns into hatred of the world. *Golden Boy* is a good show into which you can read a social message if you want to." So said Brooks Atkinson of the *New York Times* in his qualified rave of the original production of Clifford Odets's most successful play. It opened November 4, 1937, at the Belasco, for 248 performances.

Golden Boy was immediately bought by Hollywood, for seventy-five thousand Depression dollars. Luther Adler—the Group Theatre member who played the Italian-American hero onstage—was replaced by newcomer William Holden, who became a star overnight. (The film is strikingly directed by the innovative Rouben Mamoulian, who had been on Broadway in 1935 with *Porgy and Bess* and would return in 1943 with *Oklahoma!*)

John Garfield led the play's only Broadway revival, produced by Bob Whitehead for ANTA in 1952. Odets had promised the role to Garfield in 1937, but he was passed over for the more experienced Adler. Garfield was given a minor role instead; other members of the 1937 cast included Frances Farmer, Lee J. Cobb, Morris Carnovsky, Howard da Silva, Karl Malden, and future directors Elia Kazan, Robert Lewis, and Martin Ritt. Garfield soon left the play for Hollywood, where he immediately became an Oscar-nominated star—even before *Golden Boy* was filmed—in the 1938 movie *Four Daughters*.

The writing, said the critics in 1952, still packed a punch. But the melodramatic aspects, which seemed somewhat incidental in 1937, had become uncomfortably old-fashioned. The enormous impact of the original play (and the film version) led to a virtual industry in melodramatic boxing movies. By 1952, *Golden Boy* seemed overly familiar.

Odets, meanwhile, had seen his career more or less disintegrate after leaving Broadway for Hollywood. By 1960 he was pretty much washed up. (If the unsuccessful 1957 film *Sweet Smell of Success*, is any indication, though, he could still write pithy dialogue.) First-time producer Hillard Elkins approached him in 1961 with the scheme of a musical *Golden Boy*, reconfigured for Sammy Davis. The presence of a major box office star— and the offer of the book-writing job—convinced Odets to go ahead with the project.

Elkins added songwriters Charles Strouse and Lee Adams (of *Bye Bye Birdie*) and British director Peter Coe (of *Oliver!*) to the *Golden Boy* team. They proceeded through two drafts, although it was slow going; plays and musicals have distinctively different script needs, a concept that Odets could not grasp. He died of cancer on August 18, 1963, at the age of fifty-seven. As is typically the case, the show underwent constant revisions before beginning its pre-Broadway tryout in Philadelphia on June 25, 1964—with no librettist on hand. Changes were patched together by committee, with Adams and Coe more or less shepherding the script. After bad reviews in Philadelphia and Boston, Elkins called William Gibson.

Gibson was one of Broadway's top playwrights at the time, with back-to-back hits in 1958 and 1959, *Two for the Seesaw* and *The Miracle Worker.* (These turned out to be the only Broadway successes of Gibson's career.) Gibson's loyalty to Odets—his mentor and friend—caused him to undertake the chore, with misgivings. Director Coe departed in a huff and was replaced by Arthur Penn, director of the Gibson plays.

Gibson did the best he could, "keeping what was alive onstage, drawing much upon the original text, and inventing a new body of material for the love story." This from Gibson's fascinating preface

Joe Bonaparte was weighing good (music) against evil (boxing), with the easy money of the latter winning the day. Joe Wellington was fighting to get out of the ghetto; he had little reason *not* to box.

to the published version of the *Golden Boy* libretto. "It was never possible for us to bring in a truly organic show—the components we had to blend, music, book, casting, lyrics, dance, sets, were so disparate the union was not unlike a shotgun wedding, and the daily revisions to meet musical changes cost us much of Clifford's dialogue—and the reviews we garnered reflected its inner incompatibilities; but however misbegotten it was alive, and its successful delivery after such labors displeased none of us."

While Gibson, Penn, Strouse, Adams, and the uncredited Herb Ross did a Herculean salvage job, the show that finally reached the Majestic

CITY CENTER
Judith E. Daykin, President & Executive Director

CITY CENTER
ENCORES!

ARTISTIC DIRECTOR — Jack Viertel
MUSICAL DIRECTOR — Rob Fisher
DIRECTOR-IN-RESIDENCE — Kathleen Marshall

GOLDEN BOY

BOOK BY
Clifford Odets & William Gibson

MUSIC BY
Charles Strouse

LYRICS BY
Lee Adams

Based on the play by Clifford Odets

STARRING
Alfonso Ribeiro
Anastasia Barzee   Norm Lewis   William McNulty
AND
Paul Butler

ALSO STARRING
Wayne Pretlow   Thursday Farrar   Michael Potts
Rob Bartlett   Joseph R. Sicari   Morgan Burke
Kamar de los Reyes   Karine Plantadit-Bageot   Julio Monge

Eric Anthony   Kristine Bendul   Chaundra Cameron   Kyra DaCosta
Manuel Herrera   Erik Houg   Terace Jones   Gelan Lambert, Jr.
Vicky Lambert   Sharon Moore   April Nixon   Devin Richards
Angela Robinson   Janelle Anne Robinson   J.D. Webster   Patrick Wetzel

SCENIC CONSULTANT — John Lee Beatty
COSTUME CONSULTANT — William Ivey Long
LIGHTING — Peter Kaczorowski
SOUND — Acme Sound Partners

CONCERT ADAPTATION — Suzan-Lori Parks
PRODUCTION STAGE MANAGER — Peter Hanson
MUSICAL COORDINATOR — Seymour Red Press

ORIGINAL ORCHESTRATIONS — Ralph Burns
ORCHESTRATIONS RECONSTRUCTED AND ENHANCED BY — Don Sebesky

CASTING — Jay Binder
FIGHT CHOREOGRAPHER — Michael Olajide
CHOREOGRAPHER — Wayne Cilento

The Coffee Club Orchestra
Rob Fisher, MUSICAL DIRECTOR

DIRECTED BY
Walter Bobbie

Major sponsorship for *City Center Encores!* is provided by a grant from
AOL Time Warner, Inc.

The development of *Encores!* is assisted by seed support from The New York Times Company Foundation
City Center 55th Street Theater Foundation, Inc. gratefully acknowledges the significant support it receives from the
New York City Department of Cultural Affairs

Baldwin Piano, Official Piano of City Center

Joe Wellington, a contender Alfonso Ribeiro

Tom Moody, his manager William McNulty

Lorna Moon, Tom's girl Friday Anastasia Barzee

Roxy Gottlieb, Tom's investor—Rob Bartlett

Tokio, Tom's trainer Joseph R. Sicari

Flynn, a boxer Erik Houg

Wellington, Joe's father Paul Butler

Frank, Joe's brother Michael Potts

Anna, Joe's sister Thursday Farrar

Ronnie, Joe's brother-in-law Wayne Pretlow

The Kid Morgan Burke

Punks Erik Houg, Patrick Wetzel, Manuel Herrera

Eddie Satin, a promoter Norm Lewis

Felipe, Eddie's protégé Julio Monge

Karine Karine Plantadit-Bageot

Kyra Kyra DaCosta

Sharon Sharon Moore

Lopez, a champion Kamar de los Reyes

Drake, a reporter Erik Houg

Driscoll, a referee Patrick Wetzel

Ensemble Eric Anthony, Kristine Bendul, Chaundra Cameron, Kyra DaCosta, Manuel Herrera, Erik Houg, Terace Jones, Gelan Lambert Jr., Vicky Lambert, Sharon Moore, April Nixon, Devin Richards, Angela Robinson, Janelle Anne Robinson, J. D. Webster, Patrick Wetzel

The action takes place in New York City (and on the road) in 1964.
This production is dedicated to Ralph Burns (1922–2001).

on October 20, 1964, was only intermittently effective. Howard Taubman of the *New York Times* said that "the theatrical form of *Golden Boy* as a musical is as crisp as a left jab and as jolting as a right uppercut. One can have nothing but admiration for the snap, speed and professionalism of this musical. . . . But at the core of its story, *Golden Boy* hardly scores at all. Despite its constant reach for the heart, it does not land there convincingly."

Other critics agreed, giving it qualified favorable reviews despite obvious flaws. "There's something very curious about *Golden Boy*, good as most of it is," noted Walter Kerr of the *Herald Tribune*. "At the same time that Sammy Davis is winning one fight, the music is losing another to the book. And not because the book is flabby. On the contrary, the book packs so much weight that even attractive music comes as thinning-out beside it." Kerr summed up *Golden Boy* as "a more interesting musical than most," which is a gentle pat on the head but doesn't sell tickets. Especially when the nine-month-old *Hello, Dolly!* is the hit of the decade, the seven-month-old *Funny Girl* is a sellout smash, and the four-week-old *Fiddler on the Roof* has knocked the other fall musicals out of the box.

Davis managed to sell tickets, but not enough. *Golden Boy* ran 569 performances, roughly sixteen months. This would normally be enough to turn a profit, but extensive pre-Broadway fixings come at a premium; while the show was capitalized at $435,000, as it headed to town costs ballooned to $700,000. (*Fiddler*, which also needed out-of-town fixing, was capitalized at $375,000 and cost $450,000.) *Golden Boy* closed with a deficit of more than $300,000, setting a new mark as the longest-running musical to lose money. It would hold this dubious distinction until 1973, when the high-grossing Debbie Reynolds–John Gielgud–Gower Champion *Irene*—which had even more severe tryout problems and excess costs—closed after 594 performances. The current-day champ in this category is *Jekyll & Hyde*, at 1,543.

Golden Boy, the play, told of a talented fellow forced to choose between prizefighting and music; he plays the violin, and well, too. Joe Bonaparte takes the easy money offered by fighting, breaking his hand in the process. So much for the violin. (The character was suggested by a real-life musician-turned-boxer, Mike Rubino.) Joe becomes the champ, but success is hollow. When he kills an opponent in the ring, he storms off in his car and is killed in an (intentional?) crash. Joe's decision to fight is helped along by Lorna Moon, his manager's mistress. She goads Joe into the ring, wrapping him around her little finger, and you can guess what happens.

By 1960, the plot was slightly worn and somewhat hackneyed. (The satirical *Fade Out—Fade In*, another competing musical from 1964, was about the making of a film called "The Fiddler or the Fighter," with Carol Burnett as the temptress.) But what happens when you transform Joe Bonaparte from the Bronx into Joe Wellington from Harlem? (How Napoleonic!) That has to breathe new life into *Golden Boy*, especially with Sammy Davis donning the boxing gloves. Or so it seems. Because it forced a critical change in focus.

The play is about success and sacrifice. From Mr. Atkinson in 1937: "On the one hand is music, which is a creative gift that enriches everyone; on the other hand, prizefighting, which is savage and destructive. The choice Mr. Odets's hero makes is fundamental, and it goes down through the whole core of civilized life."

The musical, with Sammy Davis in the title role, inevitably is about race. Lorna is not simply someone else's girl who Joe falls for; she is

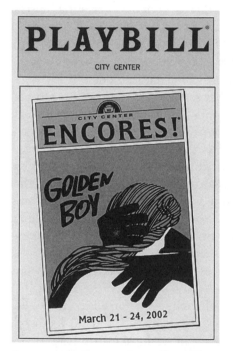

a white girl. (As everyone in the 1964 audience knew, Davis was married to blonde Swedish actress Mai Britt—a marriage that didn't run much longer than *Golden Boy*.) Joe must fight for Lorna's love, as before, but it's a very different fight than it was in 1937. Theirs is a forbidden love, etcetera, etcetera, and so forth.

The 1964 Joe was not even a musician; he was planning to be a surgeon. (His brother, formerly a labor organizer, became a civil rights activist.) When Joe breaks his hand in the play, it's the point of no return; the end of the violin, commitment to the ring. This same scene ended the first act of the musical. But to what effect? The same broken hand, but a very different impact when the fellow is not a violinist.

Joe Bonaparte was weighing good (music) against evil (boxing), with the easy money of the latter winning the day. Joe Wellington was fighting to get out of the ghetto. Under the new scheme, he had little reason *not* to box. A very different *Golden Boy*, and a stubbornly unworkable one.

Davis was apparently very good in the role (although he faced the opening-night critics with a bad case of laryngitis). His presence had a negative effect on the project posterity-wise, though. Here you had a role calling for a leading man who could sing like Frank Sinatra, tap dance like Gene Kelly, perform complicated "fight" choreography, and hold the audience in the palm of his hand like—well, like Sammy Davis in his prime. Okay, who are you going to get?

The musical more or less disappeared after Davis took it to London in 1968 for a lackluster 118 performances. Charles Strouse has been trying to get *Golden Boy* back in the ring ever since. There was an off off-Broadway run in 1984, with a new book; a regional theatre production at Florida's Coconut Grove Playhouse in 1989, with a new book; and another regional production at New Haven's Long Wharf Theatre in 2000, with yet another new book. All have failed.

The problem is the score. Yes, the score—Strouse's most exciting work, arguably—is the only reason to salvage *Golden Boy*. But the score doesn't fit *Golden Boy*; it fits Sammy Davis. I daresay that the Odets play could be musicalized successfully, under the right circumstances. But the time (1964) and the place (Harlem) that were chosen, for rather logical reasons, worked against the drama. As Gibson put it, "From beginning to end the book, wherever it had a choice of materials, it had made the wrong choice." The songwriters wrote songs to fit the book—the original version, the final version, and those in between—and to suit Sammy's stringent demands.

Strouse wrote a *Sunday Times* piece to promote the Encores! production of the play, a wonderfully candid and self-effacing essay on what happened and why. "We wouldn't/couldn't write the 'pop' Sammy Cahn–Jimmy Van Heusen songs with the Sinatra overlay that Sammy could metamorphose into jazz-sounding phrases, and Sammy wouldn't/couldn't/didn't sing *our* version of 'black.' So *Golden Boy* began its musical life as mangled jazz, strangled Milhaud, a little Stravinsky here and a little Rodelph Sholem Synagogue there."

The combination of Milhaud, Stravinsky, and synagogue jazz was the revelation when *Golden Boy* appeared at Encores! The show was a late substitution; *It's a Bird, It's a Plane, It's Superman,* a cartoonish Strouse and Adams failure from 1966, had been announced for the slot. But the villain of *Superman* plotted to blow up the city hall of a metropolis very much patterned on Manhattan. Following the events of the fall, Encores! understandably changed from *Superman* to Strouse and Adams's prior musical.

The book problems were summarily dealt with; they simply shredded it. Suzan-Lori Parks—Pulitzer in hand—had her name on the adaptation, but it was a severe operation. We went from song to song via tissue paper–thin connections, making the proceedings seem like a Cliff Notes version of *Golden Boy*. (I clocked the first act, with ten musical numbers, at forty-seven minutes.) Even so, the remains of the plot dissolved into a melodramatic muddle. There was also some song tinkering; "Can't You See It," Joe's joyous reaction to his first night with Lorna, was spotted late in the show in 1964, just before the climactic boxing match. City Center moved it to the top of the second act, where it seemed like part of a Las Vegas lounge act.

Even so, the *Golden Boy* score seemed wondrous in 2002. Especially to audiences fresh from Broadway's newest musicals. *Golden Boy* has always sounded reasonably good, though not in a class with *Fiddler* or *She Loves Me* or *Gypsy*. Compared with *Thoroughly Modern Millie* and *Sweet Smell of Success*, it seemed like Rodgers and Hammerstein at their best.

Strouse has had a long career as a Broadway tunesmith, his biggest successes being the bouncy "show tune" scores for *Bye Bye Birdie* and *Annie*. But he started as a serious musician, before he decided he'd rather eat; he went to the Eastman School of Music in Rochester, traveled to Paris to study with the musical wizardress Nadia Boulanger, and worked with Aaron Copland as well. He has written fifteen full-scale musicals to date, plus at least a half dozen unproduced ones. *Golden Boy*, his third show, is the only time we have heard the smoky, jazzlike moodiness that I suppose is the real Strouse. There were hints of it in three of his post-*Annie* musicals, *Dance a Little Closer*, *Rags*, and *Nick & Nora*; each was a spectacular failure, however, running a combined total of fourteen performances.

> **Strouse's score is the only reason to salvage *Golden Boy*. But the score doesn't fit *Golden Boy*; it fits Sammy Davis.**

Strouse was the hero of the Encores! presentation; his long-neglected music was roundly hailed. In fact, he woke up to what appears to be his only great personal review from the *Times* ever, with Ben Brantley calling it "one of the most compelling musical scores to come out of the last four decades. Mr. Strouse's music is still in your head when you wake up the next morning, and you feel the urgent need to go buy a recording of *Golden Boy*." (Compare this with Clive Barnes, then of the *Times*, on *Annie*: "The music is tuneful and supportive. It is neither unduly inventive nor memorable.") This must have been sweet vindication for the composer. I ran into Judith E. Daykin, executive director of Encores!, in the lobby on the day the reviews appeared. She told me that Strouse said it was the happiest day of his life. A wild exaggeration, no doubt; but understandable from a man whose last eight musicals, over twenty-five years, had been savagely received.

"Night Song," "Lorna's Here," "Golden Boy," "I Want to Be with You" —all are highly moving and fascinating in structure. "Don't Forget 127th

Golden Boy
Opened: March 21, 2002
Closed: March 24, 2002
5 performances (and 0 previews)
Profit/Loss: Nonprofit
Golden Boy ($80 top) played the 2,753-seat City Center. Box
   office figures not available.

*Critical
Scorecard*

Rave 1
Favorable 4
Mixed 2
Unfavorable 1
Pan 1

Street" and "This Is the Life" are high-powered production numbers, and the seductive "While the City Sleeps" is one of my favorite Strouse songs. This made for an impressive lineup at City Center. The score was greatly abetted by the music department, playing the great orchestrations by Ralph Burns. Burns died on November 21, 2001; the Encores! production of *Golden Boy* was dedicated to him.

Burns brought a new sound to Broadway when he appeared with Richard Rodgers's *No Strings* in 1962. This was his third Broadway show, actually; the first two were quick failures that went unrecorded, *Strip for Action* (which closed on the road in 1956) and *Copper and Brass* (1957). *No Strings* was followed by *Little Me*, *Funny Girl*, *Golden Boy*, *Sweet Charity*, and numerous other musicals.

While Burns received sole orchestration billing in 1964, Elliot Lawrence —the show's musical director—was credited for "additional musical scoring." Jim Tyler is known to have orchestrated "Night Song" after Davis rejected at least four versions by Burns, and I understand that other parts of the score were contributed by Larry Wilcox. (This assistance was understandable; the *Golden Boy* opening was delayed a month, by which time Burns was out of town with another musical in trouble.) When Rob Fisher and his staff went to work, they discovered that some of the original charts were missing. Don Sebesky came in to reconstruct the missing parts from the original cast album, and it all sounded perfectly swell.

Fisher and his Coffee Club Orchestra really let it rip. (When Fisher turned for his bow at the top of act 2, he was wearing a boxer's championship belt.) It was especially nice to hear Red Press in the first reed chair. Press is one of Broadway's busiest musical contractors. (A contractor is more or less a casting director for pit bands.) Unlike most of his peers, he still plays whenever possible. Press goes back forty years; he was in the pit of *Gypsy* in 1959. Sitting out in the open at Encores!, you could see who was playing what; Red's alto sax solo in "Lorna's Here" was stunning.

Alfonso Ribeiro—who at the age of twelve was Broadway's *Tap Dance Kid*, before Savion Glover came in as a midrun replacement—played Joe, and guess what? He wasn't the singer-dancer-actor-showstopper that Sammy Davis was. Still, he got through it, most of it; but he was far more comfortable when dancing. The other two principals were considerably better. Anastasia Barzee sang Lorna's songs with the fatalistic melancholy called for and paired well with Ribeiro for the big duet "I Want to Be with You." Norm Lewis—an extremely talented singer-actor still looking for his big break—gave an icy-cold reading of the Machiavellian Eddie Satin and really landed "While the City Sleeps." (This villainous evildoer was called Eddie Fuselli in the play version, when the characters came from the Italian ghetto. The role was created by Elia Kazan.)

> **Golden Boy has always sounded reasonably good, though not in a class with Fiddler or Gypsy. Compared with Thoroughly Modern Millie and Sweet Smell of Success, it seemed like Rodgers and Hammerstein at their best.**

The purpose of Encores!, first and foremost, is to present today's audiences with the opportunity to hear scores from yesterday that they would not otherwise ever have the chance to hear. *Golden Boy* is stubbornly unworkable, as a show. The score proved to be golden, though, and boy! what a treat.

The Smell of the Kill

The Smell of the Kill sorta stinks," said Michael Kuchwara of the Associated Press. "Fridge Farce B-b-b-bad to the Bone," said the headline of Howard Kissel's review in the *Daily News*; "the only thing that engaged my mind was whether I had ever seen anything stupider." Clive Barnes of the *New York Post* called it "a situation comedy that has only one situation and very little comedy," noting that "such tension as there is [is] the tension of wondering not where it will end, but when."

Elysa Gardner of *USA Today* observed that "the real mystery is how this turkey managed to get on Broadway in the first place." And Charles Isherwood in *Variety* noted that "a week after *Sweet Smell of Success* had critics fleeing the Martin Beck holding their noses, along comes Michele Lowe's *The Smell of the Kill*, a coarse, sloppy comedy about three wives who blithely decide to let their husbands turn into Popsicles when they get themselves locked in a meat freezer. No amount of time in the subzero, alas, could keep this one from stinking."

Variety said it had the makings of a hit. "With more lusty guffaws . . . than many a so-called comedy . . . , The Smell of the Kill . . . should have a good chance at a successful Manhattan transfer."

And there was more of the same, from most quarters. The critics painted a bull's-eye on the carcass of Michele Lowe's play and let launch a torrent of buckshot. It was not to their liking, obviously; but what prompted such an enraged attack?

Broadway had seen an assortment of critically maligned washouts over the course of three seasons, shows like *Voices in the Dark* and *Epic Proportions* and *Saturday Night Fever* and *Minnelli on Minnelli* and *Wrong Mountain* and *The Dinner Party* and *The Gathering* and *The Adventures of Tom*

Debra Claudia Shear
Molly Jessica Stone
Nicky Lisa Emery
Danny Patrick Garner
Jay Mark Lotito
Marty Patrick Garner

Time: After dinner
Place: The kitchen of Nicky's house in
Wilmette, Illinois

THE HELEN HAYES THEATRE
MARTIN MARKINSON   DONALD TICK

ELIZABETH I. McCANN   NELLE NUGENT   MILTON & TAMAR MALTZ
USA OSTAR THEATRICALS

PRESENT

LISA   CLAUDIA   JESSICA
EMERY   SHEAR   STONE

IN

the **Smell** of the **Kill**

A NEW COMEDY

BY

MICHELE LOWE

WITH

PATRICK GARNER   MARK LOTITO

SET DESIGN   COSTUME DESIGN
DAVID GALLO   DAVID C. WOOLARD

LIGHTING DESIGN   SOUND DESIGN
KENNETH POSNER   DAN MOSES SCHREIER

FIGHT DIRECTOR   CASTING
RICK SORDELET   JOHNSON-LIFF ASSOCIATES

PRESS AGENT   PRODUCTION STAGE MANAGER
BONEAU/BRYAN-BROWN   DAVID HYSLOP

TECHNICAL SUPERVISOR   GENERAL MANAGER
LARRY MORLEY   ROY GABAY

DIRECTED BY

CHRISTOPHER ASHLEY

ORIGINALLY PRODUCED AT THE CLEVELAND PLAY HOUSE
PETER HACKETT ARTISTIC DIRECTOR DEAN R. GLADDEN MANAGING DIRECTOR

Sawyer and *45 Seconds from Broadway* and *One Mo' Time.* What was it
that earned *The Smell of the Kill* the rankest collective critical scorn? On a
level, perhaps, with *Squonk* and *Taller Than a Dwarf.*

Yes, *The Smell of the Kill* was slight. Yes, it was outrageous. But it was
funny, with jokes cascading across the footlights like golf balls. (There
were also golf balls cascading across the footlights like golf balls, the night
I saw it at least.) It was well directed. And it was well played by three actresses, who under the circumstances gave impressive performances.

The Smell of the Kill began life in January 1999, when it premiered at
the Cleveland Play House. Regional productions followed at the Intiman
Theatre in Seattle, Syracuse (New York) Stage, the Delaware Theatre
Company in Wilmington, and the Round House Theatre in Washington,
D.C. (where it was directed by Heather McDonald, author of *An Almost*

Holy Picture). Producers Elizabeth I. McCann and Nelle Nugent optioned the property and arranged an August 2001 tryout at the Berkshire Theatre Festival in Stockbridge, Massachusetts.

This production got some highly favorable reviews. Markland Taylor of *Variety* said the producers "have the makings of a hit on their hands. With more lusty guffaws in its short length than many a so-called comedy twice as long, *The Smell of the Kill* makes murder in the suburbs killingly funny. . . . It should have a good chance at a successful Manhattan transfer."

And so a Manhattan transfer was arranged. Most of the team assembled by McCann and Nugent for Stockbridge was retained: director Christopher Ashley, scenic designer David Gallo, and lighting designer Kenneth Posner, as well as costar Claudia Shear (of *Dirty Blonde*). The other two actresses in the Stockbridge cast, Kristen Johnston (as Nicky) and Katie Finneran (as Molly), were unavailable. Both brightened the 2001–2002 season long before *The Smell of the Kill* came in, winning acclaim in (respectively) the revivals of *The Women* and *Noises Off*.

The Smell of the Kill quickly grabbed the Helen Hayes when *By Jeeves* hastily vacated. Lisa Emery, who had done such a nice job in the Pulitzer Prize–winning *Dinner with Friends*, replaced Johnston. (Emery appeared earlier in the season with Johnston in *The Women*, playing the bachelorette-writer Nancy Blake.) Jessica Stone became the new Molly; she had been a replacement Rosemary in the 1995 revival of *How to Succeed in Business without Really Trying* and was prominently featured in the Drama Dept. 1998 revival of *June Moon*.

And then came those lacerating reviews from the Broadway critics. The three actresses received empathetic personal notices; the critics seemed to go out of their way to praise the players, while ravaging the play. Director Ashley was more or less appreciated as well; everybody placed the blame solely on the shoulders of the playwright.

The plot, simply put, told of three wives with overbearing husbands. (Said husbands are very much present, delivering their lines through the swinging door to the living room, offstage right.) The boys make a trip to the meat locker in the basement; the man of the house, a former vegetarian, is now an enthusiastic hunter. The freezer door, alas, gets stuck. The wives, understandably, choose not to intercede, and within seventy-two minutes the girls are merry widows and the boys are dead meat. The action transpired in real time, by the way; a clock marked time on the wall of set designer Gallo's severely raked kitchen, which thrust the murderous action into the audience's lap.

Lowe, a forty-something playwright from Massapequa Park, was one of those writers with a handful of regional credits but no prior Broadway exposure. While *The Smell of the Kill* was clearly not a critical favorite, the author displayed a gift for the comically macabre. And her play was packed with laughs, not a given with many of today's so-called comedies.

The Smell of the Kill marked the reunion of producers Liz McCann and Nelle Nugent. As with many things in this business, success is cyclical; for about five years, McCann and Nugent were Broadway's most powerful producer-managers. I recall an ad in *Variety* circa 1982 that was headed: "McCann and Nugent: Never an Intermission!" There followed the titles and opening dates of *Dracula* (1977), *The Elephant Man* (1979), *Amadeus* (1980), *Morning's at Seven* (1980), and *The Life and Adventures of Nicholas Nickleby* (1981). Five Tony Award winners in four seasons, including two of the most memorable shows of the last twenty-five years. (*Amadeus* was revived on Broadway in 1999, with both *The Elephant Man* and *Morning's at Seven* returning a month after the opening of *The Smell of the Kill*. None with the participation of McCann or Nugent.)

This represented only a portion of McCann and Nugent's activity. They produced six other shows during these years, with a total of twenty-one between 1977 and 1985; other memorable productions included *Piaf*, *The Dresser*, and the Royal Shakespeare Company's twin bill of *Cyrano de Bergerac* and *Much Ado about Nothing* starring Derek Jacobi. McCann and Nugent also simultaneously served as general managers of more than a dozen other shows. These included three Pulitzer Prize winners in six years, *The Gin Game*, *Crimes of the Heart*, and *'night, Mother*.

Elizabeth Ireland McCann began her career working in theatrical offices in 1956. In 1960, she went to work for a producer named Martin Tahse, who would buy up the remains of touring companies of Broadway hits, cut down the productions, recast them inexpensively, and send them out on secondary tours. McCann served as general manager for Tahse's tours of *Fiorello!*, *The Miracle Worker*, *A Funny Thing Happened on the Way to the Forum*, and *Funny Girl*. She made her Broadway debut in 1960 with Stanley Holloway's one-man show, *Laughs and Other Events*, which lasted seven performances at the Barrymore. This makes Liz the oldest established, permanent floating producer-manager in New York. (Manny Azenberg's first Broadway-level job, as far as I can tell, was as company manager of *Lena Horne in Her Nine O'Clock Revue*, which closed during its pre-Broadway tour in 1961.)

The Nederlander family of Detroit bought New York's legendary Palace Theatre in 1965 and over the next few years established themselves as Broadway's second-most-prominent theatre owners. James M. Nederlander, who led the New York operation, soon started coproducing shows to fill his theatres. McCann, who had earned a law degree in 1966, was named managing director in 1968. She coproduced the 1969 Nederlander tour of *George M!* but otherwise remained behind the scenes until 1974, when she received coproducer credit on *My Fat Friend*.

Liz McCann is the oldest established, permanent floating producer-manager in New York.

Nelle Nugent began her career as an off-Broadway stage manager in 1961. In 1964 she moved up to Broadway as production assistant on the long-running hit *Any Wednesday*. She became a Broadway stage manager on the short-lived 1965 sex farce *Boeing-Boeing* and spent the next few years as assistant stage manager on a string of mostly bad plays. (In one five-month stretch, she did three Broadway shows from start to finish—and these were not supposed to be limited engagements.) In 1968 she landed on a good play, *A Day in the Death of Joe Egg*. When that show's producer mounted his next show in 1970, he hired Nugent as general manager. *Gantry*, a musical version of Sinclair Lewis's novel *Elmer Gantry*, was a one-night flop.

Nugent moved over to Nederlander Productions as production manager. She became in-house general manager in 1974, with *My Fat Friend*. Later that year—within four weeks—she did imports of two Royal Shakespeare Company productions, *Sherlock Holmes* (which was highly successful) and *London Assurance*. In 1975 she general managed Scott Joplin's *Treemonisha* and the British transfer *Habeus Corpus*, and in 1976 McCann and Nugent went out on their own as producers and general managers.

Success followed success until 1983, when things began to sour. Take out an ad in *Variety* that says "Never an Intermission!" and just see what happens. *The Elephant Man*, *Amadeus*, and *The Life and Adventures of Nicholas Nickleby* had each originated with other producers; McCann and Nugent were brought in as managing producers. As they grew more prominent, they set about creating shows of their own.

They went out on a limb with what turned out to be a full-fledged disaster. *Total Abandon*, a 1983 play about child abuse, received outraged re-

The Smell of the Kill
Opened: March 26, 2002
Closed: April 28, 2002
40 performances (and 20 previews)
Profit/Loss: Loss
The Smell of the Kill ($70 top) was scaled to a potential
 gross of $326,330 at the 597-seat Helen Hayes Theatre.
 Weekly grosses averaged about $71,000, with the bad
 reviews dropping the show from an $85,000 high in
 previews to a $50,000 low. Total gross for the eight-week
 run was $533,380. Attendance was about 51 percent, with
 the box office grossing about 22 percent of dollar-
 capacity.

*Critical
Scorecard*

Rave 0
Favorable 1
Mixed 0
Unfavorable 1
Pan 8

views and closed after one performance at the Booth. (This despite the
presence of Richard Dreyfuss, then at the height of his fame.) Next came
a revival of *The Glass Menagerie* that sounded good on paper; John Dexter directed, Jessica Tandy starred, but it simply didn't work. Three ineffective off-Broadway productions followed (including Stockard Channing in Michael Cristofer's *The Lady and the Clarinet*), after which McCann
and Nugent embarked on a full-scale rock-and-roll revue.

   Leader of the Pack, a compilation of songs by Ellie Greenwich, was unworkable; it opened in April 1985 at the Ambassador and closed three
months later. The production period was intensely stormy; it seemed to
me, as a disinterested observer, that none of the many people involved
had any idea what they were trying to accomplish, theatrically speaking.
Tension between McCann and Nugent had been high since *Total Abandon*. *Leader of the Pack* proved such a wrenchingly unpleasant experience
that McCann and Nugent simply closed their doors.

   Nugent moved into television and film, producing movies of the week
and features. McCann maintained a somewhat infrequent presence on
Broadway, with such productions as the RSC's *Les Liaisons Dangereuses*
(1987), Vanessa Redgrave's *Orpheus Descending* (1989), and the infamous
musical *Nick & Nora* (1991). McCann's career revived with the off-
Broadway production of Edward Albee's remarkable Pulitzer Prize–
winning *Three Tall Women* in 1995. This was followed by the 1998 Tony
Award–winning revival of *A View from the Bridge*; Michael Frayn's 2000
Tony Award–winning play *Copenhagen*; Albee's controversial 2001 off-
Broadway *Play about the Baby*; and—within two hectic weeks—*The Goat,
or Who Is Sylvia?*, and *Smell of the Kill*.

   McCann and Nugent responded to their brutal Wednesday morning
Smell reviews with a Friday display ad in the *Times* quoting the review of
that paper's critic Bruce Weber: "O.K., I'm not a woman and I'm not mar-

ried, so it's possible I'm just not in tune with a members-only message. (I admired *The Vagina Monologues*, but I suspect I didn't really get it.)" The producers then quoted Roma Torre, of the cable channel New York 1: "Imagine Lucy & Ethel transplanted to the 21st century. *The Smell of the Kill* is a very funny, 90-minute guilty pleasure. This comedy has enough of a black heart to make it more appealing to men than you might think." The ad concluded, in big letters, with "Get it Now, Bruce?"

Put Kathleen Turner or Rosie O'Donnell in the cast, and *The Smell of the Kill* would still be running to laugh-filled houses, critics be damned.

To little avail. You can counteract lousy reviews with good word of mouth, but you first need to get audiences in the theatre. With little advance sale, and facing stiff competition from seventeen new shows within two months, the producers had little recourse but to close after five weeks. One thing seems clear. Put Kathleen Turner in the role of Nicky—or Rosie O'Donnell in the role of Claudia—and *The Smell of the Kill* would still be running to laugh-filled houses, critics be damned.

Fortune's Fool

Alan Bates's bravura twenty-minute drunk scene at the end of act 1 of *Fortune's Fool* was, alone, worth the price of admission. So intimated roughly half of the evenly divided critics. The others opined that Bates's bravura drunk scene, alone, was *not* quite worth the price of admission—$75, plus that pesky $1.25 restoration fee. Two nights later, the reviewers engaged in another opening-night discussion of time-dollar ratio. To save you from having to thumb ahead, the party of the second part was Kathleen Turner, and they weren't talking about her line delivery.

There was a time when an evening like *Fortune's Fool* might have been a surefire moderate success. In the thirties or forties, Broadway's carriage trade would have embraced this snapshot of a time in Russia just beyond memory (circa 1850). In the fifties or sixties, the two star performances would have enraptured audiences. In the seventies or eighties, the very presence of two stars like Bates and Frank Langella—both of whom have given well-remembered performances on stage and screen—might have been enough to carry the load.

But Broadway since the turn of the new century had seen *True West, A Moon for the Misbegotten, Copenhagen, The Real Thing, Proof, The Tale of the Allergist's Wife, The Invention of Love, Stones in His Pockets, One Flew over the Cuckoo's Nest, The Seagull, Hedda Gabler, Dance of Death, Metamorphoses, The Crucible,* and *The Goat.* Five of these were still playing when *Fortune's Fool* opened, with further competition within a fortnight from a *Topdog* and an *Elephant Man.* Not to mention the aforementioned Ms. Turner.

Which makes it tough competition for twenty minutes of great acting, even when it comes from Alan Bates. He had been absent from Broadway for twenty-nine years, since *Butley* (for which he won his first Tony Award) closed in 1973. Bates made a brief off-Broadway visit in 2000, in *The Unexpected Man*, presented by two of the three top-billed *Fortune's Fool* producers.

As Kuzovkin, Bates was quite something. (He created the role in Mike Poulton's adaptation of *Fortune's Fool* in 1996, at England's Chichester Festival.) In the duly celebrated drunk scene, Bates weaved—nay, danced—his way about the stage, progressing deeper and deeper into his cups. During one stretch of the monologue, he engaged in a fierce but memorable struggle to pick up a fallen napkin while remaining angular.

Bates has always been an exceptional actor. It was my good fortune, as a teenager, to watch him onstage for two weeks straight; late in the run of *Butley*, I filled in as concessionaire at the Morosco. Fine actors can fall into the trap of overintellectualizing their performances, so that you see the actor thinking, especially on a night-by-night basis. With Bates, in 1972 and 2002, it was the character who did the thinking.

Alan Bates's bravura twenty-minute drunk scene at the end of act 1 of *Fortune's Fool* was, alone, worth the price of admission. Or maybe not.

Badgering Kuzovkin and waging onstage battle with Bates was Frank Langella, chewing the drapes as a deliciously outré "infamous, fatuous fop." Langella acted with his hands. "My worst fear, my nightmare, is that you'll find us all so very dull," he told his hosts, "and you'll scurry away back to Petersburg, flippety-floppety like a pair of little gray rabbits." Flippety-floppety went his hands, in kid gloves, and I suppose that "flippety-floppety" can describe his whole performance. He used his hands as if they were quotation marks. "Art and nature are my only vices," Langella confessed, with worlds of meaning. Late in the second act, he turned from the action to explain to the audience with arched eyes, "there's more fun to be had here than at the theatre." Which, indeed, was the case.

Langella is worlds apart from Bates, an intense charmer with a hint of danger just below the surface. He made a memorable Broadway debut in 1975 as a lizard in Edward Albee's *Seascape* and became a star in 1977 with *Dracula*. I spent a couple of months with Frank some years ago, hanging out in his dressing room. (I was managing a show he produced and starred in, and backstage was the only place to get his attention.) His most recent appearances, in *Fortune's Fool* and the 1996 revival of Noël Coward's *Present Laughter*, have displayed a wild comic talent only hinted at in his days as a leading man. I've always felt that Frank was an electric Henry Higgins waiting to happen. Perhaps Langella, who turned sixty-two in 2002, will still have the opportunity.

In another time and another place, the Bates-Langella double act

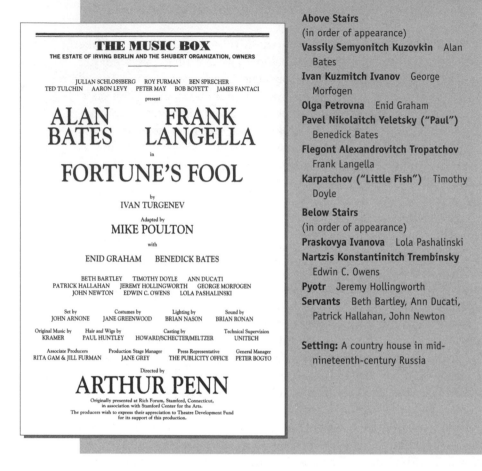

might have proved more than enough for success. But for seventy-six bucks, against such rugged competition, *Fortune's Fool* needed to offer more than an Actors' Studio demonstration of how to go way, way over the top while more or less maintaining your character's integrity.

As is my general practice, I decided it would be helpful to read *Fortune's Fool* as preparation. This was not so simple. *Fortune's Fool* was described, in ads and press releases, as "a new adaptation of Turgenev's comedy." But which of Turgenev's comedies? Ivan Turgenev (1818–1883) wrote ten plays in all, from 1843 to 1852; he then turned novelist, his work culminating in *Fathers and Sons* in 1862. All his plays are long forgotten except *A Month in the Country*, which was written in 1850 but didn't achieve success until 1879.

Turgenev titled his plays in Russian, and not without reason. Searching through the published English translations of his work, I encountered nothing with a title remotely resembling *Fortune's Fool*. (Clive Barnes, in the sole rave review for *Fortune's Fool*, told us that the play's original title —transliterated into English—is *Nakhlebnik*.) I did find something called *The Bachelor*. This appeared to have a suitable starring role for Alan Bates, so I sat down and read it.

The Bachelor told of a middle-aged fellow named Moshkin, a low-level civil servant of sympathetic character who—as the play progresses— grows on you. He has a nice-but-plain nineteen-year-old ward, for whom he arranges a marriage with a young clerk from his office. The girl is too plain for the clerk, it turns out, so he jilts her. In a startling twist in the final scene, Turgenev solves the problem by having the girl accept a marriage proposal from Moshkin himself. And it works out perfectly! The playwright has been talking about the bachelor all through *The Bachelor*, and it turns out that his title character was not the fiancé—as you'd been led to expect—but Moshkin.

I couldn't quite figure out what role Langella would play, though, and as I headed into the third act I began to suspect that *The Bachelor* surely wasn't *Fortune's Fool*. At this time, I learned from a preliminary interview that Bates was playing a character named Kuzovkin. Thumbing through my anthology—*Turgenev Plays*, translated by Stephen Mulrine—I finally found Kuzovkin, in a play called *One of the Family*.

I finished *The Bachelor*—it was too intriguing to leave hanging—and then moved on to the real *Fortune's Fool*. This, too, made for engrossing reading. But as an episode, rather than a fully satisfying dramatic piece. Kuzovkin was one of the family, which in the parlance of the time was understood to be an impecunious gentleman living on charity as a permanent house guest

> As the actors all stood their ground, waiting for something—anything—to happen, a cell phone went off. A Broadway producer, possessor of six Tony Awards, sheepishly switched it off.

at a grand estate. (Not unlike Telegin in *Uncle Vanya*, as Mulrine explains.) Kuzovkin moved in thirty years earlier, as guest of and court jester to the former owner. Ten years later, the owner died; Kuzovkin—"a poor gentleman down on his luck"—stayed on as a nonpaying guest. Eleven years later the lady of the estate died, and her daughter Olga Petrovna went off to Petersburg. Now the twenty-year-old Olga Petrovna has returned, in company with her new husband, Yeletsky.

Kuzovkin is understandably concerned about his future. A neighboring landowner—a flamboyantly wild character named Tropachov—comes along, mercilessly ridicules Kuzovkin, and plies him with drink. Tropachov pushes and pushes until he goes too far, causing Kuzovkin to explode. He melodramatically blurts out that he is not a mere foolish jester —fortune's fool—but the father of Olga Petrovna.

This is quite a scene, and Bates was rather amazing as he went from tipsy to drunk to sullen to out of control. As he delivered his final claim, he was clearly too far gone to be making it up. Turgenev arranged it so that Olga Petrovna should pass through the room just in time to hear Kuzovkin claim paternity. All in all, an effective first-act curtain.

But that was the end of it. In the second act, the action moved from the main living room to Olga's sitting room, and that's what they all did: sit. Sit and talk. Olga Petrovna and Yeletsky talked about the falseness of Kuzovkin's claim; Olga Petrovna and Kuzovkin talked about the truth of Kuzovkin's claim; Tropatchov barged in, inevitably, and talked about himself. The second act was all talk, explanation, and the emotional merging of hearts when the daughter recognized the truth of the situation, culminating in a satisfactory resolution. All nine characters— including visitors to the house whom you'd not logically expect to encounter in the living quarters—found their way into Olga Petrovna's parlor, which made for a crowded sitting room. When the extra men entered the room, the play came to a sudden halt. There they were, pacing as if in preparation for a duel, and nothing whatsoever happening.

> **Fortune's Fool was all about that one bravura drunk scene. The first hour of the play prepared us for it, and the final hour explained it; but this was clearly the centerpiece.**

As they all stood their ground, waiting for something—anything—to happen, a cell phone went off directly behind me. A producer friend of mine was sitting there, someone whose name I won't mention but who is the possessor of six Tony Awards (and counting). One of the first people, as I recall, to use that "please turn off your cell phone" announcement at his shows. He sheepishly dug through his coat pockets, found his phone, and switched the thing off. These things happen, I guess, even to distinguished Broadway producers.

But nothing else happened during the final hour of the play. *Fortune's Fool*—or *One of the Family*, or *The Poor Gentleman* or *The Parasite* (as it has also been called in a previous English-language version) or *Nakhlebnik*—was all about that one bravura drunk scene. The first hour of the play prepared us for it, and the final hour explained it; but this was clearly Turgenev's centerpiece. There was a time when Bates's fireworks—and Langella's heavyweight hamming—might have been enough to sustain *Fortune's Fool*. In April 2002, though, it was a losing proposition.

The play's anonymity is not surprising. Although it was finished in 1848, Mulrine tells us, it was banned until 1861; Kuzovkin's drunk scene

—centering around his hapless struggle to recover his rightfully inherited estate against Russia's corrupt legal system—was not to the liking of czarist censors. As far as I can tell, *Fortune's Fool* or whatever you want to call it saw very little stage time until Mike Poulton unearthed it for the Chichester Festival in 1996.

Poulton's adaptation of *Uncle Vanya* was produced at Chichester earlier that year, at which time Derek Jacobi was codirector of the festival. The Roundabout presented it at the Atkinson in 2000, with Jacobi re-creating his role in an otherwise new production with an American director. Judging from the two Broadway productions, Poulton did far better with Turgenev than with Chekhov. Two of the Chichester principals, Bates and his son Benedick (who played Yeletsky, Olga Petrovna's husband), made the trip from England. Gale Edwards directed the original *Fortune's Fool*, the same Gale Edwards who made her Broadway debut with the dismal 2000 revival of *Jesus Christ Superstar*. For Broadway, the producers enlisted Arthur Penn.

Penn was, for a brief spell, one of the theatre's most influential directors. After a decade in live television, he made his Broadway debut in 1958 with William Gibson's *Two for the Seesaw* (starring Henry Fonda and Anne Bancroft). This was followed in 1959 by Gibson's *The Miracle Worker* (starring Bancroft) and three hits in 1960: Lillian Hellman's *Toys in the Attic* (starring Jason Robards Jr., Maureen Stapleton, and Irene Worth); *An Evening with Mike Nichols and Elaine May*; and the Pulitzer Prize–winning *All the Way Home* (starring Colleen Dewhurst, Lillian Gish, and Arthur Hill). Then came three failures, one each in 1962, 1963, and 1964. (The latter was a replacement job on the Sammy Davis Jr. musical *Golden Boy*. Conversely, Penn was the original director of two other musicals, on both of which he was replaced by George Abbott: the Pulitzer Prize–winning *Fiorello!*—which he conceived, and in which he retained a slice of the author's royalty—and *How Now, Dow Jones*.) Next came the 1966 thriller hit *Wait until Dark*.

Penn began a Hollywood career in 1962, with the film version of *The*

Miracle Worker. His fourth movie effectively took him away from Broadway: *Bonnie and Clyde* (1967) established him as one of Hollywood's most
influential directors. This was followed by such movies as *Little Big Man*,
Alice's Restaurant, and *Night Moves*. Penn didn't return to Broadway until
1976, with Larry Gelbart's comedy hit *Sly Fox*. His only subsequent visits
were with two unsuccessful Gibson plays, *Golda* (in 1977, starring Bancroft) and *Monday after the Miracle*, a 1982 sequel to *The Miracle Worker*.
Since then, Penn had been inactive in the theatre; he turned eighty in
2002.

For those of you interested in such mundane matters, let me point out
that Turgenev's billing was half the size of Poulton's. Chekhov's billing on
Vanya was the same size as Poulton's, which can only mean that Chekhov
has a better agent than Turgenev. Speaking of agents and billing, theatregoers who were so bored as to spend the second act reading the small
print in the *Playbill* might have noticed that two actors, Edwin C. Owens
and Jeff Talbott, were listed under the legend "standby for Mr. Bates."
This was followed by Mr. Owens as "standby for Mr. Langella" and Timothy Doyle as "understudy for Tropatchov." Thus, Bates had two standbys
while Langella made do with a standby and an understudy. Go figure. (In
my experience, "standby" is a meaningless term used to placate agents of
understudies who are trying to get more money for their clients.)

When awards time came around, the producers petitioned the eligibility committee to consider Langella in the featured category, despite his

over-the-title billing. This move paid off; instead of two stars a-battling, Bates and Langella both went home with a Tony medallion. The producers also talked them into considering *Fortune's Fool* a new play, even though Turgenev wrote it in 1848. It has never been produced on Broadway, so how can it be a revival? Which leads you to wonder, is there a new play by Shakespeare out there?

The Graduate

The play that received the very worst reviews of the season proved to be the play that did the very best business of the season. How did the producers manage to pull it off? Very easily, it turned out. They simply settled on a property that ticket buyers were clamoring to see and went artlessly on from there.

And how did they manage to come up with such a surefire property, that from the evidence was impossible to destroy? Well, that was the hard part.

Much has been said of late around Broadway—and in this book—about the increasing tendency to adapt motion pictures to the stage. We spoke of it five shows back, and I'm afraid we'll be renewing the conversation three shows down the line.

All the discussion, though, has centered on films converted into stage musicals. It is exceedingly rare for a film to be converted into a nonmusical stage play. Television plays that are adapted directly for the stage—like *The Rainmaker* and *The Miracle Worker*—are something else again; but it has been highly uncommon to go from screen to play. Abby Mann's *Judgment at Nuremberg* was attempted just before the 2001 Tony deadline, stumbling through fifty-six performances at the Longacre. Budd Schulberg's *On the Waterfront* was attempted just before the Tony deadline in 1995, capsizing after only eight at the Atkinson. Rod Serling's *Requiem for a Heavyweight* (starring John Lithgow) was attempted just before the 1985 Tony deadline, giving up the ghost after only three performances at the Martin Beck. Each was adapted for the stage by the original author; two had originated as television plays, but they were best known for their motion picture versions.

I can't think of anyplace to research further examples. The only others I recall were a disastrous attempt at the cult hit *Harold and Maude*, which lasted four performances at the Beck in 1980; a 1957 play called *Monique*, based on the source material for the nifty 1955 French classic *Diabolique*, that expired after sixty-three performances at the Golden; and a 1945 stab at Alfred Hitchcock's *Rebecca*, which folded after twenty performances. (This last played the Ethel Barrymore, with Ethel's brother John's daughter Diana hopeless as the second Mrs. de Winter. Not coincidentally, Maxim de Winter was portrayed by Bramwell Fletcher, Diana Barrymore's husband at the time.) None of these adaptations worked, but how could they? Start with a classic film directed by someone like Hitchcock. How can a stage version hope to be half so effective?

If Hitchcock was not replaceable by the likes of Clarence Derwent on *Rebecca*, it seems reasonable to suspect that adapter-director Terry Johnson might also falter in the shadow of *The Graduate*'s Mike Nichols. Johnson was heretofore unknown in America, although his *Playbill* bio boasted that he won the Lloyds Bank Private Banking Playwright of the Year award. In fairness, if you read further in his bio you discovered that he has won two Olivier Awards for Best Comedy. But not for *The Graduate*.

Johnson did a pretty poor job of it, all told; our critical scorecard shows ten outright pans. But *The Graduate* earned a profit of about $2 million in London alone and seemed likely to be equally successful in America. Oscar Hammerstein II famously quoted his grandfather Oscar Hammerstein, who once said that "there is no limit to the number of people who will stay away from a bad show." *The Graduate* suggests a corollary, something along the lines of "there is no limit to the number of people who will stay away from a bad show unless they want to see it."

I can think of any number of local playwrights and directors who would kill to write or direct a lousy play like *The Graduate*, taking Terry Johnson's lousy reviews in stride and also his royalty checks. You choose: good reviews with bad business, or awful reviews with a new co-op and a house in Majorca.

The play that received the very worst reviews of the season proved to be the play that did the very best business of the season.

There have been numerous shows that have proven highly successful despite generally rotten reviews. Prime examples are the fabled *Abie's Irish Rose* (1922), still number three on the all-time longest-running play list, and *Tobacco Road* (1933), number two and unlikely to be challenged unless *Proof* runs until March 2008. The 2001 musical *Mamma Mia* wasn't unanimously trounced, but many critics loathed it. *Abie*, *Tobacco*, and *Mamma* had something in common, besides being common; we might as well add the non–critical favorites *Cats* and *Miss Saigon* to this list. General audiences—excluding the die-hard Broadway crowd—loved these

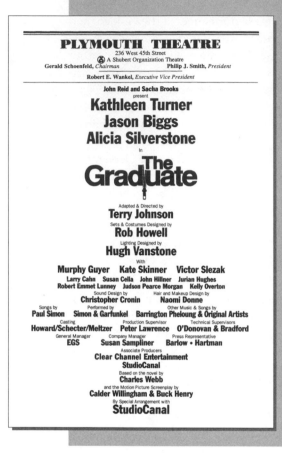

PLYMOUTH THEATRE
236 West 45th Street
Ⓢ A Shubert Organization Theatre
Gerald Schoenfeld, *Chairman*   Philip J. Smith, *President*

Robert E. Wankel, *Executive Vice President*

John Reid and Sacha Brooks
present

Kathleen Turner
Jason Biggs
Alicia Silverstone

In

The Graduate

Adapted & Directed by
Terry Johnson

Sets & Costumes Designed by
Rob Howell

Lighting Designed by
Hugh Vanstone

With

Murphy Guyer   Kate Skinner   Victor Slezak
Larry Cahn   Susan Cella   John Hillner   Jurian Hughes
Robert Emmet Lunney   Judson Pearce Morgan   Kelly Overton

Sound Design by   Hair and Makeup Design by
Christopher Cronin   **Naomi Donne**

Songs by   Performed by   Other Music & Songs by
Paul Simon   Simon & Garfunkel   Barrington Pheloung & Original Artists

Casting   Production Supervisor   Technical Supervisors
Howard/Schecter/Meltzer   Peter Lawrence   O'Donovan & Bradford

General Manager   Company Manager   Press Representative
EGS   Susan Sampliner   Barlow • Hartman

Associate Producers
Clear Channel Entertainment
StudioCanal

Based on the novel by
Charles Webb

and the Motion Picture Screenplay by
Calder Willingham & Buck Henry

By Special Arrangement with
StudioCanal

Benjamin Braddock   Jason Biggs
Mr. Braddock   Murphy Guyer
Mr. Robinson   Victor Slezak
Mrs. Braddock   Kate Skinner
Mrs. Robinson   Kathleen Turner
Elaine Robinson   Alicia Silverstone
The Hotel Clerk, The Bar Patron, The
   Psychiatrist   Robert Emmet Lunney
The Bartender, The Priest, The Motel
   Manager   John Hillner
The Assistant Desk Clerk   Kelly
   Overton
The Bellhop, The Man in Bar   Judson
   Pearce Morgan
The Stripper   Susan Cella

Setting: California, 1960s

Cast Album: Columbia/Legacy CK
   86468 (incidental music)

shows. They raved about them to their friends, and they returned to see the shows again and again.

The Graduate was something else. The people who bought their tickets to see Kathleen Turner got what they paid for, and they don't seem to have complained, exactly. But I don't think they especially liked the show. I checked around, anyway, talking to anyone I could find who had seen it. Some of them were enthusiastic that they were able to get tickets, but I didn't find anyone who seemed to actually enjoy it. I'm sure many people liked it, but I couldn't find them.

The night after I saw *The Graduate*, I was walking along Forty-fifth Street to the Music Box, to see *Fortune's Fool*. But I did not have Turgenev on my mind; rather, I was wondering what it was that made people want to buy tickets to *The Graduate*, despite the dreadful word from previews and the critically trashed tryout. As I passed the coffee bar where Oliver Morosco's theatre used to be, I heard a voice behind me say, "Oh, *The Graduate*. I think *that* would be good."

I turned to look at the speaker. She was in her early forties, a New Yorker; casually but stylishly dressed, a business executive perhaps. Or maybe a lawyer. And there, I suppose, was part of the explanation. *The Graduate* was a well-loved film, but it was also a sophisticated, witty, subversive film. The stage version, as it turned out, was anything but. I suppose that the general assumption was that anyone who chose to adapt and/or direct *The Graduate* for the stage would have the same sensibility as the people who wrote and directed it for the screen. This turned out to be woefully off the mark. But *The Graduate* sold tickets. Even after the show opened to scathing reviews, it sold tickets. I don't suppose that many theatergoers went back for a second viewing; more than a few didn't even go back for the second act. But Kathleen Turner and *The Graduate* hooked enough customers to be the hottest ticket of the season, after *Mamma Mia*.

Terry Johnson padded the scenes from Mike Nichols's *The Graduate* with material from Charles Webb's 1963 novel, upon which the film was based. Or perhaps Johnson made up all the new material, out of his own beady imagination; I don't know, and I didn't care enough to go to the effort of finding a copy of the novel and reading it. The end effect, though, was of bumping along from one remembered-moment-from-the-film to the next remembered-moment-from-the-film. Thus, we were watching not a stage adaptation of *The Graduate*; rather, "Scenes from *The Graduate*." Selected scenes, although the play took 115 minutes—plus intermission—to slog through, rather than the sleek 105 Mike Nichols did it in.

What *The Graduate* did have was star power. Kathleen Turner, who created the role of Mrs. Robinson—the stage Mrs. Robinson that is, in London—headed the cast. Turner was joined over the title by Jason Biggs and Alicia Silverstone, both of whom sported major youth-market film credits. Biggs won great renown for his relationship with the title dessert of the 1999 film *American Pie*. He made his Broadway debut next door at the Royale in 1992, at the age of thirteen, in Herb Gardner's *Conversations with My Father*. Silverstone starred as the heroine in the 1995 surprise film hit *Clueless*. Both Biggs and Silverstone presumably helped sell some tickets, although audiences at *The Graduate* did not seem appreciably younger than those at *The Elephant Man* next door. Kathleen Turner was the draw, undoubtedly; Kathleen Turner without clothes, as had been well publicized since this *Graduate* opened at the Gielgud in London in 2000.

That Turner is a major box office draw is indisputable. Or is it? She made her Broadway debut in 1990 in a steamy revival of *Cat on a Hot Tin Roof*, a hot ticket in which she was very good. Turner returned to Broadway in 1995 in *Indiscretions (Les Parents Terribles)*, in which she did not sell tickets. Not enough, anyway. This was Cocteau, mind you, as opposed to Tennessee Williams; still, it had been assumed that the presence of Turner (opposite the great Eileen Atkins) would counteract the kiss-of-death Cocteau connection. It didn't.

Turner had a wide following, that's for sure. A movie star with what one might call a "sexy" persona, she made a sensuous debut in 1981 with *Body Heat*. This was followed by such films as *Romancing the Stone* (1984), its sequel, *The Jewel of the Nile* (1985), and *Prizzi's Honor* (1985). But female stars age quickly in Hollywood. Turner peaked in 1986, at the age of thirty-two, with her delicious performance in *Peggy Sue Got Married*. She made a sultry Jessica Rabbit in *Who Framed Roger Rabbit?* (1988), but it was her voice only. In her other 1988 film, *The Accidental Tourist*, Turner was already the "older woman." Her last important film was—what? *V. I. Warshawski*, in 1991? Her more recent film credits, from 1999 and 2000, included *Baby Geniuses*, *The Virgin Suicides*, *Love and Action in Chicago*, *Beautiful*, and *The Amati Girls*. Not big box office, I'd say.

Turner followed the London *Graduate* with a pre-Broadway tour of the one-woman show *Tallulah*, which opened in Minneapolis in October 2000 and closed in Columbus, Ohio, in March 2001. A spring 2001 opening was canceled due to the pre–Tony Award cutoff booking jam; a fall 2001 opening was canceled "to allow the creative team to further develop the play," which is Broadway lingo for "we'll be killed if we try to take this thing to Broadway." The *Tallulah* cancellation made Turner very much available for the Broadway *Graduate*, which began its tryout in January 2002. Toronto, Baltimore, Boston—torrid business, horrid reviews. Maybe Turner was no longer hot in Hollywood, but *The Graduate* proved that she could, in person, still sell tickets. And how.

> Oscar Hammerstein said that "there is no limit to the number of people who will stay away from a bad show." *The Graduate* suggests "there is no limit to the number of people who will stay away from a bad show unless they want to see it."

Which takes us to the question: Do clothes make the man? Or, rather, Do no clothes make the woman?

The fact that Turner was appearing totally naked garnered *The Graduate* instant worldwide press when it opened in London. (And no, she wasn't totally naked; she was wearing a pair of white pumps.) I can't imagine that theatergoers would buy tickets to *The Graduate* simply to see Kathleen Turner naked; maybe in London, but not on Broadway. We've gone past that, I think. (Or at least hope.) But Turner and *The Graduate* sure sold tickets.

Ben Brantley, in his *New York Times* review, calculated that "with top seats for *The Graduate* going for $76.25, those 20 seconds cost close to $4 each for theatergoers interested only in full-frontal star gazing." The top ticket price on opening night, actually, was $71.25, including the $1.25 restoration fee. This was raised to $76.25 three weeks after the opening. At the same time, *The Graduate* joined *The Producers* and *The Crucible* in offering "prime" seats, in this case for $250 a pop. "The better to see you, my dear," said the well-heeled wolf.

As a former producer, I do a different sort of reckoning. *The Graduate* grossed $6,106,345 from the first preview through the end of the 2000–2001 season, thirteen weeks later. (This does not include the show's tryout tour, where it also raked in the dough.) Let us assume that the reports of Turner earning 10 percent of the box office gross were correct; this sounds right, as it is the going rate for top box office stars on Broadway. That would give her $610,635 for the thirteen weeks in New York, which—sliced into performances, divided by Mr. Brantley's twenty easy pieces, and reconstituted into sixty-second minutes—comes to approximately $17,614.46. That's $17,614.46 *per minute*. Not bad for standing around in a draft in high heels.

This is all very well and good, I suppose, and a fine way for a former film star to build a little nest egg. (The Julia Robertses of this world are now getting $20 million a film or so, but Kathleen Turner is no longer one of the Julia Robertses of this world.) Since Ms. Turner chose to disrobe herself to the public glare, I feel it pertinent to comment upon what it was we saw. Upstage, in somewhat dim light, but far bright enough. Ms. Turner was big. Big like a football player. Broad-shouldered like a linebacker. Mr. Biggs, meanwhile, was slim as a string bean. And he got to wear underwear—stylish, 2002 underwear, mind you, although the rest of the show's wardrobe was very 1963. So we had a forty-seven-year-old actress parading naked across the stage, while a twenty-three-year-old actor jumped around in his underpants.

As I checked out the entire company of eleven during the curtain call, Ms. Turner appeared to be the largest person on the stage. I heard from one of the investors that management was surprised when Turner showed up for the American production; she was very much larger than she had been in London. Not so, said a stage manager friend of mine who saw Turner in both cities and had worked with her back before *The Jewel of the Nile*. She was always large, he said, even then; but they were careful not to put her onstage with short actors and skinny actresses.

Be that as it may, Ms. Turner's relative size did not appear to bother ticket buyers. And it didn't seem to bother Ms. Turner, either. I ask, dear reader, would you parade across the stage of the Plymouth in nothing but white heels? For $17,600 a minute? How many minutes can I sign you up for?

"Mrs. Robinson, Mrs. Robinson, wherefore art thou Mrs. Robinson?" As the lights mercifully rose for intermission and the audience scattered to the bar, I looked along my row and there was Mrs. Robinson, seated on the opposite aisle. Mrs. Brooks Robinson, I mean; no, not the baseball player, the Mrs. Robinson who is Mrs. Mel Brooks. That is, Anne Bancroft. Thirty-five years older in calendar years, but from the distance of ten seats looking simply smashing. With built-in class, sophistication, and a glance that could still slice through ice. All of which were absent from the stage of the Plymouth.

This is slightly inaccurate, I'm afraid. I didn't see Ms. Bancroft at the Plymouth, in truth; it was the next night, across the street at the Music

Box. One can understand why she might have chosen to avoid *The Graduate*. (Imagine once more that you are Kathleen Turner. How would you like to play Mrs. Robinson with Anne Bancroft majestically perched in E 101? Even at those prices.) It was just as understandable that Bancroft would make it to *Fortune's Fool*; Arthur Penn had directed her in three of her seven Broadway visits.

Bancroft was there, smiling, at *Fortune's Fool* despite a rough couple of months. In February, she made a long-awaited return to the stage as Louise Nevelson in Edward Albee's new play *The Occupant*, for the off off-Broadway Signature Theatre Company. Midway through previews Bancroft developed pneumonia, forcing cancellation of half of the limited engagement. As a result of the missed performances, *The Occupant* never got around to inviting critics and therefore never officially opened.

A forty-seven-year-old actress paraded naked across the stage, while a twenty-three-year-old actor jumped around in his underpants.

Learning and rehearsing a one-woman show is a rough undertaking; a bout of pneumonia is no picnic; and returning onstage immediately following a bout of pneumonia without even a week or two in the sun has got to be wearying. Especially when you're seventy years old. All things considered, Bancroft looked pretty good, sitting there. So I did, indeed, get to see Mrs. Robinson in the flesh. As opposed to Kathleen Turner in the flesh. Not on the stage of the Plymouth, but on the night after I saw *The Graduate*.

Topdog/Underdog

And now for something completely different.

Topdog/Underdog was different, all right. By Broadway standards, anyway. Suzan-Lori Parks did not spring out of nowhere. She came to West Forty-ninth Street with more than fifteen plays to her credit. Two of them, *Imperceptible Mutabilities in the Third Kingdom* and *Venus*, won Obie Awards; *In the Blood* was runner-up to *Proof* in the 2000 Pulitzer race. But Broadway lives in a vacuum, insofar as non-Broadway plays are concerned. *Topdog/Underdog* was in many ways unlike anything ever seen on the street.

The thirty-eight-year-old Ms. Parks was indeed a rarity. There have been successful women playwrights on Broadway since *Abie's Irish Rose* —the 2001–2002 season featured four—and African-American playwrights are no longer as rare as they used to be. (August Wilson alone has had seven new plays produced on Broadway since 1984, more than any writer other than—you guessed it—Neil Simon.)

But the combination remains exceedingly rare. Lorraine Hansberry had two plays produced on Broadway, the groundbreaking hit *A Raisin in the Sun* (1959) and the 1964 failure *The Sign in Sidney Brustein's Window*. (Her uncompleted final play, *Les Blancs*, was haphazardly finished by her ex-husband and posthumously produced in 1970.) Ntozake Shange's *For Colored Girls Who Have Considered Suicide / When the Rainbow Is Enuf* was also a long-running hit, in 1976. *Mule Bone*, a play by Zora Neale Hurston and Langston Hughes, was staged in 1996, thirty-six years after Ms. Hurston's death. Both Whoopi Goldberg and Anna Deavere Smith have been represented with one-woman shows. But as far as I can tell, Hansberry and Shange are the only nonwhite nonmale writers to have seen their plays produced on Broadway, before Ms. Parks and *Topdog* came along.

Not that Parks was unrecognized on the cultural scene. Like Mary Zimmerman of *Metamorphoses*, she was a recipient of a MacArthur Foundation "genius" grant. Parks's 2001 grant was for $500,000, more than double what Zimmerman received in 1998. Which indicates that under present-day economics, it might pay to struggle unrecognized for just a couple of years longer.

Topdog/Underdog was first mounted at the New York Shakespeare Festival's Anspacher Theatre on July 26, 2001. (The play was produced simultaneously with *The Seagull*, at the Delacorte in Central Park.) George C. Wolfe, producer of the Shakespeare Festival, directed; this was the fourth Parks play during his eight years at the Public. The reaction was extremely enthusiastic, with high praise for the performances and production, along with some minor quibbling about the remarkably written but questionably plotted script. A Broadway transfer was quickly arranged, but an October date at the Ambassador was put off by the events of September 11.

Wolfe and the Shakespeare Festival turned their attention to *Elaine Stritch at Liberty*, which opened downtown in November. *Topdog* was rescheduled for an April 7 opening. Good planning, as it turned out; *Topdog* won the Pulitzer Prize on April 8, the day numerous rave reviews hit the papers.

The Pulitzer victory was in some ways foreseeable. The Drama award is voted on by a jury of five, with Ben Brantley (of the *New York Times*) serving as chair. Brantley, a longtime fan of Ms. Parks, lavishly praised *Topdog* at the Public in July; in March, he distinctly disliked *The Goat, or Who Is Sylvia?* by three-time Pulitzer winner Edward Albee. Parks won the Pulitzer; Albee won the other three main playwriting awards, the Tony, Critics Circle, and Drama Desk.

Topdog didn't win any Tonys, as it happens; Parks and actor Jeffrey Wright deservedly received nominations, while Wolfe and actor Mos Def were overlooked in especially crowded fields. But the critics—led by Mr. Brantley—tended to like *Topdog* considerably more than did audiences, Broadway professionals, and Tony voters.

That *Topdog* even made it to Broadway was eyebrow raising.

There have been many successful women playwrights on Broadway, and African-American playwrights are no longer as rare as they used to be. But the combination remains exceedingly unique.

Traditional Broadway fare it wasn't; commercial, in terms of appealing to traditional Broadway ticket buyers, it surely wasn't. A team of fourteen or so producers banded together to raise the $1.5 million capitalization, and they weren't in it for the money (as several of them candidly admitted in

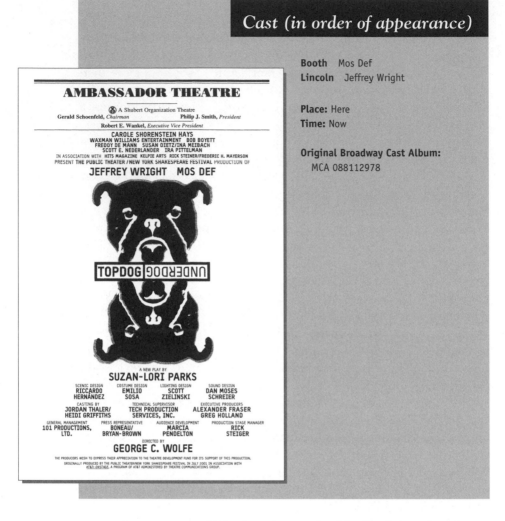

AMBASSADOR THEATRE

Ⓢ A Shubert Organization Theatre
Gerald Schoenfeld, *Chairman*   Philip J. Smith, *President*
Robert E. Wankel, *Executive Vice President*

CAROLE SHORENSTEIN HAYS
WAXMAN WILLIAMS ENTERTAINMENT   BOB BOYETT
FREDDY DE MANN   SUSAN DIETZ/INA MEIBACH
SCOTT E. NEDERLANDER   IRA PITTELMAN
IN ASSOCIATION WITH HITS MAGAZINE KELPIE ARTS RICK STEINER/FREDERIC H. MAYERSON
PRESENT THE PUBLIC THEATER / NEW YORK SHAKESPEARE FESTIVAL PRODUCTION OF

JEFFREY WRIGHT   MOS DEF

TOPDOG UNDERDOG

A NEW PLAY BY
SUZAN-LORI PARKS

SCENIC DESIGN   COSTUME DESIGN   LIGHTING DESIGN   SOUND DESIGN
**RICCARDO   EMILIO   SCOTT   DAN MOSES
HERNÁNDEZ   SOSA   ZIELINSKI   SCHREIER**

CASTING BY   TECHNICAL SUPERVISOR   EXECUTIVE PRODUCERS
**JORDAN THALER/   TECH PRODUCTION   ALEXANDER FRASER
HEIDI GRIFFITHS   SERVICES, INC.   GREG HOLLAND**

GENERAL MANAGEMENT   PRESS REPRESENTATIVE   AUDIENCE DEVELOPMENT   PRODUCTION STAGE MANAGER
**101 PRODUCTIONS,   BONEAU/   MARCIA   RICK
LTD.   BRYAN-BROWN   PENDELTON   STEIGER**

DIRECTED BY
GEORGE C. WOLFE

THE PRODUCERS WISH TO EXPRESS THEIR APPRECIATION TO THE THEATRE DEVELOPMENT FUND FOR ITS SUPPORT OF THIS PRODUCTION.
ORIGINALLY PRODUCED BY THE PUBLIC THEATER/NEW YORK SHAKESPEARE FESTIVAL IN JULY 2001 IN ASSOCIATION WITH
AT&T: ONSTAGE, A PROGRAM OF AT&T ADMINISTERED BY THEATRE COMMUNICATIONS GROUP.

Booth   Mos Def
Lincoln   Jeffrey Wright

Place: Here
Time: Now

Original Broadway Cast Album:
MCA 088112978

preopening interviews). Profit or loss, a play like *Topdog* needs to be on Broadway; where is the future of drama if we stick to easy-sell items like Neil Simon's *The Dinner Party*?

Topdog/Underdog was a tale of two brothers, one named Lincoln and the other named Booth. The characters are defined by their identity. Or lack thereof.

BOOTH: Daddy told me once why we got the names we do.

LINCOLN: Yeah?

BOOTH: Yeah. He was drunk when he told me, or maybe I was drunk when he told me. Anyway, he told me, may not be true, but he told me. Why he named us both. Lincoln and Booth.

LINCOLN: How come? How come, man?

BOOTH: It was his idea of a joke.

Which should give you some idea of Ms. Parks's writing style.

Lincoln, the elder, is the topdog. He is thus identified in the script, although that designation did not appear in the theatre program. He is not only the topdog; he is also better drawn, considerably so. He works in an arcade, presumably a Coney Island arcade (as Parks mentions "the smell of the ocean"). Lincoln—the character in the play—plays Honest Abe-in-a-box, sitting in content reverie as one customer after another sneaks up behind, stands on footprints helpfully painted on the worn carpet, and shoots him dead.

"This is sit down, you know, easy work," says Link. "I just gotta sit there all day. Folks come in kill phony Honest Abe with the phony pistol." But not so very easy; the clothes don't necessarily make the man. "Every day I put on that sh**, I leave my own sh** at the door and I put on that sh** and I go out there and I make it work."

(Parks used a similar character—a black man impersonating Lincoln for would-be Booths at a pay-and-shoot arcade—in an earlier work, *The America Play*. This was produced for five weeks at the Public in 1994, during Wolfe's first season on the job.)

Lincoln wasn't always so passive; an ace at three-card monte, the sidewalk con game, he lost his nerve when his partner was killed in action. Lincoln retired from the street corner, hiding himself in a bottle of "medicine" and a frayed frock coat. But in the *Topdog* universe, you can try to change your life but you can't change your identity (or lack thereof).

Booth is less accomplished. He's a booster—that is, one who boosts. Suits, shirts, shoes, magazines, diamondesque rings, oriental folding screens, and complete dinner sets. He is very good at it, apparently; but all he wants is—well, to run the three-card monte scam as well as Lincoln. He even changes his name, to 3-Card. But in the *Topdog* universe, you can try to change your life, but you can't change your identity (or lack thereof). Especially when your name is Booth, living in the shadow of your older brother, Lincoln.

When Lincoln loses his job as Honest Abe, he returns to his former identity as Link, the con man. But he was right when he quit throwing the cards; his luck has run out. The fortune in his fortune cookie in the first scene says "your luck will change," and it does—from ill to fatal. "My luck was bad but now it turned to worse, don't call up a doctor, just call me a hearse," he sings. In this same song—he makes up songs while sitting in the "phoney" Ford's Theatre box awaiting the next assassin—he sings, "My best girl, she threw me out in to the street, my favorite horse, they ground him into meat."

Topdog/Underdog moved to Broadway on April 7. Parks won the Pulitzer Prize on April 8, the day numerous rave reviews hit the papers.

Listen to Ms. Parks's poetry, as Lincoln describes his act. And mind her idiosyncratic spelling. "And there he is. Standing behind me. Theres some feet shapes on the floor so he knows just where he oughta to stand. So he wont miss. . . . I slump down and close my eyes. And he goes out thuh other way. More come in. Uh whole day full. Bunches of kids, little good for nothings, in they school uniforms. Businessmen smelling like two for one martinis. Tourists, in they theme park t-shirts trying to catch it on film. Housewives with they mouths closed tight, shooting more than once."

"Housewives with they mouths closed tight, shooting more than once." What an amazing image from an amazing writer!

Booth grows more and more frustrated by his inability to become 3-Card, despite adapting the name; he is even more frustrated by his inability to find Grace. The Grace in question—sometimes referred to as Amazing Grace—is Booth's girlfriend, to hear him tell it; or, more likely, his ex-girlfriend. Or maybe his imaginary girlfriend. In the end, he "offs" Grace (offstage), and —inevitably—Booth shoots Lincoln at the final curtain.

But it always comes back to identity, or lack thereof. Rooted in their parents, who abandoned the boys when Lincoln was sixteen and Booth was eleven. Here's Parks, via Lincoln, on the parents: "I think there was something out there that they liked more than they liked us and for years they was struggling against moving towards that more liked something. Each of them had a special something that they was struggling against. They bought a house and they brought us there and everything we owned figuring we could be a family in that house and them things, them two separate things each of them was struggling against would just leave them be. Them things would see thuh house and be impressed and just leave them be."

A special, undefinable thing that "they was struggling against." This image seems to be the root of the lack of identity, and the despair it brings, to a whole generation of African-American males. With no

Topdog/Underdog
Opened: April 7, 2002
Closed: August 11, 2002
144 performances (and 31 previews)
Profit/Loss: Profit
Topdog/Underdog ($76.25 top) was scaled to a potential
    gross of $517,766 at the 1,109-seat Ambassador Theatre.
    Weekly grosses averaged about $247,000, with business
    topping $300,000 through May and breaking $400,000 in
    the final week. Total gross for the twenty-two-week run
    was $5,405,007. Attendance was about 63 percent, with
    the box office grossing about 48 percent of dollar-
    capacity.

TONY AWARD NOMINATIONS
Best Play: Suzan-Lori Parks
Best Performance by a Leading Actor: Jeffrey Wright

PULITZER PRIZE
Suzan-Lori Parks (WINNER)

Critical Scorecard

Rave 5
Favorable 3
Mixed 2
Unfavorable 0
Pan 0

history—no family history, no background—identity is adrift. Booth,
Lincoln, what (after all) is in a name?

The proceedings were played out in impeccable manner, with director
Wolfe chillingly abetted by his cast, set designer Riccardo Hernández and
especially lighting designer Scott Zielinski. (Wolfe, in show after show,
seems to have a keener sense of lighting than other current-day Broadway
directors.)

Wolfe placed the action on a small platform in the middle of the Ambassador's wide stage, with a timeworn, paint-peeled door at center. The
play's first image was Booth caught in a headlight-like glare, almost as if
he was a fly trapped against a screen on a summer's night. Time and again
and again, Wolfe pinned his actors to the wall, either in full face, as it
were, or in silhouette. Shadow play, a lantern show; the weaving and bobbing stovepipe hat, the mitt of a gloved hand waving slowly to the crowd,
the extended arm attached to a pistol stealing into the picture.

This is the America play, all right.

Jeffrey Wright's Lincoln made his entrance in whiteface, wearing an
antique frock coat, top hat, and fake beard; a chilling sight, let me tell
you. Wright—a Tony Award winner for his unforgettable performance
as Belize in Wolfe's 1993 *Angels in America: Perestroika*—gave one of
the more amazing performances of the season. One part Honest Abe, a
vaudeville-tinged Uncle Tom waving to the audience with fake beard
flanking a toothsome but unreal smile. One part slick con man, with his

icy-smooth three-card spiel, confidently invulnerable as long as he still has the moves. And the other part—the scariest—the hollow shell inside. Long after *Topdog* is gone (but not forgotten), Wright's mime sequences—*Topdog* contained five or six extended pantomimes—will remain firmly embedded in playgoing memory.

Mos Def—who replaced Don Cheadle, unable to make the Broadway transfer when the dates were postponed—gave an equally impressive performance, rather astounding for a first-time actor. Let's not call him a first-time actor, though; this rap artist might never have been in a play, but he sure as hell can act.

> A team of fourteen producers banded together, and they weren't in it for the money. Profit or loss, a play like *Topdog* needs to be on Broadway; where is the future of drama if we stick to easy-sell items?

Deep in the second act, Parks gets to the heart of the matter with a cryptic exchange from a character Booth refers to as "yr best customer." That is to say, Lincoln's best customer at the arcade. But is this a real character, or merely Lincoln's inner musing?

"Does thuh show stop when no one's watching or does thuh show go on?" is the question. The answer: "Yr only yrself—when no one's watching."

For Lincoln, as both three-card monte ace and Honest Abe, the show does stop when no one's watching; he only exists in front of an audience. Booth is the opposite; he performs, as a shoplifter, *only* when no one's watching. Either way, how do you define yrself for yrself when your past is a con man's shell game, and there's no future in yr future?

"First thing you learn is what is," Link explains in his final speech before the gunshot. "Next thing you learn is what aint. You don't know what is, you don't know what aint, you don't know sh**. You was in such a hurry to learn thuh last move," he tells his brother, "that you didn't bother learning thuh first one."

And so Booth shoots Lincoln, inevitably, once more. Another America play ends, another America play begins.

The Elephant Man

There was a time when a revival, practically speaking, was a special event. Even as recently as thirty years back, revivals were relatively rare. Yes, regional theatres were full of them, summer stock lived on them, and big-name star packages plied the road; but commercial producers thought twice about bringing them to Broadway.

That was then; nowadays, Broadway is awash with revivals. Let us look at the three seasons thus far examined in the *Broadway Yearbook* series. Thumbing through the pages, I come up with an astounding thirty-five revivals: ten in 1999–2000, eleven in 2000–2001, and fourteen in 2001–2002. (This includes full-scale Broadway productions only, and not such special events as City Center Encores!, which presented concert versions of nine musicals over the three seasons.)

For comparison's sake, I've gone back forty years in the dusty old record books to find *no* revivals in 1961–1962. The total for 1959–1962, actually, was only two: John Gielgud in *Much Ado about Nothing* and Maurice Evans in Shaw's *Heartbreak House*. By the 1971–1972 season, we were up to six revivals; all failed.

So have we seen any good, old plays over the last three seasons? I made a little list, in order of appearance.

The Rainmaker. Nonprofit transfer from the Williamstown Theatre Festival (with a partially new cast). Box office name: Woody Harrelson. Original 1954 production: 125 performances, loss. Revival: 82 performances, nonprofit (profit). Scorecard average: mixed-to-unfavorable.

The Price. Commercial transfer from the Williamstown Theatre Festival. Box office name: Arthur Miller. Original 1968 production: 429 performances, profit. 1979 revival: 144 performances, loss. 1992 revival: 46 performances, nonprofit [loss]. 1999 revival: 128 performances, loss. Scorecard average: favorable.

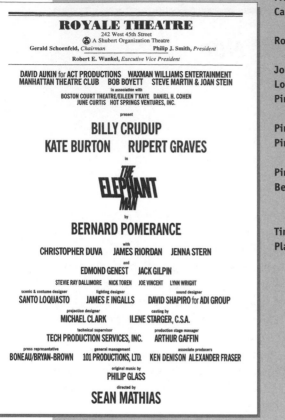

ROYALE THEATRE
242 West 45th Street
Ⓢ A Shubert Organization Theatre
Gerald Schoenfeld, *Chairman*   Philip J. Smith, *President*

Robert E. Wankel, *Executive Vice President*

DAVID AUKIN for ACT PRODUCTIONS   WAXMAN WILLIAMS ENTERTAINMENT
MANHATTAN THEATRE CLUB   BOB BOYETT   STEVE MARTIN & JOAN STEIN
in association with
BOSTON COURT THEATRE/EILEEN T'KAYE   DANIEL H. COHEN
JUNE CURTIS   HOT SPRINGS VENTURES, INC.

present

BILLY CRUDUP
KATE BURTON   RUPERT GRAVES
in

THE
**ELEPHANT
MAN**

by

BERNARD POMERANCE
with
CHRISTOPHER DUVA   JAMES RIORDAN   JENNA STERN

and
EDMOND GENEST   JACK GILPIN

STEVIE RAY DALLIMORE   NICK TOREN   JOE VINCENT   LYNN WRIGHT

scenic & costume designer   *lighting designer*   *sound designer*
SANTO LOQUASTO   JAMES F. INGALLS   DAVID SHAPIRO for ADI GROUP

projection designer   *casting by*
MICHAEL CLARK   ILENE STARGER, C.S.A.

technical supervisor   *production stage manager*
TECH PRODUCTION SERVICES, INC.   ARTHUR GAFFIN

press representative   *general management*   *associate producers*
BONEAU/BRYAN-BROWN   101 PRODUCTIONS, LTD.   KEN DENISON ALEXANDER FRASER

original music by
PHILIP GLASS

directed by
SEAN MATHIAS

Frederick Treves   Rupert Graves
Carr Gomm, Belgian policeman
   Edmond Genest
Ross, Bishop Walsham How   Jack
   Gilpin
John Merrick   Billy Crudup
London policeman   Nick Toren
Pinhead manager, London policeman,
   Will, Lord John   James Riordan
Pinhead, Mrs. Kendal   Kate Burton
Pinhead, Miss Sandwich, Duchess,
   Princess Alexandra   Jenna Stern
Pinhead   Lynn Wright
Belgian policeman, conductor, Snork,
   Countess   Christopher Duva

Time: 1884–1890
Place: London and Belgium

Kiss Me, Kate. Commercially produced for Broadway. Box office names: title, Cole Porter. Original 1948 production: 1,077 performances, profit. 1999 revival: 636 performances, profit. Scorecard average: favorable-to-rave.

Amadeus. Commercial transfer from London (with a mostly new cast). Box office names: title, director Peter Hall. Original 1980 production: 1,181 performances, profit. 1999 revival: 173 performances, loss. Scorecard average: mixed-to-unfavorable.

True West. Commercial transfer from London (with a new cast). Box office name: Sam Shepard. Original 1980 off-Broadway production: 52 performances, nonprofit [loss]. 1982 off-Broadway revival: 762 performances, profit. 2000 revival: 154 performances, profit. Scorecard average: favorable-to-rave.

A Moon for the Misbegotten. Commercially produced for Broadway. Box office names: Eugene O'Neill, Cherry Jones. Original 1947 production: closed during tryout, loss. 1957 Broadway production: 68 performances, loss. 1973 revival: 313 performances, profit. 1984 revival: 40 performances, loss. 2000 revival: 120 performances, profit. Scorecard average: favorable.

Jesus Christ Superstar. Commercial transfer from London (with a new cast). Box office names: title, Andrew Lloyd Webber. Original 1971 production: 711 performances, profit. 2000 revival: 161 performances, loss. Scorecard average: pan.

The Real Thing. Commercial transfer from London (with the English cast). Box office name: Tom Stoppard. Original Broadway 1984 production: 566 performances, profit. 2000 revival: 135 performances, profit. Scorecard average: favorable-to-rave.

The Music Man. Commercially produced for Broadway (and the road). Box office name: title. Original 1957 production: 1,375 performances, profit. 1980 revival: 21 performances, loss. 2000 revival: 699 performances, loss. Scorecard average: favorable-to-rave (with a pan from the *Times*).

Uncle Vanya. American premiere of 1996 British translation (with a new cast). Box office name: Derek Jacobi. 1973 revival (the eighth Broadway *Vanya*): 64 performances, nonprofit [profit]. 1995 revival: 29 performances, nonprofit [loss]. 2000 revival: 49 performances, nonprofit [loss]. Scorecard average: unfavorable-to-pan.

Macbeth. Commercially produced for Broadway. Box office name: Kelsey Grammer. 1981 revival (the thirty-fourth Broadway *Macbeth* of the century): 61 performances, nonprofit [loss]. 1982 revival: 21 performances, nonprofit [loss]. 1988 revival: 77 performances, profit. 2000 revival: 13 performances, loss. Scorecard average: pan.

The Man Who Came to Dinner. Box office name: Nathan Lane. Original 1939 production: 739 performances, profit. 1980 revival: 85 performances, nonprofit [profit]. 2000 revival: 85 performances, nonprofit [profit]. Scorecard average: favorable.

The Best Man. Commercially produced for Broadway. Box office name: Gore Vidal. Original 1960 production: 520 performances, profit. 2000 revival: 121 performances, breakeven. Scorecard average: unfavorable.

Betrayal. Box office names: Harold Pinter, Juliette Binoche. Original 1980 Broadway production: 170 performances, profit. 2000 revival: 89 performances, nonprofit [profit]. Scorecard average: mixed.

The Rocky Horror Show. Commercially produced for Broadway. Box office name: title. Original 1971 Broadway production: 45 performances, loss. 2000 revival: 437 performances, loss. Scorecard average: mixed.

The Search for Signs of Intelligent Life in the Universe. Commercially produced for Broadway. Box office name: Lily Tomlin. Original 1985 production: 398 performances, profit. 2000 revival: 184 performances, profit. Scorecard average: favorable-to-rave.

Design for Living. Box office names: Noël Coward, Alan Cumming. Original 1933 production: 135 performances, profit. 1984 revival: 245 performances, nonprofit [profit]. 2001 revival: 69 performances, nonprofit [loss]. Scorecard average: unfavorable.

There was a time when a revival, practically speaking, was a special event. As recently as thirty years back, revivals on Broadway were relatively rare.

Follies. Box office name: title, Stephen Sondheim, Blythe Danner. Original 1971 production: 522 performances, loss. 2001 revival: 117 performances, nonprofit [loss]. Scorecard average: unfavorable.

One Flew over the Cuckoo's Nest. Commercial transfer from Steppenwolf. Box office names: title, Gary Sinise. Original 1963 production: 82 performances, loss. 1971 off-Broadway revival: 1,025 performances, profit. 2001 revival: 121 performances, loss. Scorecard average: mixed.

Bells Are Ringing. Commercially produced for Broadway. Box office name: Faith Prince. Original 1956 production: 924 performances, profit. 2001 revival: 68 performances, loss. Scorecard average: unfavorable-to-pan.

42nd Street. Commercially produced for Broadway. Box office name: title. Original 1980 production: 3,486 performances, profit. 2001 revival: still running, profit to be determined. Scorecard average: favorable.

A Thousand Clowns. Commercially produced for Broadway. Box office name: Tom Selleck. Original 1962 production: 428 performances, profit. 1996 revival: 32 performances, nonprofit [loss]. 2001 revival: 83 performances, loss. Scorecard average: unfavorable.

Major Barbara. Box office name: Cherry Jones. 1956 revival (the third Broadway *Major Barbara*): 232 performances, profit. 1980 revival: 40 performances, nonprofit [loss]. 2001 revival: 74 performances, nonprofit [loss]. Scorecard average: favorable-to-rave.

Hedda Gabler. Commercial transfer of new translation from Williamstown Theatre Festival (and other regionals). Box office names: title, Kate Burton. 1971 revival (the fifteenth Broadway *Hedda* of the century): 56 performances, profit. 1994 revival: 33 performances, nonprofit [loss]. 2001 revival: 117 performances, loss. Scorecard average: mixed-to-unfavorable.

Dance of Death. New translation, commercially produced for Broadway. Box office name: Ian McKellen. 1971 revival (the second Broadway *Dance of Death*): 5 performances, loss. 1974 revival: 37 performances, nonprofit [loss]. 2001 revival: 108 performances, profit. Scorecard average: unfavorable-to-mixed.

Noises Off. Commercial transfer from London (with American cast). Box office name: Patti LuPone. Original 1983 production: 553 performances, profit. 2001 revival: 348 performances, profit. Scorecard average: favorable.

The Women. Commercially produced for Broadway. Box office name: title. Original 1936 production: 657 performances, profit. 1973 revival: 63 performances, loss. 2001 revival: 77 performances, nonprofit [profit]. Scorecard average: mixed-to-unfavorable.

One Mo' Time. Commercial transfer from Williamstown Theatre Festival. Box office name: none. Original 1979 off-Broadway production: 1,372 performances, profit. 2001 revival: 21 performances, loss. Scorecard average: mixed.

The Crucible. Commercially produced for Broadway. Box office names: Arthur Miller, Liam Neeson. Original 1953 production: 197 performances, profit. 1964 revival: 16 performances, loss. 1972 revival: 44 performances, nonprofit [loss]. 1991 revival: 31 performances, nonprofit [loss]. 2001 revival: 101 performances, loss. Scorecard average: mixed-to-unfavorable.

Oklahoma! Commercially produced for Broadway. Box office names: title, Richard Rodgers, Oscar Hammerstein II, Trevor Nunn, Susan Stroman, Cameron Mackintosh. Original 1943 production: 2,212 performances, profit. 1951 revival: 72 performances, profit. 1969 revival: 88 performances, nonprofit [loss]. 1979 revival: 293 performances, profit. 2002 revival: at press time, a February 23, 2003, closing had been announced, 388 performances, loss. Scorecard average: mixed-to-unfavorable.

The Elephant Man. Commercially produced for Broadway. Box office names: play, Billy Crudup. Original 1979 production: 916 performances, profit. 2002 revival: 57 performances, loss. Scorecard average: mixed-to-unfavorable.

Morning's at Seven. Box office name: none. Original 1939 production: 44 performances, loss. 1980 revival: 564 performances, profit. 2002 revival: 112 performances, nonprofit [profit]. Scorecard average: favorable-to-rave.

Private Lives. Commercially produced for Broadway. Box office names: title, Noël Coward, Alan Rickman. Original 1931 production: 256 performances, profit. 1948 revival: 248 performances, profit. 1969 revival: 204 performances, profit. 1975 revival: 92 performances, profit. 1983 revival: 63 performances, loss. 1992 revival: 37 performances, loss. 2002 revival: 127 performances, profit. Scorecard average: rave-to-favorable.

Into the Woods. Commercially produced for Broadway. Box office name: Stephen Sondheim. Original 1987 production: 764 performances, loss. 2002 revival: 279 performances, loss. Scorecard average: favorable-to-mixed.

The Man Who Had All the Luck. Box office name: Arthur Miller. Original 1944 production: 4 performances, loss. 2002 revival: 70 performances, nonprofit [loss]. Scorecard average: mixed-to-favorable.

A few observations.

> *Financial success of commercially produced play revivals.* Profit: nine. Loss: seven.
>
> *Financial success of noncommercially produced play revivals.* Profit: five. Loss: four.
>
> *Financial success of commercially produced musical revivals.* Profit: one. Loss: seven. (Undetermined: one.)
>
> *Financial success of noncommercially produced musical revival.* Loss: one.
>
> *Revivals that were generally judged to be inferior to previous productions.* Twelve.
>
> *Revivals that were arguably comparable to (or better than) previous productions.* Eight. *Adding up the categories.* Profit: sixteen. Loss: sixteen. (Undetermined: three.)
>
> *Looking at plays, only.* Profit: fifteen. Loss: ten.
>
> *Looking at musicals, only.* Profit: one. Loss: eight. (Undetermined: one.)

That final statistic is the most telling of all, perhaps. While the combined play-musical profit-loss ratio is even, the musicals are where the investment dollars are. And only one of nine commercial musical revivals recouped its costs; seven lost money—four of them total losses—and one is still running.

Let us break down revival activity into four sometimes-overlapping categories:

Nonprofit revivals for subscribers. These are regularly cranked out as part of the mission of the Roundabout, Lincoln Center Theater, and other nonprofit theatres. Results can be inspired (*Morning's at Seven*), controversial (*The Women*), or merely academic (*Major Barbara*).

Transfers of productions from regional theatres. These generally arrive with a good set of reviews, often from major New York critics. (An out-of-town rave from the *Times*—like the one lavished on Kate Burton's *Hedda Gabler* in Boston—is a key element for raising money and booking a theatre; an especially bad review from the *Times* has been known to end dreams of transfer.) It is also considerably less expensive to transfer a rehearsed production with virtually complete sets and costumes (as with *One Flew over the Cuckoo's Nest*) than to start from scratch (as with *The Crucible*).

Star-driven revivals. Any show might be cast with stars; these revivals are produced solely due to the availability and willingness of a star, such as Kelsey Grammer's *Macbeth* or Lily Tomlin's *Search*.

Big-business revivals. These revivals come from high-powered producers with preexisting touring plans. They are generally musicals, like *The Music Man*, *Kiss Me, Kate*, *42nd Street* and *Into the Woods*.

All of which brings us to *The Elephant Man*. Most people assume that it is a British play. It is not. Playwright Bernard Pomerance was born and raised in Brooklyn, although he seems to have moved to London in his twenties and remained. Biographical detail is hard to come by, but *The Elephant Man* appears

The producers proceeded under the unquestioned belief that *The Elephant Man* was a classic.

to have been his seventh produced play, of at least eleven. His first, in 1971, was called *High in Vietnam, Hot Damn*, which hints at why Pomerance might have transplanted himself. None of his work seems to have reached America other than *The Elephant Man*, which was first produced in a small theatre in London in 1977; none of his other plays seem to have been at all successful.

Pomerance's biographical tale of Joseph (John) Merrick was a surprise Broadway hit in 1979; highly theatrical, historically fascinating, and daring in its decision to have a visibly healthy young actor suggest the hero's deformities without the use of makeup. The original production was rapturously praised for its excellence; for various reasons, including the tem-

The Elephant Man
Opened: April 14, 2002
Closed: June 2, 2002
57 performances (and 23 previews)
Profit/Loss: Loss
The Elephant Man ($76.25 top) was scaled to a potential
    gross of $550,846 at the 1,078-seat Royale Theatre.
    Weekly grosses averaged about $157,000, with only two
    weeks (just after the opening) over the $170,000
    threshold. Total gross for the ten-week run was
    $1,574,221. Attendance was about 52 percent, with the
    box office grossing about 29 percent of dollar-capacity.

TONY AWARD NOMINATIONS
Best Performance by a Leading Actor: Billy Crudup
Best Performance by a Featured Actress: Kate Burton

*Critical
Scorecard*

Rave 2
Favorable 2
Mixed 0
Unfavorable 3
Pan 3

per of society at the time, it might well have been somewhat overpraised.
I originally found it interesting, but not all *that* interesting. I appreciated
the idea that prejudice can blind society to true human beauty, but I'd
had enough of it by two-thirds of the way through the play's twenty-one
brief scenes.

The revival seems to have been designed as a showcase for Billy
Crudup. The thirty-three-year-old Crudup, from the Long Island town of
Manhasset, was a rising film star. He has done memorable work on the
stage, notably so in the 1995 Lincoln Center Theater production of Tom
Stoppard's *Arcadia*. Crudup did an impressive job in *The Elephant Man*,
with the character's humanity coming through despite the actor's contorted physiognomy and thick-tongued speech.

(Note from Pomerance's published playscript: "Merrick's face was so
deformed he could not express any emotion at all. His speech was very
difficult to understand without practice. Any attempt to reproduce his
appearance and his speech naturalistically—*if* it were possible—would
seem to me not only counterproductive, but, the more remarkably successful, the more distracting from the play. . . . Anyone playing the part of
Merrick should be advised to consult a physician about the problems of
sustaining any unnatural or twisted position.")

Was Crudup's burgeoning fame enough to justify reviving *The Elephant
Man*? Seems not. Yes, he was good; but a remarkable, once-in-a-lifetime
acting exhibition it wasn't. Crudup was ably assisted by Kate Burton, giving her second fine performance of the season. He was not much assisted
by director Sean Mathias (of *Dance of Death*), who in his two Broadway
visits of the 2001–2002 season seemed drawn to startling theatricality,
even (or especially) at the expense of the text.

The producers—the show sported more than a dozen, including actor-comedian-writer Steve Martin—apparently proceeded under the unquestioned belief that *The Elephant Man* was a classic. This turned out not to be the case; the script fell flat in 2002, its original notoriety apparently owing more to novelty than distinction. Part of the problem surely stemmed from time and circumstance. In 1979, Merrick (who died in 1890) was all but unknown in America; his story was fascinating, especially as it was based in fact. *The Elephant Man* made him newly famous, compounded by two films (both called *The Elephant Man*). The first, directed by David Lynch and produced by Mel Brooks's Brooksfilms in 1980, was not related to the play. The second, in 1982, was based on Pomerance's version.

This had an unexpected effect. Many people in the audience at a revival necessarily know what's going to happen; few people at *Macbeth* are surprised by the bloodshed, while even the most innocent viewer of *Death of a Salesman* should not be surprised by the death of the salesman. But the real-life story of Merrick, when presented onstage in 1979 and onscreen in 1980, was shocking and fascinating.

The famous 1979 logo of *The Elephant Man* featured a stick figure, topped with a globe-sized head. ("Sometimes I think my head is so big because it is so full of dreams.") Contrast this with the artwork outside the Royale and on the *Playbill* cover, featuring a contorted view of Crudup's upper torso. (Crudup's torso was also on telephone booths and bus shelters around town, apparently in the hopes of attracting a larger audience.) Could it be that we went into *The Elephant Man*, in 2002, knowing too much about *The Elephant Man*? This change in viewpoint, along with Mathias's overly tricked-up production, left too many theatergoers uninvolved and unmoved.

Could it be that we went into *The Elephant Man* (the play) knowing too much about *The Elephant Man* (the person)?

The Elephant Man opened on April 14 to a scorecard average we have summarized as mixed-to-unfavorable. *Morning's at Seven* opened the following Thursday to five of ten raves (plus three favorable reviews). *Private Lives* opened the Thursday after that, April 28, with seven raves (plus two favorables). *The Elephant Man* received two Tony Award nominations on May 6, for Mr. Crudup and Ms. Burton; nothing for the revival or director.

Competition for ticket dollars was shattering, causing *The Elephant Man* to announce on May 23 that they would close on June 9. From producer David Aukin: "With the extreme competition of sixteen plays opening on Broadway this season, and a depressed economy, we are sadly unable to give the production a longer life." As it happened, they didn't even make it that long, closing a week earlier on the afternoon of the Tony Award ceremony.

Thoroughly Modern Millie

M *odern*, read the show curtain at the Marquis Theatre, followed by a Websterish string: "1) characteristic of the present and recent times; not obsolete. 2) one whose lifestyle is up-to-date; a member of the modern school of thought in relation to any subject. Occas. derog."

The folks behind *Thoroughly Modern Millie* were pulling our leg; their aims and methods were far from those of modern musical comedy, circa 2002. Their sights were unclearly set, though. What we got, approximately, was a twenty-first-century look at New York of the Roaring Twenties, filtered through a 1954 satire of stiff-upper-Britishers of the Roaring Twenties on the Lido, revamped as a 1967 satire of a 1949 satire of a 1926 satire, with a libretto seemingly patterned on screwball Hollywood comedies of the thirties.

If this sounds somewhat indistinct, it was. If this sounds muddled, it was. The results were off target; but how could they be otherwise? One thing was for certain: modern, it wasn't. Through a combination of luck and circumstance, *Millie* managed to survive a stormy reception and more or less pull through. But it wasn't easy, and it wasn't pretty.

Millie started with flamboyant Hollywood producer Ross Hunter (originally Martin Fuss, from Cleveland). Hunter earned many millions of dollars for Universal with a series of mediocre films aimed, mostly, at the women's market. His theory was that women wanted "a chance to dream, to live vicariously, to see beautiful women, jewels, gorgeous clothes, melodrama"—and that when a married couple went to the movies, it was the woman who decided which film to see tonight. It turned out that he was right, with a string of critically maligned successes like *Magnificent Obsession*, *Tammy and the Bachelor*, *Pillow Talk*, *Imitation of Life*, and *Midnight Lace*.

Julie Andrews first arrived on Broadway at the age of nineteen, as the heroine of *The Boy Friend* (1954). This was a musical satire by Sandy Wilson, which opened in the West End earlier that year (without Andrews). Andrews became a major Broadway star in 1956 with *My Fair Lady*, which was followed in 1960 by *Camelot*. She was famously rejected for the 1964 *My Fair Lady* film, the producers deciding that they needed a *real* star. Andrews made *Mary Poppins* (1964) instead, followed by the film version of *The Sound of Music* (1965)—making her one of Hollywood's hottest properties.

Before *Mary Poppins* was released, Hunter determined to present Andrews in a movie version of *The Boy Friend*. The rights, alas, proved unavailable; perhaps Wilson had seen Hunter's 1962 film version of *Flower Drum Song*? Hunter nevertheless decided to move ahead, commissioning Richard Morris to write an original-but-similar twenties satire. Morris's main credit was as head writer of TV's *The Loretta Young Show*. His one Broadway libretto was for the mediocre 1960 musical *The Unsinkable Molly Brown*. (This was filmed in 1964, but Morris did not write the screenplay.)

The Boy Friend was a well-mannered spoof of musicals of the 1920s featuring British characters and was set in Nice. The script that Morris and Hunter devised for *Millie* was set in New York, the better to incorporate flappers, tap dancers, hootch, and the like. The gold-digging heroine seems derived in part from Lorelei Lee, of *Gentlemen Prefer Blondes*. Anita Loos's best-selling novel—first published as a magazine serial in 1925—quickly spawned a hit Broadway version in 1926. A generation later, Lorelei gained renewed prominence when *Gentlemen Prefer Blondes* became a popular 1949 musical comedy. Carol Channing attained stardom in the role, singing the gold digger's theme song "Diamonds Are a Girl's Best Friend" (by Jule Styne and Leo Robin). The musical made it to Hollywood in 1953, with Marilyn Monroe donning Channing's sequins.

Sutton Foster wasn't Channing and Streisand rolled into one; not yet. But this was a girl who stepped out of the chorus and managed to carry an unwieldy show.

Millie took place in 1922, but it seemed to emulate the style of the 1949 musical comedy version of *Gentlemen Prefer Blondes* (which took place in 1928). As for the style of the scattershot plot, Morris seemed to have drawn on the screwball films of the 1930s; the film *Thoroughly Modern Millie* can be described as a Preston Sturges movie without Preston Sturges, and that is decidedly not a compliment. Hunter assembled a curious score, including some period tunes; some new ones, written to order; and some oddities (including "Jewish Wedding Song" by Saul

Millie Dillmount Sutton Foster
Jimmy Smith Gavin Creel
Ruth Megan Sikora
Gloria JoAnn M. Hunter

MARQUIS THEATRE
UNDER THE DIRECTION OF THE MESSRS. NEDERLANDER

Michael Leavitt   Fox Theatricals   Hal Luftig
Stewart F. Lane   James L. Nederlander   Independent Presenters Network
L. Mages/M. Glick   Berinstein/Manocherian/Dramatic Forces   John York Noble
and Whoopi Goldberg
present

THOROUGHLY MODERN

millie
THE NEW BROADWAY MUSICAL COMEDY

Book by Richard Morris and Dick Scanlan

New Music by Jeanine Tesori

New Lyrics by Dick Scanlan

Original Story and Screenplay by Richard Morris for the Universal Pictures Film

Starring
SHERYL LEE RALPH   HARRIET HARRIS   MARC KUDISCH
GAVIN CREEL   ANGELA CHRISTIAN
KEN LEUNG   FRANCIS JUE   ANNE L. NATHAN

With
Kate Baldwin   Roxane Barlow   Melissa Bell Chait   Catherine Brunell   Joyce Chittick   J.P. Christensen
Julie Connors   David Eggers   Aldrin Gonzalez   Gregg Goodbrod   Jessica Grové   Susan Haefner
Amy Heggins   JoAnn M. Hunter   Alisa Klein   Matt Lashey   Darren Lee   Dan LoBuono   John MacInnis
Casey Nicholaw   Noah Racey   Aaron Ramey   T. Oliver Reid   Megan Sikora   Brandon Wardell
and introducing
SUTTON FOSTER
as Millie

Scenic Design   Costume Design   Lighting Design   Sound Design
DAVID GALLO   MARTIN PAKLEDINAZ   DONALD HOLDER   JON WESTON

Orchestrations   Dance Music Arranger   Vocal Music Arranger   Music Coordinator
DOUG BESTERMAN and RALPH BURNS   DAVID CHASE   JEANINE TESORI   JOHN MILLER

Hair Designer   Press Representative   Marketing   Casting
PAUL HUNTLEY   BARLOW • HARTMAN   TMG—THE MARKETING GROUP   JIM CARNAHAN, C.S.A.

Production Manager   General Management   Production Stage Manager   Associate Producers
THEATERSMITH, INC.   NINA LANNAN ASSOCIATES   BONNIE L. BECKER   MIKE ISAACSON KRISTIN CASKEY
CLEAR CHANNEL ENTERTAINMENT

Music Director
MICHAEL RAFTER

Choreographed by
ROB ASHFORD

Directed by
MICHAEL MAYER

Originally Produced by La Jolla Playhouse, La Jolla, CA
Des McAnuff, Artistic Director & Terrence Dwyer, Managing Director

Rita Jessica Grové
Alice Alisa Klein
Ethel Peas Joyce Chittick
Cora Catherine Brunell
Lucille Kate Baldwin
Mrs. Meers Harriet Harris
Miss Dorothy Brown Angela Christian
Ching Ho Ken Leung
Bun Foo Francis Jue
Miss Flannery Anne L. Nathan
Mr. Trevor Graydon Marc Kudisch
Speed tappists Casey Nicholaw, Noah Racey
Officer Casey Nicholaw
Muzzy Van Hossmere Sheryl Lee Ralph
Kenneth/dishwasher Brandon Wardell
Mathilde Catherine Brunell
George Gershwin Noah Racey
Dorothy Parker Julie Connors
Rodney Aaron Ramey
Dishwashers Aldrin Gonzalez, Aaron Ramey, Brandon Wardell
Muzzy's boys Gregg Goodbrod, Darren Lee, Dan LoBuono, John MacInnis, Noah Racey, T. Oliver Reid
Daphne Kate Baldwin
Dexter Casey Nicholaw
New Modern Jessica Grové
Ensemble Kate Baldwin, Roxane Barlow, Catherine Brunell, Joyce Chittick, Julie Connors, David Eggers, Aldrin Gonzalez, Gregg Goodbrod, Jessica Grové, Amy Heggins, JoAnn M. Hunter, Alisa Klein, Darren Lee, Dan LoBuono, John MacInnis, Casey Nicholaw, Noah Racey, Aaron Ramey, T. Oliver Reid, Megan Sikora, Brandon Wardell
Swings Melissa Bell Chait, J. P. Christensen, Susan Haefner, Matt Lashey

Time: 1922
Place: New York City

Original Broadway Cast Album: Victor 09026-63959

Chaplin and Sammy Cahn). With Julie Andrews to sing them, it didn't matter.

The creation of Millie was complicated by the success of Mary Poppins and the inordinate success of The Sound of Music. (We should all have such complications.) Hunter suddenly had a major movie star on his hands. Universal decided to upgrade Millie, making it a lavish road show presentation. In those days, big-budget films would first open at prime theatres in major cities, like New York's Radio City Music Hall, with re-served seats at high ticket prices. Millie's budget was increased propor-tionately, its running time expanded, and its material bloated.

The effects of the upgrading were evident in the casting. Andrews, suddenly a top movie star, was joined by two other triple-A Broadway stars. Carol Channing herself came in for the oddly conceived role of Muzzy, a character who appears almost as an afterthought. Channing per-sonified the Roaring Twenties flapperette for the postwar crowd, thanks to her performance as Lorelei Lee a generation earlier. (She had first sati-rized a twenties flapper in the 1948 revue Lend an Ear, in a much-noted musical extended sketch called "The Gladiola Girl.") Channing's star had fallen in the fifties, but when Millie came along she was back on top; the 1964 musical Hello, Dolly! catapulted Channing to nationwide promi-nence.

Andrews and Channing were joined by a third stage star of enormous fame. Beatrice Lillie came to Broadway in 1924; like Andrews, she ar-rived in a British import (Charlot's Revue of 1924) and took the town. Like Channing, she was a larger-than-life clown with a deft satiric touch. She had been starring on Broadway as recently as 1964, in High Spirits, a musicalization of Noël Coward's Blithe Spirit. (This show was more or less knocked out of the box by the competing superhits Dolly and Funny Girl.) Lillie had already turned erratic, suffering from severe memory loss and dementia. Her performance in Millie—as the wildly wacky Mrs. Meers—captured her unique talents on film, although the seventy-two-year-old Lillie was at the end of her career. She barely got through the filming, lin-gering on incapacitated for more than two decades. She died in 1989, at the age of ninety-four.

The Millie movie included a fourth leading lady; Ross Hunter liked to give his audiences leading ladies. (He liked to give them Rock Hudson too, but that's another story.) Mary Tyler Moore had just finished six sea-sons on TV's Dick Van Dyke Show, winning two Emmy Awards in the pro-cess. She had also had a crack at Broadway, starring in the legendary mu-sical fiasco Breakfast at Tiffany's (1966), which shuttered during previews at the Majestic.

Millie was very much built around Andrews, with Lillie, Channing, and Moore more prominently spotted than their roles might have merited. This made *Millie* overblown on the screen, a problem that carried over to the stage version. The film was pretty haphazard, but Ross Hunter's package proved successful at the box office.

I don't suppose that anyone ever expected *Thoroughly Modern Millie* to be turned into a Broadway musical. Twenty years after the film's release, a young actor named Dick Scanlan determined that it should be translated to the Broadway stage, and he set out to convince its recalcitrant creator. Richard Morris was apparently in retirement; I can't find any writing credit for him following the 1969 film *Change of Habit*, Ms. Moore's second feature (and Elvis Presley's last). Scanlan finally convinced Morris, and in 1991 the pair started work.

Morris died in 1996. Scanlan took the just-finished draft to up-and-coming director Michael Mayer. Scanlan and Mayer hailed from Rockville, Maryland, where as like-minded teenagers they dreamed of getting out—of Rockville, Maryland—and heading toward Broadway. Mayer signed on, bringing along composer-arranger Jeanine Tesori to help bridge the incidentals; Tesori was a consultant on Mayer's first Broadway musical, *Triumph of Love*. At this point, the *Millie* score consisted of period songs, plus songs written for the original film; as work progressed, Tesori and Scanlan started writing new songs to fit the plot.

Millie was staged as a workshop in October 1999, with Kristen Chenoweth and Bea Arthur playing the roles created by Andrews and Lillie. This led to a fully staged production the following October at the La Jolla Playhouse, in La Jolla, California. Erin Dilly and Pat Carroll were signed for the leads. Dilly was one of those promising young stars who hadn't yet arrived. She created sparks singing "The Lady Is a Tramp" in the February 1999 Encores! production of *Babes in Arms*. By the final week of rehearsals in La Jolla, Dilly was gone. (She went on to play the lead in the pre-Broadway tour of *Martin Guerre*, the Claude-Michel Schönberg–Alain Boublil–Cameron Mackintosh epic that folded in the spring of 2000.)

Millie received promising but cautious reviews in La Jolla and did strong business. But strong enough for Broadway? The show needed ten producing organizations to assemble the $10 million necessary to find out. Intriguingly, one of those who signed on was performer-entrepreneur Whoopi Goldberg, who under other circumstances might have made a Mrs. Meers to reckon with. In retrospect, the most important of the producers might well have been a group called Independent Presenters Network. More about them later.

In revamping *Millie* for Broadway, the La Jolla cast was substantially overhauled. Only Foster and Kudisch, as Millie's millionaire boss, were retained. Kudisch had been with the show since the 1999 workshop. He made a Broadway splash as the conceited suitor in the 1998 musical *High Society*, followed by noticeable stints in *The Scarlet Pimpernel* (version 3.0), Michael John LaChiusa's *The Wild Party*, and as costar of the 2001 revival of *Bells Are Ringing*. Kudisch was delicious as Trevor Graydon, the blueblood Millie decides to wed; a walking sight gag, the Arrow Collar Man with Ovaltine in his veins. (Here, again, was a glint of Preston Sturges; Kudisch's performance might well have been modeled on Rudy Vallee's John D. Hackensacker III in *Palm Beach Story*, another big-buck buffoon who doesn't stand a chance at landing the perky leading lady.)

Harriet Harris, who appeared as Maggie in Nathan Lane's 2000 Roundabout revival of *The Man Who Came to Dinner*, replaced Pat Carroll as Mrs. Meers for the final week of the La Jolla run. Her material was subpar; "They Don't Know," her big and only solo, seemed to be Miss Hannigan's "Little Girls" (from *Annie*) without the showbiz know-how. But Harris filled Bea Lillie's shoes with style, earnestly munching on every piece of

scenery she could get her claws on. Harris and Kudisch did everything with complete inserity— that is, insane sincerity—which made them lovably ludicrous. These two actors understood precisely what *Millie* should have been, in a way that everyone else involved seems to have missed.

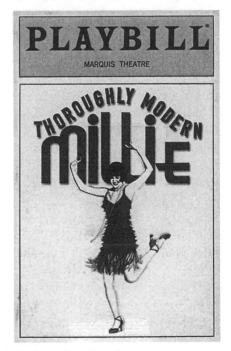

Gavin Creel came in to play the romantic lead Jimmy, giving a highly likable performance (despite some ineffective songs). The Carol Channing and Mary Tyler Moore roles were undertaken by Sheryl Lee Ralph and Angela Christian, and not happily so; without Channing's and Moore's star quality, the characters were more or less lost in the proceedings. Ralph had the worst of it, with little to do other than sing two especially poor Tesori-Scanlan songs. She did have one desperate comedy scene near the end of the evening in which—so help me—she seemed to be wearing one of Ms. Channing's cast-off wigs.

Rounding out the principals were three minor players who—oddly enough—were accorded star billing on the title page of the program. Ken Leung and Francis Jue played a pair of Chinese kidnappers, managing to be extremely charming in roles that could easily have been ethnically offensive. (The plot dealt with white slavery, which didn't seem to bother anyone, although I wonder exactly how parents explained this to their preteens.) Leung was especially droll, managing to impart the heart of a Siamese Dick Powell beneath his charade.

Hidden away among the chorus was Anne L. Nathan, as an executive secretary borrowed from *How to Succeed in Business without Really Trying*. Mayer and choreographer Rob Ashford gave her a tap specialty in the number that opened the second act, "Forget about the Boy," and she was worth her weight in gold-plating. (Paul Huntley, who did such a good job on the wigs for *Millie* and had at least nine other shows simultaneously on the boards, gave Nathan a beehive of a hairdo that tousled to the left and continuously threatened to spring off into the brass section of the orchestra pit.)

> Old-fashioned musical comedy is a musical style that Jeanine Tesori has little interest in. But *Millie* was a show that *needed* old-fashioned musical comedy writing.

As for Sutton Foster, she gave a winning performance as Millie, professionally working her way through a large amount of undistinguished material. Did she grab me with her talent, shake me by the shoulders, and knock me for a loop? Not quite. People who disliked *Millie* tended to discount Foster for her teeth-gritted determination, which seemed a bit backward. No, she wasn't Channing and Streisand rolled into one; not yet, anyway. But this was a girl who had just stepped out of the chorus, literally so, in La Jolla. She managed to carry an unwieldy show, and that was a mighty feat.

The book problems from La Jolla—which stemmed from the scattered satiric thrust of the screenplay—remained unsolved. One character or other entered to sing a song, often with a dance attached; on came another character-with-song, followed by yet another. Muzzy arrived in act 1, scene 10, with the eleventh number of the evening (including reprises). Here was yet *another* character, played by an actor given first-star billing in the program, singing the worst of the four poor new songs of the first act. This is no way to spark a lethargic evening.

And as for those songs, the expectation, obviously, was that the new songs would be better than those in the film. But no. The stage producers, somewhat bafflingly, chose to replace most of the indifferent old songs with indifferent new ones. (*Millie* reached Broadway with nine new songs.)

Tesori is one of the musical theatre's crop of promising, "artistic" composers, best known—until *Millie*—for her 1997 musical *Violet*. This was an odd-but-interesting Playwrights Horizons offering, which attempted a transfer but was unable to attract the necessary financing. Tesori also provided not-especially-interesting incidental music for the 1998 Lincoln Center revival of *Twelfth Night*, and not-especially-interesting dance arrangements for the 1998 revival of *The Sound of Music*.

Old-fashioned musical comedy is clearly not Tesori's métier, and a musical style that I suppose she has little interest in. But *Millie* was a show that *needed* old-fashioned musical comedy writing. Tunes, that's what Broadway musicals of the 1920s were about; Youmans and Gershwin led the way, with songs you could *dance* to. There was a cultural and sexual aspect to all of this; the very concept of being a "thoroughly modern" woman—to borrow a phrase—could be defined as going out unchaperoned to cabarets and dancing to fast music, snuggled closely against men to whom you weren't even engaged. That's not important for our purposes, and *Millie* the musical needn't have had an authentic score.

But the songs needed vitality. This is what Jule Styne (of *Gentlemen Prefer Blondes*) was able to do so well throughout his long career, even when the songs themselves weren't especially good. Old-timers John Kander and Charlie Strouse and Cy Coleman and Jerry Herman—all still active and looking for Broadway hearings when *Millie* waltzed in—can seemingly write this type of tuneful music effortlessly. That's not to say they write better music, simply more suited to the necessary style.

Tesori seemed to consciously avoid anything that smacked of the formulaic, resulting in a frustrating musical evening. The high spots were, quite clearly, Sir Arthur Sullivan's "My Eyes Are Fully Open" ("It Simply Doesn't Matter") from *Ruddigore* (1887), with a new lyric by Dick Scanlan; and a combination of Victor Herbert's "Ah! Sweet Mystery of Life" and "I'm Falling in Love with Someone" from *Naughty Marietta* (1910), with the original lyrics by Rida Johnson Young. A third highlight was "Muqin," a Mandarin lyric to "My Mammy" (Sam Lewis–Joe Young–Walter Donaldson) from Al Jolson's 1918 musical *Bombo*. This was frightening, folks; we had a "thoroughly modern" 2002 musical comedy with a 1967 sensibility (still evident in the book) that took place in 1922, and the best music by far came from 1910 and 1887.

As if to stack the proverbial decks, the *Millie* team came up with a garish and highly unattractive physical production. The deco look was approximated by constructing the sets out of what looked like aluminum foil. Atmosphere was added by shining colored lights on said aluminum foil. The blue lights and red lights on aluminum looked tacky; the green and purple looked especially cheesy, while the yellow—or was it gold?—gave the show a touch of jaundice. The costumes were not much better, as a whole, and I don't care if the fellow won a Tony Award. Ms. Harris's

Thoroughly Modern Millie
Opened: April 18, 2002
Still playing May 27, 2002
44 performances (and 32 previews)
Profit/Loss: To Be Determined
Thoroughly Modern Millie ($95 top) was scaled to a potential
gross of $994,201 at the 1,578-seat Marquis Theatre.
Weekly grosses averaged about $553,000, with the Tony
nominations sending business over the $600,000 mark to
a season-ending $728,000. Total gross for the ten-week
partial season was $5,256,965. Attendance was about 89
percent, with the box office grossing about 61 percent of
dollar-capacity.

TONY AWARD NOMINATIONS
Best Musical (WINNER)
Best Book of a Musical: Richard Morris and Dick Scanlan
Best Original Score: Jeanine Tesori (Music), Dick Scanlan
(Lyrics)
Best Performance by a Leading Actor: Gavin Creel
Best Performance by a Leading Actress: Sutton Foster
(WINNER)
Best Performance by a Featured Actor: Marc Kudisch
Best Performance by a Featured Actress: Harriet Harris
(WINNER)
Best Direction of a Musical: Michael Mayer
Best Choreography: Rob Ashford (WINNER)
Best Costume Design: Martin Pakledinaz (WINNER)
Best Orchestrations: Doug Besterman and Ralph Burns
(WINNER)

DRAMA DESK AWARDS
Outstanding Musical (WINNER)
Outstanding Actress: Sutton Foster (WINNER)
Outstanding Featured Actress: Harriet Harris (WINNER)
Outstanding Director: Michael Mayer (WINNER)
Outstanding Orchestrations: Doug Besterman and Ralph
Burns (WINNER)

*Critical
Scorecard*

Rave 2
Favorable 4
Mixed 0
Unfavorable 2
Pan 2

quasi-Oriental outfits were perfect—Mrs. Meers looked like she stepped
out of the window card for *Auntie Mame*—and some of Ms. Foster's costumes had just the right touch, but the chorus was awash with purple, orange, pink, and teal. *Millie* was not the worst-looking big-budget musical
in memory, but it easily earned a spot on the list.

Millie came to town just in time for the April sweeps. Critical and audience response was severely mixed; some people loved this show, some
hated it. The esteemed Ben Brantley of the all-powerful *Times* complained that "watching this aggressively eager show is like being stam-

peded by circus ponies. It's all whinnying and clomping and brightly decorated bouncing heads, and it never lets up for a second. You'll leave either grinning like an idiot or with a migraine the size of Alaska." The only outright rave among the major papers came from Elysa Gardner in *USA Today*, who gave *Millie* three and a half stars and said it "is as welcome as a gooey ice cream sundae after a week-long fast."

Two weeks after the reviews came the Tony Award nominations, with *Millie* receiving an impressive eleven nominations. Which is where the aforementioned Independent Presenters Network came in. This, according to their *Playbill* biography, was "an association of promoters, theatres and performing arts centers that brings Broadway plays and musicals to audiences in more than 40 cities throughout the United States." That is to say, people who make a living presenting Broadway musicals on tour. The road has, and will presumably always have, a number of blockbusters to contend with. But shows like *The Producers* and *The Lion King* are extremely expensive for the local promoters; they *have* to offer these shows to keep their subscribers happy, and the producers of said blockbusters negotiate accordingly. With the dearth of moderately priced product coming out of Broadway, this group of presenters banded together to support *Millie*. And support it they did, coughing up $25,000 apiece. Broadway shows no longer take $25,000 investors, but forty of them banded together makes for a nice cool million.

These promoters, theatre operators, and performing arts center executives are, for the most part, dues-paying members of the League of American Theatres and Producers. Dues-paying members of the League of American Theatres and Producers make up a large segment of the votership for the Tony Awards. As shows-with-many-producers have become the norm rather than the exception, some productions have more built-in votes than others; a handful of highly principled producers might vote against their own show for a worthy opponent, but not many can resist a shot at adding "producer of the Tony Award–winning" such-and-such to their personal *Playbill* bio.

As *Thoroughly Modern Millie* locked horns with *Urinetown*, it suddenly became clear that *Millie*

A "thoroughly modern" 2002 musical comedy with a 1967 sensibility that took place in 1922, and the best music by far came from 1910 and 1887.

had fifty-odd automatic votes in her corner, while *Urinetown* didn't. The latter show had four producing organizations over the title representing thirteen individuals, most of whom were related to Dodger Theatricals— which withdrew from the League in the fall and presumably lost their voting privileges. This built-in advantage might well have tipped the scales to *Millie*. If so, well—that's show business.

Still, *Millie* needed at least two hundred additional votes to win Best Musical—which means that they received votes from a substantial number of people who were *not* producers of *Thoroughly Modern Millie*. If *Sweet Smell of Success* had fifty voters as investors, I suspect, it *still* wouldn't have won Best Musical. Or even a hundred. It will be noted that even with those extra votes, the songwriters, librettists, and director of *Millie* did not win the awards for which they were nominated.

It remains to be seen whether the Best Musical nod will prove sufficient to put *Millie* in the hit column. It got off to a decent start following the Awards, but before it could build into a standing-room-only hit it was overshadowed by the August arrival, *Hairspray*. There have been Best Musicals of questionable merit in the past, including four in the last decade. *Kiss of the Spider Woman, Passion, Sunset Boulevard,* and *Titanic* each met a severely mixed reception, and each ultimately lost millions of dollars notwithstanding that little silver medallion. Without substantial income from touring companies, *Millie* might well end up in the same boat at *Titanic*.

I would like to go on the record as saying that *Thoroughly Modern Millie* was an exciting, innovative, and deliciously tuneful Broadway musical comedy. But I can't. All I can say is that the film version was practically impossible for me to sit through; the stage musical was barely passable. Which I suppose is a vast improvement.

Morning's at Seven

A season chock-full of revivals continued with yet another, the tenth of the semester. Lincoln Center Theater's revival of Paul Osborn's 1939 comedy *Morning's at Seven* received the strongest critical reception of the lot, although it would be surpassed seven days later by revival number eleven. But eight out of ten favorable reviews—including five outright raves—is rather lovely, thank you.

Paul Osborn (1901–1988) came to Broadway in the late 1920s, a graduate of Professor George Pierce Baker's influential 47 Workshop at Yale. From 1928 through 1958, Osborn wrote a dozen produced plays. His third, *The Vinegar Tree* (1930), was a moderate hit; his fifth was the even better *On Borrowed Time* (1938), which has seen two Broadway revivals —and, at the rate we're going, is bound to resurface sooner rather than later.

Osborn adapted *On Borrowed Time* from the novel by Lawrence Watkin. The play's success, and

One can't necessarily resolve life's inner demons, Osborn seems to be saying; the best you can hope for is to make peace with them and go on.

the failure of his next work—an original play—pegged him as a specialist in adaptations. He adapted three more novels into stage hits, John Hersey's *A Bell for Adano* (1944), John P. Marquand's *Point of No Return* (1951), and Richard Mason's *The World of Suzie Wong* (1958). The latter, Osborn's final play, was a blockbuster potboiler; Brooks Atkinson, in the *Times*, found it "flaring in style and sophomoric in viewpoint, and on the artistic level of a comic book." But a significant moneymaker.

Osborn simultaneously had great success writing adaptations for Hollywood, his credits including *Madame Curie* (1943), *The Yearling* (1946), *East of Eden* (1955), *Sayonara* (1957), and *South Pacific* (1958). He seems to have retired after the twin successes of *Suzie Wong* on stage and screen

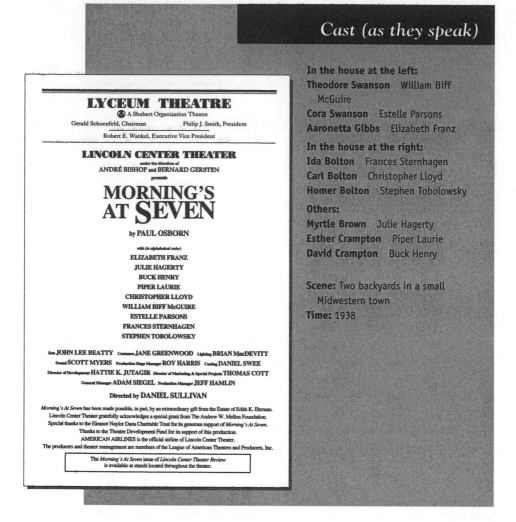

Cast (as they speak)

In the house at the left:
Theodore Swanson   William Biff McGuire
Cora Swanson   Estelle Parsons
Aaronetta Gibbs   Elizabeth Franz

In the house at the right:
Ida Bolton   Frances Sternhagen
Carl Bolton   Christopher Lloyd
Homer Bolton   Stephen Tobolowsky

Others:
Myrtle Brown   Julie Hagerty
Esther Crampton   Piper Laurie
David Crampton   Buck Henry

Scene: Two backyards in a small Midwestern town
Time: 1938

LYCEUM THEATRE
Ⓢ A Shubert Organization Theatre
Gerald Schoenfeld, Chairman   Philip J. Smith, President

Robert E. Wankel, Executive Vice President

LINCOLN CENTER THEATER
under the direction of
ANDRÉ BISHOP and BERNARD GERSTEN
presents

MORNING'S AT SEVEN

by PAUL OSBORN

with (in alphabetical order)
ELIZABETH FRANZ
JULIE HAGERTY
BUCK HENRY
PIPER LAURIE
CHRISTOPHER LLOYD
WILLIAM BIFF McGUIRE
ESTELLE PARSONS
FRANCES STERNHAGEN
STEPHEN TOBOLOWSKY

Sets JOHN LEE BEATTY   Costumes JANE GREENWOOD   Lighting BRIAN MacDEVITT
Sound SCOTT MYERS   Production Stage Manager ROY HARRIS   Casting DANIEL SWEE
Director of Development HATTIE K. JUTAGIR   Director of Marketing & Special Projects THOMAS COTT
General Manager ADAM SIEGEL   Production Manager JEFF HAMLIN

Directed by DANIEL SULLIVAN

Morning's At Seven has been made possible, in part, by an extraordinary gift from the Estate of Edith K. Ehrman.
Lincoln Center Theater gratefully acknowledges a special grant from The Andrew W. Mellon Foundation.
Special thanks to the Eleanor Naylor Dana Charitable Trust for its generous support of Morning's At Seven.
Thanks to the Theatre Development Fund for its support of this production.
AMERICAN AIRLINES is the official airline of Lincoln Center Theater.
The producers and theater management are members of the League of American Theatres and Producers, Inc.

The Morning's At Seven issue of Lincoln Center Theater Review
is available at stands located throughout the theater.

(1961). He was all but forgotten by 1980, when *Morning's at Seven* unaccountably reappeared on Broadway.

Morning's at Seven originally opened on November 30, 1939, at the Longacre, received pleasant but mild reviews, and closed after forty-four performances. The last of Osborn's original plays (as opposed to adaptations), it was one of his least successful efforts. Joshua Logan directed; his first hit had been *On Borrowed Time*, the year before. (Logan's final hit was Osborn's *Suzie Wong*; the pair also worked together on the films *Sayonara* and *South Pacific*.) Prominent among the cast of respected character actors was Dorothy Gish, who played Aaronetta; the other names are no longer familiar.

The title phrase *Morning's at Seven* is meaningless to us today; it merely looks mispunctuated. Shouldn't it be *Mornings at Seven*, implying that the slice-of-life recurs time and again? But no. The phrase is borrowed from Robert Browning's *Pippa Passes*. "The year's at the spring, and day's at the morn, morning's at seven . . ." This passage was presumably more familiar to 1939 audiences; they would have known, without prompting, the rest of the quotation—"God's in His heaven, all's right with the world."

The action takes place in the backyards of two barely detached houses in a Midwestern town. Stage right lives seventy-year-old Cora, with her husband, Thor (Theodore), and her baby sister, Arry (Aaronetta). Arry came to visit when she was seventeen and has remained for forty-eight years, making for a somewhat tense situation. Stage left lives another strained threesome: Ida, the sister between Cora and Arry; her husband, Carl, a lost soul searching for the meaning of life; and their forty-year-old bachelor son, Homer. Down the street are Esther, the eldest of the sisters, and her estranged husband, David.

This sleepy octet is thrust into action by a movie. Ida has seen a film about an unhappy bachelor who commits suicide in the final reel, and she determines that Homer must marry. He brings Myrtle, his thirty-nine-year-old fiancée of twelve years, to visit, but the poor girl ends up in the midst of several family affairs. (The poor girl, herself, turns out to be pregnant.)

All nine characters have their own private struggles, which bubble up within the twenty hours spanned by the play. All are dealt with, if not alleviated, by curtain's fall. One can't necessarily resolve life's inner demons, Osborn seems to be saying; the best you can hope for is to make peace with them and go on. Everybody kisses or shakes hands, and they all return home, leaving us with Browning's moral (though not his words). "God's in His heaven, all's right with the world."

A 1955 off-Broadway revival of *Morning's at Seven*, at the Cherry Lane, ran a more respectable 125 performances; Tom Bosley, just arrived in New York, played Homer. That, presumably, would have been that. But producers Liz McCann and Nelle Nugent, looking for something with which to follow up their successful *Dracula* (1977) and

The 1980 *Morning's at Seven* was hailed as a long-lost masterpiece, receiving better reviews than Arthur Miller (in the revival of *The Price*).

The Elephant Man (1979), settled on Osborn's long-neglected *Morning's at Seven*. (McCann had been production assistant on the 1955 revival.) They stocked the cast with respected character actors. Teresa Wright, Elizabeth Wilson, Nancy Marchand, and Maureen O'Sullivan played the four sisters at the center of the story.

Lo and behold, things worked out. The 1980 *Morning's at Seven* was hailed as a long-lost masterpiece, receiving better reviews than, say, Arthur

Miller (in his 1980 play *The American Clock* and the 1979 revival of *The Price*). A rather surprised Osborn found his orphaned play winning the Tony Award for best revival; director Vivian Matalon and supporting actor David Rounds (as Horace) also won. The revival ran 564 performances, Osborn's longest Broadway visit by far.

Twenty-two years later, the sixty-two-year-old play returned amid a veritable parade of revivals. But this was a revival with a difference, an ensemble piece featuring no less than nine flavorful roles. The tempo of the times aided in the selection; following the events of September 11, the folks at Lincoln Center Theater selected the late-Depression play "particularly as America is once again living through uncertain times." Daniel Sullivan, who had recently directed back-to-back Pulitzer Prize

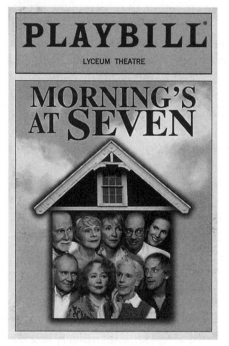

winners *Dinner with Friends* and *Proof* (as well as Cherry Jones–led revivals of *A Moon for the Misbegotten* and *Major Barbara*), returned to Lincoln Center Theater for his tenth visit.

Sullivan assembled a fine cast, led by a quartet of award-winning actresses. Elizabeth Franz captured the fussy frustration of the spinster Arry, successfully revealing her inner despair in the letter scene; the always-proficient Franny Sternhagen added some unaccustomed humor to her portrayal of Ida; Julie Hagerty, as the way-too-eager-to-please fiancée, fit right in with the group; and Buck Henry—a sometime actor better known as a comedy writer—was delightful. (Better he should have been over at the Plymouth, fixing the shambles of his Oscar-nominated screenplay for *The Graduate*.)

I was especially taken with seventy-five-year-old William Biff McGuire, perhaps because he is less familiar than most of his castmates. This singer-actor goes way back, to the original 1949 production of *South Pacific*. He returned to Broadway in 1997 in *The Young Man from Atlanta*, winning a deserved Tony nomination, and gave a lovely performance as the least eccentric of *Morning at Seven*'s characters.

The 2002 *Morning's at Seven* was hailed as a classic, receiving better re-

Morning's at Seven
Opened: April 21, 2002
Closed: July 28, 2002
112 performances (and 27 previews)
Profit/Loss: Nonprofit [profit]
Morning's at Seven ($66.25 top) was scaled to a potential
    gross of $387,501 at the 924-seat Lyceum Theatre. (The
    top was increased to $71.25 in May, with a $413,412
    potential.) Weekly grosses averaged about $159,000, with
    business falling off severely in July. Total gross for the
    eighteen-week run was $2,766,340. Attendance was about
    58 percent, with the box office grossing about 40 percent
    of dollar-capacity.

TONY AWARD NOMINATIONS
Best Revival of a Play
Best Performance by a Featured Actor: William Biff McGuire
Best Performance by a Featured Actor: Stephen Tobolowsky
Best Performance by a Featured Actress: Elizabeth Franz
Best Performance by a Featured Actress: Estelle Parsons
Best Performance by a Featured Actress: Frances Sternhagen
Best Direction of a Play: Daniel Sullivan
Best Scenic Design: John Lee Beatty
Best Costume Design: Jane Greenwood

Critical Scorecard

Rave 5
Favorable 3
Mixed 1
Unfavorable 1
Pan 0

views than, say, Arthur Miller (whose *Crucible* met with less critical enthusiasm but far stronger business). If half of the critics found *Morning's at Seven* worth raving about, I found my pleasure in the proceedings somewhat more moderate. The outing provided an enjoyable evening, thanks chiefly to the warm glow emanating from the ensemble. That might be enough under ordinary circumstances. Given the

The 2002 *Morning's at Seven* was hailed as a classic, receiving better reviews than Arthur Miller (in the revival of *The Crucible*).

unrelenting mediocrity of the spring 2002 lineup, I saw *Morning's at Seven* not as a relief but as an affirmation of how sleepy things had become.

The Mystery of Charles Dickens

At a quarter past nine, Simon Callow—as the forty-year-old Charles Dickens—complained "my misery is amazing, my blankness is inconceivable, indescribable." Having sat through the first act of *The Mystery of Charles Dickens*, I knew precisely how he felt.

The final week of the 2001–2002 season brought yet another solo show, the sixth in slightly less than five calendar months. The season also saw three two-handers and one play with an enormous cast of three. That is, nine shows—a full quarter of the season's Broadway activity—with a combined cast of twelve.

The easy reaction is: sure, this is a cheap way to make a killing on Broadway at sixty-five dollars a pop (if you can get it). But one of the 2001–2002 one-person shows, *Elaine Stritch at Liberty*, was arguably the most entertaining offering of the semester; three of the others, John Leguizamo's *Sexaholix*, Alan Alda in *QED*, and Barbara Cook in *Mostly Sondheim*, provided high entertainment value in a lackadaisical season. As for the other two, *Bea Arthur on Broadway: Just between Friends* and *The Mystery of Charles Dickens*—well, yes, they were mighty trying.

> "My misery is amazing, my blankness is inconceivable, indescribable," said Simon Callow. Having sat through the first act, I knew precisely how he felt.

Callow is a vibrant and somewhat overbearing performer, best known in the States for his screen performances in *Four Weddings and a Funeral* and *Shakespeare in Love*. *Dickens* marked his Broadway acting debut, although he visited Shubert Alley in 1989 as director of the import *Shirley Valentine*. He has numerous stage credits back in England; prominent among them are the title character in the original production of *Amadeus* (in 1979). He is a writer as well, with books about Oscar Wilde, Orson Welles, and Charles Laughton. This last is not coincidental; Callow calls to mind larger-than-life actors like Laughton, Robert Morley, and Peter Ustinov.

In 1997, Callow revived Micheal MacLiammoir's one-man take on Wilde, *The Importance of Being Oscar*; as a student, Callow had been MacLiammoir's dresser. The success of this venture impelled Callow to do the same for Dickens, in tandem with director Patrick Garland (who staged Callow's *Wilde*). Previously, Garland had been responsible for two remarkable solo shows, Roy Dotrice's *Brief Lives* and Eileen Atkins's *A Room of One's Own*. Garland was less successful with Alec McCowen's *Kipling*.

For the script, Callow turned to Peter Ackroyd, author of the 1,195-page 1991 biography *Dickens*. By browsing the Internet, I'm sorry to report, I found a book review (by James R. Kincaid) from the *New York Times*: "This new biography of Dickens waddles along like a maudlin elephant that has attached itself to us against our will." Oh, dear!

Ackroyd and Callow came up with an unwieldy framework. Here was Callow onstage, playing Dickens. But not really Dickens, and not, presumably, Callow. More like Callow playing Alistair Cooke (of *Masterpiece Theatre*) playing Callow playing Dickens playing Copperfield and Crummles and Bill Sykes and Miss Havisham.

More specifically, we had Callow (or Callow/Ackroyd); Callow playing Dickens; Dickens in his own words, presumably truthful; Dickens in his own words, with an eye on posterity; fifty-odd Dickens characters; and, most unfortunately, Dickens in his characters' words. That is, Callow and Ackroyd continually used Dickens's fictional writing as pseudo-autobiography; imagine an actor playing Tennessee Williams describing his life story, using dialogue borrowed from Stanley Kowalski. Better yet, please let's not imagine it.

Here are excerpts—considerably trimmed excerpts—from the opening moments of the play; the italics are mine. "Charles Dickens once wrote that 'the more real the man, the more genuine the actor.' Certainly *he* was writing of himself. '*I* was an actor and a speaker from a baby'. . . . *He* was an irrepressible entertainer. '*I* must have been a horrible little nuisance,' *he* said. . . . *He* would recite his favourite poem: '*I* hear him complain / you have waked me too soon / I must slumber again.' *He* had a toy theatre. . . . 'When my mother is out of breath, *I* watch her winding her bright curls 'round her fingers. Nobody knows better than I do, she likes to look so well. 'My dear boy!' cried my mother, caressing *me*, 'my own dear little boy.' These idyllic childhood days were without any question the happiest days of Charles Dickens's entire life."

As you see, Callow and Ackroyd shifted from "me" to "I" to "he" within a breath. And the "I" and "he" of the last section are neither Callow nor Ackroyd nor Dickens; they are quotes from *David Copperfield*. So we are on many playing fields at once, leading us to question Ackroyd's "these idyllic childhood days were without any question the happiest days of Charles Dickens's entire life." Does he base this statement on something Dickens said, or wrote? Or is it paraphrased from *David Copperfield*?

These changing pronouns went on for two hours, less intermission (which gave the overwrought Callow a much-needed respite, and the audience, too). Theatregoers well versed in the work of Dickens might well have had a far, far easier time of it, and an enjoyable one to boot. But how many twenty-first-century New Yorkers, do you suppose, are well versed in Dickens? This is not to say that there isn't a place for a show about Dickens; but *The Mystery of Charles Dickens*, as structured, wasn't it.

The sixth solo show in less than five months. The season also saw three two-handers and one play with a cast of three. That's nine shows with a combined cast of twelve.

Callow's *Dickens* opened September 6, 2000, at the Comedy Theatre in London and toured happily through the United Kingdom until they decided to brave Broadway just in time for the 2002 Tony Award nominations. Why, one wonders? To enable Callow and Dickens to tour under a "direct from Broadway" banner? The timing, with far too many plays vying for a limited pool of ticket buyers, was not opportune. The three British producers of Dickens were coproducers of *Noises Off*, which could easily withstand the competition; one was also lead producer on *The Elephant Man*, which decidedly could not (withstand the competition). As it was, *The Mystery of Charles Dickens* not so mysteriously died at the box office and was gone quicker than you can say *Martin Chuzzlewit*.

The evening finally worked its way around to Dickens's 1869 reading tour. Callow (as Dickens) performed a string of excerpts from his (Dickens's) novels and—in a self-congratulatory mode—told us: "He held his audience spell-bound. Wild applause, tears, cheers, wonderful happiness." Callow went through the parade of characters—Sam Weller, Sarah Gamp, Pecksniff, Uriah Heep, Squeers, Mr. Podsnap—and I felt not spellbound but bound-in-ropes, if you please.

Dickens was always exhausted after each performance, Callow told us. But not nearly so exhausted as I.

"He was always exhausted after each performance," Callow told us. But not nearly so exhausted as I.

Private Lives

*P*rivate Lives is a reasonably well-constructed duologue for two experienced performers, with a couple of extra puppets thrown in to assist the plot and to provide contrast. There is a well-written love scene in act 1, and a certain amount of sound sex psychology underlying the quarrel scenes in act 2. As a complete play, it leaves a lot to be desired.

This even-tempered opinion of Noël Coward's most successful effort—the revival of which was the third-to-last Broadway offering of the 2001–2002 season, as well as the third-to-last revival of the 2001–2002 season, and which received the finest set of reviews of the 2001–2002 season—came from Noël Coward himself.

The play's failings, said he in the introduction to his 1933 anthology, *Play Parade*, are "principally owing to my dastardly and conscienceless behaviour towards Sibyl and Victor, the secondary characters. They, poor things, are little better than ninepins, lightly wooden, and only there at all in order to be repeatedly knocked down and stood up again."

> **"There is no further plot and no further action after Act One, with the exception of the rough-and-tumble fight at the curtain of Act Two."**

The gentleman doth protest too much, I think; I suppose he thought *Private Lives* was just fine, and surely his bankbook agreed. Still, he points out—and rightfully so—that "there is no further plot and no further action after Act One, with the exception of the rough-and-tumble fight at the curtain of Act Two."

Coward knows his onions, as one of his ninepins might say. Having played Elyot, the male lead of *Private Lives*, for almost a year, he offers insight on the acting challenges presented by the play: "As a general rule

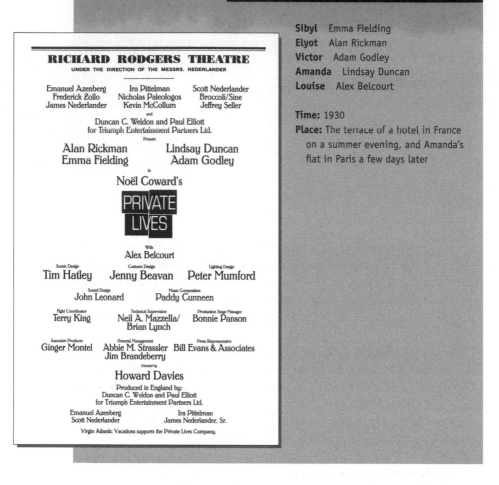

RICHARD RODGERS THEATRE
UNDER THE DIRECTION OF THE MESSRS. NEDERLANDER

Emanuel Azenberg   Ira Pittelman   Scott Nederlander
Frederick Zollo   Nicholas Paleologos   Broccoli/Sine
James Nederlander   Kevin McCollum   Jeffrey Seller
and
Duncan C. Weldon and Paul Elliott
for Triumph Entertainment Partners Ltd.
Present

Alan Rickman   Lindsay Duncan
Emma Fielding   Adam Godley

in

Noël Coward's

PRIVATE LIVES

With
Alex Belcourt

Scenic Design   Costume Design   Lighting Design
Tim Hatley   Jenny Beavan   Peter Mumford

Sound Design   Music Composition
John Leonard   Paddy Cunneen

Fight Coordinator   Technical Supervision   Production Stage Manager
Terry King   Neil A. Mazzella/   Bonnie Panson
Brian Lynch

Associate Producer   General Management   Press Representative
Ginger Montel   Abbie M. Strassler   Bill Evans & Associates
Jim Brandeberry

Directed by
Howard Davies

Produced in England by:
Duncan C. Weldon and Paul Elliott
for Triumph Entertainment Partners Ltd.

Emanuel Azenberg   Ira Pittelman
Scott Nederlander   James Nederlander, Sr.

Virgin Atlantic Vacations supports the Private Lives Company.

Sibyl Emma Fielding
Elyot Alan Rickman
Victor Adam Godley
Amanda Lindsay Duncan
Louise Alex Belcourt

Time: 1930
Place: The terrace of a hotel in France
on a summer evening, and Amanda's
flat in Paris a few days later

the considerate author provides lifelines for his actors, in the shape of sharply etched cameos for the subsidiary members of the cast, who can make bustling little entrances and exits in order to break the monotony. He may even, on occasion, actually provide a sustained plot for them to hang on to when all else fails. In the second act of *Private Lives*, however, there was no help from the author over and above a few carefully placed laugh lines, and, taken all in all, it was more tricky and full of pitfalls than anything I have ever attempted as an actor."

Private Lives was a vehicle for its author and his childhood pal Gertrude Lawrence, "conceived in Tokyo, written in Shanghai, and produced in London" in September, 1930. After a limited engagement of 101 performances in London, Noël and Gertie trouped over to New York for a January 27, 1931, opening at the Times Square Theatre. (This theatre has been defunct since 1933, although the handsome exterior—with its grand portico—is still visible just to the west of the Forty-second Street entrance of the Ford Center.) *Private Lives* was the hit of the town, running for as long as Coward wished to remain, which was 256 performances. The author cast a couple of newlyweds as his so-called wooden ninepins, bringing them along for the New York engagement. Jill Esmond played Coward's wife, Sibyl; Lawrence's husband was played by Esmond's husband, twenty-three-year-old Laurence Olivier.

If *Private Lives* is gossamer slight, Broadway has adopted the play as its favorite bit of Coward. And not only Coward; as far as I can tell, it has had more commercial revivals on Broadway than any other twentieth-century play. That's right, more than *Streetcar* or *Death of a Salesman* or *Long Day's Journey* or even *Abie's Irish Rose*. *Hamlet* has it beat, but as of 2002 *Hamlet* has been around for 399 years (to *Private Lives*'s 72); and, besides, *Hamlet* is royalty-free.

Amanda and Elyot first returned to Broadway in 1948. Or perhaps I should say Amanda returned, in the person of Tallulah Bankhead. I could tell you who played her Elyot, but the name wouldn't matter now—nor did it matter then, not when Tallu was onstage at the Plymouth. ("During the last year, Miss Bankhead has been touring it throughout America, which will probably never be the same again," said Brooks Atkinson in the *New York Times*. "Miss Bankhead is vastly interesting. She gives *Private Lives* a good shaking up, and the audience a good going over.")

Bankhead and Company—all right, it was Donald Cook as Elyot, with newcomer Barbara Baxley as Sibyl—more or less equaled the original run, with a highly profitable 248 performances. For the record, Noël and Gertie also came to town in 1948, with a revival of *Tonight at 8:30*—which lasted but 26 performances. (Lawrence appeared opposite Coward's companion Graham Payn, with Coward directing.)

Private Lives did not return to Broadway for another twenty years, but it has in the interim made up for that prolonged absence. In 1969, on the occasion of Coward's seventieth birthday, David Merrick presented a revival at the Billy Rose Theatre (now the Nederlander). With Tammy Grimes and Brian Bedford in the leads, this was a surprise hit, running 204 performances. The play returned a mere five years later, with Maggie Smith gloriously in the lead. I could tell you who played her Elyot, but the name wouldn't matter now—nor did it matter then. Sir John Standing was his name; Sir John Gielgud directed. Imported from London for a highly successful American tour, Maggie and company stopped for three months at the Forty-sixth Street (now the Richard Rodgers).

With *Private Lives* having happily made money on each of its four Broadway visits, craven producers apparently decided that it would be always thus. The worst conceivable *Private Lives* came to town in 1983, at the decidedly nonintimate Lunt-Fontanne Theatre. The better to sell tickets, my dear. Elizabeth Taylor and Richard Burton together again, how could they possibly fail? thought the producers. (The producers were billed as "The Elizabeth Group," headed by guess who.) Neither Taylor nor Burton was stageworthy, and the whole enterprise was terribly sad for 63 performances.

And then came an even worse *Private Lives*, which made Burton and Taylor look like Lunt and Fontanne. Joan Collins headlined a wretched 1992 tour, which collapsed under a cloud of unpaid bills after 37 performances at the Broadhurst. I could tell you who played her Elyot, but it didn't matter then, and the poor fellow is still actively trying to earn a living in the theatre. The once-invulnerable *Private Lives* no longer seemed a surefire moneymaker, and this fifth Broadway production seemed likely to be the last for a spell.

Private Lives has had more commercial revivals on Broadway than any other twentieth-century play. More than *Streetcar* or *Death of a Salesman* or *Long Day's Journey*.

But all it takes, it appears, is two exceptional actors to make Elyot and Amanda sizzle once more. Alan Rickman and Lindsay Duncan had sizzled together before, in London (1985) and Broadway (1987), in Christopher Hampton's *Les Liaisons Dangereuses*. The director of that dazzling production, Howard Davies, was approached to reunite his dangereuse stars in the Coward. The trio—each of whom won Tony nominations the first time round—were sufficiently intrigued. Since *Les Liaisons*, Duncan and Davies had been steadily active in the theatre; Davies has been represented, locally, with *Cat on a Hot Tin Roof* (starring Kathleen Turner) and *The Iceman Cometh* (starring Kevin Spacey). Rickman, on the other hand, found himself a high-priced movie star specializing in villains.

The new *Private Lives* was a major hit when it opened at the Albery on October 4, 2001, to critical raves and sellout business. The show was showered with seven Olivier Award nominations; Duncan, set designer Tim Hatley, and costume designer Jenny Beavan won in their respective categories. Within weeks of the opening, the limited engagement was extended to March 3, and the inevitable Broadway transfer was announced. *Private Lives* generated a U.S. advance sale of about $1.5 million, impressive although not in the league of Kathleen Turner's *The Graduate* (around $5 million) or even Liam Neeson's *The Crucible* (around $2 million).

Private Lives opened at the tail end of the revival-stuffed 2000–2001 season. It received a set of raves that made the critical bouquets lobbed at *Morning's at Seven* a week earlier look lukewarm. This *Private Lives* was, indeed, something. None of that stiff-but-terribly-brittle-upper-lip acting that made Coward famous, or that Coward made famous; Rickman and Duncan were a hot-blooded, sensual pair. This added a level of interest to viewers overly familiar with the play, a classification that included just about every critic. Something new was found in something old, and it fit the material perfectly. Well, almost perfectly. Hence, handstands from the press corps.

Which did not set the credit card machines buzzing as quickly as such sterling notices ordinarily warrant. Sales on the day after the opening were about $105,000, a decent figure but nothing to pop the Dom Perignon over. Perhaps audiences were tired of revivals, this being the thirteenth of fourteen since *A Thousand Clowns* reared its head the prior July. If *Private Lives* was not an immediate blockbuster, it dealt a fatal blow to the recently opened *The Mystery of Charles Dickens*, which didn't stand a chance; and *The Elephant Man*, which did stand a chance but couldn't withstand the added competition.

I was just as happy with the proceedings as the critics in general. Well, almost, but for a reason I can't fairly count against Davies and Duncan and company. Certainly, this *Private Lives* was one of the woefully few Broadway offerings of 2001–2002 that I truly enjoyed and wholeheartedly recommended and would have gladly returned to for a second helping. I did find that things tended to sag a bit in the middle.

Coward, in his preface, had foreseen the problem. Between the end of the first act and the fireworks at the end of the second, "there is exactly forty minutes of dialogue between Amanda and Elyot which naturally demands from them the maximum of resource and comedy experience as every night, according to the degree of responsiveness from the audience, the attack and tempo of the performance must inevitably vary. This means a constant ear cocked in the direction of the stalls, listening for that first sinister cough of boredom, and when it comes, a

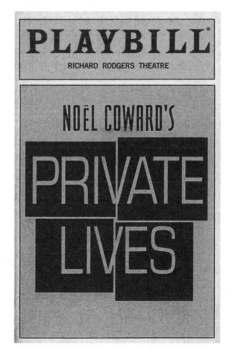

PLAYBILL

RICHARD RODGERS THEATRE

NOËL COWARD'S

PRIVATE

LIVES

Private Lives
Opened: April 28, 2002
Closed: September 1, 2002
127 performances (and 9 previews)
Profit/Loss: Profit
Private Lives ($75 top) was scaled to a potential gross of
$563,886 (for a seven-performance week) at the 1,334-
seat Richard Rodgers Theatre. Weekly grosses averaged
about $365,000, with initially strong business falling off
over the summer. Total gross for the twenty-week run was
$7,083,941. Attendance was about 73 percent, with the
box office grossing about 65 percent of dollar-capacity.

TONY AWARD NOMINATIONS
Best Revival of a Play (WINNER)
Best Performance by a Leading Actor: Alan Rickman
Best Performance by a Leading Actress: Lindsay Duncan
   (WINNER)
Best Direction of a Play: Howard Davies
Best Scenic Design: Tim Hatley (WINNER)
Best Costume Design: Jenny Beavan

DRAMA DESK AWARDS
Outstanding Revival of a Play (WINNER)
Outstanding Actress: Lindsay Duncan (WINNER)
Outstanding Set Design of a Play: Tim Hatley (WINNER)

Critical
Scorecard

Rave 7
Favorable 2
Mixed 0
Unfavorable 1
Pan 0

swiftly exchanged glance of warning, and an immediate and it is to be hoped imperceptible speeding up of the scene until the next sure-fire laugh breaks and it is permissible to relax and breathe more easily for a moment."

This suggested "speeding up of the scene" was not only imperceptible the night I attended the play, it was absent. I suppose that this sort of self-regulating is problematic when you are concentrating on the emotional interplay of the characters, as was the case in this production. This might be why this *Private Lives* seemed LONG. They even saw fit to interpolate a song; where Coward instructed Elyot to merely tinkle around at the piano, Davies had Rickman launch into a full performance of "If Love Were All." Yes, Coward wrote it, but not for *Private Lives*; it seemed a highly unlikely choice for the characters under the circumstances. And it made a long scene even longer.

But this lapsed pace was acceptable, given the overall outcome. The slightly slackened comedy was offset by the heightened emotional temperature, which made the play look ever so much more substantial. My *Private Lives* problem, such as it was, had to do with Maggie Smith. While I was only peripherally involved with the 1975 production, I saw it frequently enough for Maggie's line readings to sink into my subconscious. So much so that anything else sounded wrong. This is unfair to other performers in general, and Ms. Duncan in particular—who was, and is, a wonderful actor. But there it is. I was watching Duncan on the stage of the Rodgers, but I couldn't shake the image of Maggie in her gold-lamé gown slinking across the boards of the Forty-sixth Street—which, despite a change of name, were the very same boards.

Familiarity with one performance does not in itself count against another performance. Maggie's Elyot, John Standing, was perfectly amusing and quite winning in the role, but Rickman—from his first utterance— was clearly in another league. No Coward hero suffers fools gladly; but watching Rickman suffer them with an invisible snarl, and sometimes a visible one, was a joy. This Elyot was oh-so-sophisticated and weary-of-it-all, all right, but he was not above stomping his feet and pouting like a stubborn kindergartner.

Rickman has in the past demonstrated a keen relish for juicy acting, a trait that has made him such a valuable cinema ham. While he is a trained and accomplished actor, he has the ability to stand slightly outside his performance and *enjoy* it along with the audience. This put him in good stead for *Private Lives*; his Elyot was far less in period than others we might have seen,

None of that stiff-but-terribly-brittle-upper-lip acting that made Coward famous, or that Coward made famous. Alan Rickman and Lindsay Duncan were a hot-blooded, sensual pair.

but it turned out to be precisely the revivifying tonic that was called for. Gin and tonic, that is.

Duncan was very good, certainly, and I suppose I would have found her every bit as brilliant as Rickman were it not for the unfair competition from the invisible Maggie. But this was my problem, not Duncan's. For that matter, Tammy Grimes—who won a Tony in 1970 for her Amanda —was delicious in the role, too. Unforgettable, I should say, until I saw Maggie do the role five years later. Maggie was quite something, that's for sure. She defined the role of Amanda for me in such a way that no one else need apply. Ms. Duncan might well have the very same effect on a whole new generation of playgoers. So let's call it an evening of capital entertainment.

Into the Woods

One question arose many times during this season of too many revivals. Well, many questions arose; but one question in particular, with related follow-ups, was often asked. Was it as good as the last time? Was it better than the last time? Was it worse than the last time?

This is not, generally, a helpful question. It has a certain relevance to those who actually attended it the last time, or in some longer-ago production. We should always remember, though, that "revival" is an indistinct term. A play or musical is new to a person who has never seen it before. Or is it? Was *Oklahoma!*—the 2002 Trevor Nunn revival—new to someone who had never seen the Rodgers and Hammerstein musical before? Even if they had listened to the record hundreds of times? Or if they saw the movie? Or if they played Ado Annie in junior high school?

The 2001–2002 season saw a full range of types of revivals. *Oklahoma!* couldn't have been more familiar; *Private Lives*, *Hedda Gabler*, and *The Crucible* were also well known, at least to the theatrically literate. *Noises Off* and *The Elephant Man* were widely seen in their relatively recent, original Broadway runs (and in motion picture versions). *The Man Who Had All the Luck*, on the other hand, was fifty-eight years old—just one year younger than *Oklahoma!*, the season's most familiar revival—but the least known of all. This Arthur Miller play, the final offering of 2001–2002, ran four performances in 1944, presumably to near-empty houses. How many people sitting in the auditorium of the American Airlines Theatre could possibly have seen the original production? Arthur Miller, of course. His sister, Joan Copeland, probably. I'd be surprised if there were more than a dozen others.

Was *The Man Who Had All the Luck* as good as it was the last time? How can that possibly be a relevant question? What is more to the point is, did the new production work? Comparisons were trickier with *Noises Off*. The 2001 revival was a perfectly satisfactory comic evening, with high spots of hilarity. This should be more than enough to ensure artistic and commercial success, and it was. The 1983 production, however, was —simply—perfectly hilarious. This difference should have in no way hindered the reception of the revival, at least to first-time viewers. Good is good enough, isn't it? Had I not seen *Noises Off* in 1983, I suppose I'd have been marginally more excited in 2001. But I can't imagine that I'd have left the Atkinson in 2001 with my sides hurting and my eyes moist from laughter, as I did when I left the Atkinson in 1983.

It is not the comparison that matters, then. It's the way you feel when you're walking up Seventh Avenue, and the enthusiasm with which you relate the proceedings in the next day's phone calls. Or e-mails, as the case may be. Still, comparisons can help explain differences in the overall effect of the show, from production to production.

The 2002 revival of the Stephen Sondheim–James Lapine musical *Into the Woods* was heavily compared to the original 1987 production. So, for that matter, was the 2001 revival of Sondheim and James Goldman's 1971 musical *Follies*. Let's face it; *every* Sondheim revival is likely to be meticulously measured against every prior production of that show. Many are measured against prior productions of *other* Sondheim shows, as well.

Sondheim's groundbreaking collaboration with director/producer Hal Prince, encompassing six musicals between 1970 and 1981, ended with the failure of *Merrily We Roll Along*. (The earlier shows were *Company*, *Follies*, *A Little Night Music*, *Pacific Overtures*, and *Sweeney Todd*.) A new collaborator was found in James Lapine, author and director of the 1979 off-Broadway play *Twelve Dreams*. The pair began a collaboration that has thus far resulted in *Sunday in the Park with George* (1984), *Into the Woods* (1987), and *Passion* (1994). There was a major shift in style from the final Prince shows (*Sweeney* and *Merrily*) to the first Lapine shows (*Sunday* and *Into the Woods*). The method of storytelling was different. The Prince shows, for all **"Revival" is an indistinct term. A play or musical is new to a person who has never seen it before. Or is it?** their advanced methods of dealing with time, were more or less straightforward; Lapine's dramaturgy was something else again.

Lapine began his career as a professional photographer and graphic designer. As a director, he seems to concentrate on focus, and the effects of differing focus on the same picture. He is also very much interested in psychology; *Twelve Dreams*, which brought him to Sondheim's notice, was distinctly Jungian. As a result, Lapine's main characters tend to be psychologically developed, as opposed to the quickly sketched one-

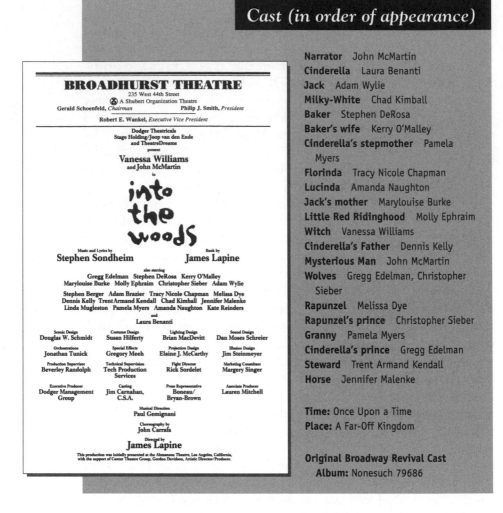

Dodger Theatricals
Stage Holding/Joop van den Ende
and TheatreDreams
present

Vanessa Williams
and John McMartin
in

**into
the
woods**

Music and Lyrics by   Book by
Stephen Sondheim   **James Lapine**

also starring
Gregg Edelman Stephen DeRosa Kerry O'Malley
Marylouise Burke Molly Ephraim Christopher Sieber Adam Wylie

Stephen Berger Adam Brazier Tracy Nicole Chapman Melissa Dye
Dennis Kelly Trent Armand Kendall Chad Kimball Jennifer Malenke
Linda Mugleston Pamela Myers Amanda Naughton Kate Reinders
and
Laura Benanti

Scenic Design **Douglas W. Schmidt**	Costume Design **Susan Hilferty**	Lighting Design **Brian MacDevitt**	Sound Design **Dan Moses Schreier**
Orchestrations **Jonathan Tunick**	Special Effects **Gregory Meeh**	Projection Design **Elaine J. McCarthy**	Illusion Design **Jim Steinmeyer**
Production Supervisor **Beverley Randolph**	Technical Supervision **Tech Production Services**	Fight Director **Rick Sordelet**	Marketing Consultant **Margery Singer**
Executive Producer **Dodger Management Group**	Casting **Jim Carnahan, C.S.A.**	Press Representative **Boneau/ Bryan-Brown**	Associate Producer **Lauren Mitchell**

Musical Direction
Paul Gemignani

Choreography by
John Carrafa

Directed by
James Lapine

This production was initially presented at the Ahmanson Theatre, Los Angeles, California,
with the support of Center Theatre Group, Gordon Davidson, Artistic Director/Producer.

Narrator John McMartin
Cinderella Laura Benanti
Jack Adam Wylie
Milky-White Chad Kimball
Baker Stephen DeRosa
Baker's wife Kerry O'Malley
Cinderella's stepmother Pamela Myers
Florinda Tracy Nicole Chapman
Lucinda Amanda Naughton
Jack's mother Marylouise Burke
Little Red Ridinghood Molly Ephraim
Witch Vanessa Williams
Cinderella's Father Dennis Kelly
Mysterious Man John McMartin
Wolves Gregg Edelman, Christopher Sieber
Rapunzel Melissa Dye
Rapunzel's prince Christopher Sieber
Granny Pamela Myers
Cinderella's prince Gregg Edelman
Steward Trent Armand Kendall
Horse Jennifer Malenke

Time: Once Upon a Time
Place: A Far-Off Kingdom

Original Broadway Revival Cast
Album: Nonesuch 79686

dimensional types found in many musicals. *Thoroughly Modern Millie*, for example.

The fact that Lapine is a director-who-writes makes a major difference in the collaborative process. Prince, as director-producer, can try to explain (and/or dictate) to his writers what he wants them to do; that is, attempt to put his unformulated ideas into words. A librettist-director doesn't need to formulate the ideas in order to investigate them; he can just sit in a room with his composer as they experiment together.

Since we're discussing *Into the Woods*, let's use the forest as metaphor. The director, outside the woods, can explain where he or she wants the writers to get to, in terms of plot or effect. The director can suggest a direction, but the director can't tell the writers precisely how to get there. The writers must choose the path to take, and sometimes the wrong path will lead to an unexpectedly right moment (in the woods). The writer-director is party to these choices, while a nonwriting director—even one so intimately involved as Prince—necessarily remains on the sidelines.

There are also generational differences. Prince and Sondheim were children of the Depression, teenagers during World War II. Lapine is a baby boomer; he was a teenager during Vietnam. (Lapine is nineteen years younger than Sondheim, twenty-one younger than Prince.)

A third difference is procedural. Prince and Sondheim—as well as everyone in their generation—came from a theatre where you wrote a show, a producer raised the money, and it opened (hopefully) on Broadway. Lapine was a product of André Bishop's program at Playwrights Horizons, where a script would be given a reading and then developed and workshopped and rewritten and given a reading once more. That is to say, unfinished work would be mounted as a tool to guide the authors, a method that was unheard of in the days when "tryout" meant a split-week in New Haven before facing the Boston critics three days later. *Sunday in the Park* underwent such a developmental course (at Playwrights Horizons), as have all his post-Prince musicals. A good thing, too, as Sondheim does some of his most creative writing once he has a stageful of actors in front of him.

Sunday in the Park focused on the pointillist painter Georges Seurat and the creation of the masterpiece we call *A Sunday Afternoon on the Island of La Grande Jatte*. In the first act, that is; in the second act, Lapine and Sondheim moved to the world of contemporary art, with the Seurat character becoming his own great-grandson. This tied yesterday to today, drawing parallels between then and now. At least, it was supposed to. It seemed to me that the writers felt the need to justify their tale of Seurat by making it *relevant*. I, for one, didn't buy it at the time. My thinking has changed, somewhat, after the Kennedy Center's 2002 *Sondheim Celebration* (which will be discussed in *Broadway Yearbook 2002–2003*).

Every Sondheim revival is likely to be meticulously measured against every prior production of that show. Many are measured against prior productions of *other* Sondheim shows, as well.

Into the Woods was different but the same. The first act interwove three well-known fairy tales, bringing everybody to a happy ending. Act 2 showed what happened "Ever After," which—as in *Sunday*—was the dark side. (Half of the main characters are killed, and three more are blinded.) This seemed rather heavy-handed to me; again, I thought, Lapine and Sondheim decided to justify their first act by drawing parallels and bopping us over the head with 'em.

The original 1987 production of *Into the Woods* was a success d'estime of sorts. The reviews were mixed, business was mediocre, and the show closed at a loss. (*Into the Woods* has been highly successful in the nonprofessional licensing field, with more school and amateur productions than any Sondheim musicals other than *West Side Story* and *Forum*. I would expect that income from these subsidiary rights eventually paid off the original Broadway investment.) Sondheim and Lapine deservedly won Tony Awards as authors—their work was far better than anything else that season—but Prince won for directing the Best Musical winner, *Phantom of the Opera*. Which outlasted the original *Into the Woods* by fourteen years, and the revival as well.

Sitting at the new *Into the Woods*, and knowing the show so well, I was prepared for another intriguing but ultimately unsatisfying evening of theatre. Within the first minute—the show eschews an overture, introducing the main characters right off the baton—I discovered that I was surprisingly *happy* to be back in the woods once more. Several minutes in, when Little Red Ridinghood introduced the title theme while doing a little side-by-side shuffle step, I felt charmed; and by the final section of the

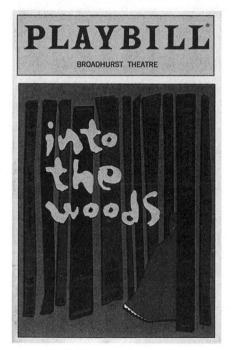

opening number, with eleven of the principals singing their way "Into the Woods" while the cow Milky-White started scrambling like crazy to do the choreography, I thought: Well, yes!

Here we had the same show; the same material; the same director, even, as they had at the Martin Beck in 1987. Was the show as good as the last time? Was it better than the last time? Or was it worse?

Opinions were split. People who loved it in 1987 tended to fault the changes; nonfans of the original praised the improvements. (The end results were more or less the same: a succès d'estime with mixed reviews and mediocre business, closing at a loss.) I found the 2002 show more enjoyable, by far. No comparison. Why? Observations, in somewhat random order.

John McMartin. Not the actor himself, but the way he and director Lapine decided to reinterpret the role of the Narrator. Tom Aldredge played it in 1987 as a crusty and somewhat foreboding fellow, a frosty, Ichabod Crane–like presence. There was a bit of humor beneath the characterization, but Aldredge left me cold. And as the Narrator goes, so goes *Into the Woods*. (Aldredge's performance in the 2002 revival of *The Crucible* was another crusty old fellow, but one with all the warmth that his Narrator had lacked.) McMartin, a leading man in such musicals as *Sweet Charity* and the original *Follies*, was the opposite of serious; a warm, friendly, lovable, and somewhat addled grandpa. His tone was reminiscent of the Edward Everett Horton voice-overs for the "Fractured Fairy Tale" segments of the *Rocky and Bullwinkle Show*. When called on to carry a coat hanger wired with fluttering "birds," McMartin fluttered as well. He fluttered, he flounced, he charmed. And brought us into the story from the very beginning.

The cow. Milky-White, originally, was a piece of—what, fiberglass spray-painted white? As inanimate as could be. It had handles, like a piece of luggage, and if I remember correctly the back legs were on wheels; the actors rolled it around as if it were a child's pull toy. Lapine changed course, here, making it a decidedly animate cow with a hangdog stare, impossibly lean ribs, and four left feet. Chad Kimball, the actor in the cowhide, did a wonderful job. This was a cow who positively emoted, somehow, garnering laugh after laugh. The biggest laugh? When Milky-White died (temporarily), collapsing like a bag of dusty old bones in a homely heap. Loved that cow, which in 1987 was nothing to love.

The choreography. John Carrafa, a former Twyla Tharp dancer, has been kicking around the fringes for years. He finally hit it big in 2001–2002 with *Into the Woods* and *Urinetown*, demonstrating that he is a choreographer with a fine comic sense. The dance numbers in this *Into the Woods* seemed to consist mostly of the company hopping around from side to side, in little skipping steps. This worked charmingly for this child-friendly fairy tale of a show. There were no real dancers in the cast, nor should there have been, but Carrafa's staging kept the energy up. (The choreography in the original production, as best I can remember it, was all but negligible.) Carrafa also took full advantage of Milky-White, who—being a fellow in a cow costume—was always valiantly two steps behind. Very, very funny; and charming.

The physical production. The last time around it was a spooky Woods. Perhaps fittingly, as it is a spooky world. The dark forest loomed upstage, constantly reminding us that anything (bad) could happen in the woods. Doug Schmidt's new set was built upon storybooks, literally, book pieces that unfolded to provide interiors. The results were ever so much friendlier. Perhaps it was the colors that did it—the reds and greens and browns, instead of the darkly inky blue of 1987. Susan Hilferty's costumes were fairy-tale perfect, richly textured and colored to match the set. So was Brian MacDevitt's lighting, which enhanced the material's quick changes of mood, taking us seamlessly from the interiors to the forest. (Matching the costumes and lighting to the scenery is obvious but easier said than done, and if you don't believe me, look at, again, *Thoroughly Modern Millie*.) Lapine also solved the problem of the Giantess, a voice-over character who is too large to actually appear onstage. He simply got Judi Dench to record the dialogue, and who can argue with that?

The kids. Lapine and Sondheim seemed to reverse course on these two characters. Little Red Ridinghood, in 1987, was played by a sixteen-year-old comedienne who looked and acted like a little old character lady. Danielle Ferland (from *Sunday in the Park*), cast way against type, was very funny in the role. The new girl, Molly Ephraim, was simply a teenager. With comic sense and spunk, mind you; but she could have passed for someone's daughter. That is, she was a real Red Ridinghood; when tragedy overtook the woods in the second act, you had a *child* to care about. This aspect was elusive in 1987. Jack's characterization was changed as well. Ben Wright was tall, handsome, and almost heroic; in the photo included in the liner notes of the 1987 CD, he appears to be the second-tallest of the seventeen cast members. Adam Wylie, the new Jack-of-the-Beanstalk, played the role as a rubber-faced fool (which is how he's described by his mother). But a boy, not a young leading man.

The prince. Gregg Edelman far outpaced the 1987 Prince Charming. Not due to talent, necessarily, but to characterization. The original chap was—well, princely. Edelman's prince had a touch of the buffoon, shimmering about the stage as if he was drawn by Jay Ward (creator of the aforementioned *Bullwinkle*). Edelman has always sung well and acted satisfactorily, in such musicals as the 1987 revival of *Cabaret*, *Passion*, and *City of Angels*. Here, for the first time I can remember, he was lovably funny.

The others. Devoted fans of the 1987 version seem to have missed the original cast. I liked the original cast, mostly, but their show didn't work for me, so I was open to new interpretations. Chip Zien and Johanna Gleason, who originated the roles of the Baker and the Baker's Wife, were both highly memorable; Gleason was especially wonderful, nabbing a Tony for her portrayal. Stephen DeRosa and Kerry O'Malley more than held their own in these roles. Yes, I kind of missed Gleason at the start; but O'Malley pulled through, while DeRosa has established himself as an inspired clown over the last few seasons. Kim Crosby made a lovely Cinderella in 1987, but Laura Benanti is a star-to-be. In fact, I think she's a star already, just waiting for her breakthrough role. Pure enchantment, which is what you want from Cinderella.

Into the Woods
Opened: April 30, 2002
Closed: December 29, 2002
279 performances (and 18 previews)
Profit/Loss: Loss
Into the Woods ($100 top) was scaled to a potential gross of
$760,960 at the 1,135-seat Broadhurst Theatre. Weekly
grosses averaged about $397,000, hitting the half-million
mark on only two occasions. Total gross for the thirty-
eight-week run was $14,731,618. Attendance was about
69 percent, with the box office grossing about 52 percent
of dollar-capacity.

TONY AWARD NOMINATIONS
Best Revival of a Musical (WINNER)
Best Performance by a Leading Actor: John McMartin
Best Performance by a Leading Actress: Vanessa Williams
Best Performance by a Featured Actor: Gregg Edelman
Best Performance by a Featured Actress: Laura Benanti
Best Direction of a Musical: James Lapine
Best Choreography: John Carrafa
Best Scenic Design: Douglas W. Schmidt
Best Costume Design: Susan Hilferty
Best Lighting Design: Brian MacDevitt (WINNER)

DRAMA DESK AWARDS
Outstanding Revival of a Musical (WINNER)
Outstanding Set Design of a Musical: Douglas W. Schmidt
  (WINNER)
Outstanding Sound Design: Dan Moses Schreier (WINNER)

*Critical
Scorecard*

Rave 4
Favorable 2
Mixed 1
Unfavorable 1
Pan 2

The name-above-the-title star. Vanessa Williams in for Bernadette Peters. Didn't much like Peters, who seemed overqualified for the role and
not especially engaged. (The star of *Sunday in the Park*, she stepped in at
the last minute to fill a casting hole as a favor to Sondheim and Lapine.)
Didn't much like Williams, who seemed lost in the woods. Maybe it's the
writing? Or more accurately, the emphasis. Put in someone who is not a
star, take her name off the top of the billing page, and have her share a
dressing room with Cinderella and the Baker's Wife. Change the attitude,
and then—maybe—I'll appreciate the Witch.

The changes. These were rather minor overall, but highly effective.
The dancing cow, as mentioned above. (This was not Sondheim's first
dancing cow, by the way; Caroline, a two-person bovine, was prominently
featured in Baby June's vaudeville act in *Gypsy*.) Lapine and Sondheim
brought a second wolf, along with three plump pink pigs, into "Hello, Little Girl." This got a laugh, as was to be expected; but it was a warm laugh,
reminding the audience that we were in a storybook world. It also soft-

ened the predatory nature of the wolf-who-eats-Red Ridinghood, as if to say—hey, there are two wolves, that's what *all* wolves do. The pair also served to balance the pair of Princes, which made things even more neat and nice. As I watched Edelman doing his sashay-of-a-softshoe, I couldn't help but remember the overly phallic costume that the 1987 wolf wore. Earthy, you might say; or vulgar, you might say. It got a laugh at the time, but it seemed a mite unpleasant for a fairy-tale musical with hundreds of kids in the audience. Edelman's wolf was second cousin to Bert Lahr's Cowardly Lion. Yes, he does swallow Red and Granny, but nevertheless he's a very nice wolf.

Other changes came in song. "Our Little World," a duet for the Witch and her daughter Rapunzel that was added for the 1990 London production, was retained here. Sondheim also brought the two children—Red Ridinghood and Jack—into the end of Cinderella's solo "On the Steps of the Palace," interspersing the lessons they learned on their journey into the woods. A minor rewrite, but one that effectively tied strings together and underlined Sondheim and Lapine's message of the evening. Amazing what a few words, in the right place, can do.

The 1987 show seemed to be a case of "wouldn't it be intriguing to take all those characters from children's storybooks and weave them into a musical?" In 2002, this became "wouldn't it be *lovely* . . . "

All of which leads back to:

The director. If the director has come up with improvements on the original show and he or she happens to be the author, why not incorporate them? Lapine did, but the new *Into the Woods* was not simply a case of textual changes. The tone of the show was considerably altered; the revival was child-friendly, if you will, in a way that the original was decidedly not. The 1987 show seemed to be a case of "wouldn't it be intriguing to take all those characters from children's storybooks and weave them into a musical?" In 2002, this became "wouldn't it be *lovely* to take all those characters . . ." And it *was* lovely. Which did elicit grumbling in some quarters, from Sondheim fans who appreciated the darker original tone. For me, the first *Into the Woods* didn't work—despite the score—and the second did. These alterations and changes were made by the original authors themselves, on purpose; so I ask: What's wrong with that?

I know Lapine, casually; I produced a show of his in 1990 but haven't spoken to him in years. So I might be wrong in this, but I have a hunch. *Into the Woods* 1987 was the work of a savvy showbiz intellectual. (Mind you, there's nothing much wrong with being a savvy showbiz intellectual.) *Into the Woods* 2002 was the work of a savvy showbiz intellectual who had spent the intervening fifteen years raising a daughter. Was the new Narrator less of a curmudgeon and more of a teddy bear, someone you'd want to read cuddly bedtime stories? Was the new Red Ridinghood less of a caricature and more of a normal teenager, someone you'd want to be your daughter? Was the actor who doubled as the Wolf and Prince Charming less of a prig and more of a goof, the type who wouldn't hurt a flea (or a cow)? Did all this pay off at show's end, when the survivors— the Baker and Cinderella, Red Ridinghood and Jack—came together as a family, in a way that the actors playing the roles in 1987 couldn't have, and sang "No One Is Alone"?

Yes, yes, and double yes. If this new *Into the Woods* failed to excite the ticket-buying public, so be it. I was happy in these woods.

The Man Who Had All the Luck

Suppose for a moment that you are a young, unknown, and talented writer, complete with the Hopwood Award in Drama from your college. Two Hopwoods, let's say, at one thousand bucks apiece. (We needn't add that the prize was funded by the Estate of Avery Hopwood, author of such dramatic claptrap as *Ladies' Night*, *Why Men Leave Home*, and the imperishable *Getting Gertie's Garter*.)

Six years out of college, your first full-length play—three years in the writing—opens on Broadway. You are unaware at this point that you will one day write one of the great plays of the twentieth century; you are unaware that you will become one of the most produced American playwrights ever; you are unaware that you will be universally honored as one of the most important writers—of any variety—of the twentieth century.

"A play you both need and will want to see. . . . It is as American as an ice cream cone; and just as refreshing, emotionally and intellectually, as an ice cream cone on a hot day."

Nor can you guess that you will be a central figure in one of the fiercest political and ideological struggles of the century, or that your so-called private life will forever be entangled with an iconic celebrity of mythic proportions. No, all you know is that you have struggled for three years on your first play, and it has finally opened on Broadway. You're too nervous, no doubt, to eat your Thanksgiving dinner; the producer, without the slightest hint of irony, has chosen to open it on turkey day. First-time producer, first-time writer, first-time director. Hmmm.

Imagine your response the next day when you read the following:

"This is a play you both need and will want to see. This is not only a touching, realistic play, with some especially fine characterizations in it, but a play with a challenging new idea in it—something very rare in the theatre. It is as American as an ice cream cone; and just as refreshing, emotionally and intellectually, as an ice cream cone on a hot day. It is a challenge to all the defeatism and self-pity of 19th century European literature and drama, from the Romanticists to the Surrealists and from Chekhov to O'Neill. This is not a play to knock you out of your seat, roll you in the aisles, cause you to dance in the street or throw your hat in the air. It is a much finer drama than that. It is a unique event."

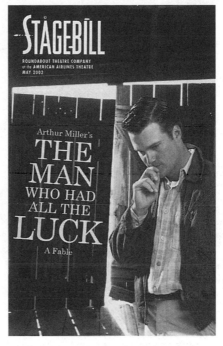

Exactly, you might exclaim. My, this critic– Burton Rascoe, of the *New York World-Telegram* —is very perceptive, isn't he?

But I'd rather doubt that Arthur Miller thought any such thing; he probably didn't even read Rascoe's notice. The *World-Telegram* was an afternoon paper; by the time it hit the street, *The Man Who Had All the Luck* was already deader than a poisoned mink, buried by the morning's pans. (More on minks later.) By twilight, a new play had already been booked to open two weeks later at the Forrest. The Eugene O'Neill, to us.

There were seven New York dailies at the time; the other six reviews were bad, real bad. Although the playwright was offered some encouragement.

Howard Barnes, in the *Herald Tribune*, said that "some subtle meaning must lurk in the sprawling stanzas of *The Man Who Had All the Luck*. It was certainly elusive. Somewhere in this mess of pottage Miller must have hidden a kernel of philosophical truth. If so, he has picked the wrong medium to reveal it. For *The Man Who Had All the Luck* is incredibly turbid in its writing and stuttering in its execution."

In the *Sun*, Ward Morehouse called it "ambling, strangely confused, and rather tiresome. This new play has some engaging moments and several likable characters wander through it, but it has more than its share of sermonizing. *The Man Who Had All the Luck* is philosophical, languid, and rambling. Perhaps Mr. Miller's luck will be better with his next one."

And here's this from John Chapman in the *Daily News*. "*The Man Who Had All the Luck* is about a fellow who tries a lot of things and they all

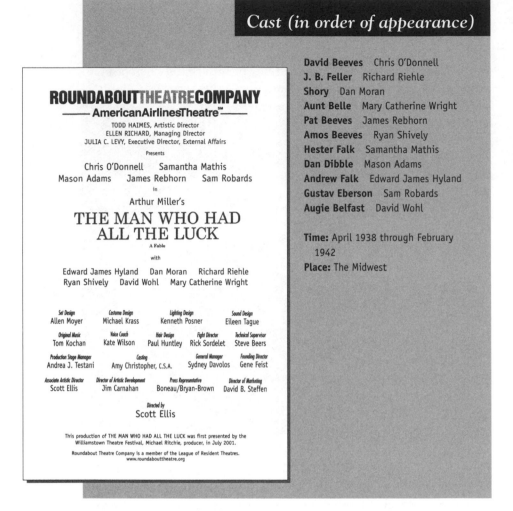

Cast (in order of appearance)

David Beeves   Chris O'Donnell
J. B. Feller   Richard Riehle
Shory   Dan Moran
Aunt Belle   Mary Catherine Wright
Pat Beeves   James Rebhorn
Amos Beeves   Ryan Shively
Hester Falk   Samantha Mathis
Dan Dibble   Mason Adams
Andrew Falk   Edward James Hyland
Gustav Eberson   Sam Robards
Augie Belfast   David Wohl

Time: April 1938 through February
   1942
Place: The Midwest

ROUNDABOUTTHEATRECOMPANY
AmericanAirlinesTheatre℠

TODD HAIMES, Artistic Director
ELLEN RICHARD, Managing Director
JULIA C. LEVY, Executive Director, External Affairs

Presents

Chris O'Donnell   Samantha Mathis
Mason Adams   James Rebhorn   Sam Robards

in

Arthur Miller's

THE MAN WHO HAD
ALL THE LUCK
A Fable

with

Edward James Hyland   Dan Moran   Richard Riehle
Ryan Shively   David Wohl   Mary Catherine Wright

Set Design	Costume Design	Lighting Design	Sound Design
Allen Moyer	Michael Krass	Kenneth Posner	Eileen Tague

Original Music	Voice Coach	Hair Design	Fight Director	Technical Supervisor
Tom Kochan	Kate Wilson	Paul Huntley	Rick Sordelet	Steve Beers

Production Stage Manager	Casting	General Manager	Founding Director
Andrea J. Testani	Amy Christopher, C.S.A.	Sydney Davolos	Gene Feist

Associate Artistic Director	Director of Artistic Development	Press Representative	Director of Marketing
Scott Ellis	Jim Carnahan	Boneau/Bryan-Brown	David B. Steffen

Directed by
Scott Ellis

This production of THE MAN WHO HAD ALL THE LUCK was first presented by the
Williamstown Theatre Festival, Michael Ritchie, producer, in July 2001.

Roundabout Theatre Company is a member of the League of Resident Theatres.
www.roundabouttheatre.org

click, but he keeps thinking that sooner or later something will flop because it stands to reason he's got to pay for it in the end. Arthur Miller, the newcomer who wrote the play, has done all his paying-up right off the bat. His first offering tries a lot of things—too many by far—and most of them flop. And now I hope Mr. Miller will go right back to work writing another piece, for he has a sense of theatre and a real if underdeveloped way of making stage characters talk and act human."

Miller did not go right back to work writing another play. He quit theatre altogether, turning to fiction instead. (*Focus*, Miller's only novel, tackled the subject of anti-Semitism. Published in 1945, it sold more than ninety thousand copies.) Within a few years he was lured back to the footlights, turning out the Critics Circle Award–winning *All My Sons* in

1947 and the Pulitzer-winning *Death of a Salesman* in 1949. So he did all right. But it wasn't just luck.

It is almost unheard of for outright Broadway flops to be given a second chance. Sure, it has happened. Leonard Bernstein's musical *Candide*, for example, played only seventy-three performances in 1956, but the composer never gave up on it; he kept revising it, and it went on to a celebrated and notably resilient life.

Eugene O'Neill's *The Iceman Cometh* was underappreciated in its 1946 premiere. (This was not helped by a Hickey who—as one of the critics reported—"in the course of his harrowing fifteen-minute speech, suffered an unfortunate lapse of memory. The audience shuddered as he stopped dead still and sought assistance from the prompter.") The play was rediscovered off-Broadway in 1956, with Jason Robards in the lead. It has enjoyed two major Broadway revivals, in 1985 (with Robards) and in 1999 (with Kevin Spacey).

O'Neill's *A Moon for the Misbegotten* closed during its pre-Broadway tryout in 1947. It finally made it to Broadway in 1957, failing once more. The third try—also with Jason Robards, in the company of Colleen Dewhurst and director José Quintero—finally established the play, which was again successfully revived in 2000 (with Cherry Jones).

And then there's Paul Osborn's *Morning's at Seven*, a forty-four-performance failure in 1939 but a Tony Award–winning hit in 1980 and winner of nine nominations in 2002 (as discussed a few pages back). I guess that the rescue of failed shows from oblivion is not as unheard of as I imagined. Still, these shows, in their initial Broadway runs, lasted at least five weeks. The original *Man Who Had All the Luck* closed after only a weekend; *Morning's at Seven* ran ten times as long.

But, then, *The Man Who Had All the Luck* was written by Arthur Miller, America's favorite living playwright. He has seen nine Broadway productions since 1991, seven of them revivals (including two *Prices* and two *Crucibles*). This is quite a turnaround for a playwright whose new work has been consistently unsuccessful on Broadway since 1968.

Miller has completed sixteen full-length plays. His five hits came within his first nine tries, with *The Man Who Had All the Luck* followed by *All My Sons*; *Death of a Salesman*; an adaptation of Ibsen's *An Enemy of the People* (1950); *The Crucible* (1953); *A View from the Bridge* (1956, from an earlier one-act); *After the Fall* (1964); *Incident at Vichy* (1964); and *The Price* (1968).

None of Miller's subsequent work has been successful. In America, anyway; England has been more hospitable to his later plays. These include *The Creation of the World and Other Business* (1972); *The Arch-*

bishop's Ceiling (1977), which closed during its pre-Broadway tryout; *The American Clock* (1980); *Broken Glass* (1994); and *The Ride Down Mt. Morgan* (presented on Broadway in 2000, although it was mounted in the West End in 1991). Two others, *The Last Yankee* (1993) and *Mr. Peter's Connections* (1998), fared poorly in off-Broadway mountings by non-profits.

Like his contemporary Tennessee Williams, Miller went from cele-brated genius to unappreciated also-ran, with each new play a reminder of fallen greatness. Unlike Williams, Miller has lived long enough to see his reputation restored and his work appreciated. Hence, a century-ending decade of all Miller, almost all the time.

It was inevitable that someone would eventually turn up Miller's long-forgotten *Man Who Had All the Luck*. (Similarly, Williams's early *Not about Nightingales* was plucked from the archives and mounted on Broad-way in 1999.) Scott Ellis, associate artistic director of the Roundabout Theatre, mounted a reading of the Miller play in 2000. This led to a full-scale production at the Williamstown Theatre Festival in 2001. Fine re-views, including a rave in the *New York Times*, were enough to get the Roundabout to bring *The Man Who Had All the Luck* back to Broadway. Whether it would have braved a commercial run is another question; a fifty-seven-year-old, eleven-character, four-performance flop without box office stars is a hard sell, even with Arthur Miller's name attached.

The play proved to be significantly more interesting than one would expect from its production history, although not surprisingly so given its authorship. *The Man Who Had All the Luck* tells of a man who—well, who has all the luck. The good kind, that is. David Beeves, an un-trained auto mechanic, is in love with Hester Falk. Old Man Falk, an exceedingly unpleasant type,

"[Arthur Miller's] first offering tries a lot of things . . . and most of them flop. . . . He has a sense of theatre and a real if underdeveloped way of making stage characters talk and act human."

refuses to allow the engagement. He storms offstage and is immediately struck dead by a Rich Old Man in a fancy car. The Rich Old Man leaves said fancy car, which is not working properly, with Beeves. A Foreign Stranger suddenly appears, picks up a wrench, and fixes the thing. This causes the Rich Old Man to stake Beeves to a grand new garage. The For-eign Stranger becomes his friend and employee; the girl becomes his wife (and he inherits Old Man Falk's property); and the state unexpectedly runs a major highway right alongside the garage, causing it to thrive be-yond expectation.

The Rich Old Man just loves Beeves—everybody just loves Beeves—and sets the boy up in mink; the old guy is a mink farmer, and the audi-

The Man Who Had All the Luck
Opened: May 1, 2002
Closed: June 30, 2002
70 performances (and 15 previews)
Profit/Loss: Nonprofit [loss]
The Man Who Had All the Luck ($65 top) was scaled to a
potential gross of $349,943 at the 740-seat American
Airlines Theatre. Weekly grosses averaged about $246,000,
steadily building from $177,000 in the comp-heavy
opening week to $298,000 at the close. Total gross for
the eleven-week run was $2,610,518. Attendance was
about 91 percent, with the box office grossing about 70
percent of dollar-capacity. (These figures are not
indicative, as the potential was calculated at the top
ticket price, but subscribers paid less.)

TONY AWARD NOMINATION
Best Performance by a Featured Actor: Sam Robards

Critical Scorecard

Rave 1
Favorable 5
Mixed 1
Unfavorable 1
Pan 2

ence gets a whole education on that fascinating subject. Everything works
out for Beeves, while everyone around him has the more ordinary type of
luck (i.e., bad). This gets the boy to thinking too much and feeling guilty.
Miller's protagonists tend to think too much and feel guilty about their
place in society, as demonstrated by the season's earlier visit from John
Proctor of *The Crucible*, this being a tendency these men appear to have
caught from their creator.

Miller's machinations remained fascinating through the first two acts
of *The Man Who Had All the Luck*, but events lurched uncomfortably
thereafter. Miller had written himself into a bit of a box, he needed to
make things happen, and some of the strings were tugged way too abruptly
for comfort. Beeves, who all along appeared to be unassuming and like-
ably modest, became a monster. Yes, this can happen to a fellow in real
life, but here it was—well, mighty abrupt. The Foreign-Stranger-turned-
loyal-friend tells us the doctor told him David is "losing his mind," and we
learn that the hero has stocked up on life insurance. You know what that
means.

Miller's well-drawn assortment of subsidiary characters also backfired.
They were an intriguing lot, certainly; each of them had his or her own
backstory, illustrating various shadings of bad luck. They all had plenty to
say, much of it extremely interesting. But all this information piled up,
clouding Miller's point. Yes, "a man is a jellyfish. The tide goes in and the
tide goes out. About what happens to him, a man has very little to say."
This we are told about seven times in six scenes, by a Saroyanesque character in a wheelchair. Some of these supporting characters have watched
their luck disappear, while others have subverted it by action. What is

clear is Beeves has got it all—all the luck—and he is, therefore, even more tortured than the rest.

In the end, Beeves once more enjoys great good luck and so averts ruin. This time, though, he has ensured his luck through conscious action; something to do with checking fish for silkworms before feeding them—the worms in the jellyfish—to the mink. Beeves continues to have all the luck; but it is okay because he has "earned" it. Or some of it. Meanwhile, Beeves's treatment of his wife and infant and friend has left a sour taste. We don't like the guy anymore, good luck or no, and I don't imagine that was Miller's plan.

One of the many subplots dealt with Beeves's brother Amos, a natural athlete with a blazing fastball. His anticipated major league career was subverted by his father, who overtrained the boy, ruined his "basebrains," killed his chances, and destroyed his life. Many of the critics in 1944 complained about the overabundance of plot; one of them, the previously cited John Chapman, suggested that "Mr. Miller would have been much happier today had he taken just one part of his plot—the part about the ballplayer—and made three acts of it. For here is something true and touching." I agree with Chapman. A lost opportunity, although Miller seemingly developed this tangent into Biff and his football in *Death of a Salesman*.

Like Tennessee Williams, Miller went from celebrated genius to unappreciated also-ran, with each new play a reminder of fallen greatness. Unlike Williams, Miller has lived long enough to see his reputation restored.

All told, *The Man Who Had All the Luck* was an incredibly interesting evening in the theatre. Interesting for its history, though not in itself. But incredibly interesting evenings in the theatre are not all that common, are they? Certainly not on Broadway in 2001–2002. So chalk it up as a success for the Roundabout and Williamstown.

Director Ellis did a good job taming the material and making sense of the dramatics. There was a fair amount of acting-at-the-top-of-your-voice-as-you-strut-around-the-stage, but hey—this was a fable. (The play was officially subtitled "A Fable," a designation absent in 1944.) Screen actor Chris O'Donnell did a respectable job in his Broadway debut. Respectable, yes, though he was understandably unable to make sense of Beeves's severe character development during the second intermission.

Ellis got several fine performances from his ensemble. Sam Robards was especially strong as Gus, the Foreign Stranger. Another Broadway newcomer (at forty), it is impossible to overlook the fact that he is the son of Lauren Bacall and the aforementioned Jason Robards. That is neither here nor there; he was very good, and that's that. (I didn't realize his lineage until reading the cast list after the play.) Mason Adams also gave a fine performance as Dibble, the Rich Old Man. Adams is a lovely actor, who had been on Broadway since the Thanksgiving before Miller got there with *Man Who Had All the Luck*. (The eighty-three-year-old veteran started in George Abbott's production of Saroyan's *Get Away Old Man*, which—with thirteen performances—was three times as successful as the Miller.) Of the others, David Wohl came off best as Augie Belfort, the baseball scout. This might have been Miller's doing; his was the briefest role, in the strongest scene, with the best writing.

It is instructive to note that *The Man Who Had All the Luck* was based on a real-life incident that the budding playwright was told by his mother-in-law at the time. (No, not Marilyn's mother.) She once knew a fellow out in the Midwest, a farmer in his late twenties who had nothing but good luck. He became paranoid that something bad would happen, and one day went and hung himself in the barn.

Miller chose not to send his hero to the noose. Not in 1944, anyway. But death was to be Miller's final leveler in *All My Sons*, *Death of a Salesman*, *The Crucible*, and *A View from the Bridge*.

The Pajama Game

I'm a time-study man," says the comedian in the opening number of the 1954 musical comedy *The Pajama Game*. "I can tell you per second exactly how many stitches go into a pair of pajamas."

The Pajama Game was adapted from a humorous novel called *7 ½ Cents* by Richard Bissell, and it's a good one. The character Hines plays a small part in Bissell's novel; he was expanded into a starring role by George Abbott, who directed and collaborated on the libretto with Bissell. Abbott was, indeed, a musical comedy time-study man.

It would be an exaggeration to call Abbott the man who invented the modern, comic musical comedy, but I'm going to do it anyway. George Abbott thought it up hisself, with a stopwatch in one hand and a laff-o-meter in the other. Any number of other Broadwayites deserve credit for one thing or another, but Abbott influenced much of what happened in the field from the late thirties to the midsixties.

An actor turned playwright turned director turned producer turned musical comedy librettist, Abbott made his Broadway debut in 1913 at the age of twenty-six. He had his first major hit as author-director with the 1926 melodrama *Broadway*, followed by *Chicago* (the play, not the musical) and *Coquette*. The thirties saw such comedy hits as *Twentieth Century*, *Three Men on a Horse*, *Boy Meets Girl*, *Brother Rat*, and *Room Service*.

Abbott entered the musical theatre in 1935, when he was a kid of forty-seven. (He directed his last new Broadway musical in 1976 and continued directing revivals until the night before his hundredth birthday in 1987.) His new career began when he was hired to stage the book sections of the Billy Rose extravaganza *Jumbo*, which featured a score by Rodgers and Hart; the experienced showman John Murray Anderson was general director of the overall production.

Abbott apparently got along well with Rodgers; both men were serious about their work and highly professional. Abbott was invited to collaborate with Rodgers and Hart on their next musical, *On Your Toes* (1936); soon Abbott was directing and producing Rodgers and Hart musicals, including *The Boys from Syracuse* (1938) and *Pal Joey* (1940). With Hart becoming incapacitated by alcohol and Rodgers concerned about his career, the latter decided to learn to produce, enlisting as silent partner on two Abbott musicals (with scores from other composers).

Abbott and Rodgers parted company in 1942 after seven shows, when Rodgers joined Hammerstein for the Theatre Guild's production of *Oklahoma!* In the forties, Abbott championed Broadway newcomers like Leonard Bernstein, Betty Comden, Adolph Green, and Jerome Robbins of *On the Town* (1944); Jule Styne of *High Button Shoes* (1947); and Frank Loesser of *Where's Charley?* (1948).

In 1954, Abbott directed *The Pajama Game*, which introduced songwriters Richard Adler and Jerry Ross; choreographer Bob Fosse; and producer Hal Prince, who had been casting director of Abbott's *Call Me Madam* (1950) and stage manager of Abbott's *Wonderful Town* (1953). Abbott also groomed Bob Merrill of *New Girl in Town* (1957); Jerry Bock and Sheldon Harnick of *Fiorello!* (1959), for which they all shared the Pulitzer Prize; Mary Rodgers of *Once upon a Mattress*

George Abbott invented the modern musical comedy, with a stopwatch in one hand and a laff-o-meter in the other.

(1959); Stephen Sondheim on his first show as a composer, *A Funny Thing Happened on the Way to the Forum* (1962); and John Kander and Fred Ebb on their first collaboration, *Flora, the Red Menace* (1965).

Abbott demonstrated a clear knack for discovering important new songwriters. He also developed an impressive array of choreographers, serving as the prime force for incorporating dance into musical comedy. Most critically, he introduced three all-important men to the book musical: George Balanchine (who did five Abbott shows), Jerry Robbins (who also did five), and Bob Fosse (who did three). Other Abbott choreographers included Gene Kelly, Herb Ross, Donald Saddler, Peter Gennaro, and Joe Layton. Mind you, musicals were only a sideline for Abbott; he kept writing and directing and producing comedies all along.

Abbott musicals, generally speaking, were fast and funny. The shows were almost always well assembled, even when they weren't good, and Abbott had his share of failures. (Does anyone remember *Beat the Band*, *Barefoot Boy with Cheek*, or *The Fig Leaves Are Falling*?) Abbott was, indeed, a time-study man, with his stopwatch and laff-o-meter.

The problem with this is that it can make the work become too for-

CITY CENTER
Judith E. Daykin, President & Executive Director

CITY CENTER
ENCORES!

ARTISTIC DIRECTOR — MUSICAL DIRECTOR — DIRECTOR-IN-RESIDENCE
Jack Viertel — Rob Fisher — Kathleen Marshall

THE PAJAMA GAME

BOOK BY — MUSIC AND LYRICS BY
George Abbott & Richard Bissell — Richard Adler & Jerry Ross
Based on the novel "7½ Cents" by Richard Bissell

STARRING
Brent Barrett   Karen Ziemba
Daniel Jenkins   Ken Page   Deidre Goodwin
AND
Mark Linn-Baker

ALSO STARRING
Gina Ferrall   Fred Burrell   Jennifer Cody
Katie Harvey   Edgar Godineaux   Herman Payne

Rebecca Baxter   Timothy Breese   Tony Capone   Caitlin Carter   Susan Derry
Joe Farrell   Anne Hawthorne   Joy Hermalyn   Ann Kittredge   Kirk McDonald
April Nixon   Marc Oka   Tina Ou   Jessica Perrizo   Josh Prince
Devin Richards   Rebecca Robbins   Angela Robinson   J.D. Webster   Patrick Wetzel

SCENIC CONSULTANT — COSTUME CONSULTANT — LIGHTING — SOUND
John Lee Beatty — David C. Woolard — Ken Billington — Scott Lehrer
CONCERT ADAPTATION — PRODUCTION STAGE MANAGER — ORIGINAL ORCHESTRATIONS — MUSICAL COORDINATOR
David Ives — Peter Hanson — Don Walker — Seymour Red Press
CASTING — CHOREOGRAPHER
Jay Binder — John Carrafa

The Coffee Club Orchestra
Rob Fisher, MUSICAL DIRECTOR

DIRECTED BY
John Rando

Major sponsorship for *City Center Encores!* is provided by a grant from
AOL Time Warner, Inc.
The development of *Encores!* is assisted by seed support from The New York Times Company Foundation
City Center 55th Street Theater Foundation, Inc. gratefully acknowledges the significant support it receives from the
New York City Department of Cultural Affairs
The Pajama Game is presented through special arrangement with and all authorized performance materials are supplied by
Music Theatre International, 421 West 54th Street, New York, NY 10019
Baldwin Piano, Official Piano of City Center

Hines Mark Linn-Baker
Prez Daniel Jenkins
Mae Katie Harvey
Brenda Angela Robinson
Poopsie Jennifer Cody
Hasler Ken Page
Gladys Deidre Goodwin
Charley J. D. Webster
Sid Sorokin Brent Barrett
First helper Kirk McDonald
Second helper Josh Prince
Mabel Gina Ferrall
Babe Williams Karen Ziemba
Virginia Rebecca Baxter
Max Joe Farrell
Anderson Timothy Breese
Pop Fred Burrell
Cutting room workers Edgar
   Godineaux, Herman Payne
Joe Tony Capone
Factory workers, union organizers,
   patrons in Hernando's Hideaway,
   etc. Rebecca Baxter, Timothy
   Breese, Tony Capone, Caitlin Carter,
   Susan Derry, Joe Farrell, Edgar
   Godineaux, Anne Hawthorne, Joy
   Hermalyn, Ann Kittredge, Kirk
   McDonald, April Nixon, Marc Oka,
   Tina Ou, Herman Payne, Jessica
   Perrizo, Josh Prince, Devin Richards,
   Rebecca Robbins, Angela Robinson,
   J. D. Webster, Patrick Wetzel

Place: Cedar Rapids, Iowa
Time: 1954

mulaic. Abbott knew what he was doing, and he knew what he wanted, and he knew what "worked" (as far as he was concerned). He called the shots, which was fine for newcomers but confining for artists who had their own creative ideas. If the list of Abbott's hits is impressive, none of Broadway's greatest all-time musicals are on it. He taught people how to write musicals, but they couldn't create with a free hand while Abbott was setting the rules.

The Pajama Game was Abbott's longest-running show (with 1,063 performances), and in some ways the most durable. A great musical? No. The score is joyously melodic, with a variety of friendly and funny songs; but they are well crafted, as opposed to inspired. The show is marvelously well put together, like clockwork, but it doesn't have the staying power of Rodgers's *Oklahoma!* or Loesser's *Guys and Dolls* or Robbins's *West Side Story* or Styne's *Gypsy* or Bock's *Fiddler on the Roof* or Kander's *Cabaret*.

Mind you, I'm a great fan of *The Pajama Game*. I've always considered it a B-grade musical comedy, but probably the best B-grade musical ever. It was highly successful in its day, hitting the record books as the ninth-longest-running Broadway musical. That was then; by the time it appeared at Encores!, alas, it was down to number fifty-six.

There was a Broadway revival in 1973, starring Barbara McNair, Hal Linden, and Cab Calloway; I was assistant general manager. Due to a back-stage crisis or two, we were suddenly left without a stage manager just after the opening. I had enough experience (almost) to bluff my way into the stage managing job for the last eight weeks of the run, so I got to know the show very well. The biggest challenge: How do you cue in the blackout drop when one of your stars is weaving drunkenly back and forth beneath the pipe? And what do you do when he steps down to the apron, out of reach, and starts singing "Minnie the Moocher"? Hi-de-hi-de-ho, indeed.

The revival was pretty poor; it was produced on a frayed shoestring, resulting in a cheap and ugly production. The cast was uninspired, and—other than Linden (as Sid), Mary Jo Catlett (as Mabel), and some of the dancers—not very good. Mr. Abbott was old and tired; hey, the guy was eighty-six! Even so, the material still worked, although the clockwork timing was a bit sluggish. The strongest element was Bob Fosse's choreography, re-created by his original *Pajama Game* assistant Zoya Leporska (who was otherwise a waitress at Serendipity). The ability to watch "Steam Heat" and the "Once a Year Day" ballet and the production number "Hernando's Hideaway" and the delectably corny softshoe accompanying "I'll Never Be Jealous Again," in more or less authentic form night after night, more than made up for the lapses.

> If the list of Abbott's hits is impressive, none of Broadway's greatest all-time musicals are on it. He taught people how to write musicals, but they couldn't create with a free hand while Abbott was setting the rules.

Before we move on, one other observation, which I related in my 1997 book *More Opening Nights on Broadway*, is worth repeating here: "One night during curtain calls the pass door opened, and Jerry Robbins—who had codirected the original with Abbott—steamed in, a-cursin' and a-mutterin'. He tore onstage, wreaking havoc among the cast, most of whom had never met him and understandably idolized him. (The few who *had* worked for J. R. no longer idolized him, but he seems to have had that effect on people.) The coast was pretty much clear by the time eighty-six-year-old Abbott came skipping through. Five minutes later, I crossed upstage in the course of my professional duties and also to find out What They Were Talking About. There, shielded from view by the factory unit, were the two legends of the American Musical Theatre: Jerry Robbins—the great man of *West Side Story* and *Fiddler on the Roof*—stood scowling like a naughty, baldpated four-year-old being scolded by his overpowering, overtowering teacher."

Given my experience with the revival, I walked into City Center knowing considerably more about *The Pajama Game* than the people who were given ten days to put the thing on. As with the prior Encores! offering, the book was cut past the point of clarity (although not so severely as *Golden Boy*). At one point, Sid ran on, pecked Babe on the cheek, and started to sing about how she made him feel like every day was a holiday. When did they fall in love? you might well have wondered. In act 1, scene 8, which was missing in action. (This act, at Encores!, was cut from ten scenes to six.) This was somewhat unfortunate, as Bissell—the novelist and colibrettist—had a marvelously folksy comic style. But for various reasons, concert presentations need severe trimming.

The Pajama Game at Encores! managed to demonstrate, quite handily, how immensely pleasurable the well-made musical comedy can be. This despite the somewhat old-fashioned material; despite lackadaisical handling of the comic material, compounded by odd casting choices; and despite a dance component that—due to reduced rehearsal time—was understandably less developed than the original. *The Pajama Game* was never intended to be an integrated dance show, not by a long shot; but the Encores! exercise demonstrated how much first-time choreographer Fosse punched up the proceedings with energy, humor, and—to use a highly technical term—pizzazz.

The Pajama Game
Opened: May 2, 2002
Closed: May 6, 2002
6 performances (and 0 previews)
Profit/Loss: Nonprofit
The Pajama Game ($80 top) played the 2,753-seat City
Center. Box office figures not available.

Critical
Scorecard

Rave 2
Favorable 7
Mixed 0
Unfavorable 0
Pan 0

What Encores! did have was Brent Barrett, belting the ballads across the footlights in a way that could make you forget all about John Raitt (who created the role). Barrett has never had a clear shot at Broadway stardom, although his vocal power is no secret; he did the same sort of rafter-ringing job for Encores! in their 2000 staging of *On a Clear Day You Can See Forever*. On that occasion, though, he was playing a subsidiary role (and making the nominal leading man look even weaker than he was). Here, Barrett was in full control. There was a time when a man with a clear, strong voice and no tricks could simply plant his feet onstage and stop a show. This is what Raitt and Alfred Drake and Dick Kiley and John Cullum could do, provided they were given halfway decent material to work with. This is what Barrett, on leave from playing the Drake role in the London production of *Kiss Me, Kate*, did in *The Pajama Game*. When he sang "Hey There," the evening's big ballad hit, you thought—now *that's* a love song.

Karen Ziemba, too, made a charming babe. ("Babe" was the character's name, I'm sorry to relate.) Her opening number, the exuberantly joyous waltz "I'm Not at All in Love," sent the show soaring even before Barrett got around to "Hey There." Her role kind of diminishes after intermission. I suppose this was Abbott's way of dealing with the weaknesses of Janis Paige (who originated the part) and the strengths of Carol Haney, the dancer who stole the show and wound up with three big numbers in the second act. Ziemba made a strong showing in her role, but it was odd watching one of Broadway's best dancers stand on the sidelines while someone else got the good material.

Which leads to the weaker aspects of the proceedings. *The Pajama Game*, even in 1954, was one-third old-fashioned musical comedy. And purposely so; the charm of the comedy was a mix of sly sophistication and corn. Bissell was a Dubuque-born, Harvard-educated former steamboat pilot with a wry way with words; the comedy, though, was considerably diluted at Encores! Hines, or Hinesie as he's called by his secretary, is an ex-vaudevillian; his old knife-throwing act is written into the plot. Where did these ex-vaudevillains go when they left the stage? Some of them landed in small-town America, charming their way into do-nothing jobs like time-study men at pajama factories.

Hines's material includes the aforementioned corny-old-softshoe duet (written to be performed with a character comedienne); a novelty number in which he's surrounded by pretty young chorines, who dance rings around him; and a "drunk" scene. (In the 1973 revival, the actor playing Hines would prepare for this the old-fashioned way, in his dressing room.) The role was originated by Eddie Foy Jr., who was indeed something out of vaudeville. His father was the comedian Eddie Foy; as his family grew, the act became Eddie Foy and the Seven Little Foys. (Hollywood transformed this into the 1955 film *The Seven Little Foys*, with Eddie Jr. narrating and Bob Hope playing Eddie Sr.)

> Throw Brent Barrett and Karen Ziemba together in a spotlight singing and modern-day musical comedy fans are bound to leave the theatre thinking they don't make 'em like that anymore.

Hines calls for a baggy-pants comedian, with a slab of ham in his pants pocket. Mark-Linn Baker, who played the role at Encores!, was simply a comic actor. Prez, the show's second banana, needs to be one of those short, dumpy middle-aged men who ludicrously picture themselves latter-day Don Juans. Daniel Jenkins, who played the role, is closer to a leading-man type; not so long ago he played the Tom Hanks role in *Big: The Musical*. The comedy in the Prez role comes from this sad sack hopelessly running after any woman he can find, humor that is of questionable workability nowadays. If Prez is young and not clearly a cartoon, he becomes unsympathetic and unfunny.

Gladys, the kewpie doll in tights that established Carol Haney on Broadway and sent understudy Shirley Maclaine off to Hollywood stardom, was likewise diminished. Deidre Goodwin did a decent job with "Steam Heat" but was not the lovable gamin the character needs to be. Gladys plays her comedy scenes with Hines and Prez, which might have been part of the trouble; the role is full of glances and glares and rolled-eye reactions to the funny business, which in this case wasn't funny. Goodwin was also for some reason removed from the cut-down "Once a Year Day" ballet, Gladys's main chance to shine in the first act.

With weak support from the featured players, Barrett and Ziemba were forced to carry the evening on their own shoulders. Highly capable shoulders they were, too, resulting in a delightful spring finale to the season. Give Barrett "Hey There" or Ziemba "I'm Not at All in Love" and place them in separate spotlights, and you've won half the battle. Then throw them together with the mock-hillbilly duet "There Once Was a Man," and modern-day musical comedy fans are bound to leave the theatre thinking they don't make 'em like that anymore. And ruing that unpleasant truth.

Curtain Calls

Honorable Mention

for noteworthy contributions to the season

There follows a highly personal list of people whose contributions, one way or another, made the season of theatregoing brighter.

Carnival
Brian Stokes Mitchell
Anne Hathaway
David Costabile
Kathleen Marshall (as director and
    choreographer)
Rob Fisher (musical director)

The Crucible
Liam Neeson
Tom Aldredge

Dance of Death
Ian McKellen
Santo Loquasto (scenic designer)
Natasha Katz (lighting designer)

Elaine Stritch at Liberty
Elaine Stritch (as actor and author)
John Lahr (author)
George C. Wolfe (director)
Jules Fisher and Peggy Eisenhauer
    (lighting designers)
Jonathan Tunick (orchestrator)
Rob Bowman (musical director)

The Elephant Man
Billy Crudup
Kate Burton

Fortune's Fool
Alan Bates
Frank Langella
Jane Greenwood (costume designer)

45 Seconds from Broadway
Lewis J. Stadlen
Marian Seldes
Bill Moor

The Goat, or Who Is Sylvia?
Bill Pullman
Mercedes Ruehl
Edward Albee (author)
David Esbjornson (director)
John Arnone (scenic designer)

Golden Boy
Alfonso Ribeiro
Anastasia Barzee
Norm Lewis
Rob Fisher (musical director)

Hedda Gabler
Kate Burton
Nicholas Martin (director)

Into the Woods
John McMartin
Laura Benanti
Gregg Edelman
Chad Kimball
James Lapine (director)
John Carrafa (choreographer)
Douglas W. Schmidt (scenic designer)

Major Barbara
Dana Ivey
Denis O'Hare
John Lee Beatty (scenic designer)

Mamma Mia!
Judy Kaye
Karen Mason

The Man Who Had All the Luck
Sam Robards
Mason Adams

Mandy Patinkin in Concert
Mandy Patinkin

Metamorphoses
Doug Hara
Mary Zimmerman (as author and
    director)
Daniel Ostling (scenic designer)

Morning's at Seven
Elizabeth Franz
William Biff McGuire
John Lee Beatty (scenic designer)

Barbara Cook: Mostly Sondheim
Barbara Cook
Wally Harper (music director)

Noises Off
Katie Finneran

Oklahoma!
Shuler Hensley

The Pajama Game
Brent Barrett
Karen Ziemba

Private Lives
Alan Rickman
Lindsay Duncan
Howard Davies (director)
Tim Hatley (scenic designer)

QED
Alan Alda

The Seagull
Meryl Streep
Mike Nichols (director)

Sexaholix . . . a love story
John Leguizamo (as actor and author)

Smell of the Kill
Christopher Ashley (director)
David Gallo (scenic designer)

Sweet Smell of Success
John Lithgow
Brian d'Arcy James
Natasha Katz (lighting designer)

Thoroughly Modern Millie
Sutton Foster
Harriet Harris
Marc Kudisch
Anne L. Nathan
Ken Leung
Paul Huntley (hair designer)

Thou Shalt Not
Norbert Leo Butz
Thomas Lynch (scenic designer)
William Ivey Long (costume
    designer)
Peter Kaczorowski (lighting designer)

Topdog/Underdog
Jeffrey Wright
Mos Def
Suzan-Lori Parks (author)
George C. Wolfe (director)
Riccardo Hernández (scenic designer)
Scott Zielinski (lighting designer)

Urinetown
John Cullum
Jeff McCarthy
Hunter Foster
Spencer Kayden
Greg Kotis (as librettist and lyricist)
Mark Hollmann (as composer and
    lyricist)
John Rando (director)
John Carrafa (choreographer)
Bruce Coughlin (orchestrator)
Edward Strauss (musical director)

The Women
Cynthia Nixon
Kristen Johnston
Mary Louise Wilson

Tony Wrap-Up
(and Other Awards)

TONY AWARDS

The 2001–2002 season's Tony Award nominations are listed below, with asterisks denoting the winners. Overlooked people who—for various reasons—might have been expected to receive nominations are also mentioned.

Best Play

Fortune's Fool (Author: Ivan Turgenev, adapted by Mike Poulton)
*The Goat, or Who Is Sylvia?** (Author: Edward Albee)
Metamorphoses (Author: Mary Zimmerman)
Topdog/Underdog (Author: Suzan-Lori Parks)

Overlooked

45 Seconds from Broadway (Author: Neil Simon)
The Graduate (Author: Terry Johnson)
QED (Author: Peter Parnell)

The Goat was clearly the best play of the season—except that a sizable portion of the audience simply didn't like it. *Topdog* arrived on Broadway with the Pulitzer and a clutch of enthusiastic reviews, but it seemed oddly out of the running. *Metamorphoses*, too, had the reviews—and it was the one play among the group that did substantial business (and by season's end recouped its investment). But the writing couldn't compare with Albee.

Best Musical

Mamma Mia!
Sweet Smell of Success
*Thoroughly Modern Millie**
Urinetown

Overlooked

Thou Shalt Not

Urinetown was clearly the best musical of the season—except that a sizable portion of the audience simply didn't like it. Wait, we already said that! This was the first case in Tony Award history of a show winning Best Score, Best Book, and Best Director—but losing as Best Musical. *Thoroughly Modern Millie* went into battle with a numerical edge; fifty-odd Tony voters were producers of the show. Even so, *Millie* couldn't have won without the support of hundreds of other voters.

Best Revival of a Play

The Crucible
Morning's at Seven
Noises Off
*Private Lives**

Overlooked

Dance of Death
The Elephant Man
Hedda Gabler
The Man Who Had All the Luck
The Women

In this strange season, it was the revivals that pretty much received the best reviews. *Noises Off* was lavishly praised in the fall, and *Morning's at Seven* was extravagantly praised in the spring. *Private Lives*, which came along the final week of the season, was favored by critics and audiences alike.

Best Revival of a Musical

*Into the Woods**
Oklahoma!

Overlooked

One Mo' Time

The highly anticipated *Oklahoma!* was one of the season's most severe disappointments. The mildly anticipated *Into the Woods* was not universally loved; but, then, neither was the original *Into the Woods*. The revival of *Woods* worked for many people, whereas few were enthused by *Oklahoma!*

Best Book of a Musical

John Guare, *Sweet Smell of Success*
Catherine Johnson, *Mamma Mia!*
Greg Kotis, *Urinetown**
Richard Morris and Dick Scanlan, *Thoroughly Modern Millie*

Overlooked

John Lahr and Elaine Stritch, *Elaine Stritch at Liberty*
David Thompson, *Thou Shalt Not*

Urinetown deservedly won in this category. The other book of award-winning caliber—John Lahr and Elaine Stritch's expertly assembled script for the latter's one-woman show—was deemed ineligible for consideration.

Best Original Score (Music and Lyrics) Written for the Theatre

Harry Connick Jr. (Music and Lyrics), *Thou Shalt Not*
Marvin Hamlisch (Music), Craig Carnelia (Lyrics), *Sweet Smell of Success*
Mark Hollman (Music and Lyrics), Greg Kotis (Lyrics), *Urinetown**
Jeanine Tesori (Music), Dick Scanlan (Lyrics), *Thoroughly Modern Millie*

Overlooked

Andrew Lloyd Webber (Music), Alan Ayckbourn (Lyrics), *By Jeeves*

Urinetown had one of Broadway's freshest scores in years; even voters who didn't like the show recognized this. *Millie*'s score was admittedly weak; *Thou Shalt Not* and *Sweet Smell* were musically ambitious but unworkable.

Best Performance by a Leading Actor in a Play

Alan Bates, *Fortune's Fool**
Billy Crudup, *The Elephant Man*
Liam Neeson, *The Crucible*
Alan Rickman, *Private Lives*
Jeffrey Wright, *Topdog/Underdog*

Overlooked

Alan Alda, *QED*
Kevin Bacon, *An Almost Holy Picture*
Jason Biggs, *The Graduate*
Mos Def, *Topdog/Underdog*
Peter Gallagher, *Noises Off*
Rupert Graves, *The Elephant Man*
Ian McKellen, *Dance of Death*

Chris O'Donnell, *The Man Who Had All the Luck*
Bill Pullman, *The Goat, or Who Is Sylvia?*
Tom Selleck, *A Thousand Clowns*
Lewis J. Stadlen, *45 Seconds from Broadway*
David Warner, *Major Barbara*

In an overcrowded field, the finest performance—in my opinion—was overlooked by the nominators. Still, I'll remember Bill Pullman's work as long as the other nominees. Alan Bates and Alan Rickman were a toss-up, with the equally deserving Jeffrey Wright an underdog.

Best Performance by a Leading Actress in a Play

Kate Burton, *Hedda Gabler*
Lindsay Duncan, *Private Lives**
Laura Linney, *The Crucible*
Helen Mirren, *Dance of Death*
Mercedes Ruehl, *The Goat, or Who Is Sylvia?*

Overlooked

Dana Ivey, *Major Barbara*
Kristen Johnston, *The Women*
Cherry Jones, *Major Barbara*
Patti LuPone, *Noises Off*
Samantha Mathis, *The Man Who Had All the Luck*
Cynthia Nixon, *The Women*
Marian Seldes, *45 Seconds from Broadway*
Alicia Silverstone, *The Graduate*
Jennifer Tilly, *The Women*
Kathleen Turner, *The Graduate*

Kate Burton and Mercedes Ruehl gave startlingly good performances, although both had some critical detractors. Lindsay Duncan was delectable with no detractors, which made her the favorite.

Best Performance by a Leading Actor in a Musical

Gavin Creel, *Thoroughly Modern Millie*
John Cullum, *Urinetown*
John Lithgow, *Sweet Smell of Success**
John McMartin, *Into the Woods*
Patrick Wilson, *Oklahoma!*

Overlooked

Craig Bierko, *Thou Shalt Not*
Hunter Foster, *Urinetown*

Jeff McCarthy, *Urinetown*
John Scherer, *By Jeeves*

Musical comedy veterans John Cullum and John McMartin gave canny performances in what were arguably featured roles. John Lithgow was the only nominee with a true star-sized role. He did a highly professional job despite being stranded in an unworkable flop, and was thus honored by the voters.

Best Performance by a Leading Actress in a Musical

Sutton Foster, *Thoroughly Modern Millie**
Nancy Opel, *Urinetown*
Louise Pitre, *Mamma Mia!*
Jennifer Laura Thompson, *Urinetown*
Vanessa Williams, *Into the Woods*

Overlooked

Josefina Gabrielle, *Oklahoma!*
Kate Levering, *Thou Shalt Not*
Elaine Stritch, *Elaine Stritch at Liberty*

The one knockout performance of the year, that of Elaine Stritch, was deemed ineligible for consideration (with the show moved into the Special Theatrical Event category). Only two of the nominees were in star-sized roles. Few voters took *Mamma Mia* seriously, leaving the award to the hardworking Sutton Foster.

Best Performance by a Featured Actor in a Play

Frank Langella, *Fortune's Fool**
William Biff McGuire, *Morning's at Seven*
Brian Murray, *The Crucible*
Sam Robards, *The Man Who Had All the Luck*
Stephen Tobolowsky, *Morning's at Seven*

Overlooked

Mason Adams, *The Man Who Had All the Luck*
Adam Godley, *Private Lives*
T. R. Knight, *Noises Off*
Denis O'Hare, *Major Barbara*

Frank Langella was unstoppable for his scenery-munching, comic tour de force.

Best Performance by a Featured Actress in a Play

Kate Burton, *The Elephant Man*
Katie Finneran, *Noises Off**
Elizabeth Franz, *Morning's at Seven*
Estelle Parsons, *Morning's at Seven*
Frances Sternhagen, *Morning's at Seven*

Overlooked

Emma Fielding, *Private Lives*
Piper Laurie, *Morning's at Seven*
Faith Prince, *Noises Off*
Rue McClanahan, *The Women*
Mary Louise Wilson, *The Women*

In a field crowded with veteran performers, relative newcomer Katie
Finneran's refreshing comic turn stood out.

Best Performance by a Featured Actor in a Musical

Norbert Leo Butz, *Thou Shalt Not*
Brian d'Arcy James, *Sweet Smell of Success*
Gregg Edelman, *Into the Woods*
Shuler Hensley, *Oklahoma!**
Marc Kudisch, *Thoroughly Modern Millie*

Overlooked

Stephen DeRosa, *Into the Woods*
Jack Noseworthy, *Sweet Smell of Success*

Shuler Hensley's Olivier Award–winning performance proved to be the
only element of *Oklahoma!* that transferred well. Especially worthy
performances were also given by Brian d'Arcy James and Norbert Leo
Butz; one suspects that a sizable number of voters did not see the
performance of Butz, as few out-of-towners visited New York during the
fall of 2001.

Best Performance by a Featured Actress in a Musical

Laura Benanti, *Into the Woods*
Harriet Harris, *Thoroughly Modern Millie**
Spencer Kayden, *Urinetown*
Judy Kaye, *Mamma Mia!*
Andrea Martin, *Oklahoma!*

Overlooked

Jessica Boevers, *Oklahoma!*
Karen Mason, *Mamma Mia!*
Debra Monk, *Thou Shalt Not*
Kelli O'Hara, *Sweet Smell of Success*
Kerry O'Malley, *Into the Woods*

Spencer Kayden gave one of the more remarkable performances I've seen in a long time, but Harriet Harris—who was indeed very good—managed to ride the *Millie* juggernaut. For that matter, Laura Benanti and Judy Kaye were equally worthy of the honor.

Best Direction of a Play

Howard Davies, *Private Lives*
Richard Eyre, *The Crucible*
Daniel Sullivan, *Morning's at Seven*
Mary Zimmerman, *Metamorphoses**

Overlooked

Scott Elliott, *The Women*
Scott Ellis, *The Man Who Had All the Luck*
David Esbjornson, *The Goat, or Who Is Sylvia?*
Terry Johnson, *The Graduate*
Nicholas Martin, *Hedda Gabler*
Sean Mathias, *Dance of Death*
Sean Mathias, *The Elephant Man*
Arthur Penn, *Fortune's Fool*
Jeremy Sams, *Noises Off*
Daniel Sullivan, *Major Barbara*
George C. Wolfe, *Topdog/Underdog*
Jerry Zaks, *45 Seconds from Broadway*

The competition here was between Howard Davies, for his stunning take on *Private Lives*, and Mary Zimmerman, whose *Metamorphoses* was unlike anything Broadway had ever seen. Some especially fine work—including that of George C. Wolfe and David Esbjornson—was overlooked in a crowded field.

Best Direction of a Musical

James Lapine, *Into the Woods*
Michael Mayer, *Thoroughly Modern Millie*
Trevor Nunn, *Oklahoma!*
John Rando, *Urinetown**

Overlooked

Nicholas Hytner, *Sweet Smell of Success*
Phyllida Lloyd, *Mamma Mia!*
Susan Stroman, *Thou Shalt Not*
George C. Wolfe, *Elaine Stritch at Liberty*

John Rando managed to withstand the *Millie* steamroller, winning for his skillful shepherding of *Urinetown*. Again, one of the most impressive directing jobs of the season—George Wolfe's work with Elaine Stritch—was deemed ineligible for consideration.

Best Choreography

Rob Ashford, *Thoroughly Modern Millie**
John Carrafa, *Into the Woods*
John Carrafa, *Urinetown*
Susan Stroman, *Oklahoma!*

Overlooked

Susan Stroman, *Thou Shalt Not*
Christopher Wheeldon, *Sweet Smell of Success*

Susan Stroman, who seems to win these things every year, was the favorite despite *Oklahoma!*'s lackluster reception. John Carrafa did what might have been the season's most creative work on *Urinetown*, but he presumably split votes with his second nomination. Rob Ashford managed to take the award for his energetic but not especially inspired work on *Millie*.

Best Scenic Design

John Lee Beatty, *Morning's at Seven*
Tim Hatley, *Private Lives**
Daniel Ostling, *Metamorphoses*
Douglas W. Schmidt, *Into the Woods*

Overlooked

Bob Crowley, *Sweet Smell of Success*
Rob Howell, *The Graduate*
Santo Loquasto, *Dance of Death*
Anthony Ward, *Oklahoma!*

Tim Hatley's overpowering tower of hotel terraces managed to snare the award from Douglas W. Schmidt's storybook world of *Into the Woods*.

Best Costume Design

Jenny Beaven, *Private Lives*
Jane Greenwood, *Morning's at Seven*
Susan Hilferty, *Into the Woods*
Martin Pakledinaz, *Thoroughly Modern Millie**

Overlooked

Jane Greenwood, *Major Barbara*
William Ivey Long, *Thou Shalt Not*
Isaac Mizrahi, *The Women*
Anthony Ward, *Oklahoma!*

Susan Hilferty's impressive work on *Into the Woods* was overlooked in favor of the somewhat unattractive garb of *Thoroughly Modern Millie*.

Best Lighting Design

Paul Gallo, *The Crucible*
David Hersey, *Oklahoma!*
Natasha Katz, *Sweet Smell of Success*
Brian MacDevitt, *Into the Woods**

Overlooked

Jules Fisher and Peggy Eisenhauer, *Elaine Stritch at Liberty*
Natasha Katz, *Dance of Death*

Brian MacDevitt, who designed 17 percent of the Broadway offerings of the season (the others being A *Thousand Clowns*, *Major Barbara*, *Urinetown*, *The Women*, and *Morning's at Seven*), managed to take the prize against three equally worthy, better-known Tony nominees.

Best Orchestrations

Benny Andersson, Björn Ulvaeus, and Martin Koch, *Mamma Mia!*
Doug Besterman and Ralph Burns, *Thoroughly Modern Millie**
William David Brohn, *Sweet Smell of Success*
Bruce Coughlin, *Urinetown*

Overlooked

Harry Connick Jr., *Thou Shalt Not*
Jonathan Tunick, *Elaine Stritch at Liberty*

As has become the habit since the institution of this award in 1997, the Best Musical winner picked up the orchestration prize as well. Bruce Coughlin's work on *Urinetown* was highly inventive (especially since he was working with a band of five), while Jonathan Tunick's charts—which sustained the high-pressure excitement of *Elaine Stritch at Liberty*—were deemed ineligible.

Special Theatrical Event

Elaine Stritch at Liberty*
Bea Arthur on Broadway: Just between Friends
Barbara Cook: Mostly Sondheim
Sexaholix . . . a love story

No contest here. Elaine Stritch nabbed the first Tony Award of her fifty-six-year Broadway career.

SPECIAL TONY AWARDS

Robert Whitehead, producer
Julie Harris, actress

Regional Theatre

Williamstown Theatre Festival

PULITZER PRIZE FOR DRAMA

Rebecca Gilman, *The Glory of Living*
Dael Orlandersmith, *Yellowman*
Suzan-Lori Parks, *Topdog/Underdog**

NEW YORK DRAMA CRITICS CIRCLE AWARDS

Best Play

The Goat, or Who Is Sylvia? (Author: Edward Albee) (Tony Award winner)

Best Musical

[No award was given]

Best Revival

[No award was given]

Special Citation

Elaine Stritch at Liberty (Tony Award winner)

DRAMA DESK AWARDS

Outstanding Play

The Goat (Author: Edward Albee) (Tony Award winner) tied with *Metamorphoses* (Author: Mary Zimmerman)

Outstanding Musical

Thoroughly Modern Millie (Tony Award winner)

Outstanding Revival of a Play

Private Lives (Tony Award winner)

Outstanding Revival of a Musical

Into the Woods (Tony Award winner)

Outstanding Actor in a Play

Alan Bates, *Fortune's Fool* (Tony Award winner)

Outstanding Actress in a Play

Lindsay Duncan, *Private Lives* (Tony Award winner)

Outstanding Actor in a Musical

John Lithgow, *Sweet Smell of Success* (Tony Award winner)

Outstanding Actress in a Musical

Sutton Foster, *Thoroughly Modern Millie* (Tony Award winner)

Outstanding Featured Actor in a Play

Frank Langella, *Fortune's Fool* (Tony Award winner)

Outstanding Featured Actress in a Play

Katie Finneran, *Noises Off* (Tony Award winner)

Outstanding Featured Actor in a Musical

Shuler Hensley, *Oklahoma!* (Tony Award winner)

Outstanding Featured Actress in a Musical

Harriet Harris, *Thoroughly Modern Millie* (Tony Award winner)

Outstanding Director of a Play

Mary Zimmerman, *Metamorphoses* (Tony Award winner)

Outstanding Director of a Musical

Michael Mayer, *Thoroughly Modern Millie*

Outstanding Choreography

Susan Stroman, *Oklahoma!*

Outstanding Book of a Musical

John Lahr, Elaine Stritch, *Elaine Stritch at Liberty*

Outstanding Music

Jason Robert Brown, *The Last Five Years* (off-Broadway)

Outstanding Lyrics

Jason Robert Brown, *The Last Five Years* (off-Broadway)

Outstanding Orchestrations

Doug Besterman, Ralph Burns, *Thoroughly Modern Millie* (Tony Award winner)

Outstanding Music in a Play

Willy Schwarz, *Metamorphoses*

Outstanding Set Design of a Play

Tim Hatley, *Private Lives* (Tony Award winner)

Outstanding Set Design of a Musical

Douglas W. Schmidt, *Into the Woods*

Outstanding Costume Design

Isaac Mizrahi, *The Women*

Outstanding Lighting Design

T. J. Gerckens, *Metamorphoses*

Outstanding Sound Design

Dan Moses Schreier, *Into the Woods*

Outstanding Solo Performance

Elaine Stritch, *Elaine Stritch at Liberty*

Special Awards

Paul Huntley, hair and wig designer, for Lifetime Achievement
Billy Rosenfield, record producer, for his contributions to the preservation of
    musical theatre recordings
The Mint Theatre Company for presenting and preserving little-known classics
The Worth Street Theater Company for its Stage Door Canteen shows for
    workers at Ground Zero

Holdovers

As the 2001–2002 season began on May 28, 2001, the following shows were playing on Broadway.

Aida   Musical. Opened March 23, 2000, at the Palace. Music by Elton John; lyrics by Tim Rice; book by Linda Woolverton and Robert Falls & David Henry Hwang; directed by Robert Falls; choreographed by Wayne Cilento. 2000 Tony Awards: Score; Leading Actress (Heather Headley); Scenic Design (Bob Crowley); Lighting Design (Natasha Katz). Still playing May 27, 2002. To date: 905 performances (and 27 previews). Profit/loss: to be determined.

Annie Get Your Gun   Musical revival. Opened March 4, 1999, at the Marquis. Music and lyrics by Irving Berlin; book by Herbert and Dorothy Fields (revised by Peter Stone); directed and choreographed by Graciela Daniele. 1999 Tony Awards: Revival; Leading Actress (Bernadette Peters). Closed September 1, 2001, after 1,046 performances (and 35 previews). Total gross for the run was $82,148,713. Attendance was about 82 percent, with the box office grossing about 77 percent of dollar-capacity. Profit/loss: profit.

Beauty and the Beast   Musical. Opened April 18, 1994, at the Palace; closed September 5, 1999. Reopened November 12, 1999, at the Lunt-Fontanne. Music by Alan Menken; lyrics by Howard Ashman and Tim Rice; book by Linda Woolverton; directed by Robert Jess Roth; choreographed by Matt West. 1994 Tony Award: Costume Design (Ann Hould-Ward). Still playing May 27, 2002. To date: 3,301 performances (and 46 previews), ninth-longest-running musical in Broadway history. Profit/loss: profit.

Bells Are Ringing   Musical revival. Music by Jule Styne; book and lyrics by Betty Comden and Adolph Green; directed by Tina Landau; choreographed by Jeff Calhoun. Opened April 12, 2001, at the Plymouth. Closed June 10,

2001, after 68 performances (and 36 previews). Total gross for the run was $3,527,176. Attendance was about 67 percent, with the box office grossing about 44 percent of dollar-capacity. Profit/loss: loss.

Blast   Musical revue. Directed by James Mason; choreographed by Jim Moore, George Pinney, and John Vanderkolff. 2001 Tony Award: Special Theatrical Event. Opened April 17, 2001, at the Broadway. Closed September 23, 2001, after 180 performances (and 13 previews). Total gross for the run was $8,169,127. Attendance was about 62 percent, with the box office grossing about 38 percent of dollar-capacity.

Cabaret   Musical revival. Opened March 19, 1998, at the Kit Kat Klub (Henry Miller's Theatre); transferred November 14, 1998, to Studio 54. Music by John Kander; lyrics by Fred Ebb; book by Joe Masteroff; directed by Sam Mendes and Rob Marshall; choreographed by Rob Marshall. 1998 Tony Awards: Musical Revival; Leading Actress (Natasha Richardson); Leading Actor (Alan Cumming); Featured Actor (Ron Rifkin). Still playing May 27, 2002. To date: 1,702 performances (and 37 previews). Profit/loss: profit.

Chicago   Musical revival. Opened November 14, 1996, at the Richard Rodgers; transferred February 12, 1997, to the Shubert. Music by John Kander; lyrics by Fred Ebb; book by Fred Ebb and Bob Fosse (adaptation by David Thompson); directed by Walter Bobbie; choreographed by Ann Reinking in the style of Bob Fosse. 1997 Tony Awards: Musical Revival; Director; Choreographer; Leading Actress (Bebe Neuwirth); Leading Actor (James Naughton); Lighting Design (Ken Billington). Still playing May 27, 2002. To date: 2,306 performances (and 22 previews), sixteenth-longest-running musical in Broadway history. Profit/loss: profit.

A Class Act   Musical. Music and lyrics by Edward Kleban; book by Linda Kline and Lonny Price; directed by Lonny Price; choreographed by Marguerite Derricks. Opened March 11, 2001, at the Ambassador. Closed June 10, 2001, after 105 performances (and 30 previews). Total gross for the run was $2,558,362. Attendance was about 46 percent, with the box office grossing about 27 percent of dollar-capacity. Profit/loss: loss.

Contact   Musical. "Written" by John Weidman; directed and choreographed by Susan Stroman. Opened March 30, 2000, at the Vivian Beaumont. 2000 Tony Awards: Best Musical; Choreographer; Featured Actor (Boyd Gaines); Featured Actress (Karen Ziemba). Closed August 31, 2002, after 1,010 performances (and 31 previews). Total gross for the run was $60,218,526. Attendance was about 84 percent, with the box office grossing about 71 percent of dollar-capacity. Profit/loss: nonprofit [profit].

The Dinner Party   Play. By Neil Simon; directed by John Rando. Opened October 19, 2000, at the Music Box. Closed September 1, 2002, after 364 performances (and 20 previews). Total gross for the run was $13,974,313. Attendance was about 74 percent, with the box office grossing about 68 percent of dollar-capacity. Profit/loss: profit.

Follies   Musical revival. Music and lyrics by Stephen Sondheim; book by James Goldman; directed by Matthew Warchus; choreographed by Kathleen Marshall. Opened April 5, 2001, at the Belasco. Closed July 14, 2001, after 117 performances (and 31 previews). Total gross for the run was $7,080,718. Attendance was about 88 percent, with the box office grossing about 77 percent of dollar-capacity. Profit/loss: nonprofit [loss].

42nd Street   Musical revival. Music by Harry Warren; lyrics by Al Dubin; book by Michael Stewart and Mark Bramble; directed by Mark Bramble; choreographed by Randy Skinner. 2001 Tony Awards: Musical Revival; Leading Actress (Christine Ebersole). Opened May 2, 2001, at the Ford Center. Still playing May 27, 2002. To date: 442 performances (and 31 previews). Profit/loss: to be determined.

Fosse   Musical revue. Opened January 14, 1999, at the Broadhurst. Conceived by Richard Maltby Jr., Chet Walker, and Ann Reinking; choreography by Bob Fosse; directed by Richard Maltby Jr.; choreography re-created by Chet Walker; codirected and cochoreographed by Ann Reinking. 1999 Tony Awards: Musical; Orchestration (Ralph Burns and Doug Besterman); Lighting Design (Andrew Bridge). Closed August 25, 2001, after 1,093 performances (and 21 previews). Total gross for the run was $68,997,054. Attendance was about 88 percent, with the box office grossing about 78 percent of dollar-capacity. Profit/loss: profit.

The Full Monty   Musical. Music and lyrics by David Yazbek; book by Terrence McNally; directed by Jack O'Brien; choreographed by Jerry Mitchell. Opened October 26, 2000, at the Eugene O'Neill. Closed September 1, 2002, after 771 performances (and 35 previews). Total gross for the run was $47,862,021. Attendance was about 84 percent, with the box office grossing about 75 percent of dollar-capacity. Profit/loss: profit.

George Gershwin Alone   Play with music. By Hershey Felder; music and lyrics by George and Ira Gershwin; directed by Joel Zwick. Opened April 30, 2001, at the Helen Hayes. Closed July 22, 2001, after 96 performances (and 16 previews). Total gross for the run was $1,055,351. Attendance was about 41 percent, with the box office grossing about 23 percent of dollar-capacity. Profit/loss: loss.

The Invention of Love   Play. By Tom Stoppard; directed by Jack O'Brien. Opened March 29, 2001, at the Lyceum. 2001 Tony Awards: Actor (Richard Easton); Featured Actor (Robert Sean Leonard). Drama Critics Circle Award for Best Play. Closed June 30, 2001, after 108 performances (and 31 previews). Total gross for the run was $3,918,862. Attendance was about 83 percent, with the box office grossing about 56 percent of dollar-capacity. Profit/loss: nonprofit [profit].

Jane Eyre   Musical. Music by Paul Gordon; lyrics by Paul Gordon and John Caird; book by John Caird; directed by John Caird and Scott Schwartz. Opened December 10, 2000, at the Brooks Atkinson. Closed June 10, 2001, after 209 performances (and 36 previews). Total gross for the run was $8,038,185. Attendance was about 68 percent, with the box office grossing about 45 percent of dollar-capacity. Profit/loss: loss.

King Hedley II   Play. By August Wilson; directed by Marion McClinton. 2001 Tony Award: Featured Actress (Viola Davis). Opened May 1, 2001, at the Virginia. Closed July 1, 2001, after 72 performances (and 24 previews). Total gross for the run was $2,479,599. Attendance was about 57 percent, with the box office grossing about 39 percent of dollar-capacity. Profit/loss: loss.

Kiss Me, Kate   Musical revival. Opened November 18, 1999, at the Martin Beck. Music and lyrics by Cole Porter; book by Sam and Bella Spewack; directed by Michael Blakemore; choreographed by Kathleen Marshall. 2000 Tony Awards: Revival; Leading Actor (Brian Stokes Mitchell); Director (Michael Blakemore); Costume Design (Martin Pakledinaz); Orchestrations (Don Sebesky). Closed December 30, 2001, after 883 performances (and 28 previews). Total gross for the run was $65,051,743. Attendance was about 81 percent, with the box office grossing about 74 percent of dollar-capacity. Profit/loss: profit.

The Lion King   Musical. Opened November 13, 1997, at the New Amsterdam. Music by Elton John and others; lyrics by Tim Rice and others; book by Roger Allers and Irene Mecchia; directed by Julie Taymor; choreographed by Garth Fagan. 1998 Tony Awards: Musical; Director; Choreographer; Scenic Design (Richard Hudson); Costume Design (Taymor); and Lighting Design (Donald Holder). Drama Critics Circle Award for Best Musical. Still playing May 27, 2002. To date: 1,926 performances (and 33 previews), twentieth-longest running musical in Broadway history. Profit/loss: profit.

Les Misérables   Musical. Opened March 12, 1987, at the Broadway; moved October 16, 1990, to the Imperial. By Alain Boublil and Claude-Michel Schönberg; music by Claude-Michel Schönberg; lyrics by Herbert Kretzmer; adapted and directed by Trevor Nunn and John Caird. 1987 Tony Awards: Musical; Score; Book; Featured Actor (Michael Maguire); Featured Actress (Frances Ruffelle). Still playing May 27, 2002. To date: 6,276 performances, second-longest-running musical in Broadway history. Profit/loss: profit. (At press time, a May 18, 2003, closing had been announced, after 6,684 performances.)

One Flew over the Cuckoo's Nest Play revival. By Dale Wasserman; directed by Terry Kinney. 2001 Tony Award: Revival. Opened April 8, 2001, at the Royale. Closed July 29, 2001, after 121 performances (and 24 previews). Total gross for the run was $6,477,718. Attendance was about 81 percent, with the box office grossing about 69 percent of dollar-capacity. Profit/loss: loss.

The Phantom of the Opera Musical. Opened January 26, 1988, at the Majestic. Music by Andrew Lloyd Webber; lyrics by Charles Hart; book and additional lyrics by Richard Stilgoe; directed by Harold Prince; choreographed by Gillian Lynne. 1988 Tony Awards: Musical; Director; Scenic Design (Maria Bjornson); Lighting Design (Andrew Bridge); Leading Actor (Michael Crawford); and Featured Actress (Judy Kaye). Still playing May 27, 2002. To date: 5,979 performances (and 16 previews), fourth-longest-running musical in Broadway history. Profit/loss: profit.

The Producers Musical. Music and Lyrics by Mel Brooks; book by Mel Brooks and Thomas Meehan; directed and choreographed by Susan Stroman. Opened April 19, 2001, at the St. James. 2001 Tony Awards: Musical; Score; Book; Leading Actor (Nathan Lane); Featured Actor (Gary Beach); Featured Actress (Cady Huffman); Director; Choreographer; Scenic Design (Robin Wagner); Costume Design (William Ivey Long); Lighting Design (Peter Kaczorowski); Orchestrations (Doug Besterman). Drama Critics Circle Award for Best Musical. Still playing May 27, 2002. To date: 456 performances (and 33 previews). Profit/loss: profit.

Proof Play. By David Auburn; directed by Daniel Sullivan. Opened October 24, 2000, at the Walter Kerr. 2001 Tony Awards: Play; Director; Actress (Mary-Louise Parker). Pulitzer Prize for Drama. Drama Critics Circle Award for Best American Play. Closed January 5, 2003, after 917 performances (and 16 previews). Total gross for the run was $32,896,994. Attendance was about 74 percent, with the box office grossing about 66 percent of dollar-capacity. Profit/loss: profit.

Rent Musical. Opened April 29, 1996, at the Nederlander. Book, music, and lyrics by Jonathan Larson; directed by Michael Greif; choreographed by Marlies Yearby. 1996 Tony Awards: Musical; Score; Book; Featured Actor (Wilson Jermaine Heredia). Drama Critics Circle Award for Best Musical. Pulitzer Prize for Drama. Still playing May 27, 2002. To date: 2,534 performances (and 16 previews), thirteenth-longest-running musical in Broadway history. Profit/loss: profit.

Riverdance   Musical revue. Opened March 16, 2000, at the Gershwin. Music and lyrics by Bill Whelan; directed by John McColgan. Closed August 26, 2001, after 605 performances (and 13 previews). Total gross for the run was $45,553,810. Attendance was about 75 percent, with the box office grossing about 60 percent of dollar-capacity. Profit/loss: loss.

The Rocky Horror Show   Musical revival. Book, music, and lyrics by Richard O'Brien; directed by Christopher Ashley; choreographed by Jerry Mitchell. Opened November 15, 2000, at the Circle in the Square. Closed January 6, 2002, after 437 performances (and 25 previews). The show went on hiatus from September 23, 2001, through October 30, 2001. Total gross for the run was $13,268,048. Attendance was about 83 percent, with the box office grossing about 54 percent of dollar-capacity. Profit/loss: loss.

Stones in His Pockets   Play by Marie Jones; directed by Ian McElhinney. Opened April 1, 2001, at the Golden. Closed September 23, 2001, after 198 performances (and 11 previews). Total gross for the run was $5,141,100. Attendance was about 69 percent, with the box office grossing about 55 percent of dollar-capacity. Profit/loss: profit.

The Tale of the Allergist's Wife   Play. By Charles Busch; directed by Lynne Meadow. Opened November 2, 2000, at the Ethel Barrymore. Closed September 15, 2002, after 777 performances (and 25 previews). Total gross for the run was $29,310,727. Attendance was about 73 percent, with the box office grossing about 59 percent of dollar-capacity. Profit/loss: profit.

Shows That Never Reached Town

Every season, numerous productions are announced for Broadway that for any number of reasons never arrive. Many of these are typically more wishful than realistic; others succumb to financial woes or tryout blues. The following shows were announced to arrive on Broadway during the 2001–2002 season. Some, though not all, are still possibilities.

Assassins   Broadway premiere of the 1991 off-Broadway musical. Music and lyrics by Stephen Sondheim; book by John Weidman; directed by Joe Mantello; choreographed by John Carrafa. With Douglas Sills. A November 29, 2001, opening at the Booth was voluntarily withdrawn by the authors on September 13. At press time, the show remained on Roundabout's future schedule.

The Boys from Syracuse   Revival of the 1938 musical. Music by Richard Rodgers; lyrics by Lorenz Hart; book by George Abbott; book revision by Nicky Silver; directed by Scott Ellis. A March 7, 2002, opening at the American Airlines Theatre was postponed, with the show finally opening on August 18, 2002.

The Car Man   "An auto-erotic thriller" in dance, adapted from the opera *Carmen*. Music by Georges Bizet; directed and choreographed by Matthew Bourne; produced by Adventures in Motion Pictures. This follow-up to Bourne's award-winning *Swan Lake* opened at the Ordway in Minneapolis in August 2001, which was followed with engagements at the Ahmanson in Los Angeles and the University of California, Berkeley. Following the events of September 11, pre-Broadway bookings in Chicago, Toronto, and Boston were canceled, forcing the show to close November 5, 2001.

Dance of the Vampires   Import of Roman Polanski's 1997 musical that premiered in Vienna, adapted from his 1967 film *The Fearless Vampire Killers*.

Music by Jim Steinman; book and lyrics by Michael Kunze; adaptation by David Ives; directed by John Caird and Jim Steinman; choreographed by Daniel Ezralow. With Michael Crawford. An April 11, 2002, opening at the Minskoff was canceled in October 2001, after which the directors and choreographer were replaced by the *Urinetown* team of John Rando and John Carrafa. The musical opened December 9, 2002, at the Minskoff.

Frankie and Johnny in the Clair de Lune   Revival of the 1987 off-Broadway play. By Terrence McNally; directed by Joe Mantello; produced by The Araca Group. With Edie Falco and Stanley Tucci. An April 2002 opening was conditionally announced in November 2001, pending the availability of the stars. In December, this was pushed off to the summer. The revival opened on August 8, 2002, at the Belasco.

I'm Not Rappaport   Revival of the 1985 comedy. By Herb Gardner; directed by Daniel Sullivan; produced by Elliot Martin and Lewis M. Allen. With Judd Hirsch and Ben Vereen. The show originated at the Coconut Grove Playhouse in the fall of 2001, followed by successful engagements at Ford's Theatre in Washington, D.C., and at the Paper Mill Playhouse in Millburn, New Jersey. An April 25, 2002, opening at the Booth was postponed when coproducer Elizabeth I. McCann left the project. The revival opened on July 25, 2002.

Little Women   Musical, based on the novel by Louisa May Alcott. Music by Jason Howland; lyrics by Mindi Dickstein; book by Allan Knee; directed by Nick Corley; choreographed by Jennifer Paulson Lee. With Rita Gardner, Kerry O'Malley, and Mary Gordon Murray. The show played a February 2001 workshop at Duke University. Plans to begin previews October 31, 2001, at the Ambassador were canceled, due in part to the replacement of original songwriters by Kim Oler and Alison Hubbard. In October 2001 it was announced that Susan L. Schulman joined the project as director.

Mack & Mabel   Revival of the 1974 musical, based on the November 2000 concert version at Reprise! (the Los Angeles equivalent of Encores!). Music and lyrics by Jerry Herman; book by Michael Stewart, revised by Francine Pascal; directed by Arthur Allan Seidelman; choreographed by Dan Siretta; silent film staging by Bill Irwin. With Douglas Sills, Jane Krakowski, and Donna McKechnie. An April 23, 2001, opening was postponed due to unavailability of a theatre, with the date rescheduled to November 2001 and, later, to January 10, 2002.

The Night They Raided Minsky's   Musical comedy based on the legendary burlesque producer. Music by Charles Strouse; lyrics by Susan Birkenhead; book by Evan Hunter. Plans for a fall 2000 Broadway opening (following a July tryout at the Ahmanson Theatre in Los Angeles) were canceled, due in part to the death of director Mike Ockrent and the withdrawal of choreographer Susan Stroman. A developmental reading of the musical was held in May 2001, under the direction of Jerry Zaks.

Paper Doll   Play, about the novelist Jacqueline Susann and her husband, Irving Mansfield. Written by Mark Hampton and Barbara J. Zitwer; directed by Leonard Foglia; produced by Randall Wreghitt and Mars Theatricals. With Marlo Thomas and F. Murray Abraham. Played a November 2001 tryout at the Pittsburgh Public Theater and a February 2002 tryout in Durham, North Carolina. An announced April 30 opening at the Cort was canceled in late February. In May, it was reported that it would open in October 2002 at the Cort, with Fran Drescher replacing Ms. Thomas. In October 2002, a March 2003 production at the Long Wharf Theatre in New Haven was announced, to star Andrea Martin and Abraham.

Six Dance Lessons in Six Weeks   Play. By Richard Alfieri; directed by Arthur Allan Seidelman. With Uta Hagen and David Hyde Pierce. Played a tryout at the Geffen Playhouse in June 2001. An April 28, 2002, opening at the Booth was announced in December but was postponed to allow Ms. Hagen to re-cover from a stroke. In August 2002, a spring 2003 booking at the Coconut Grove Playhouse in Miami—with Rue McClanahan replacing Ms. Hagen—was announced.

Tallulah   One-woman play about Tallulah Bankhead. By Sandra Ryan Hey-ward; directed by Michael Lessac; produced by SFX Theatrical Group and James M. Nederlander. With Kathleen Turner. A pre-Broadway tour began in Minneapolis on October 3, 2000, prior to an announced April 2001 Broadway opening. In December, the Broadway engagement was postponed until fall 2002 due to unavailability of a theatre. The tour closed March 18, 2001, in Stamford, Connecticut. In May 2001, it was announced that *Tallulah* would not reopen.

The Visit   A musical, based on the play by Friedrich Dürrenmatt. Music by John Kander; lyrics by Fred Ebb; book by Terrence McNally; directed by Frank Galati; choreographed by Ann Reinking. With Angela Lansbury and Philip Bosco. Plans for a March 15, 2001, opening at the Broadway were changed to a mid-April opening, and then canceled after Lansbury withdrew. A tryout at the Goodman Theatre in Chicago, starring Chita Rivera and John McMartin, opened October 1, 2001. Reaction was mixed, and a New York engagement was pushed off until sometime in 2003.

Long-Run Leaders

The following shows, separated into plays and musicals, have run more than 1,000 performances on Broadway. The productions are listed in order of their all-time ranking. Because yesterday's record-breaking run might pale in comparison to a moderate hit of today, an additional column indicates productions that were at one time among the top ten, showing the highest level achieved.

The assumption that shows are running longer today than ever before holds true—but only for musicals. The nine longest-running musicals have opened within the last thirty years, with at least one other likely to work its way into the top ten. Two currently running musicals—the revival of *Chicago* and *The Lion King*—moved into the all-time top twenty, joining *Les Misérables*, *The Phantom of the Opera*, *Beauty and the Beast*, and *Rent* in that category. Three—*Fosse*, the revival of *Annie Get Your Gun*, and *Contact*—broke the thousand-performance plateau.

Long runs appear to be a thing of the past for nonmusicals, however. All but three of the twenty-six plays to exceed 1,000 performances opened prior to 1980. The last to make the list, *Brighton Beach Memoirs*, opened in 1983 and climbed only to fourteenth place. At season's close, the longest-running current play was *Proof*, which hit 917—number thirty-three on the all-time list—before closing on January 5, 2003.

Performance totals are current through May 26, 2002. Shows marked with an asterisk were still running at press time.

Musicals				
All-time Ranking	Title	Opening Date	Number of Performances	Highest Ranking
I	Cats	October 7, 1982	7,485	I
2*	Les Misérables	March 12, 1987	6,276*	2*
3	A Chorus Line	July 25, 1975	6,137	I
4*	The Phantom of the Opera	January 26, 1988	5,979*	4*
5	Oh! Calcutta! (revival)	September 24, 1976	5,852	2
6	Miss Saigon	April 11, 1991	4,097	6
7	42nd Street	August 25, 1980	3,486	3
8	Grease	February 14, 1972	3,388	I
9*	Beauty and the Beast	April 18, 1994	3,301*	9*
10	Fiddler on the Roof	September 22, 1964	3,242	I
11	Hello, Dolly!	January 15, 1964	2,844	I
12	My Fair Lady	March 15, 1956	2,717	I
13*	Rent	April 29, 1996	2,534*	
14	Annie	April 21, 1977	2,377	7
15	Man of La Mancha	November 22, 1965	2,328	4
16*	Chicago (revival)	November 14, 1996	2,306*	
17	Oklahoma!	March 31, 1943	2,212	I
18	Smokey Joe's Café	March 2, 1995	2,036	
19	Pippin	October 23, 1972	1,944	7
20*	The Lion King	November 13, 1997	1,926*	
21	South Pacific	April 7, 1949	1,925	2
22	The Magic Show	May 28, 1974	1,920	9
23	Dancin'	March 27, 1978	1,774	
24	La Cage Aux Folles	August 21, 1983	1,761	
25	Hair	April 29, 1968	1,750	7
26*	Cabaret (revival)	March 19, 1998	1,702*	
27	The Wiz	January 5, 1975	1,672	
28	Crazy for You	February 19, 1992	1,622	
29	Ain't Misbehavin'	May 8, 1978	1,604	
30	The Best Little Whorehouse in Texas	April 17, 1978	1,584	
31	Evita	September 25, 1979	1,567	
32	Jekyll & Hyde	April 28, 1997	1,543	
33	Dreamgirls	December 20, 1981	1,521	
34	Mame	May 24, 1966	1,508	7
35	Grease! (revival)	May 11, 1994	1,503	
36	The Sound of Music	November 16, 1959	1,443	4

All-time Ranking	Title	Opening Date	Number of Performances	Highest Ranking
37	Me and My Girl	August 10, 1986	1,420	
38	How to Succeed in Business without Really Trying	October 14, 1961	1,417	5
39	Hellzapoppin'	November 22, 1938	1,404	1
40	The Music Man	December 19, 1957	1,375	5
41	Funny Girl	March 26, 1964	1,348	9
42	Promises, Promises	December 1, 1968	1,281	
43	The King and I	March 29, 1951	1,246	4
44	1776	March 16, 1969	1,217	
45	Sugar Babies	October 8, 1979	1,208	
46	Guys and Dolls	November 24, 1950	1,200	4
47	Cabaret	November 20, 1966	1,165	
48	Annie Get Your Gun	May 16, 1946	1,147	3
49	Guys and Dolls (revival)	April 14, 1992	1,143	
50	Bring in 'Da Noise, Bring in 'Da Funk	April 25, 1996	1,130	
51	Pins and Needles	November 27, 1937	1,108	1
52	Fosse	January 14, 1999	1,093	
53	They're Playing Our Song	February 11, 1979	1,082	
54	Kiss Me, Kate	December 30, 1948	1,070	5
55	Don't Bother Me, I Can't Cope	April 19, 1972	1,065	
56	The Pajama Game	May 13, 1954	1,063	9
57	Shenandoah	January 7, 1975	1,050	
58	Annie Get Your Gun (revival)	March 4, 1999	1,046	
59	Damn Yankees	May 5, 1955	1,019	10
60	Grand Hotel	November 12, 1989	1,018	
61	Contact	March 30, 2000	1,010	
62	Big River	April 25, 1985	1,005	

	Plays			
All-time Ranking	**Title**	**Opening Date**	**Number of Performances**	**Highest Ranking**
1	Life with Father	November 8, 1939	3,224	1
2	Tobacco Road	December 4, 1933	3,182	1
3	Abie's Irish Rose	May 23, 1922	2,327	1
4	Deathtrap	February 26, 1978	1,792	4
5	Gemini	May 21, 1977	1,788	4
6	Harvey	November 1, 1944	1,775	4
7	Born Yesterday	February 4, 1946	1,642	5
8	Mary, Mary	March 8, 1961	1,572	6
9	The Voice of the Turtle	December 8, 1943	1,557	4
10	Barefoot in the Park	October 23, 1963	1,530	8
11	Same Time, Next Year	March 13, 1975	1,453	10
12	Arsenic and Old Lace	January 10, 1941	1,444	4
13	Mummenschanz	March 30, 1977	1,326	
14	Brighton Beach Memoirs	March 27, 1983	1,299	
15	Angel Street	December 5, 1941	1,295	5
15	Lightnin'	August 26, 1918	1,291	1
16	Cactus Flower	December 8, 1965	1,234	
17	Sleuth	November 12, 1970	1,222	
18	Torch Song Trilogy	June 10, 1982	1,222	
19	Equus	October 24, 1974	1,209	
20	Amadeus	December 17, 1980	1,181	
21	Mister Roberts	February 18, 1948	1,157	10
22	The Seven Year Itch	November 20, 1952	1,141	
23	Butterflies Are Free	October 21, 1969	1,128	
24	Plaza Suite	February 14, 1968	1,097	
25	Teahouse of the August Moon	October 15, 1953	1,027	
26	Never Too Late	November 27, 1962	1,007	

The Season's Toll

The following people, who worked on Broadway or made an important contribution to the legitimate theatre, died between May 28, 2001, and May 26, 2002.

Josephine R. Abady, 52; died May 25, 2002, of breast cancer, in Manhattan. Director, who served as artistic director of the Berkshire Theatre Festival, the Cleveland Play House, and Circle in the Square. Broadway directing credits included the 1989 revival of *Born Yesterday* and the 1996 Circle in the Square revivals of *Bus Stop* and *The Rose Tattoo*.

Martin Aronstein, 65; died May 3, 2002, of heart failure, in Van Nuys, California. Lighting designer of almost one hundred Broadway shows, including *Tiny Alice*; *Cactus Flower*; *Promises! Promises!*; *Play It Again, Sam*; *The Gingerbread Lady*; the 1972 revival of *Much Ado about Nothing*; *The Ritz*; and the original *Noises Off*.

Steve Barton, 47; committed suicide July 21, 2001, in Germany. Singing actor whose credits included Raoul in the original London and New York companies of Andrew Lloyd Webber's *The Phantom of the Opera*; Jule Styne's *The Red Shoes*; and the Goodspeed tryout of Jones and Schmidt's *Mirette*. He also starred in the Vienna premiere of *Dance of the Vampires*.

Milton Berle, 93; died March 27, 2002, in Los Angeles. Comedian who became America's first TV superstar. He moved from amateur shows and silent films to vaudeville, radio, and talking pictures. Broadway credits included the 1920 revival of *Florodora*; *Earl Carroll's Vanities of 1932*; *Saluta*; *See My Lawyer*; *Ziegfeld Follies of 1943*; and Herb Gardner's *The Goodbye People*. He also coproduced the musical *Seventeen*.

Heywood Hale Broun, 83; died September 5, 2001, in Kingston, New York. Sportswriter and actor, whose Broadway credits included *The Bird Cage*; *Point of No Return*; *Send Me No Flowers*; *Take Her, She's Mine*; and *Little Murders*.

Ralph Burns, 79; died November 21, 2001, of complications from a stroke and pneumonia, in Los Angeles. Veteran orchestrator, whose Broadway credits included *No Strings*; *Funny Girl*; *Sweet Charity*; *Pippin*; the 1971 revival of *No, No, Nanette*; *Chicago*; *Dancin'*; *Fosse*; and *Thoroughly Modern Millie*. Films included *Cabaret*; *All That Jazz*; and *New York, New York*.

Casper Citron, 82; died January 1, 2002. Theatrical reporter and critic who covered the theatre on radio for more than forty years.

Imogene Coca, 92; died June 2, 2001, in Westport, Connecticut. Slapstick comedienne best known for her role opposite Sid Caesar on the TV series *Your Show of Shows*. Broadway credits included *The Garrick Gaieties of 1930*; *Shoot the Works*; *New Faces of 1934*; *The Straw Hat Revue*; *The Girls in 509*; and *On the Twentieth Century*.

David J. Cogan, 78; died February 7, 2002, of lung cancer, in Bedford, New York. Theatre owner and producer. Owner of the Biltmore from 1960 through 1984, as well as the Eugene O'Neill from 1965 to 1967. He coproduced Lorraine Hansberry's play *A Raisin in the Sun*.

Joe Darion, 90; died June 16, 2001, in Lebanon, New Hampshire. Lyricist best known for *Man of La Mancha* (and the song "The Impossible Dream"). Other credits included the musicals *Shinbone Alley* and *Illya Darling*.

Harry Davies, 94; died July 1, 2001, at the Actors' Fund Nursing Home in Englewood, New Jersey. Veteran Broadway press agent whose clients ranged from Florenz Ziegfeld to Neil Simon.

Martin Esslin, 83; died February 24, 2002, in London. Hungarian-born British drama critic who defined and coined the term "Theatre of the Absurd" in his 1961 book *The Theater of the Absurd*.

Gloria Foster, 64; died September 29, 2001, of diabetes, in Manhattan. Actress whose credits included *In White America*; *A Hand Is on the Gate*; *Yerma*; and *Having Our Say*.

Arlene Francis, 93; died May 31, 2001, in San Francisco. Actress and television personality whose Broadway credits included the original production of *The*

Women; Orson Welles's production of *Danton's Death*; *The Doughgirls*; the 1966 revival of *Too True to Be Good*; and *Don't Look Back*. Best known for her twenty-five years on the TV game show *What's My Line?*

Kathleen Freeman, 78; died August 23, 2001, of lung cancer, in Manhattan. Character comedienne who appeared on Broadway in Feydeau's *13 Rue de l'Amour* and *The Full Monty*. Screen credits included *Singin' in the Rain* and numerous films with Jerry Lewis (including *The Nutty Professor*).

Truman Gaige, 95; died April 17, 2002, at the Actors' Fund Nursing Home in Englewood, New Jersey. Singer, who began his career in the 1931 revival of *Blossom Time* and whose credits included *Kismet*; *Kean*; *Hadrian VII*; and *Gigi*.

Leonard Gershe, 79; died on March 9, 2002, of a stroke, in Beverly Hills. Hollywood screenwriter who wrote the Broadway comedy hit *Butterflies Are Free* and the libretto for the musical comedy *Destry Rides Again*.

Ruth Goetz, 93; died October 12, 2001, in Englewood, New Jersey. Author (with her husband, Augustus Goetz) of *The Heiress*, adapted from Henry James's *Washington Square*; and *The Immoralist*, adapted from André Gide. Film credits included *The Heiress*; *Carrie*; and *Stage Struck*.

Rachel Gurney, 81; died in November 24, 2001, in Holt, Norfolk, England. British actress best known for her role of Lady Marjorie Bellamy on the TV series *Upstairs, Downstairs*. She appeared on Broadway in the 1980 production of Shaw's *Major Barbara*; *The Dresser*; and *Breaking the Code*.

Jack Gwillim, 91; died July 2, 2001, in Los Angeles. British-born actor whose Broadway work included the musical *Ari* (based on *Exodus*); the 1973 revival of *The Constant Wife* (starring Ingrid Bergman); and the 1981 revival of *My Fair Lady* (playing Colonel Pickering opposite Rex Harrison).

Albert Hague, 81; died November 12, 2001, of cancer, in Marina del Rey, California. German-born composer whose credits included *Plain and Fancy*; *Redhead*; *Cafe Crown*; *The Fig Leaves Are Falling*; and *Miss Moffat*. He also wrote the score for the television musical *How the Grinch Stole Christmas* (with lyrics by Dr. Seuss) and appeared as an actor in the film and TV series *Fame*.

Carrie Hamilton, 38; died January 20, 2002, of cancer, in Los Angeles. Her play *Hollywood Arms*, written in collaboration with her mother, Carol Burnett, opened at the Cort on October 31, 2002. Acting credits included the role of Maureen in the first national company of *Rent*.

Sir Nigel Hawthorne, 72; died December 26, 2001, of cancer, in Baldock, Hertfordshire, England. Actor best known for his role of Sir Humphrey Appleby in the TV series *Yes, Minister*. Appeared on Broadway in the 1974 all-male production of *As You Like It* and *Shadowlands*, for which he won a Tony Award in 1991. He won the Olivier in 1992 for *The Madness of King George III* (which he also toured in America), as well as receiving an Oscar nomination for the film version.

Eileen Heckart, 82; died December 31, 2001, of cancer, in Norwalk, Connecticut. Award-winning character actress whose credits included *Picnic*; *The Bad Seed*; *The Dark at the Top of the Stairs*; *You Know I Can't Hear You When the Water's Running*; and *Butterflies Are Free*. Film credits included *Bus Stop*; *Somebody Up There Likes Me*; and *Butterflies Are Free*, for which she won an Oscar. She also won three Emmys and a lifetime achievement Tony Award.

John Herbert, 75; died June 22, 2001. Author of the controversial off-Broadway prison drama *Fortune and Men's Eyes*, which opened in 1967 and was revived successfully in 1969.

Christopher Hewett, 80; died August 3, 2001, in Los Angeles. Character comedian whose credits included *My Fair Lady* (as Zoltan Karpathy); *The Unsinkable Molly Brown*; *Hadrian VII*; and *Music Is*. Directing credits include *No Sex Please, We're British* and the 1963 off-Broadway revival of *The Boys from Syracuse*. He is perhaps best known for his role of Roger De Bris in the motion picture *The Producers*.

Peggy Hewett, 56; died March 1, 2002, of leukemia, in Southampton, New York. Actress whose credits included *Jimmy*; *A Day in Hollywood/A Night in the Ukraine*; and the off-Broadway musical *Olympus on My Mind*.

Tommy Hollis, 47; died September 13, 2001, of a heart attack, in Manhattan. Actor whose credits included *The Colored Museum*; *The Piano Lesson*; *Seven Guitars*; *Ragtime*; and *The Adventures of Tom Sawyer*.

Norris Houghton, 92; died October 9, 2001, in Manhattan. Producer, designer, and writer, best known as cofounder of the Phoenix Theatre. Credits included *The Golden Apple*; *Once upon a Mattress*; Arthur Kopit's *Oh Dad, Poor Dad, Mama's Hung You in the Closet and I'm Feeling So Sad*; *The Trial of the Catonsville Nine*; and Christopher Durang's *Beyond Therapy*.

Donald W. Johnston, 57; died January 7, 2002, of cancer. Orchestrator, dance arranger, and conductor whose credits included *42nd Street* (both the original production and the 2001 revival); the 1991 revival of *Oh, Kay!*; and the Broadway transfers of the RSC productions of *The Life and Adventures of Nicholas Nickleby*; *Cyrano de Bergerac*; and *Much Ado about Nothing*.

Clark Jones, 81; died on March 28, 2002, in Key West, Florida. Longtime television director whose long career began in the earliest days of the medium. Theatre-related credits included the *Ford Motor Company 50th Anniversary Show*, which featured Ethel Merman and Mary Martin in a legendary medley duet; the original 1955 telecast of Mary Martin in *Peter Pan*; and the first nineteen Tony Awards telecasts.

Ken Kesey, 66; died November 10, 2001, of liver cancer, in Eugene, Oregon. Counterculture personality best known for his novel *One Flew over the Cuckoo's Nest*, the stage adaptation of which was produced on Broadway in 1963 and revived in 2001.

Hildegard Knef, 76; died February 1, 2002, of a lung infection, in Berlin. German actress who played the Garbo role in Cole Porter's *Silk Stockings*, the 1955 musicalization of the film *Ninotchka*.

Jack Kruschen, 80; died April 2, 2002. Film and television character actor who appeared on Broadway in the musical *I Can Get It for You Wholesale*.

Peggy Lee, 81; died January 21, 2002, in Bel Air, California. Legendary singer-songwriter who appeared on Broadway in the dire 1983 one-woman "musical autobiography" *Peg*, for which she also wrote the book and additional lyrics.

Jack Lemmon, 76; died June 27, 2001, of cancer, in Los Angeles. Comic actor whose screen work included *Mister Roberts* (for which he won an Oscar); *Some Like It Hot*; *The Apartment*; *Days of Wine and Roses*; *The Odd Couple*; and *Save the Tiger* (another Oscar). Broadway credits included the 1953 revival of *Room Service*; *Face of a Hero*; *Tribute*; and the 1986 revival of *Long Day's Journey into Night*.

Rosetta LeNoire, 90; died March 17, 2002, in Teaneck, New Jersey. Actress whose Broadway credits included *The Hot Mikado*; *Anna Lucasta*; *Destry Rides Again*; *I Had a Ball*; *God's Favorite*; and revivals of *Lost in the Stars*; *A Streetcar Named Desire*; *The Royal Family*; and *You Can't Take It with You*. Founder of the nonprofit AMAS, for which she conceived and coproduced the revue *Bubbling Brown Sugar*.

Jay Livingston, 86; died October 17, 2001, in Los Angeles. Three-time Oscar-winning songwriter who with partner Ray Evans wrote two Broadway musicals, *Oh Captain!* and *Let It Ride*.

Alan Manson, 83; died March 5, 2002, in Jamaica, New York. Veteran actor whose Broadway credits included *This Is the Army*; *Call Me Mister*; *The Tenth Man*; *Funny Girl*; *Forty Carats*; and *Broadway Bound*.

Bill McCutcheon, 77; died January 9, 2002, in Ridgewood, New Jersey. Character comedian on stage, screen, and TV, best known for his Tony Award–winning performance in Jerry Zaks's 1987 revival of *Anything Goes*. He also appeared in two other Zaks productions, *The Marriage of Bette and Boo* (for which he won an Obie Award) and the 1986 revival of *The Front Page*.

Gardner McKay, 69; died November 21, 2001, of prostate cancer, in Honolulu. Author of the off-Broadway drama *Sea Marks*, who was best known for his role on the early 1960s TV series *Adventures in Paradise*.

Barbara Matera, 72; died on September 13, 2001, of a cerebral hemorrhage, in Manhattan. Costumer whose shop, Barbara Matera Ltd., built the costumes for many of Broadway's major musicals since 1968.

James McKenzie, 75; died February 20, 2001, of cancer, in Norwalk, Connecticut. Producer who ran the Westport (Connecticut) Country Playhouse for forty-one years and the American Conservatory Theatre (in San Francisco) for twenty years. On Broadway, he coproduced two Paul Zindel plays, *And Miss Reardon Drinks a Little* and *The Secret Affairs of Mildred Wild*.

Leonard Melfi, 66; died October 28, 2001, of congestive heart failure, in Manhattan. Avant-garde playwright whose work included *Birdbath* and contributions to *Morning, Noon and Night* and the revue *Oh! Calcutta!!*

Scott Merrill, 82; died June 28, 2001, in Branford, Connecticut. Dancer best known for his performance as Macheath (Mack the Knife) in the 1954 revival of *The Threepenny Opera*. Other credits included *Bloomer Girl*; *Love Life*; *Paint Your Wagon*; and *Seventh Heaven*.

Reggie Montgomery, 54; died January 13, 2002, in Manhattan. Actor whose credits included George C. Wolfe's *Spunk* and *The Colored Museum*; Suzan-Lori Parks's *In the Blood*; and Julie Taymor's *The Green Bird*. He began his career in 1969, as the first black clown in Ringling Brothers and Barnum & Bailey Circus.

Beni Montresor, 75; died October 11, 2001, of pancreatic cancer, in Verona, Italy. Opera designer and illustrator whose Broadway credits included costumes for the 1964 revival of O'Neill's *Marco Millions*; sets and costumes for the Richard Rodgers–Stephen Sondheim musical *Do I Hear a Waltz?*; and sets for the musical *Rags*.

Dudley Moore, 66; died March 27, 2001, of pneumonia as a complication of progressive supranuclear palsy, in Plainfield, New Jersey. English comedian and musician who achieved film stardom with *10* and *Arthur*. Broadway credits as performer-writer included the 1962 comedy revue *Beyond the Fringe*, which he first played in London in 1960; and—with Peter Cook, one of his *Beyond the Fringe* companions—the 1973 revue *Good Evening*.

Inge Morath, 78; died January 30, 2002, of lymphoma, in Manhattan. Distinctive photographer who was the third wife of playwright Arthur Miller.

Harry J. Nederlander, 84; died January 6, 2002, in Rancho Mirage, California. Eldest of the five Nederlander brothers, operators of the theatre chain started by their father.

Don Nelson, 75; died September 9, 2001. Newspaper reporter and critic who covered jazz and off-Broadway theatre (from 1973 to 1991) for the *Daily News*.

Carroll O'Connor, 76; died June 21, 2001, of a heart attack, in Culver City, California. Character actor best known for his Emmy Award–winning role as Archie Bunker on the sitcom *All in the Family*. Stage credits included the Broadway plays *Brothers* (which he also directed) and *Home Front*.

Bibi Osterwald, 83; died January 7, 2002, in Burbank, California. Musical comedy character actress best known as the longtime standby for the title role in *Hello, Dolly!* (playing the part 122 times over seven years). Other credits included the revue *Three to Make Ready*; as Lovey Mars in *The Golden Apple*; and in the national company of *42nd Street*.

Anthony Quinn, 86; died June 3, 2001, in Boston. Stage and screen actor whose stage credits included Tennessee Williams's *A Streetcar Named Desire* (as replacement for Marlon Brando, opposite Uta Hagen); *Becket*; Tennessee Williams's *The Red Devil Battery Sign*; and the 1983 revival of the musical *Zorbá*. Film roles included *Viva Zapata* (for which he won an Oscar); *La Strada*; *Lust for Life* (another Oscar); *Lawrence of Arabia*; and *Zorbá the Greek*.

Edward Padula, 85; died November 1, 2001, of a heart attack, in Southampton, New York. Producer whose credits included *Bye Bye Birdie*; *All American*; *Bajour*; *A Joyful Noise*; and *Don't Bother Me, I Can't Cope*.

Tom Panko, 74; died February 18, 2002, following heart surgery, in Manhattan. Dancer and choreographer whose performing credits included *Guys and Dolls* and *The Music Man*. Choreographic credits included *Golden Rainbow* and assistant to Onna White on numerous shows, including *Half a Sixpence* and *Mame*.

Eleanor Phelps, 94; died September 29, 2001, in Gouldsboro, Pennsylvania. Actress who made her debut in George Arliss's 1928 production of *The Merchant of Venice*. Other credits include *The Disenchanted; Forty Carats* (replacement); the 1975 revival of *The Royal Family;* and the 1976 revival of *My Fair Lady.*

Herbert Ross, 74; died October 9, 2001, of heart failure, in Manhattan. Broadway choreographer and motion picture director. Choreographic credits included *A Tree Grows in Brooklyn; I Can Get It for You Wholesale; Kelly* (also director); *Do I Hear a Waltz?;* and *Anyone Can Whistle.* Director of Neil Simon's plays *Chapter Two* and *I Ought to Be in Pictures.* Film-directing credits included *Play It Again, Sam; The Turning Point; The Goodbye Girl; Funny Lady;* and *Footloose.*

Polly Rowles, 87; died October 7, 2001, in Concord, New Hampshire. Actress who made her Broadway debut in Orson Welles's 1938 production of *Julius Caesar.* Credits included *Auntie Mame* (as Vera Charles); Noël Coward's *Look after Lulu;* the Richard Rodgers musical *No Strings; The Killing of Sister George; Forty Carats;* the 1973 revival of *The Women;* the musical *Spotlight;* and *Steaming.*

Avery Schreiber, 66; died January 7, 2002, of a heart attack, in Los Angeles. TV comic whose Broadway credits included *Dreyfus in Rehearsal;* the 1981 revival of *Can-Can;* and *Welcome to the Club.* He also directed the musical *How to Be a Jewish Mother.*

Anthony Shaffer, 75; died November 6, 2001, of a heart attack, in London. Author of the international smash hit *Sleuth* and the less successful Broadway thriller *Whodunnit,* and twin brother of Peter Shaffer (author of *Equus* and *Amadeus*). Film credits included Alfred Hitchcock's *Frenzy* and the Agatha Christie adaptations *Murder on the Orient Express* and *Death on the Nile.*

John Springer, 85; died October 30, 2001, of congestive heart failure, in Manhattan. Well-connected press agent who handled shows, films, and major stars for more than fifty years.

Kim Stanley, 76; died August 20, 2001, of uterine cancer, in Santa Fe, New Mexico. Actress who achieved instant stardom in William Inge's *Picnic* and *Bus Stop,* only to voluntarily withdraw from the stage after little more than a decade. Other credits included *The Traveling Lady; A Touch of the Poet; A Far Country;* and Inge's *Natural Affection.*

Jerry Sterner, 62; died June 11, 2001, of a heart attack, in Brooklyn. Author of two off-Broadway plays, *Be Happy for Me* and the hit *Other People's Money.*

Josef Svoboda, 81; died April 8, 2002, in Prague. Prolific Czech set designer who designed the 1974 Broadway production of Tom Stoppard's *Jumpers*.

Ron Taylor, 49; died January 15, 2002, of heart failure, in Los Angeles. Actor best known for his portrayal of Audrey II, the man-eating cactus puppet, in *Little Shop of Horrors*. He also coauthored and starred in the revue *It Ain't Nothin' but the Blues*.

Dame Dorothy Tutin, 71; died August 6, 2001, of leukemia, in Midhurst, West Sussex, England. British actress whose London credits included *I Am a Camera*; John Osborne's *The Entertainer*; Harold Pinter's *Old Times*; and Tom Stoppard's *Undiscovered Country*. She starred on Broadway in *The Hollow Crown* and *Portrait of a Queen*.

Robert Urich, 55; died April 16, 2002, of cancer, in Thousand Oaks, California. Television actor whose stage appearances included the 1983 production of *The Hasty Heart* (at the Kennedy Center) and a replacement stint in the 1996 Broadway revival of *Chicago*.

Diana van der Vlis, 66; died October 22, 2001, in Missoula, Montana. Actress whose credits included *The Happiest Millionaire*; *Comes a Day*; and *A Shot in the Dark*.

Eudora Welty, 92; died July 23, 2001, of pneumonia, in Jackson, Mississippi. Pulitzer Prize–winning author whose work served as source material for the 1956 comedy *The Ponder Heart* and the 1976 musical *The Robber Bridegroom*.

Billy Wilder, 95; died March 27, 2002, of pneumonia, in Beverly Hills. Austrian-born writer-director who made dozens of influential films, including *Double Indemnity*; *The Lost Weekend*; *Sunset Boulevard*; *Sabrina*; *Some Like It Hot*; and *The Apartment*.

Irene Worth, 85; died March 10, 2002, of a stroke, in Manhattan. Celebrated actress who won Tony Awards for Edward Albee's *Tiny Alice*; the 1975 revival of *Sweet Bird of Youth*; and Neil Simon's *Lost in Yonkers*. Other credits included *The Cocktail Party*; Lillian Hellman's *Toys in the Attic*; the 1977 Lincoln Center revival of *The Cherry Orchard*; and Albee's *The Lady from Dubuque*.

Index

Page numbers in **boldface** indicate extended discussion of 2001–2002 season shows. All people, titles, and organizations mentioned in the text have been indexed. For reference purposes, selected people who are billed on the theatre programs but not specifically discussed in the text have also been included.